Haywire

HAY

WIRE

by Brooke Hayward

ALFRED A. KNOPF   NEW YORK   1977

THIS IS A BORZOI BOOK
PUBLISHED BY ALFRED A. KNOPF, INC.

Grateful acknowledgment is made to the following for permission to reprint previously published material:

Jovanna Ceccarelli: Excerpt from an interview with Margaret Sullavan and John Keating which appeared in *Theatre Arts*, February, 1960. Reprinted by permission of the publisher.

Curtis Brown Ltd. on behalf of the Estate of Ogden Nash: Unpublished poem entitled "So Red the Rose, However You Spell It." Reprinted from a letter written to Margaret Sullavan by Ogden Nash.

Harcourt Brace Jovanovich, Inc., and Faber & Faber Ltd.: Excerpt from "The Love Song of J. Alfred Prufrock" from *Collected Poems 1909–1962* by T. S. Eliot.

The Viking Press, Inc.: Excerpt from *Madeline* by Ludwig Bemelmans. Copyright 1939 by Ludwig Bemelmans, renewed 1967 by Madeleine Bemelmans and Barbara Bemelmans Marciano. Reprinted by permission of the publisher.

Mrs. Phyllis Cerf Wagner: Excerpt from a syndicated column written by Bennett Cerf.

The photographs on pages 4, 32, 60–1, 160, and 304 appear through the courtesy of John Swope; the photograph on page 198 appears through the courtesy of John Engstead.

Library of Congress Cataloging in Publication Data

Hayward, Brooke, [date]
Haywire.

Includes index.
1. Hayward family.   I. Title.
PN2287.H377H3   792'.092'2 [B]   76-40989
ISBN 0-394-49325-7

Manufactured in the United States of America

To Josie—Johanna Mankiewicz Davis

Shortly after I began exploring my past, I wanted to stop. Josie made me continue. Halfway through, she was killed. Again I stopped. Someone told me, "Do it for Josie. She believed in this. Go on." And so I did.

Chapters

Acknowledgments

For their time, memories, and love I'd like to thank Jimmy Stewart, Josh Logan, John Swope, Martha Edens, Henry Fonda, Jane Fonda, Peter Fonda, William Wyler, Billy Wilder, Nancy Keith, Diana Vreeland, Fredric and Florence March, Truman Capote, Millicent and Paul Osborn, Bill and Greta Wright, Sara Mankiewicz, Tom Mankiewicz, Bill Francisco, Peter Hunt, Charles and Ray Eames, Joseph Cotten, Hank Potter, George Cukor, Jules Stein, King Vidor, Swifty Lazar, George Axelrod, Kathleen Malley, Kenneth Wagg, my grandmother, and most of all my brother, Bill.

For holding my hand—and often forcibly placing it back on the typewriter keys—I thank Buck Henry, Curtis Harrington, Luis Sanjurjo, and Toby Rafelson.

For her fine blue pencil, Carol Janeway. And for all this and much more, my editor and publisher, Bob Gottlieb.

—BROOKE HAYWARD

Haywire

This book *is a personal memoir; but it is also a larger story—about carelessness and guilt, and the wreckage they can make of lives.*

My family seems to me the personification of these qualities. Both my parents were exceptional in ordinary ways: they were attractive, intelligent, and well educated. It was the scope and sweep of their talent and success that made them distinctive. My mother was an actress, Margaret Sullavan, and my father a theatrical producer, Leland Hayward. They were happily married for ten years, had three children in even succession (I am the oldest), and lived in California during the thirties and early forties, a golden era not only for movies but for children who, like us, grew up surrounded by its opulent trappings. When they divorced, the impact was naturally profound and ultimately disastrous—not so much for them, perhaps, as for their children, two of whom eventually did time in mental institutions.

However, this is not primarily about my parents' lives, except as they bore directly upon our own. It is really about their children—Bridget, Bill, and me—each of whom reacted uniquely to the haphazard slew of catastrophes, looking for a means of escape.

Other people marry and divorce, leaving other children angry and disturbed. What distinguishes this particular story are the particular qualities of its protagonists, and the extraordinary effects they had on their children. Our lives were a series of extremes. A thanksgiving of riches was bestowed on us at birth: grace and joy and a fair share of beauty; privilege and power. Those blessings which luck had overlooked could be bought. We seemed to exist above the squalor of suffering as most people know it. We were envied. But there were also more expectations, more marriages (my mother four times, my father five), and more damage: more of us (three out of five) suffered mental breakdowns. My parents failed, as they succeeded—on a massive scale. And they left behind them a legacy, vested in their children, that put the odds against survival ineluctably high.

1

Endings

he had called me late the night before.

Looking back, I recall (or invent?) an urgency to her tone, but really all she'd said was "Can you have breakfast tomorrow?"

"Hmm. What time? Do you have the proper ingredients? English muffins? Marmalade, et cetera?" We'd never shaken the habit of testing one another.

"Of course, you spoiled brat. Come at ten; you shall have ginger marmalade from Bloomingdale's, *fresh* orange juice I shall squeeze personally, boiled eggs—your customary five and a half minutes. And of course there will be fascinating conversation."

"Might I have a clue?" We'd also become adept at approaching each other with oblique, occasionally fake, courtesy.

Silence, as I'd expected. Then: "Okay, do you have a good gynecologist?"

My silence. "Of course. What for?"

"Brooke, listen." She was suddenly singing. "I have never ever been so happy in my life—I think I'm pregnant."

"*What?*" I was predictably stunned, but less by that possibility than by her confiding in me. "How the hell did you get pregnant?"

"Oh," she said, giggling, "probably from a toilet seat."

"Bridget. For God's sake, have you gone mad? I mean, how can you possibly be twenty-one years old and reasonably, one hopes, *reasonably* intelligent and not have been to a—"

"Brooke, listen." She was positively frenzied with elation. "Listen, it's entirely possible that I want to get married, I'm so in love. Do you hear me? *Married!*"

This conversation was moving just out of my reach, like a smoke ring. All I could say was "Yes. I see what you mean about breakfast—yes, indeed. Might one ask who the expectant father is? No, never mind."

"Ten o'clock tomorrow. What's he like, is he nice, does he hurt?" I knew she meant the gynecologist.

"Yes, no, never mind. Actually he's from India—nice blend of exotic and imperturbable. Forget it, go to sleep."

"Okay, see you in the morning. Farewell." Farewell. Nobody but Bridget ever said goodbye to me like that; all her beginnings and endings where I was concerned were unpredictable, and most of the dialogue in between was enigmatic, a foreign language to any outsider. But for my benefit she talked in her own private shorthand, and what farewell meant was that she wanted me to button up my overcoat and take good care of myself until ten in the morning, because she would miss me in a way that would take far too much sentimental effort to express. I knew what she meant. Often I missed her while we were in the same room together.

I contemplated the phone for some time. Never had I heard her so oddly gay and forthright; as a matter of fact, we hadn't discussed sex since adolescence. Her entire inner life was secretive and mysterious, and no one dared violate it. She sent out powerful "No Trespassing" signals and I had learned to honor them. It crossed my mind that my sister was drunk.

Still, the next morning—a warm October day in 1960—I stood outside her apartment door, nonplussed by the stack of mail and the furled *New York Times* propped up against it. The door itself was slowly getting on my nerves. It didn't open when I rang the doorbell for the fifth or sixth time. It didn't have a crack underneath big enough for a worthwhile view of the interior, although idiotically I'd got down on my hands and knees and looked anyway. Nor did I have a key to unlock it. Even if she *had* been drunk the night before, which was unlikely—besides, I prided myself on being able to interpret at least her external behavior—she would have been incapable of losing track of her invitation; she was a creature of infuriating compulsion, particularly in matters of time and place, always fussing about my lack of regard for either. Ever since she'd moved from her one-room, third-floor apartment (to which I had possessed a key, much used) to the comparative luxury of an apartment one floor higher with an actual separate bedroom and view (of the building across the street), I'd felt vaguely displaced and surly. For the last year, I'd thought of that little one-room apartment as mine, an irrational attachment, since I was not exactly homeless. Until a month before, I'd been living not only in a commodious house in Greenwich, Connecticut, but also, during the week, in a *pied-à-terre* on East Seventy-second Street. My marriage to Michael Thomas, art historian and budding investment banker, so blithely undertaken during undergraduate days at Vassar and Yale, had, when removed from the insular academic atmosphere of New Haven, fallen apart. We were no longer wrapped in cotton wool; I was no longer a child bride. Now that our divorce was final, I'd moved our two small children into New York and into my own spacious apartment on Central Park West. I continued, however, to drop by Bridget's whenever I had five minutes between modeling jobs and interviews. "Just checking out my make-up," I'd announce breezily, or, "Gotta use your phone." The idea of telling my sister I'd really come to see her would never have crossed my mind.

Her new quarters did have certain advantages: twice the closet space for her warehouses of clothes and shoes, and a fully mirrored bathroom, very handy for looking at oneself from all angles while sitting on the cosmetics-crammed counter and conversing with Bridget submerged in the tub as she tested some new bubble bath. But I had never acquired the same proprietary feelings about this setup. It just didn't have the smell and cozy inconvenience of the old. And now I cursed myself for neglecting to collect the duplicate key she'd had made for me weeks ago. Becoming more and more exasperated with both of us, I rang fiercely four times in a row. Actually I felt like kicking the door. Then I thought I heard a sound from where the bedroom ought to be. Of course, it was possible that she might still be asleep. Or, more interesting, asleep with an as yet undisclosed lover. But wouldn't she have left a characteristically humorous note to that effect, right where the bills from Con Ed and Jax were now lying? I began to punch the doorbell to the rhythm of "Yankee Doodle Dandy." During countless enforced afternoon naps when we were young, we'd invented out of boredom what we thought was this highly original game, whereby we would take turns tapping out an unidentified song with our fingernails on the wooden headboards of our twin beds; the object was to determine who was better at guessing it or tapping it, or even choosing it if it was particularly esoteric. We both became fairly skillful, but this time the old signal got no response. I decided that the noise inside was either imagined or my stomach growling. Fresh orange juice and an English muffin with crisp bacon at Stark's around the corner on Lexington became increasingly crucial. I scribbled her a note and went on down in the elevator, trying to feel philosophical about the whole wasted half-hour. Clearly some matter of extreme urgency was to blame. At this very moment she was certainly racing back to meet me, caught between subways, or maybe, wonder of wonders, even springing for a cab.

I galloped across the lobby toward the heavy glass doors and sunlight. Behind the streamlined reception desk, more appropriate to a luxury liner than an apartment building, was the ruddy-faced doorman.

"Hi. Did you see my sister go out today?"

"No, Miss," he answered in a thick brogue, "but then I only come on at eight."

"Ah." I hesitated with a charming smile. "Well. Tell me something." (I tried Mother's ingratiating imperative.) "Um, what time does the mail get delivered? I mean, to the people in the building?"

"Oh, Miss, maybe just over a half hour ago."

"And the newspaper?"

"Oh, somewhere around six or seven. Just a minute, Miss." He moved to the door to let in an elderly couple with a poodle and a Gristede's shopping bag, then bolted the door open so that all the sounds of the morning spewed in. A battle of simultaneous desires was shaping up; whether to go out or stay and satisfy my curiosity. After some consideration I followed him to the immense tropical plant at the entrance. It was embarrassing—even melodramatic— to ask for a key to apartment 403, but I did anyway.

"No problem, Miss. I'll ring Pete and ask him to take you up. He's in the basement."

"No, no, no, thanks, that's too much trouble." Ridiculous. For instance, what if she had had to meet Bill Francisco, a young director at the Yale Drama School (and romantic interest), for whom she was doing some kind of production work? She had probably left a message on my service. A telephone was clearly indicated. Again, Stark's. Besides, Bridget was so intensely fero- cious about her privacy there was no telling what she'd do if she knew I'd go to such lengths to break into her sanctuary. Although Bridget was a year and a half younger, I was afraid of her. "Listen, do me a favor—when you see her, tell her I came by and rang but there was no answer and I'll call her later. Okay?"

He nodded and started to lift his hand, but I was already out the door, feeling infinitely better, and striding toward Lexington.

By the time I'd downed my O.J., read the paper, checked Belles for a negative on messages, and gone to the ladies room, the grand superstructure of the day had begun to disintegrate. Out of perverseness, I jumped on the subway and went down to a sound stage on Fourth Street to watch the shooting of Kay Doubleday's big strip scene in *Mad Dog Coll,* a gangster film that can still, to my embarrassment, be seen occasionally on late-night TV. (It was the first movie I'd ever been in; I had many difficult things to do, like play the violin and get raped by Vincent [Mad Dog] Coll, played by a young actor named John Chandler, who, on completion of the movie, decided to become a priest.) Kay Doubleday was in my class at Lee Strasberg's; it was in the interest of art, I told myself, to watch her prance down a ramp, singing and stripping her heart out.

I then ate a huge heavy lunch at Moscowitz & Lupowitz with the art director Dick Sylbert. Over coffee, he smoked his pipe and patiently tried to explain the difference between champlevé and cloisonné enamel. This meandered into a discussion of etching techniques. Having killed the afternoon to my thorough satisfaction, I took a slow bus up Madison Avenue in order to read *Time* magazine. It was an absolutely beautiful four o'clock, the best in months, and when the bus got as far as Fifty-fourth Street, I decided to disembark, fetch Bridget after first giving her hell, and buy a new pair of shoes.

About a block away from her building, a strange thing happened. I was seized by what seemed to be a virulent case of the flu. My temperature rose and fell five degrees in as many seconds. Hot underground springs of scalding perspiration seeped out everywhere, and yet I was shaking with cold, frostbitten inside and out. There was nothing reassuring about the pavement under my feet; I couldn't move forward on it. Well, I thought, by way of helpful explanation, I should be getting home anyway. Besides, after the screw-up this morning she owes me the next move; either this is repressed anger or pre-menstrual tension, but in any case how virtuous and rich I shall feel for not having bought a pair of shoes this afternoon.

I hailed a cab fast, so that I wouldn't have to waste time squatting on Fifty-fourth Street at rush hour with my head between my legs. Ah, well, I thought feverishly, "I grow old . . . I grow old . . . I shall wear the bottoms of my trousers rolled," an ague hath my ham; marrow fatigue, not enough exercise, no tennis, badminton, swimming, fencing, volleyball, modern dance, *any* dance. I missed school gymnasiums, horseback riding; all I did now was tramp concrete sidewalks and wooden stages and Central Park on weekends. Middle age was phasing out into senility. I fooled the cabdriver, though, by smiling at him so he wouldn't notice all the change I dropped as we pulled up to 15 West Eighty-first Street, across from the Hayden Planetarium. Dark and cool, its dingy Moorish fountained-and-tiled lobby always welcomed me home from the wars. I rose in the elevator, gratefully trying to snuggle against its ancient varnished paneling, and finally stood with ossified feet in the small hall outside my door. The hall was semiprivate; unfortunately it provided wizened old Mrs. Rosenbaum and myself with a common meeting ground, ours being the only two apartments opening off it. She endowed it richly with a perpetual odor of cabbage, and I with an expensive new layer of wallpaper to distract from her barbaric cuisine.

Late-afternoon sun was streaming over the planetarium's dome through my living-room windows; there was a bucket of huge chrysanthemums in the hall, which our Scottish housekeeper, Miss Mac, had strategically placed in my path so that while crashing into it I would at least know that her loyalties were divided between me and the sender, with whom I was engaged in a momentary dispute.

My two chocolate-coated children, Jeff and Willie, pounced on me like small M&Ms; without too much difficulty they had acquired Miss Mac's finely honed sweet tooth. Would I like a cup of tea? (Definitely.) Biscuit? (Definitely.) Would I like to watch cartoons on TV and had I brought any comics and there was a whole bunch of telephone messages. Jeffrey coughed violently to demonstrate that the croup with which he'd been afflicted since the first day of nursery school had in no way abated. Willie told me that while he and Miss Mac had walked Jeffrey across the park to school that morning, they had seen a flock of pigeons fly up that gave him the feeling his heart was about to break. Then, while Miss Mac was showing me a mink hat that her new beau who owned a garage had presented her with the previous evening, the doorbell rang.

It was my stepmother, Pamela.

Pamela Digby Churchill Hayward had never rung my doorbell before. It struck me as a curious hour for her to be doing so now, but she was in good form and came in and hugged the children, who loved to be picked up once a week in Father's limousine and driven directly across the Park to 1020 Fifth Avenue, where they would be given a splendid high tea, Pamela being

English, and later returned with balloons and pockets full of candy. Father and Pamela lived across from the Metropolitan Museum and that in turn lay on a straight line across the Park to me, so that whenever we looked over at Father's skyline, which was at least five or six times a day, I had the sense of being able to solve a difficult geometric problem.

"Brooke, darling," said Pamela, between ardent embraces from Jeff and Willie, "I would love to have a tour of your apartment, but do you suppose that I might have a word with you first privately?"

It was odd that Pamela had never been here since I'd moved in, particularly since she had helped immeasurably with decorating sources of all kinds, and had even loaned me her cleaning lady twice a week after she'd been exposed to my tortured voice on the telephone the day we'd moved in from the country with four times as much solid mass as there was room to hold it, a slight miscalculation on my part. Now that she had suddenly materialized, I wanted to show her just how I had distributed that mass around, but obediently led her down the hall to my bedroom.

"Shall I shut the door?"

"Yes," she said. "The children." So I closed the door and stood with my back to it, facing her.

"Darling," she said, every word penetrating the three feet between us with the distinct precision of her English accent, "I have something terrible to tell you." She paused. I gazed at her, hypnotized by the inexorable chic of her pale blue suit and the long twisted rope of pearls and turquoises banded by a row of diamonds every two inches or so that hung gracefully knotted against her silk blouse. My scalp tightened. The whole day had been put together wrong.

Bridget's dead, I thought I said to myself, not in that room at all but back in front of her apartment, unable to go in.

"My God, how did you know? *How did you know?*" Pamela was practically shouting as she grabbed at my arms, which were dangling at my sides. I was so shocked by her affirmation that I was absolutely unable to move, and yet I knew that she was as badly shaken as I by my response, so I made a tremendous effort to speak through the thick white paint that was beginning to drift down over me.

"I didn't know," I said gently, so as not to scream. "It just occurred to me." No, I said to myself carefully; no, this is definitely not happening, no. I focused on Pamela's blue eyes and powdered face.

"How did it happen?" I asked cautiously. It seemed a sensible question and my voice managed to dole out the words in level teaspoons without much help from me. Pamela looked at me closely with a split second of curiosity and approval; I wasn't behaving like a rabid dog yet, although she must have sensed that I was seconds away from foaming at the mouth. Now my vision was beginning to double-cross me; the scene seemed to be speeding out of control like a runaway train about to be derailed.

Pamela seemed to be talking to me. "We don't know the exact details yet, darling. Bill Francisco found her about four this afternoon—he had a key to her apartment and they'd had an arrangement to meet or something—so then, when she didn't answer, he went in to wait and found a disturbing note for him which she'd written last night, so he went into the bedroom and found her lying in bed."

"Wait, wait a minute." I roused myself. "What was disturbing about the note? I mean, I talked to her at around eleven last night and she sounded great—I was supposed to meet her this—"

Pamela put her purse and gloves on the bed. "I'll come back to that later—the car is waiting downstairs, so we must hurry a bit. Anyhow, when Bill couldn't wake her he called your father at the office, and Leland raced over after calling *his* doctor, who met them there. He said something extraordinary—he asked your father if she had epilepsy—it really has been such chaos ever since four, the office going crazy with phones, doctors, police, coroners, God knows what. Of course Leland said no, there was no history of epilepsy, but the doctor insisted that she appeared to be having some sort of seizure at the time of her death, and besides there were bottles of Dilantin in the medicine chest and an empty one lying on the bathroom sink. So now I gather an autopsy will be performed." She started to reach for me again.

"But she did," I said, pulling back. Even my teeth ached. "She had epilepsy." I tried opening my mouth wider to make my words more audible but it felt as if lockjaw had set in.

"Brooke, darling, what on earth are you talking about?" asked Pamela, her diction slightly more ragged than usual. My body clenched like a fist. It was useless right now, too late to go back and reconstruct in meaningless detail, to communicate at all. Still, the situation had a delicate formality, and it was probably better to camouflage myself in its rituals, at least for a while longer.

"Well," I answered, wishing I were a wild creature, not civilized, a wolf in deep silent snow, howling into the wind. "You see, she did have epilepsy. She really did. I think she sort of acquired it along the way, and when she found out definitely last spring, she didn't want Father to know about it, so she swore me to secrecy."

Last spring—April, maybe. "Brooke," she'd said, squinting at me over her new electric coffeemaker, "although you are totally untrustworthy and have never been able to keep a secret, can you *promise* me on your sacred word of honor that if I tell you one now, you will *never never* repeat it, especially not to *Father?*" That piqued my curiosity enough to elicit a promise, so then she'd told me that she was supposed to give up cigarettes, alcohol, and coffee —we each had two or three more cups after that—because she'd just recently been tested by a neurologist in New Haven who had diagnosed her as being epileptic. The story behind *that* was so incredible I'd accepted it without question; it fit in perfectly with the rest of the family folklore. She told me that she'd been in New Haven for the weekend to see Bill Francisco, and that late Saturday night she'd gone back to her room at the Duncan Hotel, after making plans with Bill to pick her up for breakfast. In the morning, however, he had been unable to find her at the hotel because she'd been carted off to the morgue: a maid had mistakenly entered the room a few hours earlier, ostensibly to clean it, and had found Bridget to all intents and purposes dead on the floor, whereupon the hotel management summoned a doctor, who could not hear a heartbeat or find a pulse. So off she'd gone to the morgue, where the name of her doctor in Stockbridge was discovered on a card in her purse. It turned out that instead of being dead she was in a state of complete catatonia, and one thing led to another— eventually the neurologist and some tests. And, said Bridget, under no circumstances was Father to find out because he would just get typically hysterical and insist on her living with a roommate, a fate literally, she said, worse than death; not only did she cherish living alone more than anything else in the world, she didn't want people thinking she was crippled or helpless or any different from before, or scrutinizing her for telltale signs of the forbidden cigarettes, liquor, or coffee. There was no purpose to her life at all, she warned me, unless she could remain free to live as she chose; she was twenty-one years old and could exercise that right at last. So we drank our extra cups of coffee with lots of cream and sugar in them; I understood her and in some basic way agreed with her.

"Brooke," said Pamela, skipping over this information in a brisk businesslike tone I admired for its British sense of mission, "you are distraught, which is understandable, but I have an enormous favor to ask of you: under no circumstances must you allow yourself to become emotional now, because your father—I am deeply concerned about him—is heartbroken, as you can imagine, and you know as well as I that if too much pressure is put on him, if there's too much stress, he could possibly have one of his bleeding attacks—and then he might die as well. That's what I'm really terrified of." Her blue eyes were urgently imploring. "What is essential at this moment is that I take you back to him—I think Josh and Nedda Logan are on their way over now—and you *must* be strong and brave, Brooke, absolutely no tears, *really*, because I cannot have him made any more upset than he already is." Right: I am a potential hysteric, who can be transformed on order into a paradigm of stoicism. "Besides, you are supposed to be an actress; be a good one tonight, please."

Only nine months earlier, Pamela had stood before me on the same kind of agonizing mission, this time on Second Avenue outside of the Gate Theatre. It was a very cold night, the first night of the year, January 1st, and I had just come out of the Astor Place subway stop and was approaching the theatre where Kevin McCarthy and I were appearing in an off-Broadway production of *Marching Song*. It was my first play and we'd opened the week before. I was shivering from the snow blown down my neck by the bitter wind and also from spasms of fear, the first palpable fear I'd ever known. Twenty minutes earlier, I'd called my stepfather from a phone booth in Grand Central Station, clumsily pouring change into all three slots because he was in New Haven and I didn't want him to think I was so cheap as to call collect. I wanted to talk to him and, with luck, to Mother, or at least send her my love if she couldn't come to the phone; she was starring in a play that was trying out there before its New York engagement. He told me that she'd just died.

Mother dead. Impossible. I had called to say Happy New Year just in time to learn she was dead.

The vast dome of Grand Central Station closed down over me in the glass telephone booth like one of the jars in which we'd caught fireflies as children, only without any holes punched out in the lid, so that I seemed to go deaf. There was absolute silence: the beating of my heart, the static on the telephone, my stepfather asking me between sobs to take the next train to New Haven, and me saying no, I had to be at the theatre in a few minutes and would come up by late train that evening—all silent—and even when I pushed open the door for air, no sound anywhere in the entire huge space of the station with its magazine stands and hot-dog stands and shoe-polishing stands and waiting rooms and information booths and entrances and exits filled as before with people, but people moving noiselessly, without echoes. I moved with them, my own footsteps on the worn marble floor and even the subway totally muffled as it lurched its way downtown. My mother, my very own mother, beautiful, warm, always more alive than anyone else in the world—alive in ways that nobody else dared to be—my mother, with her special gift for living and for giving that life to all the people who knew her and many who didn't, dead.

There was only one other person in my subway car, a drunk swinging like a monkey from pull to pull. He stopped right in front of me and leaned down, suspended by both arms. "Why," he asked in a slur, puncturing the dense membrane of silence with such ease that I looked up at him as if he were a wizard, "why would you be looking so sad, little lady? It's New Year's Day." He peered more closely. "Drink up your cup fer auld lang syne. Here's to you—"

"Are we the only two people on this whole subway tonight?" I asked him as if it were the most profound question in the whole world, desperately wanting him to go on, to tell me everything about his life before we got to my stop.

"Everyone's home with friends," he said. "Celebrating."

"Why aren't you?"

"Well, you see, I'll ride to the end of the line. They let me sleep here."

"My mother died tonight," I informed him because he was a stranger. Water began to rise in his crusty red eyes, and then he sat down quietly next to me, shaking his head. I was grateful he was there. We both waited until my stop came, and he stood up with me as I got off.

Then I climbed swiftly up to the street, my mind beginning to burn like a newspaper. First there was the energizing reassurance that I was on my way somewhere specific and solid and important. I was already wound up to play my role before the phone call, and after the shock that followed, my instincts were sharpened by the freezing air; I was supposed to give a performance, and it would have to be an excellent performance. I kept sucking in air until my lungs hurt and then coughing it out like a steam engine; it reminded me that I was alive. It was much too soon for anyone involved with the play to have heard about her death, and I wouldn't have to say anything until afterward, if then. So I concentrated as Lee Strasberg had taught us, whispering over and over in a litany, "I must *use* this, I must *use* this," and finally arrived at the Gate Theatre, rather proud of myself, knowing, as seldom if ever one does, that I was going to do a fine job. Standing at the entrance of the theatre were the producer, the director, and the stage manager of the play, an unusual but not unreasonable place for them to be. Before I could say hello, Peter Kass, the director, blurted out something to the effect that Father had just called the theatre to tell them what had happened, and to have them cancel tonight's performance.

"What?" I remember asking, waves of anger striking me. "What? He's got no right to do that, he's not the producer; it's *your* play."

But they appeared not to have heard my voice at all; as if in a bad dream, they were looking fixedly through me and beyond me, and suddenly I was grasped from behind by something dark and furry. I started to struggle violently, and then I smelled a familiar perfume. It was Pamela, her face a phantasmagoria of white against a background of black sable, and beyond her an enormous black limousine, hovering curbside like a sleek bird of prey, one wing outstretched to encompass me.

"Brooke, darling," she asked anxiously, "you know about your mother?"

"Yes," I answered tersely.

"Darling, your father has sent me down here to collect you immediately. He said you'd understand he couldn't come himself, but he's all tied up with phone calls to Bridget and Bill—come on, darling, he wants you at once. He *needs* you."

"Pamela," I said, stepping backward, "I have to give a performance tonight. Then I shall take a taxi up to the apartment."

Pamela looked totally shocked. "You don't understand, darling; your father has canceled tonight's performance."

By this time we had been joined somewhat tentatively by the three at the door plus Kevin McCarthy straight from his subway: they were all making various explanations or gesticulating concern for me. Over this poorly orchestrated ensemble, I continued defiantly, "What right did Father have to cancel *any* performance of a play he didn't produce? Mother would have wanted me to go on, she would be *furious* if she knew about all this, she would *expect* me to go on—this is completely unprofessional, and what about all these people"—I gestured toward the management and cast assembling on the dark sidewalk—"what about them, and what about *me*; why couldn't Father have come and told me in person—"

"Brooke"—there was a shrill edge to Pamela's voice, not quite a scream—"your father thinks it would be *unseemly* for a performance to go on as usual tonight. Out of *respect* for your mother, he decided to do what he did—"

"Kevin!" I shouted, abandoning all pretense of propriety. "Tell me—is this what happens under these circumstances in the theatre?"

There was a shudder of silence, then everyone started talking at once, and somehow Pamela maneuvered me toward the waiting car; once again I had the sense that I was flailing my way through my worst nightmare, in which the more I struggle for life against some nameless master strategy, the more I become trapped in its ruthless machinations. For many years as a child, the nightmare was recurrent and the strategy had a name: it materialized in vivid technicolor as a giant carnivorous dinosaur, a *Tyrannosaurus rex*, with hideous red eyes and furrows of sharp teeth that glistened hungrily in the sun. He would ring our front doorbell and settle back on his huge scaly haunches waiting for me to answer; invariably I would slip past him and, with a sudden rush of adrenalin, spread my wings and fly, soar to freedom right over his head, catch the wind and glide with it like a falcon across the desert next to our house, while just below he stalked me through the yucca and cactus, erect on his powerful rear limbs, snapping at me with salivating jaws as the wind bore me up and down and up and then, finally, down. It must have been preordained that the Honourable Pamela Digby Churchill, not yet even my stepmother, would swoop down as an emissary from my father, not only to tell me about my mother's death in the absence of his ability to do it himself, but also to collect me efficiently for a ritual gathering of the clan, in this case my brother and sister, who were separated by half the country in mental institutions—Menninger's, in Topeka, Kansas; Austen Riggs, in Stockbridge, Massachusetts.

I huddled in the rear of the limousine, overcome by its dizzying warmth and sensuality. Pamela covered my lap with a fur lap robe and gave me a handkerchief, which I balled up and held very tight. I thought, I must not be melodramatic, my mother's death is a historically tragic event, it affects many other people— but all that is inconsequential—what is essential at this particular moment, what is crucial, is to be absolutely selfish. Why, if one of my parents had to die, did it have to be my mother, when I needed her so? Why not my father? Only my mother had understood me; nobody else in the world ever had or ever would in the same way, and we had really only just begun. All of my fearful battles with her for survival and identity had been fought, and just as we had learned how to shrug off ancient rivalries, to conquer our primordial fears about each other, to throw down our weapons, cease being mother and daughter, unequal or different, now that we were two individual people who had survived together, having successfully held each other and the outside world at bay for miles and years, there was something truly senseless about life if this was the result. It was a revelation. I stared out at the dark city, feeling that we were passing under it rather than through it, and thought: You might as well think whatever you want, be as self-indulgent as you need to be. You have about ten minutes of privacy, and then the sorrow of other people to deal with, Bridget and Bill, Father. Yes, I thought, of course Father loves you, but if I, Brooke, were to die tonight, it would hardly change his life at all; he would mourn, maybe shed a few tears in passing. But ah! Mother would have known the death of someone who had actually once been a part of her; there would have been a dreadful sense of mutilation of self, blood gushing out in rivers, pain almost beyond endurance. How did she die? What was the last thing she thought about?

Until now, the idea of death had been a hazy abstraction, although, as described in close detail with more or less poetry by great or even ordinary authors I'd read since childhood, or as presented in movies, it often made me cry; I had to be taken home at the age of three, hysterical, when Bambi's mother was shot. Now I tabulated the number of times an actual death had profoundly affected me; if our dog Stewart, a pointer who'd been run over in a ghastly accident, was not counted, the tally was a meager three. Working backward, there was Herman Mankiewicz when I was fifteen and Frances Fonda when I was twelve, both close friends of my parents, and both parents of children who were close friends of mine, almost part of my own family; then there was my grandfather Colonel William Hayward, who died of cancer when I was six. The Colonel, as he was always referred to, came out from New York and stayed with us in California for a while. He knew he was dying and the idea of being an invalid confined to a wheelchair annoyed him greatly. Always an active man, he took up needlepoint, and I remembered him seated in his wheelchair—impressively upright, shoulders back, with steel-rimmed glasses and the white, freshly starched collar he'd insisted on wearing every day of his life—stitching a wondrous alphabet, which eventually hung on our wall. He started it for Bridget and me, before Bill was born, so it must have taken several years to complete; in the end it measured about six by nine feet, all squares of animals represented alphabetically (A for Antelope, B for Buffalo) and rendered in the colors of a warm desert twilight.

By the time we arrived at the Carlyle Hotel, where Father and Pamela then lived, I welcomed any distraction. Besides, I was curious about Father. How would he be affected by the death of someone to whom he'd been married for ten years and then barely seen for the next thirteen, despite the three children they shared?

He looked awful, and somehow that pleased me. It meant he must have loved her a great deal, and I'd often wondered. He looked ten years older. Maybe they had never stopped loving each other. Maybe he was the last thing she thought about.

We were in the master bedroom, gracefully filled with Pamela's antique French furniture, which had just arrived from Paris to replace the simpler hotel stock. Everywhere was the heavy scent of Rigaud candles and warm lighting, Pamela's trademarks; she always used pink light bulbs instead of white. In the dead of winter masses of fresh flowers were always in place on every surface. There was some discussion of Bridget and Bill. Bill had said on the telephone that he didn't have a dark suit or any money—he was flying in from Topeka the next day and wanted to buy the suit there. I said I wanted to go to New Haven to see my stepfather. Father said that was a bum idea, he absolutely forbade it; Kenneth had been calling every half hour and had some terrible plan to cremate Mother and have us all there while a service was said during the cremation; it sounded to him as if Kenneth had really gone crazy, and as my father, he was going to insist that all three of us children stay in the apartment with Pamela and him for the next few days until the memorial service, which was obviously going to take place whether or not there was some depressing service over her body while it was in the oven. Did I have any idea how morbid it would be to go up there to witness a cremation? Absolutely nuts, as if Bridget and Bill weren't headed enough in that direction anyway.

"But, Father," I argued, "Kenneth has nobody, no family there with him at all. Maybe he *is* desperate, and after all he's my stepfather and he's been good to me—"

"Brooke," interjected Pamela, "did you know there is a good possibility that your mother killed herself?"

I was very tired. "No, she didn't, Pamela. Kenneth said on the phone that it was her heart; it had been bothering her."

"She was very unhappy, very unhappy with the play. Sometimes these things are for the best. If she were that disturbed—"

"She couldn't have killed herself. Of all the people in the world, she'd be the last—right, Father?"

Father was silent.

I answered myself. "It's out of the question. Impossible. She had too many people who meant too much to her." Me, I thought, Kenneth, Jeff, Willie, Bridget, Bill . . .

Pamela had an indescribably sweet tone to her voice, an understanding smile. Patiently, as to a child: "She wasn't feeling well, Brooke, and she may have taken an overdose of sleeping pills." Was there no end to the horror? She had never even *met* Mother; there was something obscene about *her* telling me that Mother was dead, that she had killed herself, that she was unhappy, that one should be philosophical about these things; dangerous instincts began to rouse themselves and sniff at my heels like bloodhounds and it was too late to call them off. No aspect of this was any of Pamela's business and no rationalization could make it so. If Father was incapable of dealing with the situation, that was tough as far as he and I were concerned, but the last thing

I'd asked for was the insinuation of an outsider, particularly a lady who was working too hard at becoming my next stepmother, replacing the last one, of whom I was very fond and would have given anything to have seen standing there in her stead.

The telephone rang, galvanizing Father into the kind of action in which he was most comfortable.

"Josh, hello. . . . Ya, ya, this is a real bitch." (Father had his own personal affirmative, never yes or yeah but ya, which he barked instead of spoke.) "No, we don't know yet. Hello, Nedda, darling. . . . No, the kids are all fine. Brooke is here and the other two arrive tomorrow. . . . Ya, I definitely think a memorial service, probably in Greenwich, since she lived there, makes more sense. . . . Oh, hell, I think Kenneth Wagg is having a nervous breakdown, for Chrissake, cried hysterically on the phone. . . . Ya, of course, it's rough for all of us, but God almighty, he's come up with the worst idea I've ever heard of—the kids go up to New Haven and they all stand around having some sort of macabre service while she's being cremated. Pure crap. Christ, we don't know yet whether it was from natural causes or sleeping pills, no note or explanation—they'll have to do an autopsy. Morning papers will be full of it, goddamn reporters all over the place. . . . Right. Talk to you both in the morning. . . . Thanks. You're sweet, Nedda. . . . Okay, okay. Here, speak to Pamela."

Father was always energized by the telephone. He came over and sat on the bed beside me and put his arms around me. I sagged against his chest. He smelled of wonderful aftershave lotion, bay rum, one of the first scents I could remember; I played with his tie clip, the only one he'd ever worn, a gold facsimile of an airplane propeller with a sapphire at the center. He was so fond of it he had had Cartier's make him twenty or so over the years, all identical, just in case one got lost. His stomach rumbled and he sighed. "Goddamn gut of mine." Then he got up and paced the room with his hands in his pockets and came back and stood in front of me and sighed again.

"Brooke," he said, "little Brooke. You were the most beautiful baby I ever saw." He began to blink his eyes very fast; I could feel tears start at the corners of mine and concentrated on squinting at him. Pamela was still talking on the phone in low serious tones, and we seemed to be alone, years ago. We stared at each other and remembered the beginning. I saw his face stripped of all the time that had accumulated there, its structure fine and strong, his pale blue deep-set eyes filled with certainty instead of anguish. We grieved for ourselves, aching both for my lost childhood and his youth, when our lives, as they affected each other, had been simple.

"You see"—he frowned, desperately trying to find the momentum to lift us out of our time warp—"we really aren't sure yet how Maggie died." Come on, Pop, I cheered him on mentally, you can do it. He thrust his hands down very deep in his pockets and hunched forward, bowing his head. One hand came up with a gold cigarette lighter, which he flicked on and off, on and off. His voice crunched as if he had laryngitis. "She was miserable about the play, as you know, and herself in it. She wasn't sleeping at night—terrible insomnia. They got a doctor to come to the hotel yesterday and this afternoon to give her a sedative, a shot of some damn thing or other so that maybe she could nap before the performance tonight. Around five, after she finally fell asleep, Kenneth went across the street to Kaysey's to talk to Gabel and Margolis about the possibility of buying her out of the goddamn play. When he got back a couple of hours later, the door to her room was locked and chained on the inside and apparently she wouldn't answer his knocking. So—he went downstairs and called up; no answer. He got worried, got the hotel management to break the door in, and there she was."

"Dead."

"Ya. Brooke, hand me a cigarette, would you—over there by the lamp." Pamela was hanging up the phone.

"Leland, darling, Josh and Nedda wondered—"

"Just a second, just a second. Before he left, the doctor gave her a bottle of sleeping pills, in case she needed them later. Kenneth says they were right by the bed, and when he looked in the bottle—afterwards—there were only *two* missing. That's the hell of it—doesn't make any sense. I mean you'd think if she *wanted* to kill herself she'd dump the whole bottle down her throat." He put the cigarette in his mouth, letting it dangle while he rubbed his eyes ferociously as if to erase them. "It's possible she woke up for a second, grabbed the bottle, took a couple of pills thinking she wouldn't go back to sleep—but then why the chained door? God only knows. Maybe it was an accidental overdose like Bob Walker. It's a real bitch, though, because apparently now the hotel is crawling with reporters and every first edition in the country will be headlining suicide. Bum rap." He fell silent again. She couldn't have killed herself deliberately, not over insomnia, nor some lousy play, not when she had so many people whom she loved and was loved by—like me. I had no doubt that my strength would have been more than enough for both of us in this instance, as hers had been in the past; she would have called me—

"She would have called me, Pop, and said something. She loved me. She would have said *something*."

"Like what?"

"I don't know—like *Help*, come here, I need you, things are rough."

Pamela went over and put her hands on Father's shoulders. "Leland, the Logans thought it might be nice for all of us to come out to the country for lunch the day after tomorrow? It would be a lovely drive—and they do agree that there *must* be some form of memorial service, so we'll talk to Kenneth again in the morning and explain to him how everyone feels about it. After all, Josh was one of her oldest friends and he *is* the children's godfather, so that may have some influence."

Everything was settled, organized. Life was so easy, if one could learn how to compartmentalize it. Or be lucky enough to have somebody else to do it for you. The British certainly could teach us a lesson or two about survival. Survival of the fittest? Nothing seemed to apply; maybe that was the point.

Now, months later, in the early evening of October 18, 1960, as Pamela and I sat in the back of Father's new limousine, heading east through the Park, the sun setting behind us, recollections of our previous journey together pecked at the new skin that had taken all these months to grow. As vulnerable as this protective layer was, it sufficed temporarily, I noted apathetically; not one distinctive emotion either penetrated or emerged, except curiosity, which circled lazily like a hawk in the distance. Pamela had been somehow incorporated into the cellular architecture of this skin; I was actually not at all surprised to be sitting where I was, neither resentful of nor grateful for her presence. It was a way of life, this way of death; I wondered idly how many more times it could happen; there was my father left, and my brother. All my initial rage had subsided into inactive charcoal embers; the mechanism was easy, once you got the knack of it, nothing to do with religion or God or hope or resolution. It was much more animal, just as I had suspected the last time. The trick definitely was to stop think-ing altogether. At least for the time being. Focus on simple immediate pleasures like the sunset, or the superb whiskey sour that Monsen, my father's white-haired English butler, would soon be serving, although I didn't drink; but nothing too far into the future.

Indenting myself against the gray plush seat, I saw the three of us, my sister, brother, and I, tiger cubs, tumbling in a heap on the mossy floor of some exotic jungle, surrounded by huge fronds of foliage from a Rousseau painting . . .

"Poor Bill Francisco," Pamela was saying. "Such a sweet young man."

"Yes," I replied, yawning, "yes, I think she wanted to marry him."

Pamela pressed the button that raised the glass partition between us and the chauffeur. I much preferred it down.

"Darling, before we get home, I think I should tell you about her note to him—to spare your father going through it again."

"Okay," I agreed, wondering if Rousseau really had, as alleged, used a palette of a hundred and some-odd different greens in one painting.

As Pamela talked to me, the chain on her purse slipped back and forth through her fingers like a golden snake. "Bill arrived at her apartment around four, as they had arranged, and, not hearing her, assumed she was out. So then he looked in a folder on the desk where they used to leave notes for each other and found this—love letter, I suppose. It began, 'Dearest Bill, You must know how deeply I love you'—or something like that—the tone was very intimate, in a way, and she kept repeating 'I love you' throughout—then something about how she didn't hate him any more and didn't want him to be troubled by the vagaries of her illness—her handwriting was becoming quite illegible by this time, sliding down the page—and it ended with 'Be strong, be brilliant'—and her signature. You can imagine the panic he was in when he read it. He raced into the bedroom and found her looking as if she had prepared for bed last night and then just never got up this morning." We were almost through the Seventy-ninth Street transverse; Pamela automatically reached into her purse for a compact and lipstick. "Of course, it is impossible to interpret the exact *intent* of the letter now." She powdered her exquisite skin lightly; I could tell she'd been to the beauty salon that afternoon—probably Kenneth's—because her fingernails were freshly polished, and her auburn hair, with its natural gray streak rising perfectly from her forehead, was newly shaped.

My brother, sister, and I stretched languidly and licked each other in the late sun filtering through a hundred different greens. One time, when we were very young, Mother and Father had taken a house in St. Malo, a private beach community some thirty miles north of San Diego. I was about five, Bridget three, and Bill one. The beach was very deep as it ran down to the water, and the sand always glinted with thousands of tiny gold flecks. One evening at low tide, the shore was totally covered at the water's edge by minuscule blue and pink shells rising mysteriously out of its slick gurgling surface; they exactly mirrored the pastel colors of the sky. The three of us screamed with joy: it was the most beautiful thing we had ever seen, though no one could explain why it had happened. Every day we ran naked on the beach, until some neighbor complained about Bill's one-year-old genitals; then Mother fashioned a primitive bikini out of elastic tape and an old handkerchief, and he resumed eating all the cigarette butts he could find in the sand. Bridget and I taught him how to lie very still in the water while it foamed around us and sometimes almost gently carried us out to sea, and how to collect only the shells with tiny holes wormed through them so that we could string them together like long leis, and how to wrap seaweed around our waists like wet hula skirts, and how to scratch pictures in the sand, quickly, between waves that would erase them the next minute. It was the summer that I learned to tie my shoes, and Father had his fortieth birthday, to his great displeasure, but that morning we were allowed to taste coffee out of his cup for the first time. Many people came and stayed—three of our four godfathers: John Swope, a photographer who was always following us around taking pictures; and Jimmy Stewart, who brought me a silver necklace that I never took off, with a turquoise-eyed thunderbird dangling from it; and Roger Edens, who arranged and produced music and was married to Martha, our *only* godmother, Mother's closest friend. Roger and Jimmy played the piano and Johnny taught us this song:

Mouse, mouse, come out of your hole
And I shall give you a golden bowl.
You will sit on a tuft of hay
And I shall frighten the cat away.

Mouse, mouse, when you go to bed,
I shall give you a large loaf of bread.
You will have cheese and a plateful of rice,
'Cause I love to think of the dear little mice.

We all went around singing it endlessly. Bridget and I shared a bedroom for the first time in our lives; it was unbelievably exhilarating to lie side by side and talk to each other before going to sleep. One night, Mother stuck her head in the door and told us to stop the racket, it was bedtime; but after a safe interlude we went right on singing and giggling. The house was built around a brick patio, which she crossed again in ten minutes to say that we were being not only extremely disobedient but foolish as well, since we could be clearly heard in the living room across the courtyard where all the grownups were sitting, and if she heard one more sound, she was warning us, we would have to be spanked. Heady and reckless with excitement, we sang a chorus of "Frère Jacques" loudly in unison. Mother stormed back, yanked the Dutch door open, and switched on the light. "Leland!" she called across the darkened patio. "Come here this *instant!*" We had never seen her so angry; it was thrilling. Father came and stood sheepishly in the doorway with his hands in his pockets. "All right, Leland, you take Brooke and I'll take Bridget," she announced, marching over to Bridget's bed. "Maggie," Father murmured, "couldn't we give them one more chance?" Mother was pulling down Bridget's pajamas. "Nope," she said firmly, and started to spank Bridget. I began to giggle; by the time Father had me across his lap, I was laughing uproariously. It was my first spanking. As his hand smacked my behind for the third or fourth time, inflicting actual pain, I felt first a sensation of surprise, then of fury, both of which turned my laughter into uncontrollable sobs. I was vaguely aware of Bridget crying in the bed next to me, and then Father picking me up and carrying me outside where he leaned against a post entwined with bougainvillaea. He held me tightly against his chest, so tightly I could hardly breathe. "Brooke," he whispered to me, beginning to cry himself; unable to see his face clearly in the filtered light, I reached up and touched his eyes in wonder—his tears soaked my hair and mine his polo shirt. "Brooke," he said, weeping, "I promise you something—do you know what a promise is?—I shall never spank you again as long as I live." He kept his word.

The next time I saw him cry he was in his old maroon silk bathrobe, and it was the evening of the day Bridget died. There were other people in the study—Josh and Nedda, George and Joan Axelrod, Bill Francisco, and Pamela—whom I had to walk past rather self-consciously in order to reach him. He was sitting in his favorite armchair, heavily, as if he never wanted to rise again. His eyes were fixed absently on the seven-o'clock news; when I came and stood between the television set and him, they glimmered like milky blue stones under shallow water. I reached down and lifted the large cut-glass tumbler of Jack Daniels from his lap, where it had sunk with both his hands clasped rigidly around it, and took a sip because my mouth was so dry.

"Come here, Brooke," was all he said, so I sat on his lap and put my head against his, and his tears streamed down my cheeks. "Poor Bridget, poor little kid," he murmured over and over against my face; I kept licking his tears away as they reached my lips because both my arms were tight around his neck and I didn't want to let go. Oh, God, I thought, we used to want so badly to be grown up—all the endless games we played to evoke that miraculous state of power, Bridget and I sauntering past the hall mirror in lipstick and high heels, Bill sitting for hours in the driveway behind the steering wheel of the old Cadillac, maniacally spinning it—but given a choice of which condition was really worse, that of parent or that of child, didn't we know, even then, that parents lost hands-down? All the time we were growing up and hating the fact that it took so long, didn't we instinctively sense the agony that waited for us on the other side of the fence?

Monsen came in unobtrusively and announced dinner. Pamela moved over and rested her hand lightly on Father's shoulder.

"Come, Leland, darling, we're having your favorite—vichyssoise and chicken hash—a new recipe from the head chef at the Beverly Hills Hotel." Father blew his nose loudly. He had very dogmatic eating habits, which we children were delighted by, never touching anything remotely tinged with color: this eliminated most vegetables except potatoes from his diet, and for that matter fruit, except for strawberries (in spite of their color and his allergy to them); as for meat, he ate only chicken, lamb chops, or steak, and no more than an arbitrary two bites from the entire serving, but he consumed with passion what we alluded to as "white food" —scrambled eggs, custard, vanilla ice cream, and the Beverly Hills Hotel chicken hash.

During the course of dinner Josh recounted, with a high degree of animation for which he was justly famous, a jumble of stories about the various enterprises in which he and Father had been jointly involved, how Father had become his agent while he, Josh, was the dialogue coach for Charles Boyer in his first English-speaking movie, *The Garden of Allah*, tales about their productions of *Mr. Roberts* and *South Pacific*, about Hank Fonda and Mary Martin; they were all familiar and gratifying and went well with the chicken hash.

In Father's study, after dinner, there was the first general discussion of Bridget, and a tremendous number of phone calls were made. Bill was notified in Fort Bragg, North Carolina, where he was taking paratrooper training for the 82nd Airborne Division, one of the more successful schemes he had devised, along with marriage, to escape Menninger's. Kathleen Malley, Father's faithful secretary of thirty-one years, was on emergency duty for the evening, and all calls to the apartment had to be siphoned through her; she also had to deal with all the newspapers, which were about to go to press. While Bill Francisco sat in a daze, Pamela, Nedda, and Joan were huddled over "arrangements," and Josh strode purposefully up and down the small room, issuing suggestions on all fronts. At one point, he stopped in the middle of the Aubusson rug, right on a basket of flowers festooned with blue ribbons, and said to Father with great intensity, "You know, Leland, she really wasn't of this world at all—she never seemed to belong here. Even when she was a baby, I can remember thinking she was like a creature from some strange mythical forest, another planet—always with that faraway look in her eyes."

Father nodded. "The thing that kills me," he said, "is that I never quite knew what was going on in her head. For instance, her insane need for privacy. I mean, she never came to me and told me *anything*. So here I sit like a complete idiot, asking myself over and over where I went wrong, for Chrissake, what I could have done to make it easier for her. I thought we loved each other. I don't know. I don't know the answer to any of it. The thing that breaks my heart is the feeling of absolute uselessness."

One Sunday afternoon a few months earlier, during an inter-lude in the conversation at a family lunch, someone had asked where Bridget was. Father looked down the table at Pamela. "I forgot to ask you, darling, isn't she feeling well?" Pamela looked stricken. "Oh, Leland, for heaven's sake, you said yesterday that *you* were going to call her from the office. Didn't you get through?" Father muttered at his plate, "Oh, hell, I must have forgotten to tell Malley to ask her. Why didn't you remind me?" "What a pity," sighed Grandsarah, Father's mother (named Grandsarah by Bill), who lived in California and was visiting for a few weeks. "Maybe she'll be able to come by some other afternoon."

"Yes," Josh was saying now, "yes," kneading the lower half of his face thoughtfully. "And she was so *vulnerable*. Whenever I think of Bridget, I think of that white skin, and those lost eyes and that air of belonging in another world, so elusive, so skinny and fragile."

It flashed through my mind that I would never see Bridget again. The worst part was unraveling the word *never*. I would never be able to touch her, hug her, laugh with her in front of the objects of our evil coded gossip, use her hairbrush (first pulling out strands of her long blond hair), sometimes spend days before her birthday searching through the city for the only nightgowns she would wear (flannel, with long sleeves and small flowers), never see her again as she was the last time, just a few days ago—sitting cross-legged on a scrapbook to make the freshly glued photographs inside stick, her long arms and legs jutting out everywhere and her pale hair spilling over her face, which looked up at me quizzically as she rested it on one hand, as if she intended to stay in that position forever. "There's a sale on Kleenex and toilet paper at Bloomingdale's in a few days." She grinned at me knowingly; we would be into a lot more than paper goods. "Don't forget"—as I closed the door be-hind me—"to call."

I had found out that the coroner had roughly estimated the time of her death at around noon that day. Or perhaps a little later. So that meant, all things being equal, that I probably *had* heard a sound in her bedroom at ten o'clock that morning as I stood impatiently tapping my foot in the hall outside the door. And that, in turn, meant—this was suddenly startlingly apparent—that if I'd had a duplicate key to her apartment, or at least pursued my instinct to get one from the superintendent (Why hadn't I?

Was it haste or irritation or inane hypersensitivity about intrusion? I couldn't remember any more), I, Brooke—I would never be able to forget this—almost literally would have held in the palm of my hand the singular and now irretrievable opportunity to save my sister's life.

2

Bridget

Nancy ("Slim" Hayward) Keith:

"She was quite different from anybody I've ever known. She really was a beauty, almost transparent, both physically and spiritually. There was an aura about her, a glisten and glow to her look and to her manner. I used to say to her, 'When you've grown up and when you have mascara on, you know, those big long eyelashes black instead of white, and when you grow into yourself, you're going to be the most beautiful human being anyone's ever seen. So just bide your time. You're going to be the swan of all time.'"

Jane Fonda:

"I remember vividly the last thing she said to me. I was coming back with her on a train from New Haven; I hadn't seen her for quite a long time, because I'd been away to school and she'd been institutionalized, but this was within a year of her death. I was then studying with Lee [Strasberg] and she was living in the apartment where she eventually died.

"I was asking her questions about Riggs, and she said to me, 'The hardest part of all is coming out and having to deal with other people's problems; it's all I can do, it absorbs all of my energy just to keep myself together—and when I'm out in the world, it's slightly more than I can bear.' She was like someone who'd had shock treatment. Talking to her was like talking to someone through gauze, through heavy filters. There was the same attempt to reveal only the minimum that has to be revealed at a particular time: don't open those floodgates; don't let very much out; be as calm as you can; don't rock the boat. What that says is you must do away with anything unique or unusual about yourself or you won't survive.

"And then we went to her apartment, which absolutely shocked me because it was so conventional. I had an enormous sadness when I was there with her, because it was as if somehow she'd sold out. I couldn't believe that Bridget collected antiques. She had become terribly concerned about porcelain or the right kind of glass; it was reflected in her apartment and the way she decorated it. Somewhere along the way, Bridget was trying to fit into a mold that had nothing to do with her. Her spirit had nowhere else to go."

. . .

I didn't know it was going to be her last summer.

She spent it in Williamstown, Massachusetts, working as an apprentice at the Williamstown Theatre.

I spent it commuting frenetically between Greenwich and New York, where I then had a tiny room on the third floor of an old brownstone. Every day, I would race from fashion modeling to voice lessons to auditions for the fall theatre season to apartment hunting. Although New York City in the heat was practically unbearable, the more manic my schedule the better I liked it, particularly on Sundays when the whole city seemed to migrate to the country and I was left alone to read the newspapers lazily. Irene Selznick had given Father and Pamela, newly wed, her house in Bedford Village for the summer. It was about an hour from the city or twenty minutes from my house in Greenwich. I had a new car, my first convertible; driving it anywhere with the top down and a scarf around my hair was the most exhilarating experience I could think of.

Irene's house sat on roughly fifteen acres of beautifully landscaped property; it was called Imspond to honor the combination of her initials, I.M.S. (Irene Mayer Selznick), and an enormous pond with a rowboat. I loved going to that house; it was a one-story rambling cottage, filled with fireplaces and antique country furniture, bright handwoven rugs, wonderful quilts, and deep chintz-covered sofas, always cool inside even on the hottest day, but with a warm sense of light floating through all the rooms.

Father was deeply, instinctively suspicious of country life. His abhorrence of insects—mosquitoes, in particular—and any kind of snake amounted to a phobia, which had been a source of amusement to us as children when we lived for three years in rugged rattlesnake and coyote terrain—then the wild mountains of the Doheny Estate, now the cultivated steppes of Trousdale in Beverly Hills. To my chagrin I discovered, when I was eleven or twelve and fixated on Hemingway and Africa, that although Hemingway was a close friend and client of Father's who had many times invited him to go along on safari, Father had always declined because of the "goddamn bugs all over the place." Also he distrusted the country because poison ivy and sumac lurked there, lying in wait for the innocent wayfarer, and houses were not generally air-conditioned like apartments in the city.

This particular summer, however, he seemed to enjoy himself. Winston, Pamela's son by Randolph Churchill, came over from England, and Father promptly blew him to a course in flying instruction; aviation had always been one of Father's major passions. The other, photography, he indulged day and night by taking hundreds of color photographs of Imspond from every conceivable angle, inside and out. As usual, he would have "the best color lab in the world," *Life* magazine, blow them up to an extravagant sixteen by twenty inches, eventually to be edited by Bridget into a scrapbook for Irene. One Saturday I drove out for the day with my friend Jones Harris. Father intrepidly lowered himself into the rowboat with three cameras slung around his neck, and shot pictures of the receding shoreline with a zoom lens while I rowed; Jones, reclining languorously in the bow, inquired, "Leland, do you think you're going to be able to bring this picture in for under one million three?"

Bridget called me several times from Williamstown to report on her activities and to see if I would drive up for a visit. She was having a splendid time working backstage in a hodgepodge of production exigencies; the drive up through the Berkshires was beautiful, she informed me, and she could press me into service any day of the week. As an added inducement, I would know a lot of people: Suzie Pleshette was up there doing *Two for the Seesaw*, and E. G. Marshall and Carrie Nye and Dick Cavett; Bill Francisco was directing two productions; and, most important, our close friend Tom Mankiewicz was his assistant director, moonlighting on the side as an actor. Tom, son of the screenwriter-director Joe Mankiewicz, had grown up with us in California, but after we had moved East in 1948 we hadn't seen much of him again until the fall of 1959.

Tom Mankiewicz:

"I have tremendous memories of you and Bridget, two girls who were always just enough older than I was to really make a difference. I used to see you frequently but infrequently. I mean, Brooke and Bridget was like a traveling family act. When I was young, it was Brooke and Bridget coming over and Brooke and Bridget this and that. You were both uncommonly pretty and a very strange pair of girls to be running in and out of the house every odd summer or holiday or party when you were dragged over.

"I met Bridget again the fall of my freshman year, in the Green Room of the Yale Dramat with Bill Francisco. Bridget was going with Bill. She was lying down on a couch in the Green Room, very attractive dress, oddly made up—she had blue mascara on her eyes, that kind of thing—doing some sort of outré number. We both knew that we knew each other very well and we didn't know each other at all. Bill and she were rather tense together that evening and she wanted me to go out with the two of them to have dinner. It was about six o'clock, and I said sure. More because I wanted to get close to Bill Francisco than to her: he was the director of The Dramat—it was my first year in The Dramat—and I thought he was a terrific director.

"That night I was fascinated by Bridget. I wasn't in love with her yet; later I guess I was more in love with Bridget than I've been with anyone in my life. That night she seemed to me to be so incredibly real. And a little bit weird, which I loved. I had no idea she had been to Riggs; I had no idea that there was any trouble at all. I was just entranced by her."

The fall of 1959 was marked by a number of important events in our family.

I had entered Lee Strasberg's acting classes after an interview with him, in which, having asked me some cursory questions about my previous acting experience (none) and who my favorite actors or actresses were (Olivier, Brando, and so on), he told me that I could start immediately. As it was almost impossible to get into his classes, and I knew several people who had waited for years before a space opened up, I summoned up the courage to ask him why he was prepared to expedite the procedure in my case. He replied unhesitatingly that it was due to my mother's prominence as an actress and my father's as a producer. I boldly told him that I didn't want to be accepted by him as a student for that reason. He sighed and smoothed his fine white hair with both hands, then turned on me a dazzling smile. "It has nothing to do with favoritism, darling," he said. "Your mother and father are very talented. You might inherit the talent, see? The odds are that you will prove to be more gifted as an actress than most other people *with* experience that I interview. And your lack of experience is a blessing—it means that you have had no bad habits yet to unlearn, no preconceived ideas about how to act. I consider myself lucky to have you in my classes, darling. You will start on Monday morning."

When I related this conversation to Mother, to my surprise she agreed with him, but she may have been somewhat distracted by just having signed to act in what would be her last play, *Sweet Love Remember'd*, by Ruth Goetz. It was impossible for any of us to determine exactly why Mother ever signed for any play, since she always swore that she hated acting, and most of all the star system. At the same time, she was passionate about the theatre and much preferred it to movies, which she considered stultifying. Often her excuse for doing a play was that she needed the money, but in this case her explanation was that a ladder had fallen on her head the day she read the script.

Bridget, after two years of therapy at Austin Riggs, took a one-room apartment at 135 East Fifty-fourth Street, and commuted up to Stockbridge once or twice a month. Occasionally she would come to Greenwich to visit Mother and Kenneth; they were living in a charming house that overlooked the Byram River, with two vicious swans, an incontinent starling, an Abyssinian cat that devoured its own litters, and a crippled German shepherd. For the first time in four years, Bridget and I saw a great deal of each other. I would stop by her apartment every day; she would appear unannounced at my house in Greenwich on her way down from Riggs, and roll around on the floor with her two small nephews. She had fallen in love with Bill Francisco. I met him several times and liked him very much.

Bill Francisco:

"I met Bridget when I was in Stockbridge directing and stage-managing at that little playhouse, going back and forth between there and Williamstown. That fall, 1959, I found an excuse to write her—about getting new glasses or something. I got a lovely letter back saying, 'If you really value my opinion, please call when you're in New York.'

"Initially she was very afraid of my meeting you because she felt you were the pretty one, and that everybody who met you would fall in love with you; also you were active in the theatre and I was trying to be active in the theatre and there would be a great rapport there."

. . .

Tom Mankiewicz:

"I saw more of her and Bill. Bill took me on as assistant
director. He was very talented. He was in his early thirties then, and
blessed or cursed with a tremendously attractive face and manner.
And he cared about her. Whatever weaknesses or deficiencies Bill
had, hers were double. At least she felt that hers were double. And so,
when she became hung up on him, he was in a strange sort of cat-
bird seat—was this girl really going to shrivel and die without him? I
mean, she was beautifully bred out of great show-business stock, out
of Maggie by Leland, she was incredibly sensitive, marvelous, bright
in her own way, an ethereal kind of lady who was, also, skittish and
Bambi-like and who could immediately turn off or become upset or
depressed. I think Bill felt more comfortable with her because she
was moodier than he was."

Also that fall, my eighteen-year-old brother, Bill, decided to get
married. He was majoring in math at the University of Kansas, and
living in a small bachelor apartment in Topeka. Still wet behind
the ears from a two-year stint in Menninger's, he flew East with his
bride-to-be, Marilla Nelson, to announce his plans to Mother and
Kenneth. It was the first time Bill had been in Greenwich since the
autumn of 1955, precisely four years earlier, when he and Bridget
had left home to live with Father. Not surprisingly, things were
slightly strained between mother and prodigal son. However,
Mother and Kenneth were pleased with the liaison; not only
did they like Marilla, who bore a striking resemblance to Bridget
in coloring and build, but also they had become somewhat disil-
lusioned by Menninger's, and in this one instance their feelings
dovetailed with Father's. He was fed up with shouldering the gigantic expense. The next spring, when Bill had decided to join the
Army as a paratrooper, everyone envisioned the venture as an
effective means of tying off any remnants of the umbilical cord that
(they thought) might bind him to Topeka and the immediate
environs of Menninger's.

An engagement party was arranged by Marilla's sister in
Topeka, and Mother made plans to fly to it just before she went
into rehearsals for *Sweet Love Remember'd*.

Bridget, who hadn't seen Bill for two and a half years, suddenly professed a desire to go, too. At this point her relationship with Mother was going through one of its cycles of severe stress. She had refused to come out to the house to see Bill and Marilla, basically because she was angry at Mother and her anger at Mother inevitably manifested itself in periods of withdrawal. Nobody knew better than Mother how extremely effective this punishment was, she by her own example having instructed all of us in its subtleties for years. Bridget's was a classic case of the pupil outdistancing the master. By now her acquired skills far surpassed Mother's and, more than skills, had become involuntary and chronic, even pathological, reflex actions. As the oldest of the three of us, I had, upon reaching adolescence, taken great pride in also being the most rebellious. I saw myself as a pioneer, a pathfinder repeatedly beating my head against the barrier of Mother's authority. I, too, had become well versed in the art of psychological warfare as she taught it, but to me it had never seemed more than one of her numerous idiosyncrasies, a dreadful game whose rules I knew even when I was being too stubborn to play. The first rule was that Mother, in a state of wrath, almost never raised her voice: she lowered it drastically until it was a distant murmur. Second: the more I attempted to make contact, to explain, to argue, the more remote her voice and demeanor became. Third: I would be sent to my room with instructions not to reappear except for meals until I could apologize. (It was a challenge to see how long I could go without breaking, particularly after I saw *Lives of a Bengal Lancer*, with Gary Cooper suffering the torture of lighted bamboo sticks under his fingernails. Once I proudly lasted a week, but it was excruciating.) Fourth: when I joined the rest of the family at dinner, Mother would behave as if I were invisible, never once looking at me or addressing me. And so on. After dinner, if I tried to kiss her good night, she would turn her cheek away, and since she was a fine actress, she knew how to make her silences as eloquent as words. Bridget and Bill watched with demure interest; much later I was to wonder if these scenes didn't have more effect on them than on me. Usually after a few days I would crack and make my way downstairs for the apology scene. Mother expected a proper apology with real conviction; otherwise I was sent back and we would continue the ordeal until she was satisfied. I became adept at bursting, melodramatically, into tears at the right moment; then she would hug me and miraculously turn back into my familiar cheerful mother. Bridget and Bill would observe this ritual with angelic expressions on their faces, Bridget with a beatific smile ("You little bitch," I would mutter at her under my breath so Mother couldn't hear; Bridget would lower her eyes and smile even more mysteriously, incandescently), but I don't remember their ever having to go through this experience themselves, so they must have learned the lesson by observing me. Perhaps by not having actually to act out these psychodramas, they absorbed their impact in a more serious way than I. In any case, Bridget, in her own adolescence, would become irritatingly silent for days on end rather than face a good fight.

Now Mother and Kenneth grew concerned about the possibility that if Bridget attended Bill's engagement party the festivity of the occasion might be marred by a further incident in the current internecine strife between Bridget and Mother. Kenneth hastily sent Bridget a letter. It said that he forbade her to go to the party because her behavior to Mother, of late, had been outrageous and inhuman, and what was barely excusable when she was sixteen was now intolerable at twenty; that he would subordinate his own feelings if Bill might be unhappy at her not being there, but that since she hadn't gone a step out of her way to see her own brother on *his* visit, it was dubious that he would be disappointed if she postponed *hers*. It said that any arguments she might muster to defend herself would be hogwash and that she would have to learn someday that she could not continue to pursue a course of selfishly taking more and more without giving anything back. It said that she had forfeited all the deep love and respect he, Kenneth, had for her, that although one of the happiest features of his marriage to Mother nine years earlier had been the advent into his life of two entrancing little girls, Bridget had gone to great lengths to ruin that pleasure. It concluded with the information that he was sending the letter behind Mother's back and would only tell her after it had been mailed.

I was changing my clothes in Bridget's apartment when the mail came that day. She read the letter, handed it to me wordlessly, went to the closet, and packed a suitcase. I went downstairs with her and followed her along the street for a while but she refused to speak to me. I went on to a class at Lee Strasberg's; she checked back into Austen Riggs in a severe depression.

Kenneth was a kind Englishman of considerable equanimity. He seldom lost his temper. When he did, he recovered quickly.

Bridget did not. In December, while Mother was in rehearsals, Kenneth sent several letters to Bridget at Riggs.

In the first one he apologized for the prolonged unhappiness caused by his previous letter, and begged her to take his tantrum in her stride, as she must know how solid the foundation of his love for her really was. He explained that, in the past, Mother had always stopped him from expressing his flashes of temper but this time, to his present regret, he had eluded her. He implored Bridget to surmount the wall that had arisen between herself and Mother, and assured her there were many doors in it that Mother would crawl through if she knew Bridget would be waiting on the other side.

In the second, he enclosed a torn piece of yellow legal paper penciled in Mother's familiar scribble, which he'd rescued from the wastebasket:

> My darling Bridget
>
> I want you to know about my love for you. It is the most completely unselfish emotion I have ever known. It is forever, and needs nothing in return. I know, after these five years, that if you never write me or see me again, my love will continue just as strong and constant. So please, my darling, stop worrying about what you have or haven't done to me—the snag, of course, is that my judgment falls far short of my love—and I

The writing stopped there. Bridget did not respond, and was still at Riggs when Mother died two weeks later on New Year's Day, 1960.

Tom Mankiewicz:

"I saw more and more of Bridget. She'd come to New Haven, stay at the Taft for three or four days during final rehearsals; the week of the play she would be there every day. Everybody liked her —all the people in The Dramat who would normally hate the director's girl friend.

"We got to be really close. We knew a lot of people in common; we hadn't seen each other in a while and it was like catching up on our lives. It was during that time that I saw the chinks in her armor which made me love her more; naturally, when you're eighteen, you think you're on top of the world and can take care of anybody. I had no idea there was any kind of mental disease, if you could call it that, or withdrawal, or whatever. She didn't talk about it at all. I would say: gee, I'm sorry that you seem to be upset about this or that or so on, and she would talk about herself and her life, always, in the beginning, skirting the fact that she had been in Riggs. She didn't trust people a great deal and she was not an extrovert. If she thought she liked you, you could talk to her night after night, but it would only be after a certain number of nights that she would really start to tell you something about herself. She would test you, telling you the way she thought about things that perhaps frightened her; but she never opened herself up until she was really sure of you, and that took a long time. I found her an immensely private person who could count on the fingers of one hand the people that she would open up to. There were so damn few she was willing to let in, for whatever reason. You could sit and scream and beg Bridget to tell you what the matter was, and no matter how much she loved you, she wouldn't tell you unless she felt like telling you, and that was that."

When Mother died, I only saw Bridget cry once—right after the memorial service in Greenwich when Kenneth decided to read Mother's will to the three of us. It was the first time since Bridget had reinstated herself at Riggs that she had seen him. He took us to a small bedroom in the house while friends gathered in the living room and drank coffee. We sat in a row on the bed, Bridget, as stiff as tightly strung wire, between Bill and me. Suddenly tears were streaming down her cheeks but she did not move or make a sound. Bill and I edged closer to her and pressed our shoulders against hers. Kenneth obliviously went on reading the will.

Bill Francisco:

"What I remember most was her humor. She had a wonderful sense of humor. That's what began the relationship and that's what was always the best part of it.

"She was a very two-sided girl. There was this wonderful child-like side which was legitimate, and there was also that of a woman.

And I think one of the things that was wrong with the family relationship was a refusal to see the woman's side. I mean she was a capable, bright lady, and when we first began dating, I didn't feel I was dating a waif. Occasionally I would be aware of this other side —more after her death—how Logan and all those people felt about her, as if she was some sort of star child, strange little creature, fairy child. Which was great, but there was this other side. When your mother died—the late news came on: 'Margaret Sullavan died'—I thought, oh, my God, so I called Leland and said 'How is Bridget?' And we were both worried that she was going to fall apart, that we shouldn't leave her alone, so I came down to New York the next morning. She was shaken, obviously, but what she wanted to do was go to church and say a prayer for her mother. I convinced Leland it was all right. We left his place at the Carlyle and went back to her apartment so she could get some clothes. There was a little church across the street, and she said, 'I have to go there, do you mind?' So I stayed in the apartment; she put on a black kerchief, went off to the church, was back in fifteen minutes, no scene. She just wanted to have her moment. It was that side of her that I remember best."

In the spring of that year, 1960, my brother and Marilla got married shortly on the heels of Father and Pamela, who had been in Nevada for six weeks awaiting his final divorce papers from Nancy Hayward. Nan and Father had been married for ten years. We children were sorry to see her go.

It was damp and chilly in Topeka. Bridget and I met Father and Pamela, fresh from Nevada, at the airport and we set up headquarters in the Holiday Inn. After a rehearsal of the wedding ceremony in a drafty Methodist church paneled in dark plywood with a crucifix suspended overhead, Father took everyone to dinner at a nearby steakhouse. All the women except Pamela, Bridget, and me wore their hair in sprayed beehives. Bill was in uniform, having just enlisted. Dinner was an uneasy success.

The next day, Bridget and I, who were sharing a room, were bored to distraction. It was gray and cold outside and all we had brought were summer dresses. Besides, the Holiday Inn was in the middle of nowhere. Suddenly the door to our room burst open and there stood Peter Fonda, whom we hadn't seen in five or six years. Not only were we startled by his precipitous reappearance in our lives but also by the evidence that he was no longer fourteen years old. He notified us excitedly that he had been sitting in his aunt's house in Omaha, Nebraska, a few hours earlier, minding his own business and reading the newspaper, when his eyes lit upon an article posting Bill's wedding banns, so to speak, giving details and whereabouts of the imminent ceremony in Topeka. He'd hopped on the first plane without saying goodbye to his aunt, in order to give the groom away, being one of Bill's childhood friends.

Bridget and I were delighted. The three of us sat and talked and talked. Bill got married and we went back to talking. Peter fell in love with Bridget, so he announced, and he pocketed the white gloves she wore to the wedding.

The next morning, eating pancakes at the Holiday Inn, we found out that Francis Gary Powers had been shot down the day before, and Peter became even more excited. He said he felt like a comet traveling between two great solar systems—that of our family and that of his—only appearing when great events were taking place.

It was that spring Bridget found out she had epilepsy. Our guesswork about the origin of her bizarre fainting spells was over. Although she didn't tell me that for weeks afterward, she made a typically succinct, understated entry in her diary:

March 17, 1960: 10:30 a.m., New Haven—Saw Dr. Rogowski. Cried and cried all day.

Bill Francisco:

"Long before she went to the doctor in New Haven she knew —or believed—whatever she had was terminal. Or, at the least, debilitating enough to frighten her into that view. I had a very unsophisticated attitude. I always had this feeling she would get better, while all the time she knew she was going to get progressively worse. That much she did say. What had started with little spells was, by the time I knew her, escalating into monstrous ones that lasted for a day or two or three. She had one of these once in New Haven. I came back from a rehearsal and she was out cold on the sofa for like two days. I was panic-stricken. I thought she was dead, that she'd been drinking. I knew she wasn't supposed to drink. Every once in a while she would come to and say, 'Don't tell Father, don't call Father.' Finally, when she was better, I wanted to drive her back to New York because she was in no condition to drive. She said, 'Oh, no, I'm absolutely fine.' That steel will of hers. Well, it later turned out that she saw a doctor on the way back to New York, and he told her what she had. But she never told me or your father. Six or seven months after she died, Leland and Pamela had me to supper and all of this came up: the business about the doctor in New Haven, which I knew nothing about, and the fact that eventually—say, by the time she was twenty-four or twenty-five—she wouldn't be able to move at all. By this time, they'd been told that at the rate things were going, it would have been risky for Bridget to lead any kind of independent life. Ultimately she would have had to be contained by force. Which, of course, would have been unthinkable."

In June, she called me one Friday evening to say she was going out of town for the weekend but would I like to have breakfast with her on Monday? I was always flattered by her invitations. On Monday morning when I rang her doorbell, she came to the door looking strange and disheveled.

"You won't believe me when I tell you this," she mumbled as I followed her wobbly progress into the room. There was broken glass everywhere, overturned furniture, smashed china.

"What the hell went on in here while you were away?" I asked, aghast at the destruction. "It looks like a hurricane hit. Were you robbed?"

She pointed toward the kitchenette. "I didn't go away after all. Look." All the cupboards were open and totally empty. Half-eaten cans of tuna fish and soup, clumsily pried open, lay all over the counters and floor. The stench was awful.

"I must have done it myself." She was shivering. "It had to be me. Nobody else was here and the door was locked."

I put my arms around her. She began to cry pitifully.

"I never left," she repeated. "I must have passed out right after I talked to you on the phone, and come to just a little while ago."

It took a minute for me to grasp what she meant.

"This is what happens when I have a seizure. Sometimes I hurl stuff around, get very violent. Look at this unholy mess. I think I've broken all of my good wineglasses. I don't know what I'm doing until afterwards, when I start to come out—and then I sort of remember sort of in a dream . . ."

"But, Bridget," I said to her, my heart pounding, "you talked to me on Friday. This is Monday. Do you realize that? You can't have been unconscious for almost three days."

"Well, I must have been," she said. "Sometimes it's for a long time. The last thing I remember was leaving the apartment and putting my overnight bag down to lock the door—and then this terrible feeling. . . ." She collapsed onto the convertible sofa.

"What kind of a feeling?" I asked.

"It starts in the pit of my stomach. Kind of a rush of pain. Oh, the worst pain you can imagine. Then I begin to feel dizzy. Nauseated. Sort of a sensation I'm being sucked into the center of a black whirlpool, pitch black, whirling around and around towards the very center. Strange high-pitched voices in another language that I've never heard before, can't recognize. Voices in a foreign language—but I understand it perfectly. *Perfectly*." She shuddered.

"What do they say?"

She put her head in her hands.

"Bridget, for God's sake what do they say?"

She lay back and put her arms over her face and began to cry again.

"Bridget, I can't stand this—what do the voices say?"

"Well—there's this strange humming sound, buzzing—hurts my ears—like a dog whistle, very high frequency. I am walking down this long corridor, tunnel, endless, with lots of arched doors on either side, but I know they're locked, I can't open them. They say, in this strange language—I know it sounds crazy—but they are saying something like 'Bridget, you must open the door, one of the doors,' sort of in a chant, very high. 'Try harder—you mustn't come to the end of this tunnel—past the last door there's *nothing*, just blackness.' And the voices get louder and louder and I can't stand it any more, and then at last I open a door with all my strength, and the light comes in, the sun, and I begin to rise—and I know I'm alive, I wake up, I'm still alive after all."

"Bridget," I said gently after a while, "this is really serious. I mean two and a half days is no joke. What if you were driving a car or crossing a street or something, and you went into one of these? I promised you on my sacred word of honor that I wouldn't tell Father, but I'm beginning to think I should."

"No, no." She grabbed me. "Dr. Brenman [her analyst at

Riggs] knows all about it. It's happened before. Really. There are warnings. I know when it's about to happen. The pain I was telling you about—if I was driving, I would have enough time to pull over to the side of the road. I promise you. Look—I was outside my apartment when I began to feel it and I had plenty of time to unlock the door and come back in to lie down on the bed here. There are my purse and suitcase. I have plenty of warning. Please, whatever you do, don't tell Father or he'll make me go to a closed hospital or back to Riggs."

"But, Bridget, I don't understand. I thought Dr. Rogowski gave you medicine to take every day so you wouldn't have these blackouts. Aren't you taking it?"

"Yes, yes, of course I am. Maybe he should change the dose or something."

I made her promise me that she would go see Dr. Rogowski, and, in return, swore I wouldn't mention it to Father. And that's the way we left it.

Tom Mankiewicz:

"Throughout the winter we became closer. At that point in her life, she needed desperately to have somebody to hold on to. I think she very much wanted to marry Bill. But Bill was terribly unsure of himself, and to have Bridget fall in love with him was scary because her welfare was really completely in his hands.

"Anyway, Bill had convinced Nikos Psacharopoulos that I had to be his assistant up in Williamstown that summer. Nikos was the director of the Williamstown Theatre, which was really an offshoot of the Yale Drama School.

"Bridget wanted very much to be an apprentice and to work. And she worked her ass off. She was painting scenery and banging away with nails between her teeth. I think in many ways during that summer she was happier than she'd been in a very long time—at least she told me that and she certainly showed it. Not so much because of Bill, but because all the kids up there liked her.

"By that time I was so in love with Bridget I just couldn't see straight. She was to me the most beautiful thing I'd ever seen. She always used to wear gardenia perfume. About two days before the first opening night up there, I found a place over the mountain, about an hour's drive, that had gardenias but they couldn't send them. I borrowed Peter Hunt's car, a little red M.G., and I went over the mountain; it took me two hours to get there and back. I got the gardenias and she never knew where they came from. Every week when a play opened, I would borrow Hunt's M.G. and go get them. I guess I must have logged sixteen hours or more getting her gardenias. About twice a year, I run into somebody or some place that smells of gardenias and even now, sixteen years later, I think of Bridget, instantly."

One night in mid-August, when New York was at the height of a heat wave, I hopped in my little convertible for a cooling drive.

By the time I got to Greenwich, I knew where I was going. I stopped at my house there long enough to throw some clothes in a bag and to call Bridget in Williamstown. Although it was an ungodly hour, I told her I was about to pay her that visit she'd been suggesting for weeks. She sounded sleepy but pleased, and gave me explicit directions on how to get there. As I reached the Berkshires, the dawn came up; the land became more and more beautiful. Suddenly I understood why Bridget had often said she wanted to live in Stockbridge for the rest of her life. When I got to Williamstown, I went straight to the theatre as she'd instructed me, and there she was with Tom and a welcoming committee standing on the green.

She immediately enlisted my services as a coffinmaker; the company was in rehearsal for the second to the last show of the season, *The Visit*, which starred E. G. Marshall, and his coffin was a vital prop. I worked all morning under Bridget's careful supervision and we ended up with a very impressive black-and-gold casket.

Then she dispatched me somewhere in somebody's truck to pick up some sort of special fabric for the costumes. For me to be bossed around by my younger sister was a complete reversal of roles, and not at all unpleasant. In the afternoon she allowed me time off to watch a dress rehearsal for *The Visit*. Nikos was the director; Bill Francisco wasn't there. Tom had a walk-on as a town policeman in an absurd helmet. Bridget amazed me; she was all over the place running most of the backstage action like an old-time production manager. Everyone came to her for advice on the props, the costumes, the lighting, the scenery. I was proud of her.

She had metamorphosed into a figure of authority, the last thing anyone would ever have expected of her. As I was leaving the next morning, I told her that she should ask Father for a job on his next show. Bridget confessed that she had a secret ambition to become a producer and that it was behind-the-scenes action she really liked.

She blew me a kiss as I started back to New York, and I couldn't help thinking how pleased Mother, whose career had begun in summer stock with the famed University Players, would have been to see her so happy.

Tom Mankiewicz:

"You came up to Williamstown once that summer, and she was terribly nervous and uptight about it because she felt very much that Williamstown was her own little province. It didn't go off badly at all, but I knew she was apprehensive about the fact that you were coming up. You represented the glamorous New York Vogue influence that she was frightened to death of. She was, to herself, the girl who was crazy, and you weren't. And in fact something happened that summer that convinced her that she was crazy.

"It was the next to last week of the season. Bill wasn't there. I had gotten the gardenias and taken her to some restaurant. Afterward Nikos threw a big party at one of the fraternity houses because it was the last show of the season.

"I was sitting with Bridget on a staircase, and Nikos was about two stairs below us. Although Bridget didn't usually drink—her doctor had told her not to—that night she had a couple of glasses of wine. She was feeling terrific. We were talking to Nikos and sort of laughing; suddenly she pitched forward into Nikos's lap. Her eyes were open but they weren't. I was just absolutely panicked. People were crowding around her. Nikos told everyone to get out. We carried her into the next room. She started to scream, and the screams came from her bowels. We called the hospital; it was about one o'clock in the morning; no doctor. They had to wake one up. We must have stayed with her forty-five minutes until that doctor got there. She was talking to your mother the whole time. What she was saying was 'Mother. I've got to speak to my mother!' And we said, 'Your mother's dead.' She got very quiet, but her body was like a taut rubber band. Then she said, 'I know she's dead.' Tears were coming down her cheeks and she said, over and over, 'I never got a chance to tell her I was sorry. I wanted to tell her that I'm sorry.'

"Finally a doctor arrived. He gave her a shot, and she was terrified of the needle, just terrified; we had to really hold her down. We carried her back to the fraternity house where she was staying. The doctor ordered a nurse to stay in the room.

"I walked around crying for a couple of hours. I couldn't sleep and I went back up to the room to look at her. I would just so willingly have laid down my life for her then. If there was anything I wanted, it was to be thirty-four, my age now. I wanted so badly to be somebody who could take charge. But a fast eighteen was the best you could have said about me.

"Bridget really knew that she was sick. She knew that she wasn't in Riggs by accident and that what happened to her on the staircase in Williamstown was serious. The big suspense with Bridget was: was she getting better, or was she getting worse? She was keenly aware, when she was at family functions, that she was being observed like an exhibit. Does she look better now than a year ago? Is she in good shape or bad shape? Not because she was somebody who was subject to great highs and lows, but because she was genuinely ill.

"Bridget felt very much the pariah of the family. She had been put away somewhere—under the nicest of circumstances, the best of places; she kept saying that all the time, how much freedom she'd had there—but she felt that she had, deservedly, been put away. As far as you, her sister, were concerned, that could never happen to you. You were peaking and cresting; you were married at the time, or just divorced, but even a divorce was better to Bridget than what she was doing. You had kids; you were bopping around New York getting your apartment on Central Park West, modeling and who knows, you were going to be acting, and so on. It was very important to her because she was, as everybody is, competitive. If you had been a little uglier and less successful, I think she would have run to you.

"She knew that your father wanted what was best for her, but also felt that he was a little frustrated and bored with her. She couldn't talk to him easily. She didn't feel that comfortable with your father at all. She never knew what to think about Pamela. Bridget circled Pamela; she sniffed around Pamela a lot and every now and then thought Pamela was very nice and every now and then thought Pamela wasn't very nice. The only thing that I remember about your brother, Bill, is that she loved him very much.

She felt a kindred spirit with Bill when things went wrong with him. She talked about your mother. Bridget felt deeply that, looking back on everything, she had been unreasonably antagonistic to your mother and that she had hated her for a lot of things that weren't her fault, that there had been a time, very close to your mother's death, when your mother had wanted very, very desperately to get back together with Bridget, to talk to Bridget, to have some kind of rapprochement and that Bridget fought it, fought it hard, and tried to hurt her by fighting it at all. Then your mother died and she never had another chance.

"She was very aware that people were saying, 'Hello, Bridget, how are you?' like 'Oh, my God. I hope you're fine.' As if they were all whispering behind their fans about her, since she was the only one in the room that had been to a mental institution. She was terribly bright, Bridget, very sensitive to the attitudes other people had toward her, and she could identify a patronizing smile like 'My dear, how are you?' at a hundred yards.

"Your father, as a result of that episode in Williamstown, said, 'Get her back to New York right now.' She adamantly refused to go. There was a week left to the season and she insisted on staying out the week. The greatest thrill of my life was driving her to the airport and flying back with her."

When Bridget got back into the city after Labor Day, she changed apartments. She and I spent a lot of afternoons at the florist buying huge flowering bushes for the new space or visiting the food department at Bloomingdale's to browse through the imported delicacies. She had a passion for crystallized ginger and crème fraîche, which was hard to find anywhere else, and we both had a nostalgia for smoked turkey and Smithfield ham, which Mother, a Virginian, had seen to it were staples of our childhood.

We never talked a great deal about Mother. I was cautiously rebuilding my relationship with Bridget; if I pressed her about certain subjects, her shaky confidence in me might have regressed perhaps irreparably. I sensed she was putting me to her own private test, and just barely beginning to trust me. Any questions I might have asked her about the long bitterness with Mother were *verboten*. It was acceptable, even curiously reassuring to Bridget, if I mentioned Mother as a matter of course; not, however, if I overtly mourned for her. So we played by Bridget's rules; there was no alternative. Together we revisited all the art galleries and museums to which Mother had dragged us when we were thirteen and fifteen, the same shops and restaurants, the familiar concerts and ballets, without ever discussing why.

Sometimes she would wear one of Mother's dresses or coats, or a particular antique necklace Kenneth had bought Mother in London one year. Mother had said its delicacy would suit only Bridget. And so on her twenty-first birthday, a month after Mother died, Kenneth had presented it to her.

I tried to push Bridget into modeling or editorial work at a fashion magazine like *Vogue* or *Harper's Bazaar*. I thought she'd be very good at either, and fashion was a field in which I had connections. But she was suspicious of any interference, particularly mine.

Bill Francisco:

"*Just before her death we finally began to argue, which was great. Everything had been very lovey-dovey and kind of romantic; finally legitimate arguments could be had, really screaming fights— usually about money. 'Let's go to such-and-such a place.' 'Can't, no dough.' 'I'll treat.' 'No way.' Dutch from time to time, but no way I'd let her pay for both of us. I was making about seventy-five dollars a week, so it was very tight. And later, after the fact, I wondered if the pressure about getting married came out of the feeling 'Let's do it now, before . . .'*

"*All that crap that came out about the possibility that she killed herself because of her mother's death—I don't think anyone knew her better than I did at that time and I swear it was out of the question. She was in good shape, I was in good shape, and the relationship was working. We were both very busy setting up Broadway productions, planning this whole attack on New York City. She was interviewing writers, typing stuff, getting it organized. She wanted to be actively involved, which was wonderful. I think it was the first time she was doing something because she wanted to do it, not because she felt she had to compete. She was helping me to produce, which was great because it channeled a lot of energy that had been misdirected. That month before she died was a very active period.*"

The last time I saw her, a few days before she died, she had embarked on an ambitious project for Father: assembling and editing the hundreds of sixteen-by-twenty color photos of Imspond he'd taken all summer. Tom Mankiewicz was coming into the city that weekend from Yale, and we'd arranged to meet at Bridget's on Saturday afternoon.

When I arrived, she was squatting on the floor of the living room while the phonograph blared *La Bohème*. Tom was conducting with his eyes closed. They were engulfed in layouts and gallon containers of special glue, discards, parings of paper, scissors of every size, wastebaskets, and a lethal-looking photo-clipper. Bridget loved to entertain and always had delicious odds and ends around. While she plied us with banana cake, I noticed, over the new sofa against the wall, two narrow panels each about six feet high. They were just as spectacular as I'd remembered them from years ago: two scenes of Paris by night and day, one black, the other bright yellow, painted by Ludwig Bemelmans for Father and Nan to hang in an apartment they'd once had overlooking the East River.

"Bridget Hayward, where'd you get those Bemelmans?" I exclaimed covetously.

"Father took them out of storage and loaned them to me," she replied, coyly fluttering her long eyelashes.

"What will you trade them for?" I asked, bracing myself for the answer. She knew me too well.

"Nothing," she replied, amused but emphatic. I bargained for half an hour, offering her everything I owned in exchange, but it was no use. Once she'd set her jaw in a certain way, she was as obdurate as Mother. Tom was riveted by the scene. He even lowered the sound level of *La Bohème*.

Bridget polished off the last of her tea, and while she was playing with the cake crumbs on her plate she said to me, "Brooke, there's only one way you will ever get these paintings. I'll leave them to you when I die."

"Oh, for God's sake, Bridget," I said, thoroughly exasperated.

"Now, now," she said. "It may be sooner than you think."

"What is that supposed to mean?" I asked, really irritated.

"Nothing," she said, and she was suddenly very serious. "It doesn't mean anything except what I said. It may be sooner than you think."

We left shortly after that. As we were going out the door, I looked back at her, perched among the photos in the middle of the floor.

She laughed at me and said, "Don't forget, there's a paper-goods sale at Bloomingdale's."

"I'll phone you tomorrow," I called, starting down the hall after Tom.

"Don't forget," she called back. A few minutes later, as Tom and I were walking up Lexington, we turned to each other at the same moment and remarked how strange Bridget could be sometimes.

For the next few weeks I was busy shooting *Mad Dog Coll* and Tom was back at Yale:

"*While I was drinking in George & Harry's Bar one night, my roommate called and said, 'Listen, you'd better come back—your dad just phoned.' When I got back to my room, there was a message from my father, a message from your father, a message from my cousin Josie, and a message from you. I looked at the four messages and I knew Bridget was dead. There could be no other way that I would get four messages from those four people in the space of an hour. I called Josie and said, 'Hello, Josie?' And she said, 'Bridget's dead, kid.' Those were her first three words. And I said, 'I know, I know.' And hung up. I must have cried all night.*"

Bill Francisco:

"*I found the body. I'd been calling her all day, and thought I might drop by to see her. When I got there, the morning newspaper was still outside the door. I had a key; I went in, and there she was dead. I knew it instantly. Leland came right over. I couldn't go back in the bedroom. He went alone. Then he called this doctor and while the doctor was examining her, I went over to the desk; she kept a folder—I don't know what made me look there, but if ever I was coming to pick up something, that's where it would be— and there was the suicide note. It was so unbelievably weird. You remember her handwriting, how neat it was? Well, most of the note was like a very drunken scrawl. 'Dear Bill'—there was something like 'Be brilliant,' and an intimation of her wanting to go while things were good, before they got any worse. And then it was signed, absolutely meticulously, McFidgett, which was a name Leland called her, and I never did. She may have been so far gone she was writing the letter to both of us. Later it occurred to me she could have written it at another time in her life and just put it away in that dumb folder. Anyway, I found the note and Leland took it. By this time we were both deeply into Jack Daniels. I remember the doctor calling somebody, and people coming in to take the body away, and Leland making sure I was way down at the end of the room by the window, and not looking as the body was going out, and pouring more Jack Daniels, and Leland saying, 'You're coming home with us tonight.'"*

The next morning I was confronted with a myriad of details about the pending services. Although Frank E. Campbell was to be the funeral director, the problem was where to bury Bridget. Her will stated that she wished to be buried in Stockbridge, Massachusetts, but apparently one had to be a resident of Stockbridge to qualify for that privilege. Pamela and Harry Kurnitz (the playwright and screenwriter) drove out to Fern Cliffs in Hartsdale, New York, and came back with a glowing description that called up images of a country graveyard shaded by spreading trees. I didn't want to know too much about this aspect of the affair; I had no idea where Mother was buried and no intention of ever visiting either site. I preferred Father's only partially facetious directive that, when he met his Maker, we were to see to it that he was cremated and his ashes installed in a vase on the mantelpiece so that he could observe our every move, and rattle the vase back and forth whenever he was displeased.

Pamela asked me to go with her to Bridget's apartment for a wardrobe consultation. I clenched my teeth and picked out a blue silk dress and earrings of small turquoise forget-me-nots. Rummaging through her jewelry box, I came upon two necklaces Mother had assembled, pearl by pearl, over the years of our childhood. In weekly games of hearts, played for legendarily high stakes with a cutthroat cast of regulars—Sam Goldwyn, David O. Selznick, Herman Mankiewicz, and Father—Mother had always won. The night's winnings would be translated into the acquisition of another matching pearl. When the strands were finally completed, diamond clasps and all, they were banished to her safe-deposit box. She said they were too valuable to wear. From time to time, when she felt a mild financial squeeze, she would contemplate selling them. Sentimentality, however, prevailed. In keeping with her original intention, they were turned over to Bridget and me when we became twenty-one. Neither of us had ever had the nerve to put them around our necks. Bridget acted as caretaker, since I was notoriously lackadaisical. When Pamela saw them that day, she pointed out that they would be much safer with her (and besides, there was also a huge emerald ring of Mother's to consider). Pamela had a priceless jewelry collection that reposed in her custom-built safe—a series of drawers, each with an individual combination—which rose grandly from the floor to the ceiling of her closet. I was in no mood to defend my irresponsibility, so away went the pearls and the emerald. Ten years later, when I asked to have them back for my own daughter, they had vanished.

Pamela asked me what I wanted to do with Bridget's personal effects, all of which had been left to me. The apartment was still so filled with Bridget I could smell her perfume in the air. At my suggestion that we send all the furniture to Bill and Marilla in their dreary little house at Fort Bragg, Pamela said it was hardly worth the shipping cost, much too expensive a proposition, so what about donating it to some needy charity? "Anything," I mumbled to get out of there, "anything," and we finally left with the clothes and jewelry.

Going down in the elevator, Pamela said, "Did you know that Bridget left your father her entire trust fund? It was dear of her—she was so concerned about his financial status, she told him that since he'd supported her for so many years, she was going to do the same for him in his old age. Of course he didn't pay any attention to her, but there it is in the will. And it certainly will come in handy at this particular time."

"Yes, it was dear of her," I answered, wondering if Bridget had known that her trust fund had been set up entirely by Mother, as part of her percentage of *The Voice of the Turtle*, seventeen years earlier.

"And not only that," continued Pamela as the elevator let us out into the lobby, "but she left him her entire savings account, which seems to have about twenty-five thousand dollars in it. Amazing, isn't it?"

"Yes, indeed," I dutifully answered again, and couldn't help adding, "but of course that was Mother's life insurance. The policy came through just a few months ago." My God, I thought. Is this

what happens whenever somebody dies? These grisly discussions
about personal effects and money? Gloating about this and that?
All the way to Campbell's funeral parlor, I couldn't keep myself
from remembering a night that we'd been having dinner at 1020
Fifth Avenue: Father, Pamela, Bridget, Grandsarah, myself, and
Jones Harris, with Monsen serving. The table conversation had
never once veered from conjecture about the fabulous sums of
money that might befall Grandsarah (and thus Father, who was
already ruminating about how he'd spend it) if and when Standard
Oil decided to dig along some desolate stretches of railroad tracks
to which, in an ancient agreement with the oil company, Grandsarah had retained all mineral rights.

"I thought I'd married into an artistic family," Pamela had
suddenly interrupted, "and all anybody ever does is talk about
money."

"People in steel vaults shouldn't throw—" Jones fired rapidly, and then effectively elected to stop. Bridget had been delighted.

"Your friend Jones is marvelous," she told me after dinner.
"His father [Jed Harris] is like a caricature of *him* instead of the
other way around."

Her funeral was in the late afternoon. There was a slight
drizzle as we emerged from a caravan of black limousines at the
entrance of St. Peter's Church on Lexington and Fifty-fourth
Street. Although St. Peter's was Catholic, Bridget had often gone to
services there; she'd had a friend at school in Switzerland who was
Catholic. We ran in to avoid the reporters straggling at the entrance.

The inside of the church was faced with stone. A somber
daylight muted its stained-glass windows. The altar was banked
with white and yellow flowers. Bridget's coffin, the color of moss,
lay among them. Father, my brother, Bill, and I sat alone in the
second pew. Father and Bill both held themselves with the same
military bearing as Colonel Hayward in his wheelchair. Our shoulders were pressed, one against another, throughout the service. I
was only half aware of people sitting behind us, of friends of the
family tiptoeing down the aisles.

The service was very short. There was no eulogy. Very softly
the organ began to play Ravel's "Pavane for a Dead Infanta,"
which Bridget had learned to play on the piano when she was
twelve. As the sound echoed through the church, Father's shoul-

ders began to shake. Bill and I edged in closer, as we had with Bridget between us nine months before. I knew I would never be able to listen to that particular music again. Then Josh Logan stood up and moved to the middle of the aisle just in front of the coffin. The candles on either side were beginning to flicker as he quietly, almost inaudibly, recited the Twenty-third Psalm. "The valley of the shadow of death," I repeated after him mentally, trying to imagine what it looked like and whether I would be afraid.

Afterward, Father, Bill, and I had to go out first. As we passed, Father paused for a fraction of a second and looked at Tom Mankiewicz, who was sitting by the aisle. Tears were streaming down Tom's face. Father put his hand on Tom's shoulder and walked on. And we went out into the rain.

There was a reception at Father and Pamela's apartment afterward. The dining-room table was laden with an elegant buffet. I chose a place to sit—in the hallway on a small bench, and never moved—then Josie Mankiewicz came and sat beside me for a while, and Bill Francisco, and my brother, Bill, with Marilla. There were a great many people but the only person I remember talking to was Tom. The last time either of us had seen each other or Bridget, we had all been together. I told him I would never go to another funeral.

Tom:

"*I remember at the reception you said to me, 'I'm the daugh-. ter of a father who's been married five times. Mother killed herself. My sister killed herself. My brother has been in a mental institution. I'm twenty-three and divorced with two kids.' I said, 'Brooke, either you've got to open the window right now'—we were on the tenth floor—'either you've got to open the window right now and jump out, or say, "I'm going to live," because you're right, it's the worst family history that anybody ever had, and either you jump out the window or you live.'*"

3

The Family

ara Mankiewicz (Herman's widow):

"She had a very romantic concept of motherhood and marriage—incurable romantic, she was—and very much involved with it. Then her career started to be an interruption to her, to her duties and home; Herman used to accuse her of lying about it—that she was just crazy for her career—and she couldn't convince him that it didn't matter to her a bit. She liked the money and she was glad to make it, but she really regarded it as an imposition. She would have preferred to stay home and be strictly a mother and go to the market and go on picnics.

"Of course her phobia about your father and business—that was the stumbling block for them. She would go crazy on the subject of the telephone when he came home. She wanted him to be a husband and father, and any interruption—no matter who the client was —the more important, the more outrageously she behaved. Terrible, and you know Leland was not a husband and a father. He was never cut out for that role. I mean, this was a man-about-town, a bon vivant, a gay, carefree, marvelous guy, with big ideas of finance and involvement in business, and suddenly she wants him to come home at 5:30 and sit down and play with the children or everybody go on a picnic or do something that was so foreign to him—he hadn't been raised that way himself. But it was a gay house, even when he was miserable, and she had him raising vegetables on Evanston Street; he became absolutely domesticated. He loved it for a while, or he tried to convince himself that he did. That was what she wanted. Then the summer in St. Malo; she was very happy, very content. She would have liked to have him there constantly; he would come Friday and stay until Tuesday, something like that. He made compromises even though there was nothing for him to do and he was not what you call a beach fellow.

"And he did it for a number of years, with exceptions; you know, he insisted on the telephone thing and that was the subject of very serious quarreling. And everybody talked to her about it— David [Selznick] and Herman—for God's sake, Maggie, they told her, this is a guy with enormous interests and you've got to let him go on. No, she wouldn't hear of it. It wasn't her idea of a home."

California

I never saw my mother sign an autograph.

In December, 1943, when I was six, Bridget, Bill, and I left Los Angeles on the Super Chief for our first trip to New York. It was wartime, before easy commercial air travel. In the next few years, we came to know all the porters on the Sante Fe Railroad very well.

Mother had just opened in *The Voice of the Turtle*, the first play she had agreed to do in seven years. Bridget, Bill, and I hadn't seen her since she had gone East for rehearsals in late September. We had never been separated from her; we had some hazy knowledge that she was a movie star but we didn't know what that was, although once when I was four, and considered old enough, Father had taken me to the set of *Cry Havoc*, and I'd been frightened by parachutes and dead bodies hanging from the trees, and concluded that Mother had an exciting occasional job.

While dressing for dinner one night a week before she was due to leave Los Angeles for rehearsals, she had found Father unconscious on the bathroom floor. An ambulance had come to the house and taken him to Cedars of Lebanon Hospital, where, we were told the next morning, he had almost died from internal hemorrhaging. Exploratory surgery was performed for bleeding ulcers, but none was discovered, nor was any cause for what had happened. By the time Bridget and I were allowed to go to the hospital to see him, Mother had left for New York, in a state of frenzy, unable to change rehearsal dates.

Our expectations about the hospital were shaped by Father's many bedtime readings of *Madeline* having her appendix out: "Madeline soon ate and drank. On the bed there was a crank, and a crack on the ceiling had the habit of sometimes looking like a rabbit." Father was eating custard, which Bridget regarded suspiciously; he informed us that Dave Chasen, not the doctor, had saved his life by squeezing ten pounds of raw sirloin, daily, into one large glass of blood and sending it over from his restaurant (in spite of the fact that it was wartime and even Chasen's supplies were rationed). He also announced, scornfully, that the doctor had ordered him to quit smoking, drinking, and working so hard—an impossible combination. During his stay in the hospital, Father, out of boredom, grew a dashing mustache. He came home for Halloween and after a few weeks went to New York for Mother's opening. We were left with our nurse, Miss Mullens, and our tutor, Miss Brown.

Miss Brown was asked to take the three of us to New York for Christmas. She was a young, serious, dark-haired woman with glasses, and handwriting that we admired and tried to emulate. Miss Brown had become an honorary member of our family. She made it unnecessary for us to go to school, entirely to Mother's satisfaction. Mother had paid a dutiful visit to my kindergarten class at Brentwood Town and Country the previous year and, sitting discreetly in the rear, had become chagrined when she discovered that the class was learning to count with lima beans and that the teacher's control of English grammar had lapsed, unforgivably, as she had admonished us not to play tag and "those kind of games" in the classroom. Bill was still too young to go to school, but Mother, theorizing that the entire California school system was inadequate, took Bridget and me out the next day and we never returned. After that, Miss Brown came to our house every morning at nine o'clock, and sat with us at the long dining-room table where we learned to read and write and do arithmetic until noon. Miss Brown banished the standard reading primers from our education; instead, we cut our teeth on the most beautiful books she and Mother could find, such as *Tanglewood Tales* and *Sinbad the Sailor*, which were illustrated by Edmund Dulac, and on Father's choice, Eugene Field's *Poems of Childhood*, which was illustrated by Maxfield Parrish and contained some of Father's favorite poems. Father never tired of reading us "The Dinkey-Bird" (goes singing in the amfalula tree), "The Duel" (The gingham dog and the calico cat), "The Fly-Away Horse" (Oh, a wonderful horse is the Fly-Away Horse), and "Wynken, Blynken, and Nod" (one night, sailed off in a wooden shoe—sailed on a river of crystal light . . .). My entire concept of what the world looked like and what life promised was shaped by the sensuous textures and sinuous lines of Dulac's fantasies, the exotic blues and purples and thick-lipped heavy-lidded sentinels of slender youths that populated Maxfield Parrish's visions. Bridget and I learned to read quickly and voraciously.

The Super Chief was a beautiful train. It had a parlor car with a huge curved sun window at the far end and lots of card

tables with waiters in white jackets hovering nearby. Bridget and I
appropriated the upper berths in our compartment: it was a good
way to travel. We liked the nights best when the train became pure
sound and motion and we lay on our berths staring out through
little curtained windows at the invisible black countryside.

In Chicago we changed to the Twentieth Century Limited.
During the layover in Chicago, we were whisked off by Mother's
younger brother Sonny, who had started a law practice there. He
gave us our first bath in three days and lunch at the Pump Room.

We fell in love with New York City at once. It was a city of
firsts for us. When we got off the train, our very first snow was
falling. Mother and Father took us on their laps in a horse-drawn
carriage through Central Park and we stuck out our tongues, laughing, and caught snowflakes; we felt them tingle and dissolve. There
was a pair of turtledoves in a huge white cage in the apartment at
the Hotel Pierre, and *"The Turtle's"* author-director and producer,
respectively, John Van Druten and Delly (Alfred de Liagre), waiting for us with an enormous bowl of our first caviar. Mother
ecstatically spooned it onto slivers of toast and then into our
mouths, and we obediently reveled in it, rolling it around our
mouths and popping the tiny eggs like salty little grapes against our
palates, even asking for more. Mother was like the Pied Piper of
Hamelin: we would willingly have followed her anywhere, and a
great deal of our pleasure must have derived from hers.

She took us to the Central Park Zoo our second morning,
and in the afternoon to her real passion, the Bronx Zoo, thereby
setting a pattern that never varied in the cities we visited over the
years: a prompt, mandatory visit with the animals. She would
spend hours talking to the keepers in the monkey house of any zoo
in any city of any country she happened to be in, submerging
herself in all available data pertaining to chimpanzees. Mother had
long schemed about adopting a baby chimpanzee into our family.
With that end in mind, when I was three and Bridget a year old
(before Bill had been born and perhaps despairing that he ever
would be), she had Roger Edens and Father bring us out to the M-
G-M zoo on the back lot one afternoon after our naps. We were all
dressed up in our coats and very excited, especially when we caught
sight of Mother at a distance in an elegant black dress with a white
picture hat, and a young chimpanzee cradled in each arm. We all
rushed toward one another, but when Bridget, who got to her first,

reached up to hug her, the two chimps, seized by jealousy, let go of Mother's neck and attacked Bridget with a vengeance. She had to be taken off, screaming and covered with tooth marks, to the hospital to be bandaged. This incident put a crimp in Mother's adoption plans, much to Father's relief. (The only animals Father could tolerate were seals, preferably seal acts at circuses observed from a safe distance, although occasionally we could wheedle him into accompanying us to the Central Park Zoo if we arranged it for feeding time.)

We went for the first time to the Museum of Natural History, where I shivered at the sight of the huge blue whale floating over my head in the main hall and the vast rooms inhabited by dinosaur skeletons, the first fleshless bones I'd ever seen. While we were standing with noses pressed against the glass behind which lay a tawny African landscape with its appropriate spiral-horned eland and tufted gnu (shot and donated by Grandfather Hayward), a young black woman tapped Mother gently on the shoulder and said, "Excuse me, Miss Sullavan, can I please have your autograph?"

Mother mumbled something and shook her head. We clutched possessively at her coat, amazed that a stranger would know our mother's name. The young woman repeated her question a little more plaintively.

Mother drew herself up and regarded the intruder with a cold eye. "I beg your pardon," she said crisply, "but I think you have the wrong person. I am not Miss Sullavan."

The stranger was now as confused as we. "*Margaret* Sullavan," she said, thrusting forth a piece of paper and pencil, but Mother was already moving away.

"Come along, children," she said, "and we'll have a quick look at the mummies, which you will love."

"But, Mother," we exploded on the way down the marble stairs, "*aren't* you Margaret Sullavan?"

"Yes, that is my professional name," she answered, but before she could say anything else, we pounced on her with glee, clamoring all together, "But then you've told a lie, Mother, why did you tell such a terrible lie to such a nice lady? You don't let *us* tell lies! She looked so sad when you said that—why didn't you want her to know who you are?"

Mother sighed and waited for us to stop. "You see," she said patiently and with slow emphasis on every word, so that she would never have to say it again, and she never did, "there are a lot of people in the world who think if they get the signature—autograph, it's called—of someone who is famous down on a piece of paper—sometimes even *collect* these signatures in books—that that will somehow make them more important. Well, I feel sorry for them because they think they can have some part of *me* by having me write my name for them, but that doesn't mean I approve of it, and besides, I certainly don't want to be famous or looked at when I walk down the street or take you children to a museum." Here she gathered us in her arms as we were about to come to the mummies and spoke with such intensity that we felt swept up and purified by some glorious hurricane: "I think people who try to intrude on other people's privacy or personal life in any way—and you children are my personal life—I think those people are rude and silly. Now, look—look!" she exclaimed, her eyes widening with excitement and her low magical voice stretching until it seemed it might snap and carry us with it, so that we sighted down her outstretched hand, with its crimson enameled nails glistening like Fabergé charms, at the room that danced before us and at the gold-inscribed sarcophagi tilted so that we could see their stained linen-wrapped contents.

One cold night, Father took me to the Morosco to see Mother in *The Voice of the Turtle*. Mother disapproved vociferously, but Father had his way. "Your mother is the best actress in the world—I ought to know, for God's sake—after all, I've been her agent for eleven years." And when Mother protested: "Come on, Maggie, let her sit backstage, can't possibly hurt her; for God's sake, she may never see you in anything as good again." And so I sat backstage in the wings in my pajamas and bathrobe and saw my first play. Mother took me with her to her dressing room whenever she came offstage to change; I was enthralled watching her apply layers of mascara to her lashes and lipstick out beyond the natural lines of her own mouth ("My mouth is just a straight line, the horror of all Hollywood make-up men, and so is my crooked tooth and my mole and high forehead and lousy chin"), and move swiftly from one change to another without a superfluous motion or sound, while her maid slipped one dress over her head and removed another, leaving her hair and make-up unruffled. At the end of intermission, the stage manager would knock—"Two more minutes, Miss Sullavan"—and Mother would grab her pink swan's-down powder puff, dab her nose with a last fillip, and snatch my hand, whispering, "Come, darling, hurry, hurry or they'll *murder* me!" and we would race to the wings where I would plop down in my chair and Mother would just keep on going as Sally Middleton. During one change, as she slid into a silvery dress, she admonished me breathlessly, "Now, don't be horrified by this next scene; everybody thought this play was very immoral when they first read it, because of this scene, but remember it's only make-believe. I close my eyes and pretend I'm somebody else, and so must you, but don't forget I'm *really* your mother and it's your father I *really* love, and you and Bridget and Bill." But the audience and even I gasped audibly when, at the end of the second act, Elliott Nugent took a pair of pliers from the kitchen drawer because the zipper had stuck on her silver dress, and, wrenching it as hard as he could, stepped back as the dress fell to Mother's feet, leaving her standing in nothing but a slip as the curtain came down. "Your mother," reiterated Father as we all piled into a car afterward, Mother ignoring the crowd pressed against the car brandishing pens and paper, "your mother is the best actress alive today."

"Oh, Leland, you're just hopelessly biased," she said, laughing. "Let's go have a chocolate soda." And we did.

The Voice of the Turtle was an enormous hit. Mother was under contract to stay with it for a year, so after Christmas, Father, who had business to attend to on the Coast, took us home. In those days the train trip lasted four days and three nights. Father was somewhat impatient with that particular mode of travel; he'd had his own airplane for years and, before the war introduced gas rationing, had flown it across the country hundreds of times. In his office at 444 Madison Avenue hung two brightly colored maps showing his former air routes between New York and Hollywood, which he used to fly several times a month, logging an average of seventeen or eighteen hours a trip. Before he'd married Mother in 1936 (owing to my imminent birth, which also necessitated Mother's buying her way out of *Stage Door*, a play by Edna Ferber, coincidentally another of Father's clients), Father'd been equally in love with Kate Hepburn. He claimed that at one point, with both actresses (and clients) safely separated by three thousand miles, Mother on the stage in New York and Kate making a movie in Hollywood, he would take off in his plane from New York to complete some deal in California, pause to refuel in Kansas City, and place phone calls to both coasts, one assuring Mother that the next two weeks of separation would be a living hell, and another to Kate ardently apprising her of his arrival in Los Angeles. He used to reminisce wistfully that Kate was the classiest dame he ever knew, because among other things, when he eloped with Mother, she'd sent a congratulatory telegram saying, "DEAR MAGGIE, YOU HAVE JUST MARRIED THE MOST WONDERFUL MAN IN THE WORLD. BLESSINGS, KATE." Mother burned up the wire in a rage of jealousy.

Father's real love, though, was flying. My first memory of him was at breakfast one morning on the brick terrace of our house in Brentwood, Los Angeles. He'd already taken up one of his planes for a pre-dawn spin before going to the office. While he drank his coffee and read the newspaper, cursing Hitler, I sat on his lap in the sun and lovingly held his ears, which were bright red and rigid with cold. "They'll go on buzzing for the rest of the morning," he declared. "I'll probably go deaf from flying in an open cockpit. To tell you the truth, I'd give up the agency in a minute"—he snapped off a piece of toast—"and absolutely everything else in the world except you and Bridget if I could spend the rest of my life in an airplane. The only snag is I have to bring home the goddamn bacon."

On his desk, in his elaborate offices on Wilshire Boulevard in Beverly Hills (which we occasionally visited with Miss Brown to observe how he brought home the bacon), were models of his favorite planes and a chrome lighter in the shape of a plane, but dominating everything else in the plush linen-and-leather-upholstered room was an immense aerial map of Thunderbird Field, an air-training center for national defense that formed the nucleus of Southwest Airways, Inc.

Father was chairman of the board of Southwest Airways. He started it with Jack Connelly, an engineering inspector for the Civil Aeronautics Authority, with capital raised from clients and friends like Jimmy Stewart, Henry Fonda, Cary Grant, Hoagy Carmichael, Gilbert Miller, and Johnny Swope (who became secretary-treasurer, as well as instructor). In the fertile Salt River Valley of Arizona, near Phoenix, against a purple backdrop of mountains, he built Thunderbird Field in 1940 with the cooperation and gratitude of the United States Army, which, understaffed at the outset of the war, was offering contracts to civilian operators who could supply flying facilities and qualified instructors to train the burgeoning ranks of their cadets. Father and Jack Connelly leaped at the chance. As a test pilot, Jack had flown the Douglas DC-3, the four-engine DC-4, and most of the large aircraft built on the Coast, and had no trouble assembling a crew of the best instructors in the business.

Thunderbird was built from the ground up in ninety days. Father, with his indomitable sense of the aesthetic, lined up Millard Sheets, a well-known Western artist, to design it. It was dazzling. Sheets laid out the entire training field in the stylized shape of a gigantic thunderbird, the Indian god of thunder, lightning, and rain, so that viewed from the air, the observation tower formed the head, the administration building the body, the barracks the wings, and the gardens the tail feathers. He eschewed traditional drab Army colors for those of the Southwest desert, the green of sage and cactus, the cream of yucca in bloom, the streaked gray browns of sand, the terra cotta of adobe, and everywhere the tomato-red insignia, a thunderbird with lightning bolts as plumage.

The organization was soon turning out Army pilots at the rate of ten thousand a year, but to handle the Army's stepped-up program, Father moved into high gear and built Thunderbird II, which trained air cadets from mainland China through an arrangement with Chiang Kai-shek, who sent over a select group of officers from the Chinese Army. They arrived in lots of fifty by a circuitous route through Chungking and Kunming and then over the Burma Pass to evade the Japanese blockade. Father made frequent trips to Washington to pitch his cause with General Hap Arnold, and finally got not only a contract but a loan of $200,000 from the government. He put John Swope in charge of Thunderbird II, and then moved swiftly to build Falcon Field, forty miles east of Thunderbird, near Mesa, Arizona, for the training of young British pilots. By the time the novices had completed their twenty weeks of training, they were able to swoop out of a pitch-black sky and make a blackout landing in their big North American AT-6's on a field lit only by a couple of small flare pots. John Swope said the Chinese were the smartest and most disciplined of all, and that although language was their greatest barrier, they understood instruction easily and took to the air as if it were second nature.

Although this De Mille–like enterprise lost money at the start and Father and Jack were deeply in debt by 1941 ("Over a million dollars," said Father nonchalantly; "don't tell your mother or she'll shoot me"), they next augmented the operation with a large repair depot to overhaul engines and training planes. Then, looking to the future, Father maneuvered an Army contract to haul high-priority military cargo over a censored Pacific Coast route, a scheme that resulted in the expansion of Southwest Airways, Inc., into Pacific Airlines, eventually bought by Howard Hughes.

Mother entered into the spirit of the whole venture with characteristic gusto by taking flying lessons and getting her solo license. In 1940, Father was spending so much time in Arizona that she went on a vigorous house-hunting expedition in New Mexico. Always having hated pretentiousness of any kind, with a singular revulsion for life in Hollywood, she passed up all available grand haciendas (sprawling behind their high walls from Taos to Santa Fe) for a spare adobe bungalow on Rio Grande Boulevard in the little country town of Albuquerque, because it had a view of the Sandia Mountains through the cottonwoods in the back yard.

Before Bill was born, Bridget and I were flown there many times with our nurse, Miss Mullens; in those days, commercial airplanes had berths, and we would take off from Los Angeles in the middle of the night, lulled to sleep by the roar of the engines. William Wyler, the film director, who had been briefly married to Mother in 1934 (and was also another of Father's clients), happened to be on one of these flights with us, and persuaded Miss Mullens to let him borrow Bridget and me for the landing; he emerged from the plane and descended the staircase with one of us on each shoulder, while Mother and Father stood gaping at the bottom.

The first thing Bridget ever said was "Father's in Albu-quer-que," and the first movie she and I saw, at ages one and three, was in Albuquerque's single movie theatre on a warm desert evening while we were waiting with Mother and Father for the train to Santa Fe. The movie was *King Kong*, which Mother thought we'd enjoy because of the gorilla element. However, Bridget began to scream halfway through the underwater chase sequence, not having yet recovered from her recent chimpanzee trauma, so that Mother and Father, white-faced, rushed us out of the theatre and over to the train station platform. We all sat on a bench under the stars while Father pointed out the constellations he flew by at night and Mother, who claimed to be tone deaf, sang us the only two songs she knew until the train came: "Pack Up Your Troubles in Your Old Kit Bag" (and smile! smile! smile!) and our all-time favorite:

> *Nobody loves me, everybody hates me,*
> *Going in the garden to eat worms;*
> *Great big squishy ones, little tiny wriggly ones,*
> *Oh, how the big ones squirm.*

To celebrate the graduation of the first Thunderbird cadets, Mother and Father gave a tremendous party at our home in Brentwood. Brentwood was then mostly fields of avocado trees. We lived at 12928 Evanston Street, a block down from Jimmy Stewart and Johnny Swope, resolute bachelors who shared a rented house, and half a block away from the Fondas. Across the street lived the screenwriter Bill Wright, his wife, Greta—blond hair wrapped in braids around her head, Bavarian peasant dresses nipped in by laces at the waist, and a fascinating, deep German-accented voice—and their two majestic German shepherds, Sergeant and Major, for whom we had great respect.

Number 12928 was a simple white colonial, set well back from the street; its most luxurious features, which persuaded Mother to buy the house, were the splendid drooping pepper and acacia trees that lined the driveway and spilled their red berries and white blossoms on the gravel. Towering over everything along the street were giant deodora pines, under which Bridget and I once found a hummingbird caught in a carpet of needles, its iridescent blue-green feathers reflecting the sun in such a way that we thought it was a rare creature from the sea miraculously beached on the shores of our garden.

Just before Bill was born in 1941, Mother and Father decided to build an addition onto the original house to accommodate the new arrival. We called it The Barn, and that's just what it was: a red barn, attached to the main house by an open breezeway, into which we children were moved with our nurse. It was a two-story building, designed with single-minded practicality. The downstairs, left as one great room roughly sixty by eighty feet, boasted a floor that was parqueted in redwood blocks to withstand our tricycles and roller skates, and a long trestle table with benches at which we ate and had our morning lessons with Miss Brown. Two overstuffed denim-covered sofas flanked, at one end of the room, an enormous fireplace and mantelpiece that held my doll collection. The phonograph and a small rocking chair (in which Bill would sit and rock for hours at a time while recovering from a serious mastoid operation when he was barely a year old, one side of his head shorn of its golden curls, to Mother's sorrow) were at the other. An upstairs balcony ran around three sides of the house, so that we could lean against its pine railings and look down on the entire room below us, or out at the play yard and the Victory garden beyond through the panes of the vast picture window along the fourth side. There were four bedrooms and a sewing room that opened onto the balcony, each with checked gingham curtains and bedspreads individually colored (mine had green, Bridget's yellow, Bill's red, the nurse's blue) and doors painted to match. The upstairs bathroom was about twenty feet long and had three sinks and toilets of gradated heights and a tub big enough to hold all three of us comfortably at the same time. Our meals were prepared downstairs in a kitchen with an oilcloth-covered table, in the center of which stood a detestable bottle of cod-liver oil. By the front door was a coat closet in which Bridget and I periodically locked Bill, with the threat that he would be devoured by a wolf concealed in the dark behind the coats and galoshes. Bridget and I, discovering that Bill was much more fun to dress up than our dolls, secretly renamed him Mary and trained him, under duress, to curtsy. (Curtsying was an enviable social grace outlawed by Mother, who brought us up to shake hands in a forthright way in spite of the fact that all her friends' daughters with whom we played curtsied gracefully in their plumped-up organdies and shiny black Mary Janes.) One day, she brought Ginger Rogers (*exhausted*, Mother said, with the soles of her feet raw and *bleeding* from rehearsing some dance routine with Fred Astaire) over to The Barn to meet us. Bridget and I proudly produced Bill, his glorious curls restored, in a white challis dress sprigged with roses, outgrown by me and then Bridget. "How do you do," he lisped to Ginger, curtsying faultlessly as he had been rehearsed under dreadful threats about the hall closet; "my name is Mary." Mother let out a squawk of horror. Bridget and I were forbidden ever to dress him up again and the wolf was banished from the hall closet.

The Barn was pre-empted for the Thunderbird graduation party, and Bridget, Bill, and I had to spend that night in The Other House, as it was referred to. The preparations went on for days, with specially made homespun tablecloths and napkins and pillows, and pots of red geraniums and pink petunias all over the place. The festivities started in the afternoon and went on until dawn the next morning. Father allowed me to pick out what he was going to wear. His closets were as wonderful to me as the Arabian Nights; he had overseen their construction along an entire wall of his upstairs study, with particular attention to shoe racks and drawers for shirts and handkerchiefs. Father was a born collector. He had at least three hundred pairs of shoes, which rose in neat rows to the ceiling out of my sight. Of all these, he wore only six or seven pairs in rotation, he told me once when I begged him to dress for dinner in a pair of dapper white-and-tan saddle shoes that had caught my fancy. He also had a spectacular collection of shirts, and would never travel anywhere even for a week without thirty or forty of them. But it was his handkerchief collection that was really wondrous, housed in three huge drawers according to size and color. Bridget and I used to throw off our bathrobes whenever Father was dressing to go out to dinner, and wind each other up in our favorite handkerchiefs like saris, then dance madly around the study while Father shaved and splashed bay rum all over himself and us.

For the party, Father reluctantly agreed to wear the saddle shoes as well as an odd assortment of apparel that I laid out on the bed, including a white handkerchief with a Christmas tree Miss Mullens had helped me embroider.

Mother's taste was Spartan in comparison to Father's. She was always happiest in baggy old pants or shorts, barefoot or in sandals, but that day she exchanged her beloved gabardine shorts ("my uniform" she called them, and was still wearing the same pair sixteen years later) for a long dress of gay patchwork squares, designed by Adrian, in which she dashed about testing various seating arrangements. Bridget and I were speechless with admiration. Never had two people been more beautiful than Mother and Father. From time to time Mother would exclaim that she would never give another big party; then she would grab Father and whirl in his arms across the grass, her dress and his saddle shoes flashing among the tables on the lawn, to a waltz that only they could hear.

Suddenly, there was a small "combo" playing real music and hundreds of people strolling in the late-afternoon sun. Bridget and I flitted from one person to another in our pajamas and pink-eyed rabbit slippers, drunk with people and music. Every grownup we knew was there, our entire world; even Jimmy Stewart came home on leave, in his strange uniform. People clustered around him, congratulating him on having just been made a lieutenant; he had got an early draft number, the first or second pulled out of the hat, and gone into the Air Corps as an instructor up at Mather Field. He said everybody up there was leery of him, didn't know what to do with him, and wanted to make him a morale officer, which made him sick to his stomach. He kept on bitching about it to Father and Father bitched to Ken McNaughton, an Air Force general who had been instrumental in helping him establish Thunderbird. From then on, Jimmy was on his way: first he went to Albuquerque and flew bombers, then to four-engine school and up to Boise, Idaho, where he ended up with his own combat crew. Once he got into flying, he said, it was all right, and once we got into the war and he was sent overseas to England, everybody was in the same boat and nobody paid any more attention to him. There were lots of Air Force officers, like Ken McNaughton and Hap Arnold at the party, in a tight group around Jimmy. Bridget and I wriggled our way through their legs so that we could try on his hat and listen to what they were saying: what a wonderful soldier he was, and a great patriot and a great aviator and a great Air Corps man. Hoagy Carmichael had our upright piano carried up the stairs of The Barn to the balcony, where he sang and pounded away while everyone danced; when he got tired, Hank Potter took over on the piano and Dinah Shore sang for three hours. All night we lay in The Other House and listened to the music and wished we were grown up, too.

We lived at 12928 Evanston Street for the first seven years of my life. Although I was able to recall in detail what Mother wore on my first birthday, Bridget's arrival, in 1939, when I was one and a half, always drew a blank. Father and Mother used to tell us that when they brought her home from the hospital and up to the nursery for my inspection, I gathered my forces for a long instant, reached murderously into the bassinet, and pinched her with all my strength, then, for the next six months, did not speak to either Mother or Father or allow them to touch me. Father said pensively he would follow me through the garden and try to take my hand, but I would snatch it away without saying a word. After a lot of sulking, I rejoined the family.

Bridget was a sensational baby. She had almost white hair

and double-jointed hands like Mother; she could stick her fingers out so that they would all remain straight until the last joint, which she would crook without bending the rest of the joints along the way. When she learned to play the piano, the tips of her otherwise horizontal fingers were bent at right angles to the keyboard; watching her play the piano was something like watching the Chico Marx routine with trick fingers, in which he'd point at a piano key and shoot it, touching it as he shot. As a baby, she would lie grinning from ear to ear in her crib, one foot through the bars, while our dog sat on the outside licking her toes. Her hair was so white it didn't look quite real, nor did her complexion, which was so fair I always supposed—or wished—I could see through the transparent layers of skin and blood vessels and muscle to the center of her being. Bridget's eyes were bluer even than Father's, the color of irises before they've been open very long to the sun— cornflowers, said Mother, and called her "my little white mouse," but I called her Brie, because I couldn't pronounce Bridget, and that became her name to us. Nobody else in the family had ever had hair that color. "Oh, Bridget," people would say to make conversation when she was learning to talk, "where in the world did you get that hair?" She would fix them with a long solemn look of her blue eyes; then her mouth would turn up at the corners. "God," she would answer, "God." She was light-boned, easy to pick up, and so delicate I used to worry that wind might blow her over; the bluish tinge just below the surface of her skin gave the illusion that she was just slightly bruised.

"She was an original," said Bill Wright. "There was a fey quality of Irish fairy tales about her. You were a pretty baby, Brooke, much prettier than she was, but she had a strange quality—she had Maggie squared or cubed in her."

We used to see Bill and Greta Wright practically every day. Either they'd come over for a swim or we'd skip across the street to see if we could tempt their dogs to bark at us. Next to their house was a vacant lot, which we turned into a communal vegetable garden; we supplied the manpower in the person of George Stearns, our cigar-smoking chauffeur, and Bill Wright supplied the water from his nearby hose. For days, Bridget and I followed George and his cigar through the rows of corn, copying every move, examining handfuls of corn silk, poking at dusty summer squashes, and squealing when he picked the first ripe watermelon, which he held dramatically above his head and dropped on a sharp rock so that red pulp splattered all over us and we licked it off each other. George lived in an apartment over our garage. Elsa and Otto, the German cook and butler, lived there, too. Father used to say that Elsa was a bum cook but he could never part with her because she could make two things better than anybody else: scrambled eggs and flower arrangements. Otto's moment of glory came every Halloween when he disappeared to engineer his gigantic pumpkin extravaganzas, meticulously decorated with contrasting faces of prunes and popcorn, corn from the garden and its silk (for hair), gourds, and sprays of asters and chrysanthemums.

We had many nurses over the years, but the only two we ever cared about were the first and the last: Miss Mullens, who came when Bridget was born, and Emily Buck, who came when I was five and stayed for six years. Miss Mullens toilet-trained us on an antique china potty, kept under the bed. She wore a starched white uniform and white polished shoes, but Emily refused to wear anything but baggy old blue jeans (except on her day off, when she wore a plaid cotton dress that smelled of Clorox).

Mother loved house-hunting. She would go house-hunting at the drop of a hat. Any excuse would do. On the way to the hospital in acute labor the morning I was born, she begged Father and Martha Edens (our godmother) to stop the car because she saw a "For Sale" sign somewhere along the way. Every house we lived in was bought because Mother happened to be driving past it at a fortuitous time, either when we were due for a move or when the house was too enchanting to pass up. Number 12928 was no exception. Greta Wright was looking for a house and Mother couldn't resist going along. So they bought the houses across the street from each other. I had just been born and more space was needed anyway.

For Father, the installation of a complex telephone system took priority over everything else before a move could be considered. He found himself ensconced at 12928 before the telephone was installed, a drastic hardship. The Wrights had taken possession of their house a few weeks earlier and had their telephone. Father would race over first thing in the morning, afraid he might lose a possible twenty-thousand-dollar cash deal between home and Beverly Hills, make a couple of phone calls just in case, and then go to the office. Sometimes he'd appear at the Wrights in the middle of the night to make a phone call or two.

The telephone was the source of Mother and Father's bitter-
est fights. Mother hated the agency business because of the telephone; it might ring at any time—in the middle of dinner or in the
middle of a badminton game, a dissertation or conversation. The
phone would ring and Mother would roll her eyes heavenward,
while everyone within earshot would mock-cringe or put their
hands over their ears and get ready. "Flesh peddler!" she would
yelp, in her own peculiar blend of Southern drawl and outraged
exclamation. Then, for the benefit of her audience, she would
stamp her foot half seriously, half comically, and assume a pose,
arms akimbo: "Leland Hayward, I can't *stand* it another minute.
D'ya hear me? This is an ultimatum. I'm going to tear that damn
telephone out by its *roots* if it rings again in the next five minutes!"

Father was addicted to the telephone as much as Mother
despised it. He never wrote a letter if he could send a wire, and
never wired if he could telephone. He was happiest when he was
conducting business on his office sofa with three or four telephones
at hand, his head deep in a cushion at one end and his feet
comfortably crossed at the other. That way, between conversations
he might catch a quick nap. Everyone, even Mother, agreed on one
thing: Father was the best agent in the business, even if it was a
lousy business. In the early nineteen-forties, when he himself was
in his early forties, he had about a hundred and fifty clients,
including Mother and her two ex-husbands (Henry Fonda and
William Wyler), Greta Garbo, Ernest Hemingway, Jimmy Stewart, Ginger Rogers, Edna Ferber, Gene Kelly, Fredric March, Judy
Garland, Myrna Loy, Montgomery Clift, Gregory Peck, Boris
Karloff, Billy Wilder, Kurt Weill, Josh Logan, Dashiell Hammett,
Charles Laughton, Ben Hecht, Charles MacArthur, Helen Hayes,
Herman Mankiewicz, Lillian Hellman, Fred Astaire, Gene Fowler,
and on and on. Eventually, in the mid-forties, he was to sell his
"stable," as he referred to it, to MCA, and become an equally
successful Broadway producer, with A *Bell for Adano, State of the
Union,* and then *Mr. Roberts,* but it was as a Hollywood agent that
Father became something of a legend.

His appearance was at odds with his profession. He was a
distinguished-looking man. Tall and thin (hair parted debonairly
in the middle when he was younger—graying and close-cropped like
grass later on, a trademark in time), with an air both haggard and
elegant, he strolled in white flannels and yachting sneakers through

the corridors of the major studios of a Hollywood that had never seen anything quite like him before. The prevailing notion was that agents were a breed apart, somewhat déclassé, that they all had foreign names, like the Orsatti brothers, or spoke with heavy Russian-Jewish accents and came straight from handling vaudeville acts on Broadway. Father captured Hollywood's imagination by inventing a new style; he was an outrageous Easterner who wore linen underwear and came out on Wells Fargo. It was said that his office was the first in Beverly Hills ever furnished with antiques, and that his manner of dress, Eastern college, influenced Fred Astaire and changed Hollywood fashion. Fred was, in fact, his first client. One evening in 1927, out of a job and bored, Father was making his customary rounds of the New York nightclubs and stopped by the Trocadero to have a drink with his friend Mal Hayward (not related), the proprietor, who was in a gloomy frame of mind. Business was poor, said Mal, slumping at the table, because a new place, the Mirador, had just opened up across the street and was taking away his customers. He was so desperate, Mal groaned, that he would do anything to get his hands on a big attraction, even pay an act like the Astaires as much as four thousand dollars a week. Father went straight over to the theatre where Fred and Adele were appearing in *Lady, Be Good*, and talked them into a deal. They played the Trocadero for twelve weeks, and he collected his commission of four hundred dollars ("The easiest money I ever made," he used to say wistfully) every Saturday night.

People seeing Father for the first time would ask, astonished, "Is *he* an *agent?*" He was considered by many people, both women and men, whether in the business or not, to have been one of the most attractive people they ever knew. "Gentleman" was the word most often used to describe him. "He was a gentleman agent," said George Cukor, "a darling man. I loved him even though he was a buccaneer. By asking such outrageous salaries for his clients, I think he was responsible for jacking up the agency business into the conglomerate empire that it is today." "In my opinion," said Billy Wilder (who was to direct *The Spirit of St. Louis* for him in 1955–56), "his enormous success in this town, beyond his being very bright and knowing it inside out, was due to the fact that the wives of the moguls were crazy about him. I do not mean to imply that he had an affair with Mrs. Goldwyn, but Mrs. Goldwyn was just crazy about him. So was Mrs. Warner. *All* the wives were crazy about him and kept talking about him, because he was a very attractive, handsome, dashing man. He should have been a captain in the Austro-Hungarian Army—something like that. He was certainly miscast as an agent. If I were to make a picture about an agent, a very successful agent, and my casting director brought in Leland Hayward, I would say, 'You're out of your mind! This is not the way an agent looks!' That was part of his success. Just charmed the birds off the trees, the money out of the coffers, and ladies into their beds." And super-agent Irving ("Swifty") Lazar, in his succinct vernacular, referred to Father as a "high-class gent." Said Swifty, "He was my idol. He had a gift for closing deals, he never had the time to dicker—*he* should have been called 'Swifty' instead of me." (Swifty was given his nickname by Humphrey Bogart because he made three deals for Bogart in one afternoon.) "Leland was a real beauty. A prince. The best there was. You won't see anybody like him pass this way again. . . ."

In a way Father was a prince. He came from a well-to-do Nebraska family, spent his youth in Eastern prep schools and a year or so at Princeton before flunking out with a perfect record of non-passing grades. The next five years were a rebellious flurry, in which he chose to estrange himself from the interests of the rest of the family—or, at least, those of his father, Colonel William Hayward.

Father was fond of telling us that he'd been a late starter, having drifted around the country for a couple of years as press agent for United Artists, a job that paid fifty dollars a week and was so tedious he used to pass the time away in countless, small, hot Midwestern towns by inventing elaborate stories for fan magazines about every movie star he'd ever heard of; this got him fired by United Artists, who were paying him to write stories only about United Artists movie stars. Over the next few years, he restlessly held down and was fired from fifteen or twenty such jobs as a press agent, talent scout, or general contact man in New York and Hollywood. In 1927, galvanized by the release of the first talkie and determined to have a piece of the big money that he sensed was about to be made in movies—from studios suddenly desperate to import talent from the theatre, performers trained to speak and writers who could write plays for them—Father became an agent. He dug a manuscript by a struggling writer and friend, Ben Hecht, out of his trunk, sold it to M-G-M, and used the small commission to take the train back to New York where he talked John W. Rumsey, president of the American Play Company, into letting him work there for no salary but half the commission on anything he sold. The American Play Company was a well-established literary agency, basically concerned with authors and playwrights, but Father argued eloquently that it ought to set up a new department just to handle motion pictures; it was obvious to him that there was a new demand, and that staggering wages could be secured from a Hollywood starved for just about anyone who could read, write, or speak.

He was already indelibly marked by the contagious enthusiasm that characterizes a great salesman; in a sense it became his credo. "If you ever want to get hold of somebody," he would instruct us, "for God's sake don't beat around the bush—always ask to see who's in charge, even if it's the President of the United States. Don't screw around with anyone in the middle. The middle is always a little soft." And: "Listen, in this business, if you want to make a lot of dough—and why else would you be in this business?—you've got to remember one thing: there's a direct ratio between what you're selling and the amount of pandemonium you can stir up about it."

The bulk of his own agency's business was, naturally, in motion pictures. On a quiet morning, he might call the executives of five or six studios—Warner Brothers, Columbia, Paramount, M-G-M, RKO, for instance—to tell them, excitedly, that they should check the box-office receipts and reviews of some play that had just opened in New York (having himself arranged to handle its motion-picture sale an hour before). Then, having satisfactorily charged the atmosphere with the necessary delirium, he would leave the office before they could call back, have a relaxed lunch with a client at the Brown Derby, and maybe do an hour or two of leisurely shopping. By the time he got back to the office, there would be twenty properly hysterical phone calls waiting from the studios, all bidding against one another, and Father would calmly close the deal for a record price.

Although it was his particular style to map out deals for prodigious sums of money in a high-pitched frenzy while reclining with his feet draped over the top of his sofa, and it may actually have appeared, from time to time, that he was relaxing, there was no real slack in his routine even when he came home from the office. Father never stopped working. He was indefatigable. In this one respect, Mother and Father were similar, for all their many disagreements about a common life-style. They were both so alive, so insuperably optimistic. To watch them together was dizzying, hypnotic. One was aware of infinite potential, possibilities undreamed of—possibilities of magical endurance and energy, magical vitality. To watch them both was to strain one's own ability to keep abreast, to tread bottomless water; finally, it was to know the real meaning of exhaustion.

Bridget, Bill, and I did not concern ourselves with the matter of their telephone altercations; it had always been there, a constant, a family routine. We were satisfied by its predictability and sense of combativeness. Other people, their friends, were aware of it less comfortably. Our house was the perpetual headquarters for activity of any kind, riotous badminton matches or card games—hearts was a house favorite, since Mother always won—diving exhibitions in the swimming pool or roller-skating down the middle of San Vincente Boulevard, and the central participants were usually the same: Johnny Swope and Jimmy Stewart, Martha and Roger Edens, the Herman Mankiewiczes, the Wrights, and sometimes the Hank Fonda and Eddie Knopf clans from down the street. Johnny remembers that when Father came home from the office every afternoon he would gratefully rely on the buffer zone of friends to provide enough distraction for him to sneak in some phone calls. Mother also liked to have Johnny and Jimmy hang around; whenever Father went off on trips to New York, which was quite often, it was nice to be able to avail herself of the company of Hollywood's two most eligible bachelors.

The three of them had been close friends for years; they had started together in the University Players, a summer stock company in Falmouth, Massachusetts, which had also been the breeding ground for talent like Hank Fonda, Myron McCormack, Mildred Natwick, Kent Smith, Charles Leatherbee, Bretaigne Windust, and Josh Logan. Johnny Swope met Mother at the end of summer, 1931, when the company had ambitiously decided to extend its activities for a winter season of repertory in Baltimore. The winter before, Mother had become the first of the Players to hit the big time by landing a job as understudy to Elizabeth Love in the road company of *Strictly Dishonorable* and then the lead in *A Modern Virgin*, in which she got rave reviews although the play itself was lambasted. John Mason Brown wrote in the *Post* that "Miss Sullavan is in reality what the old phrase calls a 'find.' She has youth, beauty, charm, vivacity and intelligence. She has a bubbling sense of comedy and acts with a veteran's poise. And she deserves a far better fate than the kind of leading part in which she made her début. Last night the evening was hers, as many other evenings should be in the future." She rejoined the University Players when *A Modern Virgin* closed. The company lived in the Kernan Hotel, a run-down nineteenth-century building of which the Maryland Theatre, winter home of the aspiring young rep company, was part.

That was the winter (1931) that Mother and Hank Fonda got married, having carried on a stormy love affair over several summers of stock. An astute Baltimore *Post* reporter noticed that they were on a list of people who had just taken out marriage licenses; the day before Christmas he burst in upon the startled company assembled for breakfast in the Kernan Hotel dining room, and demanded further information. Mother grabbed a piece of toast and fled from the room, protesting, "Marry Fonda! Are you mad? Just look at him! Who'd ever want to marry him?" Hank raced after her, not only to avoid the reporter but to repair his wounded vanity. Bretaigne Windust, the head of the company, parried with the explanation that Mother and Fonda mysteriously had taken out marriage licenses at least twice before: perhaps they were making a collection of them. Mother, when she later heard this, enthusiastically elaborated on his story, "Yes, yes, that's it. We're collecting them, one for every city we're in together—New York, Baltimore—soon we'll have quite an exhibit."

Although nobody in the company believed either of them would actually go through with it, and neither did they, Mother and Hank were married at noon on Christmas Day in the dining room of the Kernan Hotel, with the dense odor of boiled cauliflower hanging over the assembled group. After a tearful ceremony, everyone sat down to an economical combination wedding breakfast–Christmas dinner, from which Hank departed somewhat precipitously, since he was starring in the matinée of *The Ghost Train*. For her honeymoon celebration, Johnny Swope took Mother that afternoon to see Greta Garbo in *Mata Hari*. He became so engrossed he almost forgot that he had to make an entrance in the third act of *The Ghost Train* as a police inspector. Suddenly, with no warning, he bolted the movie house, ungallantly leaving Mother behind, and ran without stopping all the way to the theatre and up onto the stage, just in time to pick up the wrist of the corpse and pant his one line: "Hmm, bitter almonds."

At the end of that season, Hank and Mother set up house-keeping in Greenwich Village. Since Father was already Mother's agent, he also took on Hank—still a struggling young unknown—as a client. Although Johnny and Father met each other then, they didn't become close friends until 1936, when Mother and Father got married, four years after Mother and Hank parted company.

By that time, Johnny (who at Fonda's urging had come out to California to become an assistant director) and Jimmy Stewart were sharing a house on Evanston Street. Father lost no time getting them both interested in flying airplanes. Jimmy had a slight head start, taking his first lessons on a little asphalt strip that used to be called Mines Field and is now International Airport. The airstrip was surrounded by acres of celery and lettuce fields, and every time a plane took off or landed, the air jumped with thousands of jackrabbits.

Father gave me, at age three, a hard lesson in both flying and philosophy that I have found difficult to forget since. For a long time I'd begged him to take me for a ride in his plane, although, having never seen one, I had no idea what a plane actually was other than a machine that flew noisily through the air.

One afternoon he came home early from the office and announced that this was it; the big day had come. He had George Stearns bring the car to the front of the house. Almost running a temperature from excitement, I clambered in. Mother and Bridget followed. Bridget was not yet two and hadn't been talking long; she had even less an idea than I of what an airplane might be, but she had picked up some of my euphoria and for the entire car ride murmured to herself in a singsong voice, "I want to go up in an airplane, I want to go up in an airplane." We drove for a very long time through parts of Los Angeles that I'd never seen before, flat stretches of irrigated farmland (which in a year or two would be covered with acres of sinister camouflage) and oil wells pumping— like monstrous woodpeckers, Mother said. All the while Bridget chanted, "I want to go up in an airplane," and I sat, fermenting with ecstasy, unable to speak a word. We came at last to a hangar and an airstrip with a red windsock flapping in the breeze. Father parked the car, and the four of us walked out to the asphalt strip. It was a beautiful day, warm and clear, with a sudden strange loud hum in the air. "There!" shouted Father, gaily throwing his head back and his arms out as if to embrace the sky. "Look up, quick, look up!" Right over our heads roared a small airplane doing aerobatics. "He's doing some stunts for you—now here comes a slow roll," yelled Father, "and watch this, he's starting into a loop-the-loop!"

"Where—where?" wailed Bridget desperately, pointing in the wrong direction, as Mother knelt down and tried to turn her head up.

"Look up, Brie, *up!*" called Father, his voice almost drowned out by the airplane hovering upside down over us. "Attagirl, Brooke, what d'ya think—isn't that beautiful?" At that moment the plane slowly began to lose altitude, as if on purpose, and, gathering momentum, nose-dived into the asphalt before us. It caught fire almost on impact. I screamed with delight, thinking it was part of the show, and started after Father, who was running toward the blaze, but Mother caught me and yanked me around so I couldn't see anything but her face.

"Don't look," she kept saying over and over, but I couldn't hear her very well, even in the silence after the engine had gone dead, because my ears were still ringing. "It's an accident, it's an accident." Although I didn't know what an accident was—at least not that kind—I didn't dare disobey her. Bridget clutched Mother's neck and said insistently, "I want to see an airplane, I want to see an airplane." There was a lot of commotion behind me, people and trucks whizzing past. Father came back after a while. Mother stood up. "Leland, darling," she said to him, "let's go home."

"Nope," he replied. "I promised Brooke she could have a ride in my plane and that's what we're going to do. Right?"

"Right," I said, much relieved.

"Come on, everyone," said Father cheerfully, taking my hand and striding across the strip. "Come on, Maggie. Listen." He stopped to make a sweeping motion in the direction of the charred wreck on the runway before pacing on. "Remember this, Brooke. You, too, Bridget, are you listening? If you're ever in an accident that you can walk out of, no matter what kind, keep right on going as if nothing happened at all. Airplane, car, whatever—get back in and keep going. Fall off a horse, get right back on, even if you're scared to death. Only way. Know why? Because otherwise, about five minutes later, you'll be even more afraid and won't ever want to try it again. Right. Got it?" And there we were, staring up at his plane. It was called, he said with pride, a Howard, and it was a beautiful dark blue, the color and shape of some sleek underwater creature. I was so dizzy with excitement and love that he had to reach back to haul me up the steps, and then get Bridget, who had curled up into a little ball and wouldn't let go of Mother. We all sat behind him while he put on his earphones and started the engine; a mechanic in a blue jumpsuit spun the propeller, and the plane started down the runway gathering speed. It lifted off into the air, curving around in a slow arc so that we were pressed down into our seats, and Father turned, grinning, to yell back at us, "How'd you like that?" I never wanted to come down again. Bridget spent the entire ride chanting, "I want to go up in an airplane, I want to go up in an airplane," disregarding Mother, who would squeeze her and say, laughing, "Brie, you are in an airplane, silly. This *is* an airplane, darling."

All the way home, Father animatedly talked to Mother about technical matters: how every airport had its own pattern for instrument landing, how really lousy it was to land by instrument in bad weather. I was too worn out to ask what happened to the stunt pilot; later it seemed that if it was really important to know, Father would have told me, so I forgot about it.

I can't imagine a childhood without Johnny and Jimmy in it. Johnny was around even the night I was born. It was the Fourth of July, and Mother, who was getting bored with being so pregnant, cajoled Father and Johnny into taking her out to dinner and then down to the amusement park on the Santa Monica Pier. They all tried for the gold ring on the merry-go-round, but Father was much too elegant to set foot on the roller coaster, so Mother and Johnny rode on it seven or eight times—and also the Ferris wheel, for good measure—while Father tried in vain to get them off. They threw darts, rode bumper cars, watched fireworks, paid a visit to every booth and rode every ride until two in the morning, when they went home and Johnny passed out on the sofa exhausted. He awoke at dawn, boiling hot and in a state of suffocation, because the cat had lovingly wrapped itself around his neck and gone to sleep, too; when he disentangled himself from its steaming fur and leaned over to see what time it was, he found a note pinned on his chest, which said, "Dear Johnny, when you wake up you will be a godfather. Congratulations." He ran frantically around the house but it was empty. Nobody had been able to rouse him from his stupor for the big event, so he drove down to the hospital and consoled himself by taking pictures of my bare behind, which was identified by a little piece of tape with my name on it.

Johnny was a wonderful photographer. He'd taken up flying and photography at the same time, and used to say that he learned photography by taking pictures of Bridget, Bill, and me. From the very beginning, he practiced the theory that if we never saw him without his camera we would never be self-conscious if he pointed it at us, and he was right. He was always hanging around, ready to document every move we made, every step we took, and we allowed him to study us in depth, assuming, naturally, that he was one of us.

On weekends, Jimmy and Johnny were permanent residents. Jimmy had met Mother in 1930 while he was majoring in architecture at Princeton and she was touring in the road company of *Strictly Dishonorable*. He had no intention of becoming an actor; in fact, he obtained a scholarship to go back to Princeton for his master's degree in architecture. Josh Logan, who was a class ahead, had persuaded him to join the Triangle, because he could sing and play the accordion. Josh also brought him into the University Players, not as an actor but as an accordion player in the tearoom that adjoined the theatre in Falmouth. He lasted one night in the tearoom, because it was unanimously decided that his music spoiled people's appetites; then he was given various jobs—property man, some small parts—and finally was hired by Arthur Beckhart, New York producer, to play the chauffeur in *Goodbye Again*, a part that lasted two minutes in the first act and that put an end to Jimmy's architectural career.

By 1936, he was a contract player at Metro, working all the time but getting only small parts in B movies. At Mother's suggestion, Universal tested him for the leading man in *Next Time We Love*, a movie in which she was about to star, and he got the part. He played a newspaper reporter and she played a young actress who gave up her career to marry him. They were both particularly fond of the scene in which Jimmy had to go away on some assignment, leaving his young wife and baby behind. Jimmy felt that the situation called for a tear or two on his part, and had no difficulty filling his eyes for the first take, but the baby threw something at him and they had to cut. The second take was likewise ruined by the baby, and the third and fourth. By the fifth take, Jummy was unable to summon up any more tears. He didn't know about glycerin, which is often used in movies to stimulate tears, and, in any case, would probably have been too embarrassed to ask for it, so he went behind the scenery, lit a cigarette, and held it to his eyes in the hope that the smoke would make them tear up. This experiment transformed his eyes into two raw blobs, and he almost threatened to shoot the child. Mother was delighted, particularly by the cigarette.

After he was drafted at the beginning of the war, Jimmy would come back to Evanston Street on leave, most of which he'd spend on our badminton court. During his first leave, I was in bed with a cold, lying grandly in the fourposter (canopied in green checks) of my new room in The Barn. Unexpectedly he slipped upstairs to pay me a visit during my nap time, when I was supposed to be asleep but was instead sneaking a forbidden look at some Beatrix Potter books, which tumbled loudly to the floor when I caught sight of Jimmy in uniform. He rolled me up in my bedspread like a sausage in wrapping paper, while I howled with laughter, and then perched me on his bony knee to tell me a story.

When Johnny Swope finally got married, in 1943, the ceremony took place at our house. He'd fallen in love with Dorothy McGuire, a young actress who had just starred in the stage and movie productions of *Claudia*. Johnny had swept her up romantically to Santa Barbara to be married at the historic old mission there, but to his chagrin was turned away because he was not a Catholic. Father suggested our house and that was that. Johnny had wisely avoided bringing Dorothy around before; past experience had taught him that Mother had a subtle way of overwhelming the girls whom he and Jimmy might bring over.

For Bridget and me, the wedding was the most exciting thing that ever happened at 12928. Bill was two years old and, as far as we were concerned, too young to appreciate the importance of the occasion. All the same, we allowed him to help us with our wedding present, a painting that depicted Dorothy in a red dress holding purple flowers, surrounded by the rays of the sun, while Johnny stood apart (separated from her by the three watery figures of us children) in a brown suit and porcine bowler stuck with a red feather; over all floated the message "DEAR JOHNNiE AND DOROTHY. I HOPE YOU LiKE YOUR WEDDiNG. LOVE BROOKE AND BRie AND BiLL." It was a very small wedding on a glorious July day, late in the afternoon. Our shadows fell in a procession on the wide lawn as we stood in a semicircle under the gnarled olive tree, banked with pots of flowers. Bridget and I were flower girls. Jimmy, who was stationed at the Air Force base in Albuquerque, flew in to double as best man and piano player of the wedding march: he ticked off the wedding march inside the house and then ran back out just in time to be best man.

Halfway through the ceremony, Bridget and I were jarred out of the trance into which the occasion's solemnity had beguiled us by Bill tweaking our eyelet lace pinafores and whispering confidentially, "I have to go to the bathroom, I have to go to the bathroom." Bridget scornfully snatched her skirt away and I pondered the petals in my basket, but his complaint became rapidly more desperate and audible.

"Ssh," said Bridget in disgust. "*Sssh.*"

Bill closed his eyes dreamily and began to chant, "I have to go to the bathroom, I have to go to the bathroom—"

Bridget flapped her sharp elbow at him and hissed, "*Ssssh!*"

"Ow," said Bill, then began wetting his pants slowly while he continued to sing, at the top of his high-pitched voice, "I have to go to the bathroom, I have to go to the bathroom," throughout the remainder of the mercifully short ceremony until he was carried off by our nurse Emily.

While pouring the champagne afterward, Otto, our German butler, informed Johnny that he was taking lessons in photography and would consider it an honor to be permitted to shoot the official wedding pictures. Johnny turned over his camera (which, of course, he'd brought along) and posed with Dorothy in the doorway. Shortly after that, Elsa and Otto were arrested as German spies and we found out that Otto had been enrolled in a photography school for less than patriotic purposes, but Johnny said he couldn't have been very good at his second trade because his photographs were so terrible.

. . .

Birthday parties were events of great consequence in Hollywood, and even though Mother deplored everything in or about Hollywood—keeping aloof from its social functions and disdaining its tribal customs, particularly as they related to stardom—she relented when it came to our birthday parties. Possibly one of the reasons for this was that after she took us out of school we so seldom saw other children except those of her friends on weekends. In no other way did Mother conform to the prevailing behavior of the Hollywood star, since she never had any great ambition to be a star at all. It wasn't a glamorous career and its by-products that she really wanted, but a family, and I suspect that in the matter of birthday parties she felt obligated, more for the sake of her children than herself, to overcome her disapproval of the life around her.

At a typical Hollywood party, there would be twenty to thirty children (at ours, Johanna Mankiewicz and her cousins Tom and Chris, Danny Selznick, Jane and Peter Fonda, the Scharys—Jill, Joy, and Jeb—Maria Cooper, Christina Crawford, and Jonathan Knopf were the hard-core regulars), each with his or her own governess. When we all sat down to eat, there would be an attentive line-up of white uniforms packed in close formation behind us. A ritual, even competitive air infused all these parties, from the entertainment (magicians or clowns, caravans of ponies or elephants transported by truck for gracious rides around the ancestral lawns) to the menu (creamed chicken in a ring of rice garnished with peas, ice cream molded in a myriad of shapes and flavors—frozen animals in nests of green cotton candy were *de rigueur* at our house—and the birthday cakes themselves, angel food, swagged and flounced with boiled frosting like hoop skirts under white ball gowns). Joan Crawford's daughter Christina was the most envied party hostess because invariably she offered the longest program: not only puppet shows before supper and more and better favors piled up at each place setting but movies afterward; besides, her wardrobe was the fanciest—layers and layers of petticoats under dotted swiss or organdy, sashed at the waist with plump bows and lace-trimmed at the neck to set off her dainty yellow curls.

The Hayward parties were the most boisterous, largely because The Barn seemed to inspire a lack of decorum. Our guests would arrive with their governesses and parents (the latter would soon disappear into The Other House for a quiet drink), laden with presents and attired in crisp frocks or shorts with knee socks; curtsies would be made (by all the girls except Bridget and me) and shy greetings exchanged, and then pandemonium would rage. In front of The Barn was an enclosed play yard, stocked with jungle gyms, swings, rings, and slides, and within fifteen minutes not a dress would be clean or a knee unskinned. Covered with grass stains, the panting guests would assemble at the vast trestle table. There—under the stern jurisdiction of Emily (in her one good dress), who, arms crossed, eyed the entire company like a stage manager faced with a tricky production number—trouble began in earnest. By the time the creamed chicken was served, Jane Fonda and I usually would be throwing paper snappers across the table at each other; oblivious to Emily's barked admonitions, we would swiftly move on to the peas and rice, packing them into mushy little balls—stained with brilliant vegetable dye from the favors— which we hurled at anyone who hadn't already joined in, until we achieved total participation. At my fifth birthday party, I fell passionately in love with Tarquin Olivier, seated on my left, because he led off with a round of piercing battle cries in an English accent.

Tarquin, two years older than I, was the son of Jill Esmond and Laurence Olivier. Evacuated from London during the war, he had been brought by his mother to live in California. The name Tarquin Olivier was the most beautiful I had ever heard. I used to lie on my bed in a reverie—seeing the four posts as guardian angels, with glowing satin robes and creamy wings flowing to the floor— and dream of Tarquin and myself building sand castles on the beach at the grand old Carlsbad Hotel in Oceanside, where, for a summer, the Hayward and Mankiewicz families formed a colony. One weekend, Father drove Tarquin down from Los Angeles to visit us. Every afternoon we ate tomato sandwiches on toast, dripping with mayonnaise—then, while the grownups sat in canvas deck chairs on the beach, Tarquin and I dug deep moist tunnels through which we squirmed, excited by our bare skin and the proximity of our wriggling bodies. On the morning of Tarquin's seventh birthday, his mother, Jill, brought him over for a swim.

"Mother," I asked, somewhat anxiously, "what are we giving Tarquin for his birthday?"

"Umm," said Mother, squinting at Tarquin, "let's see.

Tarquin," she kicked off her shoes and squatted down, making herself no taller than he—she never liked to address children from any height at all—"tell you what. If you can *guess* exactly what it is—one guess is all you get—then, by gum, that's what we're giving you for your birthday."

Tarquin cocked his head with interest and dangled his foot thoughtfully in the water. "A watch," he answered, his voice rising with hope, "a real wristwatch!"

Mother shook her head sadly. "Uh-uh. 'Fraid that's way off. What we're giving you is much more special than a watch, something that nobody else has. How would you like"—Mother gave me a wink and stood up—"a darling little roly-poly bug?" She opened her hand and there, in the crack of her palm, was a potato bug, rolled into a tight gray ball.

"Oh, no!" cried Tarquin. "You're teasing me!"

"Why, Tarquin," said Mother, "don't you have any idea what wonderful pets roly-poly bugs make? You can take them anywhere."

"Phew!" said Tarquin. "All I want is a wristwatch. Are you teasing me, Maggie?" Mother began to laugh, and for the rest of the morning he followed her around the pool, not quite sure what to anticipate at his party that afternoon, but politely hoping for the best.

After Jill and he left, Mother carefully placed the potato bug between two layers of cotton in a small empty bracelet box, which she then wrapped as a gift. "Don't worry," she told me conspiratorially, "he'll open this and be *horrified*, but it's just a joke—I've already sent over his real birthday present."

Bridget and I carried the box to the party, my chest throbbing with both delight and fear. Tarquin was standing regally—taller and more handsome than he'd ever been before—silhouetted against the pastel party dresses of what seemed to be hundreds of admirers fluttering on the steps of the house. It was an awful moment. I handed him the box, betraying him, my first love. His face was radiant with joy; the size of the box clearly indicated there was something precious inside. I squeezed my eyes shut, praying that the potato bug had somehow changed into a wristwatch, but it hadn't—he lifted the top layer of cotton and there was the little gray ball. Mute, Tarquin stared at it, while all our friends shoved and pushed each other for a look. Bridget and I were humiliated; there was no way to explain. Fortunately, the real present was quickly produced and we were restored to favor. As a result of this episode, I immediately wrote a poem entitled, "When You Kiss Me, Kiss Me with a Smile."

Bridget, Bill, and I knew that we were the envy of all our friends because we lived in our own house, apart from our parents. The Barn was ours, it belonged to us, every inch of it had been created with us in mind. We derived an enormous sense of pleasure from the possession of something so large, a *house*, entirely tooled to meet our needs. We were aware that ours was a unique situation. It was satisfying to feel superior to and different from anyone else our age, to be envied by all our peers because we could make as much noise as we wanted and bicycle and roller-skate and pull wagons around our own private living-room floor. The Barn was an ideal playhouse.

But sometimes we longed to know what it was like to live like other children, in one house, surrounded by family. And sometimes late at night, I would wake up—feeling alone—and quickly check to make sure there was light filtering through the crack under my door. One time the crack was dark, and I called, Emily, Emily, Emil-ee. When she didn't come, I was so frightened I forced myself to feel my way downstairs and outside, to traverse the breezeway to The Other House on tiptoe, inch by inch, because I thought the wind rustling the mottled leaves of ivy was alive, a weasel or a fox breathing through the vines as he followed my passage. When I came to the other side—The Other House—although it was only thirty feet away, I felt that at last I had reached civilization after a very dangerous journey through the wilderness. I found Emily in the kitchen, exactly where I thought she would be, chatting with Elsa and Otto over a cup of coffee. They all made a big fuss over me and I forgave Emily because she let me snuggle on her lap—the best place I ever sat—with a cup of cocoa, and comforted me with the promise that, never, ever, for the rest of life, would she forget to leave the light on downstairs or go away and leave me again, except on her day off.

To us, Emily was everything in the world. We loved her totally because she belonged to us; she was entirely ours in a way that Mother and Father never were. We loved them from a distance; we admired them as we admired the sun and moon, adoring their beauty and constancy, their infinite power. They were gods; we worshipped them. But we loved Emily in a different way.

Emily started working for us as a relief nurse and ended up

staying full time. On her days off she went home to her husband, Ed Buck, and once or twice, giving in to our entreaties, she took us with her to their little house with hibiscus bushes growing up either side of the front walk. Emily had no children of her own, and considered us hers, which suited us perfectly. Mother and Father used to say fondly that Emily was the homeliest person they'd ever seen, but the kindest. We, however, thought she was the most beautiful, and said so. She had stringy mouse-colored hair, which hung limply in one stage or another of a bad permanent. Her eyelashes and eyebrows were sparse and did less to define her eyes than the discolored hollows under them. Two deep furrows ran from her rather bulbous nose to the corners of her mouth, where they were intersected by a great system of other lines. Her skin was pitted in some places like old tarmac and in others dislodged by moles or wens; it seemed to be permanently redolent of coffee and as nicotine-stained as her teeth. Emily, like Father, smoked three packs of cigarettes a day, preferably Camels, and when they became scarce during the war, she took to rolling her own. On special occasions she wore lipstick, a dark purplish color. She'd apply it carefully to her angular lips, then smack them together and blot most of it off with tissues.

"Poor Em," we'd sigh, inspecting the varicose veins in her calves, which gave her trouble when she stood too long. "Someday we'll take care of *you*." Then Father would interject while she poured him a cup of her coffee, which he preferred to Elsa's, "I hope to Christ the three of you children take care of *both* of us when you get to be twenty-one years old and I'm doddering around in a state of financial ruin." Emily would guffaw, and say, "Oh, good Lord, Mr. Hayward, don't start that again," and we'd giggle and chorus, "But, Father, we'll never make enough money to take care of *you*." Father would lower his teaspoon into the coffee, carefully submerging three lumps of sugar, one for each of us to suck, and shake his head. "God knows, children, it won't be easy. But that's what children are for, to take care of their poor old senile parents. You're all smart as hell; you'll get good grades at school—you'd better, by God—I'm counting on you to keep me from the poorhouse. . . ."

"But, Father, we're not allowed to go to school."

"Oh, yes, that's right. Well, someday—now, let's see—let's get right down to business. Brooke, what do you want to be when you grow up?"

This was a game we loved, although the answers never changed. "A painter and a writer."

"No money in that. Bridget?"

"I want to grow up to be a housewife with ten children."

"No hope there whatsoever. Disaster. My last chance—Bill?"

"When I grow up, I'm going to be either a fireman or the President of the United States."

"Well, couldn't you marry a very rich girl while you're at it? This is just awful. Promise me that *one* of you at least will be considerate enough to marry somebody with a lot of dough for the sake of your beloved old father. After all, I think I deserve to be supported in some kind of style. . . ."

Father's mother, Sarah Tappin—Grandsarah—moved to Los Angeles in 1943. She had raised champion cairn terriers with her third husband, Lindsley Tappin, at their country house in Wilton, Connecticut. After he died, she decided to come out to California to see her only son and three grandchildren, so she sold the house, packed her station wagon with one poodle, twenty-six of her favorite cairns, and Archie, her black caretaker, and drove all the way across the country herself (since Archie had never learned how), stopping twice a day to take the dogs out of their individual wicker baskets to feed and exercise them.

Father had bought her a house on Magnolia Boulevard in Van Nuys. Every Sunday we would drive over to the Valley, holding our breaths and making wishes as we came to the entrance of the tunnel through the mountains; then, as Sepulveda Boulevard began its serpentine descent to the lovely clear expanse below, Father would take his foot off the gas as a gesture toward rationing, and the car would career around the curves, speeding up and slowing down under its own momentum.

My grandmother's house was dark and cool and filled with beautiful dusty mysteries. Beyond the verandah that ran all around it, softening its borders with six feet of shade, lay the gardens, several acres of them, bounded by high walls and fruit trees gleaming in the sun. Pomegranates overlapped persimmons, peaches and cherries intertwined, a lacy forest of citrus—tangerines, lemons, grapefruits, and oranges—gradually gave way to thick meandering shrubbery, dappled with sweet-skinned kumquats and guavas that

Grandsarah made into jelly each fall. We squinted through the shadowy living room toward the blinding green sunlight, bewitched by the contrast between inside and out. Sunday lunch at my grandmother's house was the most compelling adventure, the most seductive paradise we knew. We were overcome by desires; we wanted to possess everything that we saw or smelled or tasted, to touch it, hold it, take it away with us so that we could have it forever. In her house we became pirates.

First we headed for the cupboards where she kept her three-odd sets of wineglasses, each with a goblet or two missing, just to make sure none had been broken or rearranged since the previous Sunday. We had, after interminable bickering, staked out our individual territories, and for some reason the wineglasses from which we drank our ginger ale, pretending it was champagne, seemed to exemplify our intangible conquest. "Grandsarah," I would say, stroking my glass, which had small green bumps blown onto its surface, "you must take good care of these glasses. Right now there are two missing, so—"

Grandsarah chuckled, amused by my ill-concealed longing.

"Don't worry," she said cheerfully, poking at the chicken frying on the big stove, "I'll take good care of them for the next ten years, and then—give the gravy a stir, would you, Viola?" Viola came twice a week to clean and on Sundays to help with lunch; she was black and so fat it took her some time to lower herself, grunting, into a sitting position and quite a bit longer to get up from one. Both Viola and Grandsarah laughed at everything we said and let us do whatever we wanted—spoiled us rotten, said Father, but that's what grandparents were for.

Bridget's glass was etched with red leaves. "Mine, too?" she asked, holding it up for more ginger ale, which was forbidden at home.

"Yes, yes." Grandsarah smiled broadly. "Now I think these mashed potatoes are done just the way your father likes them—yes, and yours, too, Bill. And in ten years when I'm seventy, I'll probably be dead anyway—nobody should live past seventy—and then I'll leave them to you."

"Oh, no, Grandsarah," we'd wail, simultaneously terrified that she would ever die and pleased at the prospect that the glasses would finally be ours. "Don't die, Grandsarah, don't die—what would we do without you? You're going to live to be a hundred."

"Seventy's old enough, old enough. Don't want to push my luck," said Grandsarah.

Fried chicken was the traditional Sunday lunch because Father loved it, and as Grandsarah said, he was her only son and the most wonderful person in the whole world. We all sat around her pink wrought-iron-and-glass table while the grownups talked and laughed a lot, dogs pushed their way in and out the French doors to the patio, and Bridget, Bill, and I shoveled speckled vanilla ice cream into our mouths. "My God, that was good, Mother," Father would say, putting down his napkin. "Now, there is one thing in this room I have *my* eye on, wanted it for as long as I can remember."

We would all look toward the sideboard where a portable antique liqueur cabinet sat. "Now, Mother," Father would continue to our huge enjoyment, "you know how much I need this." He would fondle its dark mahogany sides and open its hinged top to show off the perfect set of crystal decanters and liqueur glasses arranged inside. "You have no use for it whatsoever, Mother, for God's sake."

"Oh, Leland." Grandsarah's eyes twinkled as she smiled and patted her hair, which was pinned in a roll. "I use it when we play poker." (Grandsarah had a weekly poker game with Junior and Irene Egan, whom she had met while traveling around the world in 1910.) "Besides, Leland," she continued, "you know perfectly well I've never been able to refuse you anything at all—you'll get it out of me one of these days." Then she'd hug him and laugh some more.

"How about my next birthday?" Father would ask.

"Good Lord, Mr. Hayward," said Emily, "you're worse than the children."

After lunch we'd follow Grandsarah down to the kennels at the back of the property to watch her feed the little dogs yapping in their runs. For years she was the foremost breeder of cairn terriers in Los Angeles, until the zoning laws changed and the kennels fell into musty disrepair. Even then we would go down to the end of the garden, through the sunny tangle of irises and narcissus in spring, lilies and roses in summer, to play hide-and-seek in the overgrown ruins that were haunted by mildewing, spider-infested wicker cases and shards of earthenware feeding bowls.

Crisscrossing the gardens was a maze of concrete paths that

had taken Archie and the gardener months to lay and that was inscribed at intervals with Archie's duly noted progress—"OCT. 1943, HALFWAY"—and the occasional graffiti of Bridget, Bill, and me, who had immortalized ourselves in the wet cement under Archie's drowsy supervision.

"Grandsarah," we would clamor before leaving, "it's time to look at your treasures." To us, her house glittered with treasures: small boxes with dogs enameled on them, silver trophies from dog shows, and the big oil painting over the fireplace that depicted, in deep perspective, all the champion terriers she had ever raised, posing grandly in their wiry coats of different colors against a green Connecticut landscape.

"Can I have that someday, Grandsarah?"

"No, I asked for it last time. She said—"

"No, me, me—"

"When I die, children, when I die."

And the jewelry boxes, filled with charms and earrings. Our lust had dropped all its disguises somewhere in the garden during the long hot afternoon. "Ooh, what's this, a moonstone heart? Can I have this when you die?"

We were motivated not just by avarice but also by our first intimations that people grew old and did not live forever, that maybe we could capture her forever as she was at that moment by simply dividing up her possessions.

"Oh, Grandsarah, don't forget, *please*, you promised to leave this old photograph to me."

And she, understanding, found nothing macabre in our articulate greed and inarticulate desire to stop time.

"I won't forget, I won't forget, you darling children. You tickle me, you really do. You're almost as darling as your father was when he was little."

We pestered her for stories about Father when he was a little boy, unable to conceive of such a time. "It's a long way back to make my poor old brain go," Grandsarah would say, with a laugh, sitting in her plum-colored armchair with her slender ankles crossed on a footstool. Then she would shake her head and look down at her lap. "Things were easier then, more fun."

"Oh, come on, Grandsarah, *please*." She wavered, we pressed, awed by the history she embodied. She was born November 7, 1882, in Nebraska City, Nebraska. "It was just a little bit of a town, where nothing much ever happened, just a little country town with one packing house and a few thousand people, farmland all around for miles." Her mother was Eloise Coe and her father Franklin P. Ireland, a lawyer from Newburyport, Massachusetts. We would lean against her chair, trying to imagine what it was like to grow up in a time and world with scant electricity and no cars at all. In good weather the Irelands harnessed their team of matched bay horses, Claude and Cora, to a trap; in winter Claude and Cora pulled the sleigh. For her fifteenth birthday, Grandsarah was given her own horse and trap, and thought she would faint from excitement. The only paved road in Nebraska City was Main Street, which was laid in brick along the ten or twelve blocks of its shopping and business district. The horse-drawn fire engine was the great attraction in town—"nothing else to get excited about." There was no place to swim except the Missouri River and that was too dangerous. The weather was "hotter'n hell" in summer and sub-zero in winter. In the daytime Grandsarah wore checked gingham dresses with petticoats and drawers and in the evening she wore organdies with puffed sleeves. (Bridget and I nodded approval.) Although she had no brothers or sisters, she was never lonely. There were parties and dances everywhere, all the time. The Irelands often covered their twenty-foot fishpond with oak planks, waxed them, and danced.

Grandsarah went to boarding school but never finished the last year because she was beginning to fall in love with Will Hayward, the son of Monroe Leland Hayward, U.S. Senator from Nebraska. Grandsarah first met Will when she was sixteen and he was twenty-one, a dashing young graduate from the University of Nebraska where he had starred on the baseball and football teams and was president of his class of '97. When the Spanish-American War broke out in 1898, Will exhibited signs of the adventurous streak that was to underscore his life, and promptly gave up his new law practice in Nebraska City and volunteered for service. He was placed in command of the 2nd Nebraska Infantry as captain and, after serving through the war and the Philippine insurrection, was mustered out in 1901 as a colonel.

Grandsarah thought he was irresistible, with blue eyes and a dimple in his chin: "The best-looking man I ever saw—always took good care of himself, played football night and day." After divesting herself of another beau, she married him in March, 1901, when she was eighteen. The wedding created an uproar in the Ireland family, who thought she was much too young, but her father stormed and wept to no avail. The Haywards were a clan of Baptists as diehard as the Irelands were Episcopalian; a compromise was reached, according to Grandsarah's directive, in which she and Will were married by a Baptist minister ("I didn't care who *did* it") in an Episcopalian ceremony ("not as boring"). They moved into a two-story house that Will had had built for her, and right after they were married, he brought home the first car in Nebraska City, a Locomobile. On September 13, 1902, she gave birth to Father. He was much adored, being an only child, and his nurse from infancy, Mary Coots, stayed on with Grandsarah for the next thirty years just to keep an eye on him.

Will Hayward, in 1901, became Nebraska's youngest county judge. A newspaper account of the period said, "He was an ardent bowler and paid for a telephone booth at the bowling alley so when someone wanted a marriage license he could be called to the courthouse." He ran for the State Congress in 1910 and was defeated. Grandsarah used to say he never got over it. To mend his broken heart, they went on a trip around the world. With Father in tow, they traveled by boat from San Francisco to Japan and China, making their way back through Europe. Although Father was only eight years old, he had persistent memories of the journey, highlighted by his various illnesses in every country they passed through.

When they returned to the United States, the Haywards, accelerated by a new sense of discovery, moved to New York City. Grandfather joined the law firm of Wing & Russell, and Grandsarah took ballroom ice-skating lessons every day in Central Park. Father went to school at Horace Mann. Still, despite the lure of pretty shops and a bracing social climate, life wasn't moving quickly enough. In 1911, Grandsarah went back to Omaha, Nebraska, and divorced Will Hayward. ("I just got bored with him and he was probably as bored with me.") Her family and friends were scandalized; divorce was immoral and totally improper. Grandsarah, high-spirited as always, married a very wealthy man, Shepherd Schermerhorn, the vice-president of the United Fruit Company. They lived at 375 Park Avenue and traveled to South America every winter. Father, allegedly hating them all, went to a series of boarding schools—Garden City, Pomfret, and finally Hotchkiss, from which he graduated.

Grandfather, meanwhile, distinguished himself as a lawyer and soldier. Appointed Assistant District Attorney under Charles S. Whitman, then District Attorney, he ran Mr. Whitman's successful campaign for Governor of New York in 1914. He went to Albany as Governor Whitman's counsel and became Public Service Commissioner of New York in 1915, a position he resigned in 1918 to devote all of his time to the black 369th Infantry Regiment of Harlem, which he recruited, trained, and then commanded. The 369th was among the first fighting units to land in France; it served at the front under fire for 191 days, the longest period of fighting endured by any unit of the American Expeditionary Force. Highly regarded by the French, the regiment was sometimes used as shock troops because of its striking power. It was cited for valor and, after the Armistice, became the first Allied unit to enter Germany. Grandfather, known to his men as Colonel "Fighting Bill" Hayward, received the Croix de Guerre, and was made an officer of the Legion of Honor.

In 1919 he married Maisie Manwaring Plant. At this point, if Father was listening, he'd interject scathingly, "That barmaid," because Maisie was first married to Mr. Manwaring, who managed a restaurant in a small town near New London, Connecticut, where Maisie helped him by waiting on tables until she caught the eye of the old and fabulously wealthy Commodore Morton Plant. In what many people considered an act of pure calculation, she ran off with him and had her son's name changed to Plant, then sat back and inherited Mort's vast fortune when he died shortly afterward. There was no doubt, though, that old Mort was crazy about her, Grandsarah would say, because he traded his house at Fifty-second Street and Fifth Avenue (the site of the present store) to Cartier's in exchange for a string of pearls that they'd tracked down—after an extraordinary worldwide search—to match, perfectly, one he'd already given her.

After Grandfather married Maisie, they lived in her stone mansion, a palatial structure that took up the entire block at Eighty-sixth and Fifth Avenue and that featured both a boiserie room, which had been the Duke of Wellington's study, and a Fragonard room, which was eventually given to the Metropolitan Museum. Father had ambiguous feelings about the whole setup and wildly resented the difference in the way he and his stepbrother, Philip Plant, much the same age, were treated. Phil Plant was outrageously pampered by his mother. She put at his disposal

unlimited sums of money to squander on every facet of his budding
playboy career; when Father, however, once lost a two-hundred-
dollar bet, *his* father, a stern disciplinarian, refused to lend him the
money and taught him to pay his gambling debts by selling every
possession, every piece of clothing he owned, except for a couple of
clean shirts. "Even my cuff links," growled Father; "it was a helluva lesson. I never, to this day, have ever been able to gamble
again, not even on the stock market." Father did develop a kind of
sympathetic regard for his stepbrother. "Phil Plant was really awfully damn nice to me, although he was a strange man—once bit
off a man's ear in a bar fight. And he used to take his mother—all
decked out in million-dollar paste copies of her million-dollar
jewels; she always kept the originals in a safe-deposit box and never
took them out except to look at them, too scared to go out in the
real McCoy, goddamn stingy barmaid—he used to take her out
dancing all night." In 1925, Phil eloped to Paris with Constance
Bennett; before their divorce in 1929 and her subsequent marriage
to the Marquis de la Falaise, she disappeared to Switzerland for a
while and returned with a child who she claimed was Phil's, and, as
such, the heir to his fortune. A famous paternity suit resulted, and
after Phil's death there was a protracted court battle in which
Maisie claimed that Peter Bennett Plant was really an English
child, adopted by Phil out of gallantry well after his and Constance's divorce proceedings had been initiated. Years later the case
was settled out of court, financially to Maisie's satisfaction.

Grandfather was appointed U.S. Attorney for the Southern
District of New York by President Harding in 1921, and later
became the senior partner in the law firm of Hayward, Jones, Nutt
& Murray. With his relish for politics, he became chairman of the
State Republican Convention in 1920 and a delegate to the National Convention in 1924. Also in 1924 he ran, unsuccessfully,
against Theodore Roosevelt, Jr., for the Republican nomination for
Governor of New York. Still, there was another side to his nature,
an old ache, a wildness and lust for adventure, never quite satisfied
by the perimeters of civilization. At times, when it seemed to him
that his life was becoming too sedentary, too socially refined, he
would be afflicted by migraine headaches so prolonged and agonizing, Father said, he would pound his head against the walls of his
room to ease the pain. Big-game hunting became his favorite avo-
cation; he took Phil Plant on several expeditions to East and

Central Africa, returning with those many trophies for the Museum of Natural History, and captured live polar bears for the Bronx Zoo in an exploration trip to the Arctic.

When Father flunked out of Princeton in 1920, after his first year, his father—to whom he referred thereafter as "the Colonel" —stopped his allowance and got him a job as a reporter, at twenty-five dollars a week, on the New York *Sun*. The *Sun* soon fired him, and Father, disgruntled, went up to Princeton and talked the dean into reinstating him. Several months later he left college again, to marry Lola Gibbs, a legendary Texas beauty who was considered to be that season's loveliest débutante; it was said that a moan of dis-appointment crescendoed through New York's débutante ranks when their most desirable bachelor defected to her. True to the pre-cepts of Fitzgeraldian romance, Father and Lola were divorced after two years and remarried after seven, doubling the length of the experience to four years the second time around. Two years after that, in 1936, Father married Mother.

Grandsarah stayed married to Shep Schermerhorn for about ten years ("I never could stand a man for more than that"), divorced him, and in 1924 married his closest friend, Lindsley Tappin, who died in 1941. "Well, thank goodness," she'd say, clapping her hands together as if slamming a book shut, "that takes care of that. I'm all talked out, children, talked out of everything, even my wineglasses and scruffy trinkets. I'd give anything to see the three of you go to work on Maisie." She'd place her feet carefully side by side on the pink-and-black Victorian rug and push herself up out of her armchair to put her arms around Father. "Just crazy about him—never loved anyone as much in my life."

"Absolutely true," Father would agree complacently as she rocked him back and forth. "I don't think Mother's ever said a cross word to me."

"Oh, Leland, how could I? How could I? Such a darling boy—almost as good-looking as his father. I was never very stern with him—probably should have been, but I couldn't help it. Always talked to him like a brother." She'd squeeze him and laugh some more with such gusto we'd all join in. "Now, children, it's time to pick some fruit for you to take home. Let's go see what's ripe before the birds get it all."

My grandmother would put on her straw hat with cherries all around the brim, and take the three of us, each fighting for one of her hands, out into the dying sunlight. We'd jump up and down beneath the trees, hurling ourselves against branches that glowed with strange sweet fruit—overripe persimmons and pomegranates already beginning to crack. And while the seeds trickled down our chins, staining them like blood, she, laughing her wonderful laugh, filled our paper bags until we could hardly lift them. It seemed, for those few minutes, that whatever had been eluding us all day had fallen into our sticky outstretched hands like the fruit itself.

Father produced his first play, A Bell for Adano, in the fall of 1944. Although his interest in the theatre was longstanding, it was said that his move away from the agency toward production was a capitulation to Mother, to her dogmatic insistence that the agency business was beneath him.

Several times that year, Bridget, Bill, and I crossed the country on the Super Chief to visit Mother, who was under contract to stay with "The Turtle" until December. Whenever we returned, we wrote her hundreds of letters on every conceivable kind of stationery in handwriting that changed every week under Miss Brown's tutelage. "Dear Mother, I love you. Bill is playing. Love, Bridget." "Dear Mother, I am going to play the wedding march when someone is married. Love, Brooke." "Dear Mother, I love you, I can read. I can play the piano. I have a loose tooth. Love, Bridget." "Dear Mother, I miss you. One of my upper teeth is coming in now. It feels funny. Bridget is eating fast now, Bill is eating a little faster too. Oh I want a little kitty. Love, Brooke." Bill sent pages of odd scribbles and Father sent notes on his blue Memo from Leland Hayward paper, in a scrawl so large there were only three or four words to a page, "Darling—Enclosed are some exhibits from your children—love letters, rare paintings + expressions of Bridget's soul— Also my heart, my love, my every thought, my desires— Living without you is horrible. Each month I love you more and the whole world less— You're everything there is in life to me. Without you it is pointless and silly—I wish we had been born + always lived together— I did not have lunch with Garbo today—Leland." And in anticipation of a trip to Europe planned for the two months' vacation she had that summer, he dispatched a message that took up three full pages of Western Union paper:

MAGGIE DARLING AM CALLING YOU LATER BUT WANTED YOU TO GET THIS FIRST. I HAVENT GOT THE ASTAIRE CONTRACTS YET AND WONT HAVE THEM BEFORE THE MORNING. I WANT TO MAKE A DEAL WITH YOU AND I GIVE YOU MY SACRED WORD OF HONOR I WILL KEEP IT ON BROOKE AND BRIDGETS HEAD OR ANYTHING YOU WANT. I WANT YOU TO LEAVE TOMORROW AFTERNOON AND COME HOME, STAY HERE AND WE CAN GO AWAY FOR THE WEEKEND ANYWHERE YOU LIKE AND LEAVE HERE MONDAY OR TUESDAY AFTERNOON FOR NEW YORK AND SAIL NEXT SATURDAY, LEAVING YOUR TRUNK AND MINE IN NEW YORK. AM BUYING THE TICKETS FOR NEXT SATURDAY NOW SO HAVE TO GO. I KNOW THIS IS UNREASONABLE AND AWFUL BUT IF I WERE TO LEAVE TOMORROW NIGHT IT WOULD BE REALLY CATASTROPHIC. I JUST CANT TELL YOU HOW AWFUL IT WOULD BE AND WHAT IT WOULD DO. I COULD LEAVE HERE BY THE END OF THE WEEK AND BY THE END OF THE WEEK I MEAN FRIDAY OR SATURDAY BUT I HATE BEING HERE ALL ALONE AND AM GOING CRAZY BEING HERE ALL ALONE. BESIDES THAT I THINK YOU OUGHT TO SEE YOUR CHILDREN AS BROOKE IS REALLY GETTING OUT OF HAND ABOUT YOU. IF YOU WANTED ME TO AND DIDNT WANT TO COME ALL THE WAY BACK HERE I WOULD BRING BROOKE ON TO NEW YORK BUT WHAT I WOULD REALLY LIKE MOST OF ALL WOULD BE TO HAVE YOU COME BACK TOMORROW AND I GIVE YOU MY SACRED WORD OF HONOR AGAIN THAT WE CAN LEAVE HERE MONDAY OR TUESDAY AFTERNOON AND SAIL NEXT SATURDAY. IF YOU WILL DO THIS FOR ME I GIVE YOU ANOTHER SACRED WORD OF HONOR, I WILL DO ANYTHING YOU ASK OF ME ANY TIME NO MATTER HOW UNREASONABLE. IF YOU WONT, I WILL BE ON IN TIME TO SAIL THIS SATURDAY BUT IT WILL BE REALLY AWFUL THE THINGS IT WILL DO. ALL MY LOVE LELAND.

(Father often wired people to warn them he was about to call or called them to warn them he was about to wire them. He liked to spend his dinner at Chasen's or "21," depending on which city he was in, calling or wiring people from his special table with a telephone at hand. One night he put in a call to his client Dashiell Hammett, who was three thousand miles away. "Dash," he said tersely, "I sent you a letter this morning. You'll get it sometime tomorrow." "Is that all?" asked Hammett. "That's all. It explains itself," answered Father and went back to his lamb chops.)

Mother sent us back long letters, almost conversations. To Bridget, on her fifth birthday, she wrote, "My darling Bridget, It's

Sunday and I'm sitting all by myself in my new apartment trying to guess what you and Brooke and Bill and Father are doing. And feeling very sad because in four days it will be February 10, a very important day for you and me—and I won't be there to share it with you. Five years ago I was getting pretty tired of waiting for you to make your appearance into this world—you were very late in coming—and of course Father and I were terribly excited and curious—would you be a boy? What would you look like? And what should we name you? My darling Bridget, I hope you have a wonderful birthday—and I hope we don't ever have to spend another one apart. Get right up this minute and give Brooke and Bill and Father kisses for me—I love you all so— If I were there I could give you five smacks on the fanny and one to grow on. I love you, Mother."

In the fall of that year, three momentous events took place almost simultaneously: Father left us to go East for rehearsals of *A Bell for Adano*, Grandfather died of cancer, and Mother, unilaterally deciding the time had come to leave California, bought a farm in Connecticut.

She wrote us, "Darlings, I'm so excited about your teeth coming in, Brooke, and about yours going out, Bridget! Do you think I'll be able to recognize you when I come home in *two months now?* Bill, don't knock any of yours out.

"Grandfather's funeral was very beautiful. It looked like this." (She drew a diagram of his coffin, draped with the American flag, with two big crosses of lilies at its head and a wreath from his soldiers at its foot.) "A large choir sang hymns, and then everyone joined in 'My Country, 'Tis of Thee.' Then before the pallbearers took the casket out, about fifty of his old colored soldiers marched out ahead, some of them crying because they'd lost such a good friend. Father and I didn't cry because we were so happy that the Colonel was peaceful and quiet now after so many long months of suffering and misery. In the last World War—27 years ago—he organized all the colored troops and took them to France to fight. They were very brave and adored your grandfather. And he would have been very touched to see how many came to say goodbye to him. He was a fine honest brave man and you can be very proud of him. He was of you.

"As far back as last Christmas we knew he had a terrible disease and would have to die. So you see even Maisie is not too unhappy about it. She has known for a long time that the sooner it happened the better it would be for the Colonel. Maisie has a magnificent marble mausoleum in the country. Her son, Philip, is in it—and now the Colonel will be there too." (According to Father, Maisie wheedled him into arranging all the details of the funeral—which he envisioned, according to his view of the Colonel's character, as having a military austerity and dignity—then ordered, on her own initiative, a six-thousand-dollar bronze casket, "the most expensive casket in New York," while he argued that all the Colonel would have wanted was a simple pine coffin. But what Father resented was that afterward, she, one of the richest women in New York City, had the bill sent to him.)

On weekends, Mother and Father sometimes stayed with Paul Osborn (the playwright who had adapted *A Bell for Adano* for the stage) and his wife, Millicent, at their house in Connecticut about two hours outside of New York City. One Sunday, they all piled into the car for a drive through the New England countryside. It was late September, just before the rolling hills ripened into mounds of gold. On a narrow road two miles outside the little town of Brookfield, Mother exclaimed, "Stop the car!" She pointed through the maple trees at an old farmhouse. "That's exactly the house I've always wanted. Let's go ask if it's for sale."

With typical impatience, she ignored the loud outcry of objections from the others—it was Sunday; there was no "For Sale" sign; she couldn't just pick a house at random, for God's sake; it would be rude, not to mention embarrassing, to barge in on the owner—and blithely strode across the grass to ring the front doorbell. A few minutes later, she returned triumphant. Not only was the owner, Mrs. Elroy Curtis, charmed by her unexpected guest but amazed at her well-timed arrival; by coincidence the house was going on the market in a week.

"Darlings!" Mother wrote us. "What do you think of this place Father and I found in the country, not far from the Osborns'? Instead of one red barn it has three! And it has a brook, and it's not far from a river where we can fish, and apple trees, and a small swimming pool and chicken houses, and a couple of cows and a few sheep, and woods and a wonderful great attic where you can play, and a nice school not too far away. . . ."

Shortly after that, *A Bell for Adano* went into rehearsal. Mother was beginning to count performances until her run with

"*The Turtle*" ended. "Darlings—Leland still hasn't arrived—it's Sunday afternoon and he was due to fly in this morning—but you know he's like a mosquito the way he hops around. I can never get my finger on him before he's somewhere else again. I'm very lonesome all by myself here— Forty-eight more performances—six more weeks!!! Bless your hearts—I love you, each one of you so much— and miss you much more than you can ever know—and you can't know until you grow up and have to be separated from your children —Mother."

During out-of-town tryouts of "*Adano*," Father, who disliked writing real letters himself and customarily dictated all his correspondence to a secretary, sent us a rare example of his penmanship. "Darling children—Mother and I are in the country today at the new house. It is cold and there is snow on the ground. Agnes the cow and the sheep want to stay inside out of the cold air. Agnes makes wonderful milk and cream so thick you can't pour it. I have been away in a place called Boston—which is a beautiful city. In about another week I am going to another city called Baltimore which I love very much. The reason is because before Mother and I were married she was working there and I used to go there to see her all the time and we had wonderful fun together. We used to eat codfish cakes all the time. We will be leaving for home in a little over four weeks now and are both so excited we can hardly wait. I think Christmas is coming soon, too. I love you all a great deal. So does Mother and we both send you millions of kisses—Father."

"Oh, my darlings," scribbled Mother hastily, "*four* more performances—and I have never been so excited in my life. . . . I think when I see you, my three wonderful grown-up children, I shall just sit down and bawl like a baby. You've never seen me cry, well I have a small tear in my eye right now thinking about you. This will be my last letter; did you know Father's produced a play and that it's a terrific smash hit—which means that so many people want to see it that there are not enough tickets? It's a very fine play about our soldiers who go into conquered lands and try to teach the people a good way of life. You can all go see it next spring. I love you all so much that it makes me want to cry. That's a silly way to show how happy I am, isn't it? Just think, we'll all be together again—forever and ever— Ten kisses apiece on my favorite spots— God bless you! Mother."

With *A Bell for Adano*, Father became an overnight success as a Broadway producer. But all Bridget, Bill, and I knew was that it was Christmas and Mother and Father had finally come home.

It was our last Christmas at Evanston Street. Not a single detail of the usual preparations escaped Mother's unwavering sense of tradition. Out came the antique German crèche, and on the mantel knelt a flock of carved angels with gold-leaf wings and halos like Fra Angelico paintings; thousands of Christmas cards were wedged around all the books in the library, solidly covering them. In The Barn, a thirty-foot fir tree, like an apparition from the *Nutcracker Suite*, rose dramatically to the ceiling. As usual, it was so high the top branches had to be decorated precariously from the balcony, and it took everyone who passed by, working in shifts, several days to trim. Bridget and I, in angel costumes, flitted around the mountain of packages that slowly began to compete in height with the tree; whenever Emily's back was turned, Bill, coached by us, tried to scale his way to the top where all new shipments were consigned. Most of the presents were sent, it was explained, by complete strangers, fans of Mother's who had probably seen our names in movie magazines. "Horrifying!" exclaimed Mother. "I'll let you open them all on Christmas Day—that part's the most fun anyway. Then Emily will store them all away for a rainy day." From previous experience we knew that "rainy day" was another way of saying that the entire mountain would be hauled off in a truck to a children's hospital after the holidays. (Mother had one longstanding fan who kept track of all kinds of dates, and on Bridget's fourth birthday sent her a diamond brooch, allegedly a valuable family heirloom; for once, Mother was at a loss.)

Christmas mornings were altogether overwhelming. We invested them with so many expectations, such conjecture and petty rivalry, that when they arrived like long-awaited guests, we were stricken by shyness. The big question was whether or not Santa Claus would come through. That year, Bridget, Bill, and I, with Emily and George Stearns in tow, had spent several days on his trail. After unsuccessfully canvassing all the Beverly Hills department stores, we pinned him down at Sears. Our desires were precise. Bill asked for a flashy red fire engine with an extension ladder, and Bridget, as she did every year, a life-size doll baby with all the attendant paraphernalia. I had never been interested in dolls; to me they were clumsy facsimiles of life, with their artificial smiles and limbs, and I couldn't understand how Bridget could spend hours dressing and undressing them or sticking bottles of water into their mouths to wait, fascinated, for what would come out the other end. I had spotted, in the toy store, a doll's house, which I instantly coveted; the idea of moving furniture from one room to another made perfect sense, I confided to Santa Claus. What I remember about Christmas morning that year was coming downstairs, cautiously negotiating each stair as if it were slippery with ice, and, at the bottom, Mother and Father waiting to lead me to the center of the room and a doll's house, surpassing in magnificence anything I had ever imagined, towering, it seemed, over the tree and everything else in The Barn. It was a marvel of craftsmanship, a Gothic confection of some twenty rooms, every one wallpapered, carpeted, hung with a tiny chandelier, and crammed, like San Simeon, with a prodigious supply of furniture. George Stearns stood beside it, beaming; he had built and decorated it entirely himself, working secretly every night for weeks—an old hobby, he said, carving and cabinet work, and a great pleasure to discover he had the skill to make some furniture for me to move around. Mother nudged me gently. I had forgotten to say thank you. My legs felt so wobbly I didn't quite dare reach inside to see if the furniture really moved. "Brooke," Mother whispered, "George has worked so long and so hard on this doll's house and it's so very special—of course you know Bill won't be interested, with all his cars and fire engines—but do you think you're grown up enough now and generous enough to share it with Bridget? I'll bet you are. Think! Wouldn't it be nice for her to be able to play with it, too?"

I thought. That question, Mother's simple question on Christmas morning, 1944, about the doll's house that George Stearns built was to me the most complex question anyone had ever asked. I thought for a whole minute while my heart stopped and my eyes blinked and my face flushed with fury. It was a trick question, two-sided, flipping back and forth, now-you-see-it-now-you-don't, the trick of a supreme magician who could—with cunning legerdemain under a silk handkerchief—transform a few seconds of tranquility into an eternity of chaos. The truth: no, I did not, under any circumstance whatsoever, wish to share the doll's house with Bridget (unless, uncoerced, the next day, or week, or

year, I felt like changing my mind and giving it to her outright). Or
the truth: yes, of course I wanted to share the doll's house with
Bridget, because not only would that please Mother and demonstrate how generous and grown up I really was but because I knew
that I loved Bridget very deeply and identified with her yearning as
she tentatively touched the miniature grandfather's clock in the
miniature hallway. (Get your nasty little fingers out of there, I
wanted to scream, until I give you permission.) Bridget was bliss-
fully oblivious of my pain, my conflict. I had not, before that
question, ever been *conscious* of hating her or of loving her so
absolutely. I never felt, or had the ability to be unaware of feeling,
the same way about my sister again. And I could never bring myself
to play with the doll's house. Eventually it had to be given away.

Then it was spring. The time had come to leave, even
though nobody seemed to know exactly why. We were moving not
to a house just around the corner but to a farm in a distant place
called Connecticut. For years Father had maintained that California was, deservedly, about to be bombed into the Pacific Ocean
by the Japs, but now the war was almost over, and in any case
Father didn't pretend to be naturally inclined toward a rural existence. Mother, on the other hand, was enthralled with the idea of
country life, and enthralled the three of us with her descriptions of
it. We did know, in a subtle way, that she hoped to wean Father
away from the agency business, the bulk of which remained, for
him, in California, and that she wanted to decontaminate the
atmosphere in which we were being brought up. It was phony, she
claimed, all phony—Hollywood, New York, movies, the theatre.
She wanted to retire and never work again, to become a real wife
and mother. We had no idea at all what that meant, and neither,
apparently, did Father, who swore that he didn't believe a word
of it.

"Goodbye," Mother wrote in our scrapbooks above a series
of Johnny Swope's lovingly detailed photographs of the house
and grounds. "Goodbye to the red barn— To 12928 Evanston
Street— To the scarecrow [a symbol of our Victory garden, that
quarter acre of lawn plowed under and laid out in rows of vegetables, where Bridget, Bill, and I were diligently picking green
caterpillars off the tomato vines at a penny apiece when V-E Day
was announced on the radio]— Goodbye to the stable where Sonny
[my pony] lived— To the tree on the terrace and our statue [a

primitive stone sculpture of three small children gathered in their mother's arms]— To the birdhouse— The weather vane on Elsa and Otto's house— And the angel! [a recumbent wooden figure in white relief against the sky, blowing a trumpet to the winds that spun him around and around on top of The Barn]—Goodbye." The last picture was of the driveway, where, somewhere in the gravel, my first tooth still lay—and where, at the far end, between the pepper trees curving over them, the front gates were drawn across the entrance, tightly shut.

Connecticut

We came to Brookfield, Connecticut, in 1945 with the last spring lilacs. From the moment of our arrival, the three of us ran wild. There was nothing to stop us, really—at least nothing like the previous physical boundaries or disciplines. We developed a new awareness of time; it, not Mother or Emily, seemed to discipline and define everything, even the space around us, the pastures and meadows and woods, which changed perceptibly from hour to hour, from morning to evening, from season to season. We also found that we could change like the seasons, as could our attitudes about each other, even Mother's about Father. And we acquired the unforgettable knowledge that violence and danger lay everywhere, under any surface, around any corner, even in the most deceptively beautiful and serene places.

The farm itself was named Stone Ledges. It was a ninety-five-acre estate and lay on a natural shelf in the hillside fields that rolled down to it, continued beyond as gently sloping pastureland, and leveled out way below in mysterious woods and stagnant marshes. Most of the land was situated on one side of a little country lane, Long Meadow Hill Road, and bordered its length with low stone walls. On the other side, also belonging to the property, was a lush meadow of corn and alfalfa, grown as fodder for the livestock, and, in the far corner, a fragrant patch of waist-high clover, which, on hot summer days, was our secret refuge. The field, enclosed by split fences, sloped up to a dark pine forest; at any point along the crest of the hill, one could look down and catch glimpses of the white clapboard farmhouse through towering maple trees, hundreds of years old, whose massive trunks and spreading foliage formed a solid ring around it.

There were three red barns, as Mother had described in her letters, scattered around the property: the main barn, large enough to contain a hayloft and sheep pen, to which we added a modern annex for milking the cows; an adjacent barn where the tractor and other heavy machinery were kept; and, off to the other side of the house, a third barn, which was a general storeroom for tools, paints, and carpentry equipment. There was even a fourth barn, considered to be a unique feature, because at some point it had been converted into complete guest quarters and linked to the main house itself by a series of interconnecting service rooms. These rooms—a laundry room, a storage pantry, and a dairy room—were, in a form of reverse snobbism, our favorite part of the house. They had a peculiar quality of seeming to be the center, the heart of the house, and at the same time the stillest place in it. The floors were paved with flagstone, ground down by age and wear to a fine cool smoothness, unlike any other surface our bare feet encountered inside or out.

The main house was a rambling colonial structure built in 1781 and skillfully renovated in the thirties. Every room retained its original fireplace or stove, wide-planked pine floors, and low ceilings punctuated with exposed beams. Leading up to the bedrooms were two angular staircases, tilted with age and impossible to go up or down except in single file. Over everything ran a vast attic, cedar-lined and studded with dormer windows that, like a captain's walk, commanded a 360-degree view of the countryside. The attic was the only place in the house that could resist Mother. She repeatedly attacked it with the intention of transforming it into a playroom for the three of us, but was always defeated by the unbearable summer heat or winter cold that it sucked in from every direction.

She had her way everywhere else. As if lifted from the pages of an exhaustive botanical catalogue, flowers of every color or variety, single-stemmed or in bouquets, were strewn across all the walls of all the rooms; floral chintzes covered every chair and couch, flower-printed curtains hung from every window. The house was filled with braided or hooked rugs, rustic colonial furniture, hurricane lamps, and a second profusion of flowers from the cutting garden—roses, tiger lilies, peonies, snapdragons, sweet peas— bunched on each table in every room.

Father couldn't stand any of it. The flowers gave him terrible hay fever. We could tell exactly what room he was in by following

the explosive sound of his sneezes. "A-a-a-a-*choo!* A-a-a-a-*choo!*"
They had a unique cadence, starting with a prolonged howl of
agony and ending like a violent expletive. Mother teased him
mercilessly and called him a hypochondriac as, room by room, he
sank limply into one flowered chintz chair or another, wiping his
eyes with a soggy handkerchief and gulping down antihistamines
by the handful. His legion of allergies had no place in her scheme
of things, and besides that, it was important that he set a good
example to the three of us, to whom, worst of all, he had passed
them on in one dire form or another. Something about Brookfield,
Connecticut, not only instantaneously activated them but bred
new, unheard-of mutations.

"Just my luck," Father would moan, secretly pleased at the
power of his genes and also the fact that he was not altogether
alone in his misery. "A case of god-awful history repeating itself
right under my nose—a nose that can hardly breathe any more, by
the way, it's so damned stuffed up, thanks to the fifty different
kinds of pollen that have contaminated my respiratory system.
Well, it may be too soon to tell whether the three children have
inherited any of my good points, but by God it's obvious by now
they've inherited all of the bad, poor things—it's triple jeopardy."

To Bridget he bequeathed his skin, a skin so sensitive that it
would break out in hideous rashes or eczema or hives at the suggestion of an allergen wafting through the air an acre away. Hives were
one of Father's specialties. He got them from eating strawberries or
shellfish. Once he was put in charge of Bridget and me for one of
our cross-country trips from New York to California ("Make sure
they brush their teeth twice a day and wash their hands before
meals and change their dresses once in a while and go to bed at a
reasonable hour," Mother warned him), and, in a reckless gesture
before assuming his unaccustomed duties, he treated himself and
us to strawberry sundaes ("God, I'm going to regret this," he said);
as the train left Grand Central Station, his eyes began to puff up
with red blotches and then, inch by inch, the rest of his body. For
some reason he had forgotten to bring his ever-ready pigskin suitcase stuffed with pill bottles and ointments like a miniature phar-
macy (and outfitted with a collapsible stand on which Father
could perch it while he pored over its contents); so, unmedicated,
he rolled himself up in a sheet and retired to his berth in our
private compartment, where he lay like a caterpillar in a cocoon

without saying a word for the entire four days and three nights. Bridget and I had a wonderful time running up and down the aisles and ordering whatever we wanted in the elegant dining car; occasionally we would prod Father into a semi-sitting position, pry his swollen lips open with a soup spoon or straw, and siphon liquids into him. Emily and Bill met us in Los Angeles, and we went straight from the train station to the doctor's office.

However, it was Bridget who polished off the topic of hives in our family, carrying it to extremes Father had never dreamed of. Inexplicably she got them for the first time at lunch soon after we arrived in Brookfield, gorging on fresh strawberries and Agnes the cow's celebrated double cream. Within hours she had to be taken to the nearest hospital, seven miles away in New Milford. Still, as bad as it was, the sight of Bridget with hives was nothing compared to the ghastly spectacle of Bridget with a ripe case of poison ivy. A crimson rash would spread like wildfire over her slender little body, ruthlessly sparing no area, not even the cracks between her toes. Then came a period of unendurable itching that sometimes necessitated tying her hands down or stuffing them in gloves so that she couldn't claw at herself. The next day began a long cycle in which, concurrent with the overall swelling of her body that would deform it past recognition, the rash consolidated itself into grotesque blisters that erupted, burst, oozed an evil sticky fluid, unbelievably erupted again, became open lesions, and crusted over at last into a solid orange scab, like a grisly coat of armor, which cracked and bled when she moved. We would soak her for hours in tubs of Epsom salts and boric acid, compress her with wads of cotton-soaked medicinal remedies like Burow's solution, pour calamine lotion over her, swab her with anesthetic salves, and wrap her in yards of gauze to keep the flies off.

"Oh, my God, Maggie!" exploded Father at his initial glimpse, having been spared the first stages by sequestering himself in New York City for a few welcome days of business. "The child's got leprosy, for Chrissake! What the hell are we doing in this godforsaken place, anyway? It's the tail end of civilization—she never looked like that in Los Angeles, never before in her life."

But she looked much worse many times afterward, because poison ivy was just a common weed on the farm, hard to avoid brushing against even when we became familiar with its distinctive three-leaved configuration—a seductive plant, shinier and greener than any other in the summer, turning, in the fall, to glossy red. Bridget developed the unerring instinct that wild animals have about their natural enemies; she could *feel* a clump of poison ivy growing behind a tree or stone wall and would stop in her tracks, with her nose to the wind, quivering, until Bill or I led her past it. Since we ran around all summer barefoot and practically naked, Emily took the precaution of scrubbing her down every evening with a big cake of smelly carbolic soap—a suggestion of Dr. McKenzie, the kindly Brookfield doctor, who had become resigned to making at least one emergency house call a week on behalf of one or another of us. Often in the middle of the night, he chugged up to Stone Ledges in his old car, shaking his head with sleepiness and disbelief. "Nothing like preventive medicine," he said, as the incidence and virulence of Bridget's rashes steadily increased. "This stuff should disinfect an army." But the soap was of little use. Bridget could get a major case of poison ivy even when she stayed in the house and went nowhere near it. Mother and Dr. McKenzie took a long time to figure out how, but they finally deduced that if Bridget so much as patted a dog that might have walked through a patch of it days earlier, she was in trouble. Or, in the autumn, when the farmers burned their fields, in which, of course, poison ivy grew along with everything else, the slightest contact of the smoke on her skin—even if she was standing a long distance away, fully clothed, with only her face exposed—did the trick.

As for Bill and me, we inherited all of Father's other allergies, the most prevalent of which was, on a farm, hay fever. There were variations: if Bill ingested certain shellfish, his throat swelled up to the point where he couldn't breathe and required hospitalization; and it was said that, at birth, I was so allergic to all milk ("including your mother's and anything else we could round up, goat, monkey, whatever," Father used to say with a semblance of pride) that until some weird formula was devised, nobody was quite sure how to keep me alive. But by and large, Bill and I were besieged with hay fever much worse than Father's. We—particularly I—might come down with an attack if we walked through any enclosed space with dust in it, dust or animals or hay. Barns. Cows, sheep, horses, chickens. A serious enough attack landed us in bed, sneezing and wheezing. "Lousy respiratory systems, just like your father," Father would remind us comfortingly when he came upstairs to visit us, propped up with our bed trays in the heavily vaporized room, steamy and pungent with eucalyptus oil, sealed off by Emily from the rest of the house. I was more allergic to more things than Bill, and wheezed louder, convincing myself that eventually I would stop breathing altogether and die and that nobody except Emily believed me or cared, except maybe Bridget and Bill, who, on the other hand, might be only too delighted to have me out of the way so they could divide up my books and games. Whoever was sick was regarded by the others with light-headed relief and, only as an afterthought, compassion. It was really at mealtimes that the absence of the bedridden sufferer was disturbing, when the dining-room table—at which, at long last, we were allowed to eat with the grownups—was overcast with a nagging sense of loss, of broken unity, as whichever two of us who weren't disabled tried to ignore the empty chair of the third.

Bridget, far more than Bill or I, took an interest in the gruesome details of our maladies. Around this time, when she was six, her ambition shifted from becoming a housewife with ten children to becoming a doctor; not a bad idea, we all agreed, since the family could certainly use a good one in permanent residence, and besides she had a knack not only for precisely remembering the intricate names of hundreds of medicines prescribed for one ailment or another but also for matching them up to the correct symptoms—almost before they appeared—of the correct person. In addition, her poetry revealed a newspaper reporter's relish for disaster:

> *Alas and Alack! Alas for poor Brooke*
> *She was washing the garage*
> *And got caught on a hook!*

> *Alas and Alack! Alas for poor Brie*
> *She fell in the gutter*
> *And hurt her poor knee!*

> *Alas and Alack! Alas for poor Bill*
> *He was gardening the garden*
> *And poisoned a pill!*

> *Alas and Alack! Alas for poor Mags*
> *She was under the house*
> *And turned into rags!*

Alas and Alack! Alas for poor Land [Leland]
He was down at the beach
And got lost in the sand!

Alas and Alack! Alas for poor Em
She was making a dress
And ripped up the hem!

Alas and Alack! Alas for poor Edwin [Emily's husband]
He was inside the chest
And ate an Ephedrine!

Bridget and I shared a room, and more than once, awakened by one of my nocturnal coughing attacks, she would turn on the light, hop briskly onto my bed, and, with clinical composure, put her ear on my chest to assess the condition of my bronchia. If she diagnosed my condition as serious enough—that is, if I managed to convince her that each rasping breath was my last—she would vanish, phantomlike, into the cavernous darkness of the hall to rouse Emily. The sight of Emily was such a comfort that I would burst into tears of gratitude and self-pity, thereby worsening my condition. "Em," Bridget would whisper matter-of-factly, "her wheeze is getting worser and worser, and something tells me she's probably going to wheeze to death this time. Just put your head on her chest and listen. I think you'd better call Mother and Father and Dr. McKenzie right this minute. What she needs is a shot of Adrenalin."

While waiting for Dr. McKenzie to arrive, Emily would prop me up with pillows, murmuring, "Shush, shush, there's nothing to be afraid of; what a brave girl," Bridget would pitter-patter around the bed with a bottle of Tedral, Mother would rush in tying her bathrobe and exclaiming, "What is this nonsense? Of course you're not going to die, darling, I promise you," and if Father was around, he would sit at the foot of my bed and reassuringly intone his favorite passage from Bemelman's *Madeline:* "In the middle of one night, Miss Clavel turned on the light and said, 'Something is not right!' And, afraid of a disaster, Miss Clavel ran fast and faster, and she said, 'Please, children, do—tell me what is troubling you?' And all the little girls cried, 'Boohoo, we want to have our appendix out, too!' 'Good night, little girls, thank the Lord you are well! And now go to sleep!' said Miss Clavel. And she turned out the light—and closed the door—and that's all there is—there isn't any more."

Mother refused to be fazed by any of these crises. Once she had determined a course of action, she hacked her way through any opposition like a well-tempered steel blade; she had made up her mind about living on the farm, and that was that. She had made up her mind about our allergies, too: they were troublesome but temporary. We would outgrow them. Nature would take care of itself. All the cells in our bodies were being sloughed off like dead skin every seven years, replacing themselves with nice fresh ones ("Oh, no! Another seven years of *this?*"), and until then, the more exposed we were to whatever it was that triggered the allergies, the more resistance our immunological systems would build up. However impatient this theory made us, we clung to it like drowning rats, and it was, in any case, impossible to disbelieve anything Mother told us, because she was so convincing. She didn't seem to talk, like other people, but to communicate information physically, as if she were leaning into whatever she was saying, not only with her voice—which even in a whisper crackled with electricity—but her entire body. "Absolutely! Positively!" The words hummed with the intensity of powerful incantations.

As totally as she projected the absolute essence of her own feelings, she absorbed totally—was penetrated by—the feelings of whoever was around her. It was a rare ability, but she never analyzed it; for her it was as simple and necessary, as natural, as breathing in and out. ("Come on, Brie, it's so *easy*—just take a deep breath in," she would say, patiently teaching Bridget, who was afraid of the water, how to swim. "Then blow it out. See the bubbles? In and out, that's right; do it in rhythm, in and out.") As far as we, her children, were concerned, whatever we felt she felt it more. When we were sick and felt terrible, she felt worse. In order to reverse that process step by step before it got out of hand, she decided—when Mother made a decision, she would, mentally, plant her feet wide apart and clench her fists—first, above all else, not to transmit to us her feelings of alarm; second, to underplay the seriousness of the situation by discussing it with us only in matter-of-fact terms and then as little as possible (even though she herself would have read voluminously on the subject and consulted every conceivable medical authority); and indeed, third, to overplay the humorous aspects, which were, of course, always the grimmest.

It was a wonderful performance, to which Mother applied all her favorite theatrical principles, and in a sense, Mother acted out much of what she believed, but so effortlessly, with such skill and conviction—and charm—that by the time she finished, what started out as a performance had changed into something infinitely more real than most reality. Much of the time, nobody, least of all she, could tell the difference. To us, when we were very young, life seemed like an exciting game, invented, explained, and directed by Mother. She was basically mischievous and fun-loving—"Come on! Come on, sillies, don't be afraid, just do exactly what I do. You'll see, it'll be fun!" she would urge us—and so she thought being sick, like everything else, should be as much fun as possible. To that end, she would get in bed with us herself and read aloud until she was hoarse, or show us how to crayon and watercolor and finger-paint, which we adored because not only was she talented at doing all of them herself, but at teaching us how, too.

Father was as fun-loving as Mother, but his idea of fun was not necessarily the same. It certainly wasn't living in Connecticut. But he tried. He decided to take up baking bread. Sunday was Father's bread-baking day and he spent most of it in the kitchen sprinkling flour everywhere and waiting for his dough to rise. "Now here comes the best part," he would say, punching away at the contents of three or four gigantic bowls. "God, that feels good." We would hang around the kitchen with him on the pretext of keeping him company, for which he was openly grateful; what we were really after, pushing and shoving each other from side to side ("Okay, kids, cut that out and make it snappy!" Father would say, snapping his fingers at us for emphasis), was the first look when the loaves came out of the oven and the first taste when they were cool enough to tear apart and slather with fresh butter. Bill, who was born during food rationing and had never seen butter before, used to eat it by the handful and considered the bread an intrusion. Father became such an expert at baking bread that he moved on to croissants and brioches. Popular demand, however, forced him back to the old plain white loaf.

He also had a brief fling at carpentry. Since one of the barns was a workshop, equipped with an assortment of every imaginable kind of tool, and since Father was naturally attracted to equipment and collections (although usually of a more sophisticated nature), one day he found himself out there puttering around. After several trips to the hardware store—to him, the most stimulating place within miles—for the purchase of some extraneous saws, he ambitiously started work on his first and last project: he tried to lower a side table he'd found in the barn to a reasonable coffee-table height. With measuring tapes and levelers and two sawhorses and a big vise and a splendid array of saws, he began; first one table leg and then another, around and around, down to the specified length; then, unable to get them exactly even, he sawed on, cursing, a quarter of an inch at a time, until the table leveled off without wobbling, two inches above the floor.

Father began to reach the point where, from tedium, he took desperate measures. One day Paul Osborn, who lived only five miles away (a blessing), came over for a visit and located Father on the screened porch, looking off into space. "Christ, I'm bored," said Father. "Paul, do you want to have some fun?" "Yeah," answered Paul, unable to imagine what Father had in mind. "Come on," said Father urgently; they went upstairs and while Paul watched, Father systematically, bedroom by bedroom, took down all the flowered lace curtains, gathered them up in a huge bundle, carried them down to the laundry room, and stuffed them in the Bendix washing machine. He shut the door, which had a big glass observation window in it, pressed the button, and said, "Now watch—all hell's going to break loose in a minute," and the two of them stood there and watched while the wad of curtains was pumped round and round and round.

The more bored Father became with life on the farm, the more fervently Mother threw herself into every aspect of it: the vegetable garden, the flower garden, the apple orchard, the peach and cherry orchard, the maple trees and the squirrels in them, the welfare of the livestock, the pigs and chickens, the maintenance of the heavy machinery, barns, tools, the harvesting of corn and alfalfa, the making of butter and ice cream, the curing of beef and bacon, and even the lives of Andrew Tomashek, the Czechoslovakian farmer, and his eleven children.

Andrew was in charge of everything. He lived up on the main road overlooking the alfalfa field in a small, teeming, ramshackle house. Of his eleven children, Young Andrew, at twelve, was the oldest. Young Andrew, also his main assistant, was shyly omnipresent and well muscled; I immediately replaced the memory of Tarquin Olivier with dreams of Young Andrew, whose taciturn behavior I mistook for unspoken desire. Although Mother had hoped that eight-year-old Cyril Tomashek would be a good playmate for us, he scotched that possibility by committing, one pleasant morning, the most heinous act I had ever witnessed. I had a pet squirrel, Mr. Duchin, who fell, newly born, from a maple tree the day we arrived at Stone Ledges, in what was indisputedly a good-luck omen, and whom I had nursed to healthy maturity with the same maternal solicitude Bridget showed for her dolls. Mr. Duchin grew up to assume a position of lordly privilege and was given his own private screened porch to sleep on; the rest of the time he went everywhere I went, perched on my head or shoulder, scampering up and down my bare back and tracking it with fine white scratches, and begging for nuts as he clicked his sharp little rodent's teeth, which amused everyone except Father. "Get that goddamn weasel out of here!" he'd exclaim as Mr. Duchin joyously leaped around the house, showing off; "you know I'm allergic to him." Cyril Tomashek stopped by the screened porch one morning at feeding time to watch me idly scattering nuts and raisins around. We said hello; he was always aggressively shy with me, though fascinated. Remembering Mother's instructions, and feeling, at that moment, as if I had the upper hand socially, I chatted away at him to put him at his ease. It worked. From the corner of my eye I observed him edging closer and closer. Suddenly, his hand flashed out and grabbed Mr. Duchin from my shoulder by his beautiful tail. I screeched and clawed at him, but Cyril fended me off laughing, and playfully began twirling Mr. Duchin around his head like a lasso. In the ensuing fracas, he dragged all three of us out the door. In a flash, Mr. Duchin was gone, streaking toward the maple tree out of which he'd fallen as a baby. Halfway up he stopped and chattered ferociously at us, switching his mangled tail, then made his way toward the dense foliage, which rustled for a minute and closed around him like water around a stone. He never came back, although we called him for days, and I never spoke to Cyril Tomashek again, despite his sullen apologies.

At Stone Ledges, when, as part of Mother's program of general participation, Bridget, Bill, and I were graduated to the dining-room table for all our meals, an era began. It was a new game with a new set of rules, in which sitting around the dining-room table under Mother's aegis became a vital experience. The rules were: perfect manners, excellent appetites, and stimulating non-stop conversation. Even when—especially when—one of the three rules was broken, the dynamics of the situation were interesting. Our dining-room table was a big round pine one that could seat as many as twelve, with a revolving lazy Susan on which all the serving dishes were placed (so that we had to contain ourselves from spinning it around and snatching at food as it went by); it was built by slaves in the South before the Civil War, and Mother, who came from Virginia, never relinquished that innate pride Southerners have about anything to do with their heritage.

The rule about our manners was partially enforced by Father (at Mother's insistence that he become more involved), who, loathing all forms of disciplinary action because of *his* father, would reach across the table with a huge paddle that he kept by his chair and, in what we all knew was a self-mocking gesture, rap the offender lightly on the head. The next rule, good appetites, was hard for anyone to enforce, because Bridget and Bill were such impossible eaters. They both were finicky and slow, and always had been. I had memories of Bridget as a tiny child, all alone at the long table in The Barn—while I rode in circles around her on my tricycle, having long since finished my breakfast—unable to touch her boiled eggs. She hated them, she couldn't get them down, they were too soft and runny; there was mucus in them, horrible stringy white stuff that made her gag when she tried to swallow. Whatever nurse we had then—it was before Emily—would make her sit at the table until she finished every mouthful. One day she refused to eat her eggs and sat, looking down at her plate, through the entire morning, my lunch, the afternoon, and my dinner. I protested: the nurse was mean, I was lonely and had nobody to play with, the eggs were all cold and hard and how could anybody want to eat them? They would make Bridget sick to her stomach, they made me sick just to look at them, and I would tell Mother. The nurse rapped me on the knuckles with a spoon, I burst into tears, Bridget burst into tears, and we were both sent to bed. Bridget's eating habits did not improve, especially when Bill got old enough to keep her company, but not until Connecticut, when they actively affected the whole family three times a day, did Mother step in personally. It was quite a challenge. By that time, Bridget and Bill had become adept at scooping whole platefuls of food into their napkins with lightning speed and stealthily discarding the refuse after dinner. They had to be watched closely. Once, when Bridget was sick in bed for about a week and all her meals were brought up to her on a tray, it was remarked that she had never, despite her illness, displayed such an extraordinary appetite; every single dish was sent back to the kitchen licked clean. Mother and Father were so proud they drove into New Milford to buy her a doll, but before they could present it to her, Emily gave our room a thorough cleaning and discovered, under Bridget's bed, the accumulation of an entire week's meals. Instead of the doll, Bridget got a spanking. When all punishment failed to make a dent, Mother decided the best solution was a full-out reward system. She drew up two identical charts on sheets of cardboard, of which the middle parts were as compartmentalized—with a series of carefully ruled horizontal and vertical pencil lines—as graph paper, and the borders as lavishly decorated with flora and fauna as the pages of a medieval Book of Hours. She tacked these up on the dining-room walls. According to the speed with which Bridget and Bill were able to devour all their breakfast, lunch, and dinner every day (the charts were subdivided into meals, days, weeks, and months), their progress was studded with stars—red, green, blue, silver, and gold—each color representing a higher degree of achievement. Although neither of them ever received a gold star, this system produced results and a great deal of rivalry.

As for the third rule, it was expected that all conversation be entertaining, lively, all-encompassing, and, insofar as possible, conducted with decorum. No interruptions were permitted—no newspapers at breakfast (a sore point with Father), except on Sunday mornings the *New York Times* crossword puzzle to sharpen our wits—and no subject was exempt if it could be introduced with a modicum of style; furthermore, anything of any interest that had occurred between one meal and the next, even if it was an embarrassing misdeed on the part of one of us, was brought up for required general discussion. Presided over by Mother, the dinner table was like a mirror in which all our behavior was reflected, a family tribunal, a microcosm of our total lives. Whoever missed a meal because of sickness, or was excused from the table for misbehavior, lost track of things and had to be filled in later.

. . .

That fall, the fall of 1945, Bridget and I went on the school bus to the public school in Brookfield. After years at the gentle hands of Miss Brown, school came as something of a shock. Moreover, we were extremely conspicuous for several reasons. The fact that we were the children of a celebrity who had mysteriously settled in that distant territory set us apart from the first day of school; it seemed the entire community knew about us, and were both suspicious of and flattered by our presence, although we couldn't figure out why. Mother had successfully isolated us from the remotest idea of what a movie star was; the only movies we'd ever seen were *King Kong*, *Dumbo*, *Bambi*, and *Snow White and the Seven Dwarfs*. As if we didn't feel foreign enough, we looked it. There was the matter of our hair. Mother, who disliked beauty parlors, always cut not only her own hair but ours. One sweltering day in August, she experimented on Bridget and me: waving her professional shears around, she clipped off first our long braids, and then, unable to resist the temptation, continued snipping away bit by bit, until, like Father's table, there was almost nothing left. Our hair was shorter than Bill's. "Oh it's so be*com*ing! You both look so wonderful and cool! And aren't you lucky, to *look* just like boys without having to *be* them!" We believed her until we got to school.

That first day was a catastrophe. It was bad enough being stared at like aliens, but to be ridiculed by our peers, taunted, pointed at, left alone at recess and lunch with only each other to talk to—we were outcasts in a monstrous country. And by far and away the worst part was the sense of confusion and betrayal we felt. It was one thing to be different from everybody else, but to find it out like that? Why hadn't Mother told us? "Mother," we shouted, charging through the vestibule, the kitchen, the dining and living rooms, to find her at last, supervising the hanging of a side of beef in the cold-storage room. "Why didn't you tell us how terrible it is to be a movie star? What *is* a movie star? Why can't you be like other parents? And why did you tell us our hair looks adorable when everyone else thinks it just looks funny? And why can't we take our lunch in paper bags?" (Mother had made a project out of decorating our new lunch pails with her fingernail polish.)

"Oh, my darlings, what an awful day you've had!" Mother appeased us breathlessly. "Now listen to me. Sometimes people are cruel just because they're jealous and insecure and they don't know how else to get attention. You must learn not to pay the *slightest bit* of attention—that's just what they want, and if you act hurt they're one up on you—you must just ignore them—but be polite! And say to yourselves, 'Sticks and stones will break my bones, but names will never hurt me.' And never be afraid to be different— you don't want to be exactly like everyone else. How boring that would be!"

And so we went back to school and never quite fit in. We were way ahead of our grades in every subject, which made us self-conscious, and our clothes and shoes were unlike anyone else's, as were our sandwiches—cut in triangles, with the crusts neatly trimmed off, and stuffed with exotic fillings like cream cheese and olives or deviled ham, while the other children brought hunks of salami and cheese and gooey chocolate-covered marshmallows, which were forbidden us because they were bad for our teeth.

Bill was excluded from the nightmare of school because he was too young. Up to this point, Bridget and I had thought of him as a younger extension of ourselves, with a few savory, even enviable physical characteristics thrown in (one of Bridget's first paintings, for which Mother was hurriedly called to a conference at nursery school, was entitled "Bill with a Beetle Crawling up His Pants"; in the painting, the infant Bill stood facing front with his arms outstretched and his blue suspender shorts raised to display, in scrupulous detail, what could only be a black beetle securely affixed to the tip of his penis), whom we could mold and pattern as we wished. Either he was beginning to change or we were; it was hard to tell. He even *smelled* subtly different from us, and as he instinctively moved away from the center of our control, we were only too happy to let him go—just as long as we could yank him back if we felt like it.

"Dear Bill," Bridget coaxed him in her best handwriting on her best notepaper, "would you be so kind as to get in bed with me? It will be very kind if you do. Love, Bridget."

Or, if he fell from disfavor, a harsh denunciation in blue crayon, written October 21, 1945:

Bill is a duck.
Bill is a toilet.
Bill is a wee wee

Bill is a B.M.
Bill is a frog
Bill smells terrible
Bill is a dish of ice cream.

(relenting, as usual, at the last moment).

Although we went on assuming that Bill was our property, we also began to be aware that there were more than anatomical dissimilarities between him and us. His personality was toughening up. Of the three of us, his disposition had always been the best—that is to say, the least moody or mercurial—but he was starting to get into the kind of bold trouble that would never have occurred to either Bridget or me to think up.

One night after we'd gone to bed, Mother was making the rounds of the house. She noticed, feeling absurd, that all the classic ingredients of a conventional horror story were present: she was all alone, a little nervous; it was Emily's day off and the cook and butler slept in another wing; Father was in New York City rehearsing his new play, *State of the Union*; there was a storm raging outside, thunder and lightning, windows banging, floors creaking, and branches scraping the side of the house. On her way up to bed, she turned on the light in Bill's room for a minute to make sure he was all right. He was lying in Grandfather's big mahogany bed, sound asleep and covered with blood. Mother thought he was dead, murdered. In a second she had him in her arms. The pillow and sheets were blood-soaked, his scalp was scored with gashes, and there were tufts of hair all over the place; she looked around wildly and suddenly noticed, under a glass ashtray on the bed table, a bloody razor blade. She shook him awake. "Bill!" she shrieked. "What have you done to yourself? Why?" Bill looked at her with total calm. "Oh," he answered, yawning, "I fell out of bed." If there was anything that made Mother see red—like waving a flag in front of a bull, as she said—it was a lie. "I'll give you one more chance to tell me the truth," she'd say, "while I count to ten. Ready? Now think carefully. One, two, three, four . . ." In this instance Bill was as obstinate as she. He stood his ground, hoping that she would go away so he could go back to sleep, and wondering what would happen if she didn't. She went to the bathroom and got his hairbrush. "This is going to hurt me a lot more than it's going to hurt you," she remonstrated, a line of dialogue that accompanied our spankings as inevitably as "Think of the poor starving children in China" went with dinner. Bill was resolute. He got his first spanking. Then he and Mother fell into each other's arms and they both cried and he promised that he would never never tell another lie, and she said, "Now tell me the truth; what really happened?" And after thinking for a minute, he answered, "It was just an accident—I banged my head on the headboard." She spanked him again. By this time, Bridget and I were sitting bolt upright in our beds across the hall, speculating in excited whispers about what crime our four-year-old brother—the treasure, the apple of his mother's eye—could possibly have committed to produce such an uproar. The sounds coming from his room coupled with the sounds of the storm outside were horrendous. They went on for a long time. He held out for thirteen different stories and thirteen spankings. Bridget and I didn't know that until the next morning at the breakfast table, when we also found out why he had lied. It was very simple. Buck Crouse and Howard Lindsay, the authors of *State of the Union,* had spent the previous weekend at our house. Bill, after watching one of them shave Sunday morning, had salvaged the used razor blade from the guest-room wastebasket for some useful future occasion, which came along sooner than he expected: Mother made the unpleasant announcement that he needed a haircut and she was going to give it to him. Bill, who had seen the damage that Mother's scissors could do, waited until the night before the scheduled event, got out his secret razor blade, and hacked away at his locks in the total darkness, occasionally missing his hair and nicking his scalp. ("My big mistake," he told us later, "was to hide the razor blade under the ashtray afterwards—I forgot it was glass and she could see through it the whole time.") But what he then did to cap off the morning, that morning after thirteen spankings—an endurance record that left Bridget and me baffled, yet extremely proud of him—seemed so exquisitely perverse to us that he passed heroically into some eternal hall of fame. When Mother came into his room to say good morning as if nothing had happened the night before, she found the walls of his bathroom decorated with freshly squeezed toothpaste, tubes and tubes of it. "Bill," she said, shocked, "why on earth did you make this mess?" "I didn't mean to," he responded, innocently widening his eyes; "it just happened. The toothpaste slipped out of my hand," and Mother froze. "I'll give you one more

chance to tell the truth," she began. "Here I go—one, two . . ."
Bill had his fourteenth spanking before breakfast. He was unable
to sit down for a week.

State of the Union, which opened in November, was a success. Father was away more and more, attending to business in
New York and on the Coast. He would drive out to see us on
weekends, trying, with as much good humor as he could muster, to
disregard the menace of wild goldenrod, which bloomed crazily all
over the place during the autumn months and which he felt was
somehow deliberately bringing his hay fever to a peak. By staying
indoors and never venturing out, he thought he could lick not only
that problem but a new and even more fearful one that had
unexpectedly presented itself: snakes. Copperheads had been seen
sunning themselves near the house; Andrew had taught Mother
how to pin them down with a pitchfork and deftly sever their
heads. Once Father knew of their existence, he was in a state of
panic. "God help us all," he'd groan if the word "snake" was
mentioned. "Ashes to ashes, dust to dust, if the lions don't get us
the pythons must."

The best thing about living on a farm, said Mother, was
being able to observe firsthand all the miracles of nature. She was
disappointed for us that we would have to wait until spring to
witness Agnes the cow giving birth to a calf; there was no more
thrilling and beautiful experience in life than watching the first
moment of it take place. "Crap," said Father. "There are a helluva
lot more beautiful and thrilling moments to watch that I can think
of—almost any moment you could name, as a matter of fact,
except the moment of death, which might possibly give it a run for
its money."

"Now, Leland," said Mother, "have you ever seen an actual
birth? You know damn well you haven't, so you don't know what
you're talking about."

"Maggie, darling," said Father, "guess what? For once you're
right, you're absolutely right. I don't know what I'm talking about,
and what's more, I don't want to know what I'm talking about, nor
will I go on talking about it if it's what I think it is. I have
deliberately spent my whole life, all forty-odd years of it, avoiding
contact with pain, and that includes the *sight* of it, and when
Agnes the cow gives birth to her damn calf I want more than
anything to be as far away as possible. Hear that, children? I have

no one to count on except you. Notify me wherever I am, day or night, the instant Agnes or any other animal around here goes into labor, so that I can take the next plane to California."

That did it. Although she knew he was only half serious, Mother disapproved of what she called his fastidious attitude and worried that its influence on us would be stronger than hers. A few days earlier, our dog, Stewart, had been run over in a dreadful accident right in front of the house. Stewart was a young pointer given us by Jimmy Stewart to replace Mr. Duchin. He'd rushed to the edge of the driveway to bark at a motorcycle roaring past on Long Meadow Hill Road, a seldom-traveled byway, and the driver had swerved deliberately onto the gravel to run him down. Bridget, Bill, and I were squatting in the middle of the driveway; it was midday, the best time of day to hunt for tiny pieces of glinting mica mixed in with the gravel. The motorcycle hit Stewart so hard it knocked him twenty feet out onto the road, where he lay whimpering, totally disemboweled, with two legs severed. Steaming lumps of blackish-red blood, almost indistinguishable from the shiny hot tar itself, lay all around him. We screamed for Mother and he died in her arms a few minutes later while the three of us stood on the side of the road sobbing.

This incident had a disturbing effect on us and Mother verbalized her concern. While she didn't want us going through life totally desensitized to violence, neither did she want us to be delicate hothouse flowers; it was important to instill in us an overall sense of balance and continuity. As to the matter of what to protect us from and how, she was ambivalent. There was, on her part, a hunger for simplicity, a great romantic notion of living a simple life, as opposed to what other people thought of as romantic, which was living in Hollywood. She felt it was imperative to shield us from the consequences of her career as an actress, because to her they represented life at its most dangerous—that is unreal, illusory. It was equally imperative to expose us to the simple facts of nature, because they didn't just represent life, they actually *were* life; they had substance, whether or not that substance was pleasant. To dramatize what she meant, and at the same time counteract in us what she suspected were the unhealthy beginnings of squeamishness, she came up with an unusual idea.

"The most honest-to-God revolting idea you've ever had, Maggie," we could hear Father protesting from the next room where he, Mother, and Emily were in a huddle.

"Children!" announced Mother breezily. "I have an idea for an experiment. Although your father pretends he doesn't approve at all, he's willing to give it a try. . . ." The idea sounded intriguing. We would all go together down to the chicken coop, and watch Mother take a lesson from Andrew Tomashek in how to chop off a chicken's head. Andrew performed this chore every Saturday morning in order to provide us with chicken for Sunday dinner, and once we saw how simple and perfunctory it was, just a chore like any other—and if even Mother could do it—it would prove to us that there was nothing so terrible about the sight of blood, or death, for that matter, when it was a question of necessity.

So we all trooped down the dirt path to the chicken coop. We had about three hundred chickens, so the coop was sizable; there were nesting houses and a shade tree in the middle, and under the tree a broad flat stump, bloodstained and scarred with old hatchet marks. It was a warm morning; while Mother was explaining to us the highlights of what we were about to see, such as the chicken flapping around the enclosure for a minute or two after its head had been chopped off, and how not to worry because even though it was really dead, its nervous system, interestingly enough, continued to twitch involuntarily for a little while just like a worm's or a snake's, Father shuddered and began to perspire. I stared at the pasture beyond the coop, intent on the long grass shining as a light wind moved through it and wondering if it wouldn't be more fun to go farther on down the dirt path to the swimming pool, which would be lovely and cold, freezing, since it was fed by natural springs (water so pure we could drink it right out of the ground, and so icy it made our foreheads ache), which also fed the brook running through the pasture just below.

"Maggie," I heard Father saying, "I'm really lousy at these things, no help at all—I'll stand outside the coop and wait."

"Me, too," I said, grabbing his hand.

"Come on, you two, don't be fainthearted," called Mother, concentrating on how to hold the axe and taking a few practice strokes at the stump under Andrew's direction. Father and I walked around the side of the coop and stood in the pasture. Father leaned down and picked a thick blade of grass, which he stretched out tight between his thumbs and pressed against his lips to blow on; it made a strange buzzing whistle. I hooked my fingers through the chicken wire with my back to the action, listening vaguely to the sounds of chickens squawking as Andrew chased them around and of Father blowing on his blade of grass; if I squinted, I could just see—or imagine—against the pale shimmer of the lower pasture, the wide loops of the brook meandering along. . . .

"Brooke, Leland," called Mother, "come here—Bridget and Bill will set a good example for you. Look how brave they're being." I glanced back; Bridget, Bill, and Emily were grouped around the stump; Andrew had a chicken expertly pinned down on it, and Mother had raised the axe.

"Don't look," said Father without turning around. "Think about something wonderful. Vanilla ice cream with chocolate sauce—Christ, I can't stand the sight of blood, I can't stand the sight of suffering, I hate pain. Look at that big bird out there, what do you think it is? A hawk? Beautiful the way it catches the wind. God, I wish, I wish I still had my airplane—" Behind us there was the loud thump of the axe, chickens squawking, Bridget and Bill squealing. I looked back again. The body of Mother's chicken was flopping all over the coop, headless, with fountains of blood spurting out.

"Oh, no," I said, stuffing my head against Father's stomach.

"Let's walk up to the house," said Father, shaking his head.

"But Mother will get mad at us," I wailed.

"She already is," answered Father, pulling me along. "Your mother is a remarkable woman, the bravest person I know, and I happen to be the most squeamish. That's that. Your mother can't understand squeamishness at all, and she can't tolerate what she can't understand. If she wants to call me a coward, I can't argue with her—she's a hundred percent correct. One drop of blood and I almost faint. Christ Almighty, when I hemorrhaged, couldn't stop bleeding, I thought I would die from fear long before I bled to death." He smiled down at me. "Cheer up. You take after me, so at least we can keep each other company—we'll be in hot water together at the lunch table, kid."

That was the first time I had a glimmering of insight into the difference between Mother and Father; up to then I had seen them as counterparts of the same person, Mother and Father, with diametrically opposed points of view, perhaps, but the same identity. It was also the first time I had to make a choice between them, but while disobeying Mother or in any way allowing myself to fall short of her expectations was a terrifying position to put myself in, I wasn't sure there was a choice after all. (Which was worse, my watching her kill a chicken or her anger at my not watching her kill a chicken?) I was very grateful that I had Father, who was much bigger and smarter than I, to express myself for me.

Shortly after this, Mother decided to compromise and divide her time between Connecticut and California. In order to keep up with Father, who had refused to totally sacrifice his business in Los Angeles, she bought another house in Beverly Hills as a base of operations and kept the farm as a backup residence. As willful as she sometimes appeared to be, Mother was capable of acute introspection; she was a harsh self-critic, far harder on herself than on anyone else, always the first to blame herself for any problems that arose. At times she kept diaries in which, along with animated descriptions of daily events, could be found stern remonstrances regarding her own behavior if it fell below some invisible standard she'd set for herself. In a memo to herself during her pregnancy with Bill five years earlier, she wrote:

I am guilty of growing old, losing my sense of fun and humor. I take my responsibilities too seriously. I've become smug, both with Leland and the children. So I must read this every day because I need to be reminded that I'm becoming a tyrant. From now on, I must make myself have fun with Brooke and Bridget and to hell with discipline. Brooke is sensitive and shy and I have frightened her and cowed her. Leland loves his airplane and his friends and I have taken his pleasure in them away. I am really going to restore them, and find Brooke's confidence again.

Honest to God.

California

Jules Stein, founder of MCA:

"*I can see him just as if he was standing right here and trying to sell me a bill of goods on something. I can see his smile, his drive, his conviction. He always had that radiant effervescent smile—rarely ever saw him when his face wasn't shining—ready to tell you something or sell you something.*

"*I would have hated to have been trying to convince a client* to come with us [MCA] if Leland was trying to get him for his organization. Then we bought his agency—this was in 1944—and his clients turned out to be our most important clients. As a matter of fact, when I look back even today at the list of clients he represented, the lists we got at that time, it's bewildering. He overshadowed everybody in the business. Even our list was secondary to his. I was just flabbergasted to think that he had so many important people—not only performers, but writers and directors—he had the best cross-section of artists in the whole field. He was by far the outstanding man in the entire agency field in California, but he was never quite satisfied with himself. He was always reaching for something further. I was perhaps perfectly happy to be the top agent in town, but he not only wanted to be an agent, he wanted to be a creator and he wanted to be a producer and he didn't want to stick to any one thing even though he was a success in it.

"I remember at one time when he was married to your mother and you were all out in the country, she insisted that he could not have any telephone calls. And he just couldn't stand it. It was too much for his blood, so he used to go to the drugstore or country store, maybe half a mile away, and call up the office to find out what was going on. The theatrical world and the agency world was his world. It was his life. I was amused by your mother's attempts to keep Leland in line. I think if she hadn't done that she still would have been married to him until he died."

Henry Fonda:

"He could sell the proverbial snowball to an Eskimo. He didn't show any interest in me until he saw me in New Faces. Then, when he did, it was typical of him that he took over. The summer of 1933 I was playing summer stock at the Westchester Playhouse in Mount Kisco—your mother momentarily gave up Hollywood to come back and play in Coquette with me, Kent Smith, Myron Mc-Cormack, Mildred Natwick, Josh, and Josh's sister Mary Lee. It was one of the all-time summer theatre triumphs.

"In the middle of that summer at Mount Kisco, I got a wire from your father, asking me to come to California. I wired him 'No.' I wasn't interested in films; I still hadn't hit New York the way I wanted to. He wired me back—I'll never forget it—one of those telegrams that just went on for page after page, clipped together at the top—all the reasons why I was an idiot, and why I should come. I wired him back with the one word 'No.' Then he got me on the telephone. I hadn't been home to Omaha for a long time, so I'd taken a week off and flown home for a visit. Somehow your dad knew that's where I was. Your persuasive father. He said, 'It won't cost you anything. I'll pay for your goddamned airplane fare and your hotel. You'll meet some people and it'll be easy for you to make a decision. Don't be an idiot.'

"So I wound up flying out to California. He met me at the airport. It was terribly hot, in the middle of August; I remember that I had on a seersucker suit, which was wilting on me. He took me to a suite at the Beverly Wilshire Hotel. I went in to shower and shave and clean up; when I came back out again, he was in the front room with Walter Wanger. I'd never heard of him before. He had no idea who I was either, or whether I was any good. We sat there, and within half an hour or so I was shaking his hand on a deal your father had sold him. He had dragged Walter Wanger over, and I don't know what he'd said, but I was shaking hands on a deal for one thousand dollars a week. And it was my deal: I could go back to my beloved theatre in the winter and come out the next summer to do two pictures for one thousand dollars a week. I went down in the elevator with your dad and out on the sidewalk in front of the Beverly Wilshire Hotel, still in shock. I turned to your dad and said, 'There's something fishy.' I just couldn't believe it. And he laughed and laughed. That's how I got here."

Josh Logan:

"He used to insult the heads of studios while settling one haunch on their desk corners. 'Sam,' he would say, 'why don't you stop cheating the public and do a good picture instead of just talking about it? Now, I have a writer . . .' Or, 'Harry, stop convincing people you're ignorant. I know you've got more sense than they give you credit for, and I've been explaining that to Garbo, but she doesn't believe me. Why don't you put her in a picture that— Hold it! I've got just the one for you!' "

· · ·

The new house was in the mountains above Beverly Hills on a wild tract of ranchland belonging to the Doheny family. It was at the end of a rutted dirt road called Cherokee Lane (now a four-lane highway). In those days (1946), as far as the eye could see there was nothing but mountains covered with scrub oak and sagebrush and occasionally a plume of white yucca; off to the west was a perfect view all the way to the ocean, and on a clear day we could see Catalina Island.

The land rose from the dirt road up to the house in a series of deep terraces defined by brick retaining walls and paths: on the first level was a row of pepper trees beside the garage, then up some brick stairs was a tangerine and grapefruit grove where the path split into two further sets of stairs, which continued on, circling a steep flowering slope as they went, and passing on the right a guest house and on the left a sunken garden planted with gardenias and roses. At the top, set well back by lawns and olive trees and a wide brick terrace with a spectacular view, was the house with its back to the mountain that rose behind it. It was a small, unpretentious, one-story house; Mother spent some time remodeling and enlarging it before we could move in. She said she bought it just for its privacy and location—total wilderness with Beverly Hills five minutes away. The inside of the house, when she finished, was arresting: this was a period in which she and Father avidly collected paintings by Miró, Soutine, Picasso, Dufy, Vuillard, Bonnard, and Mondrian, and Mother thought it would be a good idea to complement them with a bold modern background. The living room had a cathedral ceiling, which slanted up to a peak; one side was painted pale chartreuse and the other lavender, to give the illusion, said Mother, that half the ceiling was perpetually shadowing the other half. Over the fireplace hung a rather somber monochromatic Grant Wood, my favorite painting, in which wheat-covered hills rolled to the horizon like waves, accentuated by the path of an unseen reaper exactly following the contour of the land. The fireplace underneath was Mother's pièce de résistance, a cavernous slash of color that immediately caught the eye; its entire inside was painted a fiery reddish orange, as if it were incessantly ablaze. The dining-room walls were irregularly striped with tumbling pink watermelon slices, a motif carried through to its ultimate conclusion with the dining table: a twelve-foot-long rectangle of thick plate glass supported by two huge, green, egg-shaped pedestals, custom-designed to resemble upended watermelons from which slices had been carved vertically—big pink slices, sprinkled with black seeds—that reappeared horizontally as bases under the pedestals.

While we were still in Connecticut and Father was in California readying the house for our arrival, he wrote me,

Darling Brooke:

I am writing you a special, all by yourself letter because the poem you sent me was wonderful.

Our new cook seems very good. I told her that she had to cook wonderful food for my family so they would stay out here with me.

I am doing all kinds of things to the house to get it nice for you. The curtains are being cleaned, the rugs are being cleaned, and tell your mother I just got her fifty pounds of sugar and soap.

Do you remember the plants in the dining room? Well, they have all grown so much that you can't see out of the dining-room window. Pretty soon, they'll climb all over the room. Your mother likes everything to look like a jungle, but nevertheless, this morning I got hold of Kay, the Japanese gardener, and told him he had to clean it out enough so we could see through the window. Do you remember the book of Ludwig Bemelmans' about the old lady in Africa with the airplane? Well, the dining room looks a good deal like that.

You don't miss me half as much as I miss you, so hurry up home.

Much love,
Your Father

Typically, the feature of the house that Mother most loved, its rugged isolation, was the very one that Father found most disagreeable. Given an opportunity to purchase, for a minimal sum of money, all the acres and acres of surrounding land known as the Doheny Estate, he turned it down without hesitation, not wanting to believe that such rough terrain would ever be worth anything; fifteen years later he cursed himself for not having the foresight to know that, owing to sheer greed and the improved land development techniques that kept pace with it—Beverly Hills real estate being in particular demand—the Doheny Estate mountains would be hacked into ziggurats, graded and filled and studded with expensive houses on view lots, and promoted into the most valuable real estate in Los Angeles.

In those days the sky belonged to patrols of turkey buzzards circling it leisurely, the hills swarmed with jackrabbits and deer, and at night packs of coyotes gathered on our lawn to howl at the moon. To Father's horror, the ground was infested with snakes, both rattlesnakes and their natural enemies, kingsnakes, a differentiation in species that interested him not at all. Since no fewer than two rattlesnakes a week were seen around the house, Bridget, Bill, and I weren't allowed to wander out alone until we were given lessons in how to kill them if necessary and how, if we were bitten, to use the emergency anti-venom kit stashed in a kitchen cupboard. Father, for all his alleged queasiness, devised his own method of dispatching rattlesnakes, one that at least allowed him to preserve some distance from his victims both alive and dead: observing that the dirt road, which acted as a powerful conductor for solar heat, was the most likely spot for snakes to congregate, he would, regularly, hop in the car and pick them off with it, grimly bouncing in and out of gullies, slamming the car into reverse to back over any he'd missed, and sometimes, as they scattered before him, chasing them up and down the dirt road for hours.

For Bridget, Bill, and me, the years 1946 and 1947 were spent in a mishmash of educational systems, depending on whichever appealed to Mother's mood of the moment. Bridget and I went to Westlake, a private school for girls in Beverly Hills, until Mother concluded that it was too snobbish—we had been singled out by several older students as being the children of a movie star, and that distinction was somehow more insidious in Beverly Hills than in Connecticut. Then, for a period, we went back to public school, joined by Bill, who was at last old enough and delighted not to be left behind every morning: the Warner Avenue School had a reputation for being "progressive," and Mother had an unlimited capacity to be enchanted by anything new. Her love affair with progressive education ended as soon as she discovered that the beautiful handwriting Miss Brown had laboriously tried to inculcate in us for years wasn't taught at the Warner Avenue School until fourth-grade level, and that not only were our classmates still back in the dark ages *printing* their names at a snail's pace, but also they had yet to find out what long division meant.

After that, it was back to the good old days of Miss Brown, and Miss Brown alone. Once again she came to the house and tutored us every morning from nine to twelve. Three afternoons a week, now that we were older and presumably needed supplementary companionship, we were picked up by the Tocaloma Girls' and Boys' Club station wagons and taken off, with a group of our peers, to the Santa Monica Ice-Skating Rink or the Rocking Horse Stables, or, on Saturdays, to amusements farther afield like Knott's Berry Farm.

It never occurred to us that this was an unusual arrangement, since any other to which we might have compared it was equally unusual. Even so, it would have been unthinkable to argue; we were brought up on the premise that to argue with one's parents was fundamentally bad manners and bad manners were intolerable. ("I will forgive you anything you ever do if you do it with good manners," Father would say, handing us Munro Leaf's book *Manners Can Be Fun*. "Except tell a lie," expostulated Mother.) And, manners notwithstanding, it would have been hopeless to argue with Mother, because whatever she said was dogma. We had learned that the fine art of wheedling, effectively practiced by our friends on their parents, was a waste of time with Mother. It was fruitless to try the time-honored plea, "But everyone else we know gets to . . ." because that, to Mother, was the most unpardonable excuse of all, showing a singular lack of individuality. "It couldn't matter less to me what everyone else you know is allowed to do," she would say, trying to be patient. "That is certainly no criterion of right or wrong, only of their parents' taste, which is not necessarily something I have to or want to emulate. I have a responsibility to you and that is to teach you a set of values which is good and strong enough not to be influenced by—corrupted by—anyone else's, no matter how attractive theirs may seem to be. You have to learn to think for yourselves."

She meant it. There was no getting around her if she disapproved of something. Comic books were barred from the house under penalty of death, she said, because they were strictly for the mentally retarded, as were radio programs; if we felt the need for entertainment, we could read, instead of comics, books—any books we wanted, which meant that by the time we were nine or ten we had run out of our own and were rifling through Mother and Father's library. There were no extenuating circumstances whatsoever for the presence in the house of Coca-Cola or candy, the pure embodiment of tooth decay; Mother was always able to point to this policy with justifiable pride, since as a result of it, none of us ever had a single cavity and, furthermore, never developed the trace of a sweet tooth.

We did not miss school at all, nor did we feel particularly deprived of playmates; we had each other, and as additional companions Danny and Diane Snodmuller, the children of the Dohenys' caretaker, who lived across the road in a shack behind the heavy wire fencing that marked one corner of the property line. We were fascinated by everything to do with Danny and Diane: they were twins, they were poor, they were adventurous, they never had to take baths, they were a perfect age for us (halfway between Bridget and me), they taught us how to do cartwheels, they slept in a real tree house, and they had stacks of comics. Mother, of course, did not know about the last, or she would not have encouraged us to spend so much time over at their house. Danny and Diane were wonderful. They had to go to public school every morning, so we would walk with them down to where the dirt road ran into Coldwater Canyon, just to get in a game of tag before either the bus arrived for them or Miss Brown for us.

Afternoons if the weather was good, we'd put on our cowboy boots and set off in a tight band to roam the sagebrush-covered hills, sometimes aimlessly, sometimes on the trail of scorpions and lizards and flowering cactus. Danny and Bill practiced peeing at distant objects and became proficient at hitting anything within a radius of ten or twelve feet, while Bridget, Diane, and I watched enviously and tramped around looking for nice scorching rocks, which made especially satisfactory targets because they sizzled and steamed like dry ice when the urine hit them.

From the very beginning, Bridget kept herself slightly aloof from our unruly activities. She was not a tomboy and made no bones about it. She had neither the stamina for these excursions nor any interest in the typically rough games the rest of us liked to play at that age, where we chose sides and were pitted against each other for a rowdy chase sequence of cowboys-and-Indians or pirates. She would join us because we would coax or shame her into it, when she would really have been much more comfortable playing with her dolls or drawing a picture or reading. Bridget always seemed content to be alone, but this was partly because she felt so ill at ease with the alternative; whenever the three of us expanded into a larger group, it became an unfamiliar, disorderly, and threatening competition with which she couldn't cope. Yet she didn't want to be left out, either; there was a conspiratorial element that attracted her, and nowhere was this element as apparent as in our friendship with Jane and Peter Fonda.

The Fondas went back forever in time as we knew it, and were to go forward forever in time to come. Our families were united in the most abstract but intricately woven pattern. The Haywards and the Fondas: our mother had been married to their father and, after they had divorced, almost remarried him; our father was their father's agent and eventually, with *Mr. Roberts*, his producer. It seemed we had been born into a conspiracy and had no choice except to carry on. Brooke, Jane, Bridget, Peter, Bill. We graduated very nicely in age, all of us together. The spread was perfect. When Jane and I were nine, Bridget was seven, Peter was six, and Bill was five. Not only were we a conspiracy but an extended family, perhaps by accident, perhaps by design. Who knew? We talked about it among ourselves, but certainly our parents never discussed it with us and I can't remember how or when we discovered that once upon a time, before any of us had been thought of, our mother and their father had been married and very much in love. We had all grown up half a block away from each other in Brentwood, and had simultaneously moved away, we to our farmhouse in Connecticut and the Fondas to an enormous piece of property up on Tigertail Road. Bridget, Bill, and I were often taken there to play; our station wagon would pull up the long dirt driveway, we'd all pour out, and the five of us would go absolutely crazy.

Although Jane and I as the oldest were the ringleaders in most of our capers, it was Peter who, casting around madly for a way to make a contribution, first stumbled on the idea of smoking. He staged his corruption scene well, looking forward to an *occasion*, the next time we all got together. Bridget, Bill, and I were driven over after school one day; Peter was waiting for us expectantly out by the gas pump that the Fondas had installed to fuel their tractor. He was sitting under an umbrella in his red wagon with a display of cigarette butts he'd been assembling from ash-trays around the house, and a supply of paper Stork Club cigarette holders he'd filched from his mother. We were all sitting around smoking and coughing—with Peter in a state of glory, about to conclude his lesson by showing us how, if we punched holes in the butts, they would burn up and we wouldn't have to drag as much —when his mother's masseuse caught sight of us and rushed back into the house to report us. "Mrs. Fonda, all the children are smoking!" That was the end of it. Jane and Peter were punished by having to chain-smoke a full pack of Pall Malls each until they retched (Jane, being more clever than Peter, pretended to get sick right away, but Peter held out and kept smoking until he actually got sick and vomited), and, as usual in these matters, the Hay-wards were banished from Fonda territory for weeks.

The Fonda territory was nine acres of farmland that Hank had built up from scratch: redwood fences, compost heaps, a chicken coop, a stable, a tennis court, a pool, and lovingly planted trees—oak trees, beech trees, fruit trees, and behind the pool, his real pride and joy, pine trees, with special retaining walls con-structed around them to hold in the water that was needed to soak the arid ground. Hank used to stand and water them for hours in the hope that someday they would grow big enough to surround the house.

There was a big open field up in back—the North 40, Hank called it—where Bill and Peter used to have rock fights. One of them would position himself in a trench and the other in the log cabin that Hank had built as a playhouse, and with a characteristic lack of antagonism, they would chuck rocks and pieces of brick at each other, using ashcan tops as shields. One time, incited by Jane and me, the five of us hid behind the pine trees and methodically threw rocks, pine cones, clods of earth, anything we could find at every car that passed us on the road until finally we hit one. Its enraged owner got out and chased us across the field, but we were too nimble for him—all except Peter, who was nabbed in a clump of beeches, whereupon Jane and I, overflowing with adrenalin and bravado, wheeled around and went back for him, screaming at the man to let go of him that minute. Frances Fonda made an appear-ance, and the Haywards were sent home fast.

Another time Bill and Peter, out of idle curiosity, struck a match and set fire to the dry grass in the North 40. Pleased with the results, they settled down to see how quickly the blaze would spread, which was so much faster than they had anticipated that they had to jump up, scamper down to the tennis court for some empty tennis-ball cans, race over to the pool to fill them with water, and then dash back up to the fire. By that time it was raging out of control, so the fire department had to be called; before the afternoon was over, one fireman had been bitten by a rattlesnake and the whole North 40 burned up.

As soon as the Haywards were allowed to return after that episode, Jane and I plotted a sneak attack on the old doctor who lived at the top of a sinister brush-covered hill adjacent to the Fonda property. We had been observing him—or the lack of him, since he seldom showed himself—for some months, patiently biding our time and waiting for the perfect opportunity to catch him in one of his evil scientific experiments. The ideal moment to strike turned out to be Halloween. Gladly followed by the others, we inched our way up the hill on our bellies, maneuvering toward our objective with supreme stoicism through the burrs and brush and cactus. We had almost made it, when suddenly, down in the Fonda driveway, we heard the loud clanging of the dinner bell: it was our *governesses* imperiously recalling us to the house. We stumbled all the way down the side of the hill, crashing into trees, scraping our knees, tearing our clothes, total wrecks when we arrived at the bottom, where we were lectured very heavily about rattlesnakes, tetanus, polio, how thoughtless, how could we have—? Peter, who had an unpredictable temper, was so infuriated by having the thrust of our insurrection deflected that a few minutes later, when the two governesses lined us up on the embankment in front of some oak trees for a group snapshot, he lunged forward and bit ours (a relief nurse who was substituting on Emily's day off) on the leg, sinking his teeth in and drawing blood. She squealed and almost fell into the gulch behind her.

While the rest of us engineered these pranks with a heady life-or-death spirit, merrily devoting all our creative—and what we thought of as brilliant—energy to them, Bridget remained on the outside, hovering, bemused. Jane Fonda remembers her as being "slightly on the edge of things. Just sort of never in the center of the action. I've known several children who have leukemia, young, eleven- or twelve-year-olds, and know they're dying—there's something very different about them. First of all, they look different.

There is a kind of pale, translucent quality about them but they seem extremely mature. They're not silly and they don't rough-house the way other kids do, and Bridget was something like that."

To me, at that time, Bridget was becoming very irritating. Since I was older and usually the only one of us able to do it, it was my responsibility to talk her into being a part of any group activity; in my more dispassionate moments I was capable of understanding her reticence, but in the heat of the fray it made me impatient, and if she became stubborn, flatly refusing to enter a game that we couldn't play without another person—or, worse, threatening to tell on the rest of us if she was apprehensive about one of our daredevil schemes—I couldn't stand it. What exasperated me most was trying to figure out why, if she put up so much resistance that we would finally decide to go ahead without her, she would then stick out her lower lip, scrunch up her face, and burst into tears. Everything would come to a standstill when one of us—generally me—went to find a referee like Mother or Emily. Bridget would refuse to budge, sobbing that it was nobody else's business and besides she didn't want to be singled out to a grownup as not fitting in. "But, Bridget," Mother would comfort her, trying to make her laugh by rubbing their noses together, "you must *always* come to me if you're unhappy—at least that way I can *help* you, silly." And Bridget would whimper that that would make her feel like a tattletale and it wasn't our fault and she couldn't explain what the matter was, anyway. "Now, children, surely you can *all* play nicely together, there's room for everyone," Mother would admonish us. "But, *Mother*, that's the whole point, she doesn't want to play—do you, Bridget?" Bridget would remain silent and for Mother's sake sulkily rejoin us, occasionally getting caught up in whatever we were doing enough to enjoy herself. As time went on and she took Mother's advice, however, her behavior grew more frustrating; she would burst into tears and scuttle off at the drop of a hat to inform Mother we were being mean to her. "Crybaby, crybaby," we would run back and forth shouting harder and harder. Mother would storm after us to lecture us about being bullies, we would defend our side of the situation to Mother, and Mother would soothe Bridget. "If you were really smart, my darling Brie, you would just ignore them, go your own way and not give them the satisfaction of letting them know they can make you cry. If you behave as if they're not upsetting you—I'll tell you a secret—they won't try to bother you any more. That's human nature." And Bridget would stalk around humming to herself, pretending we were invisible so that we would have to proceed without her anyway.

She was still small and skinny—"the runt of the family," Mother teased her affectionately—and everything about her coloring was so pale, her skin, her hair, her eyelashes and brows, that once she asked Mother if she might be an albino, and Mother said of course not, if that were so her eyes would have been pink instead of blue. Still, she gave the impression of being frail and sickly, so that whenever we went to the doctor for a checkup, Mother had her tested for anemia, but it always turned out that, except for her sensitive skin, she was healthier than Bill and I, who were in bed a lot with bronchitis and ear infections. "You see?" Mother assured her. "Appearances mean nothing. Don't let them boss you around any more; you're really much stronger than either of them."

As long as Bridget was alone with Bill and me, she seemed happiest, as if, making all allowances for daily warfare, we were the underpinnings of her security. At least with us, she thought she knew exactly where she was: sandwiched halfway between us in age and size and able to predict, more or less, what effect her behavior would have on us emotionally. It wasn't a case of her being dependent on us, because although she was, she was also very much her own person, but the one thing about her that nobody—not even she—could measure or value was the extent of her originality. She looked different, she was different, she *knew* she was different, and that meant different from Bill and me, a comparison heightened by the knowledge that to begin with, the three of us were all different from other children. And no matter what Mother said, we weren't at all sure that different meant better when events seemed to contradict that concept—as, in fact, did Mother herself at times when she would expound at length on the importance of our leading "normal everyday lives" like other people. It was confusing. Bridget constantly forced herself—or was forced by our example— to contend with the idea of conformity, and it was more painful for her than for Bill and me: she was softer and had a longer way to go. It was also more difficult for her to cope with that curious ambiguity in our upbringing: on the one hand, we were wildly encouraged to have the spunk to be totally nonconformist and to take pride in expressing ourselves uniquely; on the other, we were forbidden to deviate from a strict set of rules that perpetually disciplined us to have consideration for other people and faultless manners with which to deal gracefully and tactfully with any conceivable social situation. "Children should be seen and not heard" was the doctrine around our house, "but if they are heard, it better be good and interesting."

Insofar as rules can provide a margin of safety for children, Bridget was secure with them and wrote and illustrated an extensive "Book of Rules" when she was seven; however, even though it appeared that she was more comfortable with them than Bill and I, who were always chafing with disobedient inspirations, they had a more inhibiting effect on her, one that was reinforced by witnessing the punishments that were meted out to Bill and me. This seemed to endow her with a pious quality, which really got on our nerves. Even more aggravating, sometimes, was the assumption on her part that as one of us, she owned the other two; we were her possessions and it followed, of course, that our possessions were her possessions.

I wrote her sternly, when I was nine and she was seven, to set the record straight:

Notice! (To Brie)

1. Do not touch anything here while I am gone. If you want your dolls, take them and leave my horses alone.
2. If anything is touched by you (I can tell whether they are or not) you will have some fittable punishment.
3. Don't play game until I come home from Club. Leave baskets alone. I have everything arranged nicely, just the way I want.
4. If you do not heed these warnings I will have to speak to Emily.
5. Will play with you when I get home. (Brooke)

Bill continued, in isolated grandeur, to invent trouble of a magnitude that left Bridget and me awed. There was a reckless, abandoned, spur-of-the-moment aspect to his nature that we found foreign but admirable. There was no telling what the morning might bring. He reminded us of a cat depositing some dreadful new species of prey on the doorstep. Since both his looks and his disposition were angelic, Mother and Father decided to pass off this rebellious streak as a momentary phase of development.

Bill had his own room adjoining Bridget's and mine, with French doors that led out to the front of the house. A few days after Mother had it redecorated and painted deep blue—a nice masculine color, she said—we all came down with chicken pox. On her way into Beverly Hills, Mother stopped by our respective beds to see what we would like from the toy store to cheer us up. "A jar of Vaseline," said Bill. "Whatever for?" asked Mother. "Just to have," answered Bill. "No books or crayons?" asked Mother. "No, thank you," replied Bill, "just Vaseline, please. My very own jar. To keep under my bed." Mother thought it was an adorable request. In the middle of the night a car crashed into a eucalyptus tree on the dirt road, and over the earsplitting wail of police and ambulance sirens came even more earsplitting wails and thumps from the direction of Bill's room. The house was suddenly lit up and, in mass confusion, everyone—Mother, Father, Emily, Bridget, and I—converged on Bill's room at the same moment, where we crashed into each other and slid the length of the blue linoleum floor, which had been heavily greased with Vaseline. Bill, just before going to sleep, had been inexplicably seized by a compulsion to smear his entire jar of Vaseline over every inch not only of the floor but also of the freshly painted walls. Later he was awakened by the commotion outside and, having forgotten all about his slippery art work, jumped out of bed in the darkness to see what was going on only to land loudly and painfully against the bureau on the other side of the room.

Father determined that since Bill's major passion in life was hoarding money, the most effective way of punishing him would be to dock his weekly twenty-five-cent allowance. Usually before Bill was able to pay off one punishment in full, he would, owing to a lapse, have accumulated another. He was always behind. Once he was given a tool kit, and after impulsively drilling a large ragged hole through the wall between his room and ours, he ended up owing Father thirty-seven weeks of future allowance.

The only money that Father liked to hoard was small change, and that was really because he kept it in a special bank, a large hollow glass brick—like a glass construction brick in appearance—with one narrow slit on top into which he emptied his pockets each night. The bank looked beautiful as it slowly filled up with pennies and silver and sometimes the green of folded dollar bills all mixed together, but the best part was the ceremony of opening it, which took place when Father could no longer cram in another dime. He would tie a string around the heavy glass, tell us to stand back, light a match to the string, and with deep satisfaction watch while the glass shattered and money exploded all over the place.

For us, by far and away the most interesting place in the house to be when Father came home from work was his room. It was loaded with all kinds of gadgets and paraphernalia. We loved to follow him in there and rifle through his cuff-link and watch collections. (The only jewelry Father ever wore was a pair of simple gold cuff links initialed "LH," his airplane-propeller tie clip, and a watch, but nevertheless he had fifty or sixty pairs of cuff links, some—the ones Bridget and I grabbed first—set with precious stones, and his passion for timepieces of any style or vintage was so comprehensive that he had amassed well over a hundred fabulous clocks and watches, of which his favorite was a thin hundred-dollar gold piece with a secret catch that could be flipped open to reveal a watch miraculously half as thin as the coin itself). Or we would scribble with innumerable pens on innumerable variations of his blue-on-blue personalized stationery, and fiddle around with anything at all that belonged to him while he made a deal or two on the telephone. Although he had sold his agency to MCA, claiming that it tied him down too much, he couldn't resist keeping a hand in the business and just moved his offices from his own building at 9200 Wilshire Boulevard to the MCA Building on Santa Monica Boulevard. He also remained on the board of TWA and continued as chairman of Southwest Airways, which had a milk run up and down the West Coast.

Although Father was by no means paternal by nature, he was beginning, as we grew more capable of expressing ourselves and establishing a verbal rapport with adults, to take as much interest in us as we had in him.

"Your mother and I have absolutely opposite points of view about children," he stated one evening, trying to teach us how to play chess. "She's most fascinated by them when they're babies, and babies categorically don't interest me at all, little pieces of hamburger meat—and listen, no question about the fact that, as babies go, you three were sensational—but the point is, now that you're getting older and I can see how your brains are starting to work, thank God, now *that's* an interesting process to me, and I feel as if *I'm* part of it. It's about time."

Father was always on the move, packing his overnight case engraved with the logo *LH* 10%, flying back and forth between New York and California even more frequently than before—working much too hard, said Mother. Bridget, Bill, and I were so accustomed to his trips that we accepted them as a matter of course. However, we looked forward to his return home, even from the office, with such excitement that the minute he walked in the door we jumped all over him and wouldn't let him out of our sight until bedtime. Then, even if he and Mother had to go out, we would cling to him and beg him and badger him and trap him in our room until he had given us the latest installment of a marvelous, labyrinthine, never-ending tale he improvised for us in what had become a nightly routine. One night when he unexpectedly couldn't come home for dinner, we were so disappointed that we wouldn't eat. The next morning I wrote him a letter at his office,

Dec. 5, 1946

Darling Father,

I am very unhappy that you are not feeling well, and it was pretty lonely last night without you.

Mother had supper with us and this morning she had breakfast with us too.

Bridget and Bill have gone to school. I am all by myself writing this letter to you, with a great deal of love.

You should have heard the coyotes last night! I didn't hear them, but Emily did, and she said that they were awful.

Bridget, Mother, and Emily are making doll's clothes for Bridget's rubber doll.

Anyway I miss you more than anything.

Lots of love,
Brooke

One afternoon when the Tocaloma Club station wagon pulled up to our garage to let us off, an ambulance was waiting. While everyone watched, aghast, two attendants in white came down the steps carrying a stretcher with Father on it. Before we could move, the stretcher vanished into the back of the ambulance, doors closed, red lights began to flash, and, with an ominous sound, the ambulance was gone.

We had never seen Mother cry before. It was very serious,

she said: Father had hemorrhaged again from the strain of working too hard. He needed lots of rest and blood transfusions and would be in the hospital for a long time, and we couldn't go with her to visit him in the hospital until he was out of danger, because it wasn't allowed, but we could help a great deal by being very brave—that would help her to be brave, too—and by saying prayers for him every night and every day as well. We were heartbroken. It was terrible to see Mother cry and terrifying to remember what Father had said to me that day when he and I had walked away together from the chicken coop; if, as he'd said then, the sight of a drop of blood made him afraid to death, suddenly I knew how much more afraid he would be at the idea of bleeding, literally, to death.

He didn't bleed to death, although he was in the hospital for a long time; everyone was very relieved, Mother reported to us, that he didn't have to be opened up again, but we felt, during that time, as though somehow somebody had died anyway. The air inside the house changed color and became dark gray as if all light were filtered through drawn shades, reminding me of the heavy gray velvet on the walls of my grandfather's room—the room in Maisie's house where we visited him once just before he died— even the windows and fourposter bed draped in gray velvet with gold tassels, impressive and hushed, until Grandfather, alone, without the nurse's help, went into his bathroom. "Excuse me for a moment," he said courteously, closing the door behind him, and we could hear him coughing and coughing, viscerally, as if he would never stop, while Father, agonized, stood at the window's gray light, playing with a gold tassel and looking down at the traffic on Fifth Avenue.

Also the house was quiet because around this time Mother, too, became ill. An old back injury was acting up, and she was confined to her bed under heavy sedation, while a stream of doctors came and went. Mother had never gone to bed sick before then, although we knew she had a bad back, because she'd often made fun of herself for having to keep a thick magazine like Vogue on hand to slip under her right buttock whenever she sat down. This unorthodox procedure, prescribed years earlier by an osteopath who thought she needed to support her right hip a little, was, she claimed, the only remedy that kept her from having chronic backaches.

Emily made us walk instead of run through the house, and, to our further consternation, forbade us to go anywhere near Mother's room. "No, I'm not trying to be mean," she said when we demanded querulously to see for ourselves how Mother was coming along, "and yes, I realize that when *you're* sick in bed you like to have company. But it's a funny thing. Everything's the opposite when you get to be our age—and Mrs. Hayward is a spring chicken compared to me—you find out there's nothing to make you sicker quicker than the combination of noise and pain."

Shortly after both she and Father recovered, Mother—surprisingly—decided to go back to work. John Van Druten and Alfred de Liagre were taking *The Voice of the Turtle* to England and she agreed to go with it. She had fallen in love with England ten years before and to do *"The Turtle"* there was an irresistible temptation, she told us, but she would only be gone for six months at the most—and less, if English audiences didn't like the play. In May, 1947, we put her on the train for New York with the warning to eat more and smoke less. The concept of six months as a stretch of time had very little meaning to us at all. "It's not forever, I promise you," Mother said sadly, hugging us goodbye.

From England she wrote us letters, long monologues, that vividly described its postwar ravages: the bomb damage in London, the queues for heavily rationed food, the pervasive feeling of envy and bitterness toward Americans, which, although she realized was impersonal, hurt her, and the guts and spirit of the English people for having lived through such devastation.

Her observations, as always, were intermingled with elements of both gaiety and depression. In one sentence, feeling rejected and lonely, she would complain about the rude and inhospitable attitude of English country inns; in the next, cross at herself for feeling rejected and lonely, she would extoll their charm and the extraordinary beauty of the English countryside. Whenever possible, everyone went sightseeing, which she loved, but typically, no matter how lonely she claimed to be, after just a few days with a group—even of close friends—she felt a compulsion to get away from it, to be alone. She was dissatisfied with the rehearsals of the play and the incompetence of the backstage crews and, when *"The Turtle"* opened in Manchester, with its reception ("Oh, dear," she wailed to Delly, "is this what we came to England for? Where, oh, where is our slick little play?"), although, in fact, it got good reviews.

Every week, as we had promised, we wrote to her, since she

assured us that our letters meant more to her than anything, even a steak in rationed postwar England.

From Bridget:

Dear Mother,
    Brooke had the mumps and I am expecting them. . . .

Dear Mother,
    I have the mumps at last! Brooke's party has to be postponed all because of me. Father is in Hawaii. He sent us some leis and bathing suits. Bill's is just like shorts and a blouse. Ours are a much better kind than we had before. When are you coming home? Are you still having nothing to eat but tea? You should see Emily. She has no teeth left. . . .

Dear Mother,
    Yesterday in club we went to the beach and Brooke and I got a sunburn. Half of my vaccination was sticking out from under my bathing suit and it got sunburned too. So now half of my vaccination is pink and half white. . . . Are you getting more food? I have almost forgotten how you look and talk. . . .

From me:

Dear Mother,
    How are you feeling? When are you coming home? I certainly miss you. I wonder what I'm going to get for my birthday. Bridget has the mumps and Bill has a bee sting on his foot. He can't walk. Grandsarah came over yesterday and asked about you. She talked to Father on the telephone. He said he is very lonely. Emily has all her teeth out. She looks very funny. Her mouth is out of shape. I wish I knew what you look like, I have forgotten how you talk. . . .

Dear Mother,
    Last night I had my ear opened. Now I can't go in

swimming this whole summer. I can't get my head wet.
Bridget has a rash. Bill has no ailments at all! . . .

Darling Mother,
 I hope the play isn't a success so you will come home.
It is wonderful weather out here. We are all tanned like
berries as Emily said. Have you had another egg? I must
admit I have forgotten what you look like. . . .

And from Bill:

Dear Mother,
 Yesterday I almost broke my ankle. To ducks are dead.
Love and xxxxxxoxo
            Bill

Dear Mother,
 We are playing nice. Today we had a tea party. The
ducks feathers are white. I miss you xxooxx
                    Bill

Dear Mother,
 The ducks are eating the snails. I miss you ooo
                       Bill

Dear Mother,
 Brooke saw a snake. xoxoxo
                 Bill

Dear Mother,
 I had a wonderful time at camp. I am getting a banner
for being the best camper. I love you.
                        LOVE
                        Bill

Dear Mother,
 I had a very nice time at camp. The ducks have laid some
eggs.
                    xxLOVExx*Bill*

Dear Mother,
 The day before yesterday I caught 12 fish.
                    LOVE
                        Bill

To my dear Mother from William L.H.
The poem by Bill—"Something and Nothing"

PART ONE

If I had something,
What would I do with it?
But, I have nothing, so what?
But, I must have something.

PART TWO

Too bad,
Ha! Ha! Ha!
So, too bad,
How can I help it?
Well, what would I do with it if I did have it?
That's the part I don't understand.

PART THREE

If I had something,
So I don't have anything?
I don't know,
Well, how can I help it?
Ha! Ha! Ha!

Bill Hayward

By the time Mother came back, we really couldn't remember what she looked like. Father went to pick her up and then suddenly there she was, just exactly the same as always, breathless from running up all the steps, not scrawny and dried up like a prune as she had written us, but beautiful, all familiar golden, with shiny golden hair parted in the middle and bangs across her forehead. We couldn't let go of her; there wasn't enough of her to go around, nor enough of us either, scrambling and scrabbling and scratching to be the first, nor enough time to tell her every single thing that had happened since she had left: weekly dinners with Grandsarah and kickball games with Martha Edens; inches grown, weight gained; the great snail invasion when we stuck snails down each other's shirt and Father paid us to collect them in jars with salt at the bottom, which made them ooze bubbly green slime and shrivel up; the five-foot rattler coiled right under Father's window one morning that so shocked him when he looked out that he got sick to his stomach all over it, and we kept the rattles to show her as proof of its size; Emily's new false teeth; Bill's new real tooth, on and on.

Then she told us every single thing that had happened to her since she left, which made us want to go to England immediately, and after that she said, "My darlings, there's one more thing I have to tell you—or really Leland and I have to tell you—and I guess I've put it off until the very last because . . ."

Father stood with his hands in his pockets, looking toward the ocean. It was a very clear afternoon, one of those when you could see all the way to Catalina. By the subtle change in her voice, we knew that we should pay attention and stop trying to walk in single file along the narrow brick wall at the edge of the terrace.

"Now stop wiggling around for a minute and come over here. Please. So I can look at you. Just for a minute, then you can go right back."

We came and stood before her, somewhat gravely, in keeping with her voice.

"I suppose this is a kind of family conference that concerns just the five of us."

We looked over at Father, who hadn't shifted his position.

Mother spoke rapidly and earnestly in the tone of voice that she used when she was explaining something new: "What I have to tell you is a little sad and unpleasant but certainly not the end of the world." She paused and we tried to stand still politely. "You know how much, how very very much your father and I love each other, have always loved each other—and that's one of the reasons you came to be—and of course we shall always love each other. But you see, sometimes grownups have disagreements, just like children, and get on each other's nerves, and when that happens, it's really best, rather than argue and argue, to separate for a little while—maybe a week or two or four—just a trial period, however long it may take to think things over from a more objective vantage point. You yourselves know how hard it is to come to an agreement when you're right in the middle of a squabble. But that doesn't mean at all that you stop caring about each other, does it?"

We listened very carefully. It occurred to me that Father had not moved since the beginning of this explanation, and really not at all for about fifteen minutes before it began, as if he were watching for turkey buzzards or flying saucers; it was the time of the flying-saucer scare and we all used to stare up at the skies, imagining. . . .

"Also it is imperative that you understand that I'm not talking about divorce. This is not the same thing at all."

I glanced at Father's back and longed to be standing over there beside him. Divorce. Now there was a word. Where had that come from, sailing out of the clear blue-and-gold sky like the shiny pebble that Bill had once thrown at me, and that I, innocently mistaking it for a piece of mica, hadn't bothered to duck, so that it hit me squarely on the forehead between the eyes, making them sting. Father had removed himself from all this, probably because it was infinitely worse than watching Mother chop the heads off chickens, although this time I wasn't lucky enough to be outside the coop with him.

The more frantically my thoughts darted around, the stiller I seemed to stand. Father, I thought, hanging on to his arm in my mind, what is she talking about? Divorce. Explain to her about the night with all the stars, the night you told us, remember?

One night just a month or so earlier, while Mother was still in England, Father and Bridget and Bill and I had all lain together under a blanket on the big chaise longue on the terrace, and while we gazed fixedly at the shimmering black sky and waited for flying saucers and falling stars, Father had told us stories about when he was a little boy. Then he had said, "But the worst thing that ever happened to me—ruined my whole life, really, at least what was left of my childhood—was when my mother divorced my father. Terrible. Terrible. I was only ten, and I never forgave Mother for it, never understood it. So capricious. Ten years old. It cut me in half. Divorce, it's the most awful thing in the world. I ought to know. You three are very lucky, you'll never know how lucky you are. That's one thing you'll never have to go through, no matter what, I promise you on my sacred word of honor." Ten years old; that's exactly what I was. "Ten years old, and I love you a great deal—Father," he wrote in his very own handwriting on the round gold locket he gave me for my tenth birthday. We had never heard about divorce before, except from Grandsarah, who had skipped those details, and we were overwhelmed by pity and love for Father, cut in half when he was a little boy ten years old. Father, what about the promise, I reminded him, trying, in my mind, to shake his arm harder, but I could tell just by the way he was standing, that he already knew. . . .

"Furthermore," Mother was saying, "you will see that this won't really be as painful or make as much difference as it sounds. Although Leland won't be staying here—he'll be at a hotel—you will see him just as much as ever, probably more. He'll come and have dinner with you when he can, just as he does now. You see, one of the biggest problems of his kind of business is that, even more than now, he will find it increasingly necessary to travel, to spend so much time away from home—in New York, for instance —that we will hardly ever be able to see him anyway."

"But, Mother," said Bill. Bridget and I looked at him, astonished at the interruption. Father half turned away from the ocean toward us.

"Yes, my darling," said Mother, kneeling down and kissing the top of his head.

"But we are in California to be with Father," blurted Bill. "Isn't that why?"

"Yes, my darling," said Mother. She paused for a long time, then stood up and looked over at her gold cigarette case on the table. Nobody moved.

"Now it's silly of me to make this all sound too serious," she said, changing the matter-of-fact inflection in her voice to one of levity. "You all look stricken and there's no need to be. Everything will be practically the same, you'll see." She smiled at us in a secret way, knowing how to make us giggle. "Only you must treat this just like going to the bathroom; it's not something you talk to other people about. Even if they're nosy and ask. All right? This must be just between the five of us. And Emily."

We were tongue-tied. Father walked over slowly with his eyes down. He didn't say a word either. Oh, please, I thought with all my strength, the way I did whenever he said he wished he could put me in his pocket and take me with him. He raised his eyes, and in that moment I knew from the look in them why he wasn't able to say anything at all.

"Don't worry, darlings." Mother smiled. "We both love you, each of you, more than you will ever know. Now go on and play with what's left of this beautiful afternoon." And she turned toward Father.

"Father." I said his name involuntarily. He looked at me

again, blindly, and that made me want to cry. I forgot what I wanted to ask, there was so much. "Are you going right now?" That was just a fragment of what I wanted to know, but I couldn't bear the look in his eyes.

"No. Oh, no. Of course not. Would I ever go without hugging you goodbye?"

I put up a hand to shade my eyes so that he wouldn't see them; I was afraid they reflected his. "A bear hug?"

"Until I squeeze you to death." The familiar answer made us smile tentatively.

"Are you staying for dinner?" asked Bridget.

"Well, we'll see."

"What hotel are you staying at, the Beverly Hills Hotel? Are you going to take all your clothes with you? Now? Do you have to?"

"No, no," said Father. "I'll be right here for a little while and I won't go without telling you." He looked at us very hard and we looked back for a minute before obediently turning away.

But what, I wondered as we walked in silence across the lawn in the direction of the playhouse, what if Mother's not right and there is a difference from now on? What if he never comes back again? What if after two or four or six weeks—? But he had promised. And Father never broke a promise. I knew, because he had promised me he would never spank me again, that summer night in St. Malo, and he never did.

After that, nothing ever seemed the same again.

It was as if the first decade of my life had been roped off from the rest of it. I thought of it that way, that first decade of my life, when I thought of it at all, which I tried not to. For one thing, there was no way to approach it without crossing a barrier of pain. Sometimes I blundered across, forgetting. Then all I could do was cross my fingers and pray that next time the pain would be less.

Once I was back inside, I felt crazy and alone, as if I were talking to myself. That was another thing. Bridget and Bill were no help: they claimed they recollected barely anything, less and less as those years receded. Bridget finally swore she could remember nothing that had happened in the first seven years of her life. That was odd, I thought; part of the disparity, because on the other side of the pain was a time when everything was radiant, when every detail had such absolute clarity, every color such vibrance, that it would be impossible ever to forget. Or to duplicate. By comparison, time afterward was fogged over. By comparison, my more recent history had, for me, the remote impact of photographs or postcards shown in the wake of a stunning event witnessed firsthand. Either I couldn't see as clearly or some quality was missing, gone forever.

4

Mother

P̶eter Fonda:

"I remember your mother more than I remember my mother. She would drive us around in that 1946 Chrysler Town and Country, you and Bridget and Bill and Jane and me and Maggie only. No governesses. Right down to the nitty-gritty time, to Kiddie Land or wherever it was that we'd take our ride. With her in the Town and Country with the top down. How else would I remember this car which I only rode in maybe a dozen times during my life? The color of it, the texture of it, the color of the beautiful upholstery—and your mother driving this huge Chrysler, you know, your petite mom, heading down the highway with the top down having a gas with all of us kids screaming and yelling. It was green, forest green. Great metallic paint. Beautiful hood, Chrysler hood, great chrome. The dash was wood, so beautiful, full of varnish. Your initials painted on the door, 'bBb,' little 'b,' big 'B,' and little 'b' in kind of an oval. It was our dream. It was all beautiful, varnished wood, polished metal, chrome, and flowing blond hair, all of us giggling and laughing. . . ."

So Red the Rose, However You Spell It

Margaret Sullavan, Lovely Meg,
Tell me the reason, pray,
That you spell your name, O bewitching dame,
Sullavan with an a.
Do the Murphys fashion their tag with e,
Or the Finnegans with a y?
The way you spell could amaze John L.,
The Sullivan with an i.
Margaret Sullavan, star alone,
Spell it your own sweet way;
The fairest of sights in twinkling lights
Is Sullavan with an a.

OGDEN NASH

Henry Fonda:

"She was not an easy woman to categorize or to explain. If I've ever known anyone in my life, man or woman, who was unique, it was she. There was nobody like her before or since. Never will be. In

every way. In talent, in looks, in character, in temperament. Every-
thing. There sure wasn't anybody who didn't fall under her spell."

Life, however, went on normally; that was very important, Mother
said.

She said also—in another family announcement, at which
Father was not present—that she and Father were, after all, getting
divorced. There was no chance of a reconciliation, because he'd
fallen in love with someone else.

Bridget, Bill, and I darted sidelong glances at each other.
We had learned that the best camouflage was to keep very still and
not call attention to ourselves. I knew it all the time, I told
myself—not the part about falling in love with someone else, but
the divorce part, and what difference would the reason make now?
Actually, it did make a difference, the more I pondered it in the
silence that followed that revelation, and maybe it was ruder not to
ask questions out loud. For instance, if Father had fallen in love
with another woman, did that mean he had fallen out of love with
Mother? That didn't make sense unless he had been pretending all
this time. Did love just stop? Run out? If so, where did that leave
Bridget, Bill, and me? Didn't he belong to us any more? Had he
ever loved any of us at all? How could anyone stop loving Mother?
She was perfect. Obviously if it was possible to stop loving her, it
was more possible to stop loving us.

Mother was sitting in her bedroom on a settee, the one
Bridget had crayoned orange when she was a year old, eliciting the
first spanking in our family. That reminded me of Father's promises: he'd kept the one about never spanking me again, broken the
one about divorce. Fifty-fifty. Maybe that wasn't a bad score; I
wasn't sure. I wasn't sure I'd ever trust him again. Mother's hands
clenched in her lap, her knuckles as white as her fingernails were
red. Her head was bowed. I was dizzy with emotions, proprietary
about Father, protective of Mother. My eyes began to sting.

"Stop frowning, Brooke," said Mother, cocking her head.

I cleared my throat. "I'm thinking."

"I know, but one of these days you're going to look in the
mirror and see two big creases permanently *stuck* in your forehead.
What then?"

I'll stop thinking, I thought, and cleared my throat again.

"Come over here," she beckoned me teasingly, "and let me wipe them off. Just a little spit—"

I dug in my heels. "Is she pretty? Is she as pretty as you?"

"Good gooby, yes! Prettier. You're just used to me."

"Nobody could be prettier—"

"Now I can just tell from your expressions you're dying to know her name and you don't dare ask."

We nodded.

"My poor darlings. Don't worry, I'm all right. I'm not going to cry or do anything embarrassing. Her name is Nancy Hawks. Some people call her 'Slim,' because she's wonderfully tall and thin. She's nice and funny and beautifully dressed—"

"You know her? You've met her? Where?"

"Uh-huh. Many times. Here and there. She was married to Howard Hawks for a year or so—he's a well-known movie director —and they've recently divorced. Maybe she was lonely when Leland was alone and lonely. . . . That can happen."

"Are they going to be married?"

"Probably. I don't really know. Maybe after our divorce is final. It takes some time. Oh, dear—that's still to come, the messy part, dividing everything up. Everything but *you*. I want you all to know, and so does your father, that whatever happens, he will go right on loving you all in exactly the same way, just as much, always. His feelings for you will never change. Of that you may be absolutely sure. Those feelings, the feelings parents have for their children, aren't the same kinds of feelings that they have for each other. Parents don't always love each other wisely or forever, although we all suppose we're going to. Being grown up is no guarantee against making mistakes. Lots of them." She shivered and wrapped herself in a sweater she had worn for as long as I could remember, a white sweater with the black initials "MS" knitted all over it. "Pugh. Now I'm preaching. I'll bet you can't wait to get as far away as possible from this boring tirade. I don't blame you."

. We shook our heads, flattered that she was confiding in us, feeling very close to her.

"Are you jealous?" Bridget inquired, curling up beside her. "Ooh, your legs and feet are cold. Do you want some socks? You need Emily to take care of you."

"No, I need you. All of you. You're much better than an old pair of socks."

"Are you jealous?"

"Well, yes, I was. At first. You see, I've known for a while. It's one of the reasons I decided it might be best for me to go away for a few months, far away to England. Leland and I talked about it. It was a calculated risk, but I thought maybe, that way, with a little distance between us, we could get some perspective. Re-evaluate our feelings, perhaps bring them back to life. It seemed that here we were flogging them to death. But leaving didn't work either. . . ."

Years later, she said: "So typical of your father. As soon as I arrived in England, walked down the gangplank of the boat, there was talk: a friend greeted me with the news that Leland had gone right off to Hawaii with Slim for a lovely two-week vacation—quite openly, so that it hit all the stinking gossip columns immediately. My pride was lacerated, every corpuscle in my body hurt. I felt as if my nose had been rubbed in it. Publicity—that kind, in particular—had always been a dirty word to me. The neurotic measures I took to keep my private life out of the claws of those hyenas!—as your father knew better than anyone. So, of course—as he could have predicted, not being exactly a moron—I lost my temper, became totally discouraged with the whole thing, just plain gave up. Is that what he intended? I've often wondered since. Then I didn't know, and suddenly didn't care either. When I got back, he begged me not to leave him; I felt he'd already left me."

Years later, he said: "Your mother has always been the most impossible woman I've ever known, and I've known them all. That's my business, for Chrissake. Actresses. What the hell did she expect? I implored her not to go, we had lengthy discussions about it; at her insistence we both consulted psychiatrists—and you know what bullshit I think that is— By the way, it was kind of interesting, after I'd gone in for a couple of sessions, my doctor, a woman doctor—absolutely wonderful woman, I decided as a result of this —told me: 'Leland,' she said, 'there is no question that you are crazy, but you also happen to function better than anyone I've ever seen, and what more can you ask out of life? There's no point in my treating you; it would be a waste of your money and would probably throw the whole mechanism out of whack. Stay the way you are.' Well, naturally, I just thought she was the most sensational—nuts about her. Anyway. Your mother, in her usual headstrong manner, decided to go to England. Her shrink's advice. I kept telling her how ill-advised a move it was right at that time— I told her that, told her how vulnerable I was. She knew. There was no big deal. She was nobody's fool. I was a damned attractive man. Women adored me, I adored them, but that didn't mean I was behaving like Don Juan, for God's sake. Basically I'm absolutely monogamous. Basically romantic. Faithful. As long, that is, as I know I'm cared about. I'm not very demanding, and, by God, I can put up with a great deal more horseshit than most men. But there came a point—and Maggie was perfectly aware of this, since I informed her of it myself—past which not even I could continue to go out night after night by myself, alone, while she was, arbitrarily, thousands of miles away. Connecticut. After years, I started having an affair. Nothing original about that. I honestly didn't know what the hell I was supposed to do next. She decided for me. Chose exactly the wrong course of action. Six months in England. 'Maggie, why,' I asked her, 'why in God's name should I sit around twiddling my thumbs and examining my navel while you go off and do whatever you please? That just isn't fair.' I have never, in my life, known such a perverse woman. And you know something about your mother? She was the most enchanting, wonderful, delicious human being in the world—God, she had a marvelous sense of humor, kind of offbeat and naughty—until I slipped a wedding ring on her finger. And even that was her idea. She was the one who wanted to get married; she wanted the divorce. Called all the shots. She was adamant. I begged her for once in her goddamned life not to be so bloody pig-headed; it didn't seem to me that I'd committed the crime of the century. And there were the three of you—'My God, Maggie,' I kept saying, 'what about the children?' No use. She'd made up her mind, she was furious, her pride was hurt, and she wouldn't back down. Never could. Until it was too late. She always got her own way. Always . . ."

Years later, Millicent Osborn (she and Paul remained close friends of both Mother's and Father's) said:

"I thought a great deal of the divorce was Maggie's fault, Maggie's doing, really, not Leland's at all. It all goes back to this attitude that she had. It was really an essential arrogance, although she didn't know it, of wanting things the way she wanted them without regard for what Leland wanted. Leland wanted to remain in California. This was his whole life. She wanted Leland to give up the movie business, to come to New York and be a producer. She was so unhappy about Leland's working after he got home, she wanted him to give up the agency business. I thought it was unfortunate, and in a way arrogant of Maggie, that without consulting Leland, without thinking of Leland's wishes, she went and bought a house in Connecticut when his whole life was in California. To go and buy a house because you have independent means and yank your children away from the center of their existence and the center of your husband's existence is certainly a very destructive step.

"Things began to go wrong because Leland was alone so much of the time in California, and it was quite natural for him to see other people. According to Maggie, she began to have great emotional difficulty when he began to go around with Slim. But I think that all goes back to Maggie's image of herself as a femme fatale. I know she would never have worded it that way, but the thought that she could be rejected by a man was absolutely out of the question, because it had never happened before. I remember she told me once that she was brought up in the South with the understanding that a woman has to be enchanting, that she had to charm every man she ever came across no matter what the circumstances. The enigma of Maggie. She was like a Fitzgerald creature, the Southern belle. But there was nothing substantial about her flirtatiousness; it didn't mean anything. It was a reflex action. Now, in Maggie's career, and as a woman, she had always been the siren, and here, suddenly, was Maggie reaching the age of forty, wasn't she, and her husband was more interested in another woman and she heard rumors all over about it. Of course nobody in the world would be as hurt by infidelity from a husband as Maggie. Nobody in the world. To her it was a most shattering blow. Her pride was utterly devastated. I think this was the most needless divorce, because they were crazy about each other. Even when she was divorced and had given him up, she still wanted him. . . ."

Years later, Sara Mankiewicz said:

"She was always madly in love with your father. The divorce came as a most terrible shock to her. You see, she told him to leave. This was her idea in the beginning. He didn't want the marriage to break up for anything. Then she had dreams of a reconciliation. Everything was going to be happy and wonderful, she was looking forward to it, and I think that's when he told her, 'Look, this is just no good. Let's not pretend.' And that afternoon I went up there, she told me, 'He doesn't really want a reconciliation. He really said *he doesn't want to be married to me.' It was absolutely chilling. She was miserable, she was unhappy, she was disappointed, and that really, I think, was the beginning of the end. . . ."*

Years later, many people said many things. But a few hours later, when Mother had gone out to dinner and we were eating alone, Emily said that she was shocked, simply shocked, she had no idea. Usually in such a close household—certainly in every other household she'd worked in—but here there was no inkling, she had never heard Mr. and Mrs. Hayward raise their voices in any bad arguments, just the ordinary everyday ones, the normal wear and tear. Not even from the deepest recesses of the house late at night when the children were asleep, when most people yell at each other if they're going to.

Bridget pushed her mashed potatoes around her plate, mounding them over the uneaten part of her hamburger. Using her fork as a trowel, she patted them into a castle, than squashed the castle into a crater so that melted butter slid down the sides and congealed in the fork grooves. She stuck the rest of her string beans on top like spikes.

"Stop playing with your food," Emily reprimanded automatically. She sighed. "That just shows you what remarkable parents you have. Both wonderful people, the most thoughtful people I've ever worked for. They kept their problems to themselves, didn't want to inflict them on anyone else. That's good breeding, good manners. Neither one of them ever complained or spoke a bad word behind the other's back."

We had never heard Emily so upset, and were very impressed.

"Maybe they were trying to set a good example," suggested Bill.

"Yes," said Emily. "That's right. Good Lord, I'll miss Mr. Hayward. Such a gentleman. It won't be the same, not having him to boss around just like one of you. Always sneaking cigarettes from me, bless his heart. Now I won't have anyone to make coffee for except myself. Won't be the same. And Mrs. Hayward, she must be heartbroken, but I've never seen her act sorry for herself. Not once in all the time I've been with you."

"Do I have to drink all my milk tonight?" asked Bill, batting his long curly eyelashes at Emily.

"Shut up, Bill, you're interrupting," I interjected impatiently.

"Now, now," said Emily. "First of all, what's the matter with your milk, Bill? And secondly, young lady, we don't allow 'shut up' around here."

"Be quiet, then," I muttered, wishing Emily would get back to the topic of Mother and Father.

"It's too warm now," Bill continued, "and I hate warm—"

"That's because you've let it sit for half an hour—no wonder," I retorted.

"Who's interrupting who?" asked Bridget slyly.

"Who asked you to butt in?"

"And there's disgusting yellow stuff floating around on top," went on Bill, unperturbed.

"That's just cream." Emily tasted his milk. "Ummmm. Delicious."

"I'm full," said Bill. "Just tonight. Please?"

"No dessert, then," sang Bridget, virtuously looking at her empty glass.

"Children." Emily shook her head with resignation. "You must all be worn out—I can always tell when you get snippy. Why don't you excuse yourselves nicely from the table and I'll run you a hot bath. Now, tomorrow—this will be a hard time for Mrs. Hayward. We must all treat her extra special nice."

"Oh, Emily," we said, "we know *that*."

At bedtime, after Emily had turned off the lights and kissed us good night, Bill crept into Bridget's and my room and got in bed with me.

Over the next few days, the three of us held long whispered conferences. We concluded unanimously that the best way to treat Mother (and indirectly ourselves) was to get her married off again as quickly as possible. This idea was not, we pointed out to each other, disloyal to Father. On the contrary, it would be in everyone's best interests. Clearly we needed a man around the house; it would be terrible to have Mother moping, however bright a face she might put on for our sakes. The ideal stepfather would be clever enough not to try to replace Father, who was irreplaceable; he would be rich, rich enough to buy me a horse and stable, a doll hospital for Bridget, a miniature car with a real bona-fide engine for

Bill to drive around in; he would sweep us up lock, stock, and barrel to innumerable exotic places all over the world, where, fluent in six or seven languages, he carried on his enigmatic business of a so highly dangerous but earthshaking nature that he could never reveal it, and he would make us all, particularly Mother (on whom he showered pearls and diamonds), laugh a great deal.

When we mentioned our solution to Mother, she smiled ruefully and said it was very thoughtful of us, but she didn't think she ever wanted to get married again. It just wasn't that easy to fall in love. "First you have to find the man."

There were at least two possibilities.

There was Charlie Feldman, an important Hollywood agent (and, as such, a friendly rival of Father's), whom we seeded as a front runner because the morning after he took Mother to dinner for the first time ("Oh, you really are incorrigible," she protested to us; "I've known him for *years!*"), he lavished on her a heavy gold bracelet hung with an emerald-studded Taurus. ("Well, well, how did he know what month your birthday is?" Her reaction, we perceived hopefully, was studied nonchalance. "Oh, for heaven's sake, he makes it his business to know everything about potential clients. Signs of the zodiac—what nonsense. It's much too flashy, and I'll never wear it." But she did.) At the same time he sent gold identification bracelets for Bridget and me, already inscribed with our names correctly spelled (mine usually wasn't), which Mother had a much more difficult time explaining away.

Also there was a tall handsome Arizonan, George Gregson, who had many things to his credit. For one, he was a widower; his wife, the lovely (to judge from a photograph we once saw) daughter of Dr. Edwin Janss (head of the Janss Corporation, which had developed all of Westwood and Holmby Hills—another plus), had been killed in a tragic automobile accident right after the second of their two children had been born. George, fortunately for us, had never married again. His daughter, Patsy, was by now a year older than I, and son, Eddie, a year younger, the ideal ages for step-siblings. Mother and George met perfectly: drinking champagne at a white-tie party, with, in the background, a *ton* of fresh caviar heaped in the hollow back of a huge swan magnificently carved from a block of ice. Patsy, Eddie, Bridget, Bill, and I met perfectly, too: at the Ringling Brothers Circus, when it was still held in a big tent with a terrific, steaming, smelly sideshow. We all bought chameleons on little leashes to pin on our shirts and afterward went back to the vast Janss estate, which fronted what seemed to be a mile of Sunset Boulevard (from which it was set back by another mile of driveway) in Holmby Hills; there the children lived with George and their grandparents, and there, in the splendid greenhouses latticed with a jungle of orchids, we set our chameleons free. That afternoon, I fell madly in love with Eddie, even though he was a year younger, and fantasized about a double wedding. The idea of marrying my stepbrother had an undeniable cachet. Patsy was as crazy about horses as I: not only that, the Jansses owned Conejo Ranch (which the Janss Corporation eventually developed into Thousand Oaks, a gigantic industrial park and shopping center in the San Fernando Valley), where they invited us to go riding whenever we wanted. George, who had an endearing habit of saying "Cheerio, pip-pip" with a Southwestern twang, and even looked a bit like a cowboy with his steel-blue eyes, sprouted overnight, like Jack's beanstalk, into the towering position of top contender for Mother's hand. It was spontaneous combustion, as far as we were concerned.

And then, one bright November day, just before Thanksgiving, off the train at Pasadena and into our lives stepped an Englishman. The mere fact of his nationality ranked him, sight unseen, as a redoubtable challenger; in addition, the scrupulousness with which Mother primed us for his arrival was so noticeably intensive that we were predisposed to scratch all the preliminaries and hand her over without even a token interview on behalf of our own self-interest. A period of probation or courtship seemed redundant: we knew enough. His name was Kenneth Wagg, and he had four sons ("with such en*chant*ing looks and *ex*quisite manners"), who, ranging from thirteen to four years old, flowed around us age-wise with agreeable fluidity. He had featured in Mother's letters from England as a heroic fellow who had saved her from starving to death by keeping her supplied with two cups a day of Horlick's Malted Milk, a putty-colored powder whose brand name made us snicker when we considered the ramifications of advertising it ("Hor-lick's? Tch, tch, Kenneth"), whose heavy cloying taste we found more palatable disguised with chocolate anything (eventually, for consumption in this country, Kenneth was to devise Horlick's Malted Milk Puffballs, plain or chocolate-coated—only the former in our house—a sort of highly nutritional candy, too esoteric for sale anywhere but in specialty drugstores), and whose every incongruity made it a vital factor in our destinies.

Kenneth's affiliation with Horlick's had an appealing maverick edge. Although he came from a fine old banking family and had been traditionally groomed and educated (at Eton and Oxford) to carry on in Herbert Wagg & Co., he had chucked his banking career when, after marrying the beautiful Katherine Horlick, his father-in-law, Jimmy Horlick, invited him to join *that* family concern. Katherine and Kenneth had recently divorced; she (heedlessly, said Mother; picturesquely, we thought) was now living in Egypt, having left him to bring up their four children alone with the help of a nanny. His position as president of Horlick's Corporation in Racine, Wisconsin, meant that he made frequent trips to the United States, of which this was ostensibly one. He was also assistant to the managing director of the parent company in England, which led Bridget, Bill, and me opportunistically to contemplate our potential future in Europe.

The minute we laid eyes on Kenneth Wagg, we knew we'd hit the jackpot: he was as good as gold. And that was an interesting paradox, since he had no wealth to speak of. How he was going to support us in the style to which we were accustomed, when he had four sons to educate expensively in England, gave us no pause; we became instant converts, prepared to adapt ourselves to a monastic life of poverty and sacrifice, because Kenneth's most outstanding quality, which he wore like a medal ready to turn over to Mother whenever she was ready to accept it—a quality his rivals had lacked to one degree or another (we intuited, once we saw the real thing) —was the depth of his feeling for her. He was madly, overtly in love. By some cocky inference we assumed that meant with us, too, but just to play it safe, we set about wooing him. Since Kenneth had already produced a slew of boys, Bridget and I were well aware that the onus of this task fell on us, and were gratified to detect, within minutes of meeting him, that he was openly susceptible to the novel enchantments of little girls.

That afternoon we threw ourselves into our seduction of Kenneth with a vengeance, monopolizing him for a grand tour of the house, which included our wardrobes, cajoling him to sit next to us on the piano bench and play the bass in duets, flirting with him over interminable games of pick-up-sticks, and giggling appreciatively when he said words like "lorry," "petrol," "la*bor*at'ry,"

and something that sounded more like "squiddle" than "squirrel."
By the time we were halfway through dinner, it was Kenneth who
had seduced us. We were absolutely entranced by everything he
said or thought or did. He taught us to master the British method
of holding one's knife and fork, particularly attractive to Bridget
and Bill because not only was it the reverse of American (knife
kept in the right hand, much simpler), but also involved dexter-
ously pushing food onto one's fork in various layers, allowing for
considerable creative leeway.

"Kenneth," I said the next morning, trying to make him feel
at home, "isn't it silly for you to waste money staying at the Bel Air
Hotel when you could marry Mother and move in with us?"

Mother was speechless with embarrassment but Kenneth, to
our relief, looked delighted.

"Nothing would give me more pleasure," he answered fervently, "but unfortunately your mother—"

"Brooke," spluttered Mother, regaining her voice, "I'm
going to have to explain the conventions of courtship to you—"

"Mother," Bridget interrupted, coming to my rescue, "I've
never seen you blush before" (which was true).

"If the house isn't big enough for the three of us and Kenneth's four sons," Bill said diffidently, "we could all move into the
Bel Air Hotel."

"Or I could design a new house altogether," resumed Bridget. "I've always wanted to be an architect. A real honeymoon
cottage, with my *very own* room" (giving me a sidelong look).

"Me, too," said Bill.

"I'm going to work on it right away," Bridget mused.
"*Everybody* can have their own room. That makes nine bedrooms
unless"—she grinned—"Kenneth and Mother want to share theirs;
that'll save some space."

"If you ask me, it would be much better to move into the
Bel Air Hotel," remarked Bill hopefully.

"Children!" shrieked Mother in mock distress. "Enough of
this line of torture. You're disgracing me. Poor darling Kenneth—if
you keep this up, you'll subvert your own objective and drive him
away forever. He's not used to such radically forward behavior from
children—or adults. Remember, in *his* country—even in *this* country, for God's sake—"

"Oh, I think they're absolutely correct," said Kenneth,

beaming. "The person you have to convince, children, is your mother. She's causing me no end of difficulty. Allow me to enlist your help at once; undoubtedly you carry more weight with her than I. I seem to be as effective as a gnat."

"Oh, no," moaned Mother, "this is unendurable."

"Oh, yes!" we all chorused gleefully.

"Before you get too carried away with yourselves," demurred Mother, executing a little tap dance, which was a sign she was about to win her point, "perhaps I should remind you"—mid-routine she paused emphatically right in front of Kenneth—"that I am not yet even a gay divorcee, so *don't count your chickens*," and, punctuating each word with a series of steps, she continued to tap her way around the room.

Kenneth, who had to leave for Racine after Thanksgiving, returned almost immediately to the Bel Air Hotel for Christmas, precluding any doubts we might have had concerning his intentions. We joyously dragged him to the Farmer's Market for the purchase of six-dozen ant colonies, which had caught our fancy that year as the perfect gift, and conned him into helping us wrap and deliver them to friends all over the city.

Although we had no doubts about Mother's intentions either, having quizzed her about them, we were beginning to suspect the future would be slightly harder to pin down than we'd anticipated.

"The trouble is, you see," she explained to us, "that I think I have fallen in love with him. And that is trouble, real trouble."

We waited, accustomed to the contradiction implicit in Mother's strongest feelings.

"When I was in England," she went on earnestly, "at first I was so terribly unhappy about Leland and homesick for you and miserable about the play that when this gentle kind Englishman came along and made me so terribly *happy*, I found all sorts of excuses for falling in love with him. He paid a great deal of attention to me, he made me forget how sorry for myself I was feeling, he reintroduced me to a way of life that was gracious and leisurely and to people who took the time to be charming, all the things that I had known as a child growing up in Virginia and had forgotten existed, although some part of me must have hungered for them ever since, I suppose. At the same time, half of me knew that I would never see him again and if I did, we would probably dislike each other. So I assumed I was deluding myself: how could I fall in love with a man as different from—let's say your father—without its being loneliness or perversity? Or a bit of both? And the less we had in common, the easier it was to pretend love. He was no part of my past and seemed to have no stake in my future. Then, when I came home, I was even sadder and lonelier than before, because I had to face reality again and all the ugliness of the divorce. Then, when Kenneth came back into my life at Thanksgiving, I was happy all over again. But I told myself that I couldn't take it too seriously or count on it at all, since we would be separated most of the time by six thousand miles. Besides, I thought maybe I was just using him to make myself feel cheerful. The minute he left for Racine, I knew I was hooked. In real, honest-to-God hot water, as I said."

We waited some more.

"In love, you mean," Bridget responded finally.

"Yes, I'm afraid so," said Mother resentfully. "And I've told Kenneth that he'd better be careful. It's come as something of a shock. It's the last thing in the world I want. I've warned him I'll make him pay for this—and if he's smart he'll run away as fast and as far as possible."

So we thought it was the best Christmas we ever had.

Although they weren't to be married for another two and a half years, Mother and Kenneth's relationship was established for once and for all. In January, 1948, they went East. Mother had known for some time that she was afflicted with otosclerosis, a form of deafness caused by the growth of bone over the middle ear. She was anxious to meet the world's foremost specialist in the disease, Dr. Julius Lempert, who had invented the Lempert or fenestration operation, a delicate piece of surgery in which a new opening or window is bored through the mastoid bone and a new drum grafted over the aperture. After her first consultation with Dr. Lempert, she called us to announce excitedly that he was the most fascinating man she had ever met and had so impressed her she was checking into his private hospital on Seventy-fourth Street, the Institute of Otology, to undergo the operation at once. She had always made light of the fact that she was going deaf in her left ear and made equally light of the operation, which was to be a long and serious one.

"Oh, I wish you were here so that you could meet Dr.

Lempert," she raved. "He looks exactly like a gnome out of *Grimm's Fairy Tales*. It was love at first sight. I'm so crazy about him I've decided to bequeath him my ears, or what's left of them when he's finished. And now someday I, too, can be a valuable scientific specimen in his museum. You can all come and point at my fenestrated ear bones and giggle and say, 'We used to know the person who belonged to these quite well.' "

The operation was a success and restored full hearing to Mother's left ear. Afterward, although she dutifully returned to Dr. Lempert every two years for some kind of dreaded maintenance visit in which she let him "fool around with my window," and even conceded to wear a protective plastic cap over her ear whenever she washed her hair, she in no way obeyed any of his other instructions to cut down on her diving, shooting, or flying.

As soon as she was released from the hospital after ten days in bed, she caught a cold that delayed her return to California for some time.

"Dr. Lempert is furious with me," she told us morosely on the phone. "He won't let me budge. Actually I don't care so much about whether or not his beautiful operation is ruined as the fact that Kenneth has just abandoned me."

We commiserated, knowing perfectly well Kenneth had planned to go back to England at the end of January and was more upset than she.

"He won't be back for two months," she despaired. "I really hate him for this. If only he were here, I could show him how much."

"But remember you promised to take us all to England this summer."

"By then it will be too late," she growled. "I'll have forgotten all about him. I've already given him fair warning—I'll be just fine for a week or two; then the letdown will set in. He's promised to help me by writing long letters, pages and pages every day, until they bore me; that will be somewhere in the next couple of months—April, let's say, for good measure. Then he can start tapering them off until we're reduced to postcards once a year."

"I'll bet he's got some secret old girl friend in London," suggested Bridget provocatively. "Maybe he leads a double life. The English are meant to be good at that."

"Dr. Jekyll and Mr. Hyde," I said.

"A werewolf or vampire in disguise?" Bill's voice rose hopefully.

"If so," replied Mother, "he doesn't stand a chance. Two can play that game. I'll have my revenge. Thirty years from now, I'll return to haunt him when he least expects it. He'll be sitting, one night, on his broad bottom beside his bucktoothed wife—the woman for whom he callously left me, that terrible winter so long ago in New York—having a cup of tea in front of his sooty coal grate, when my youthful ghost shall slowly rise from the embers like a Phoenix and twine itself around his body."

"You don't have to wait thirty years for your revenge," Bridget said, snickering. "I have an idea. Guess what happened last night. Brooke grew bosoms. They're not very big yet, but we can soon send her over to England to seduce one of Kenneth's sons."

"Brooke, darling, bosoms!" exclaimed Mother. (I looked down at my flat chest self-consciously.) "Oh, how exciting! Can't you tell them to wait until I get home before they get any bigger? I feel as if I'm missing everything."

"You'd better hurry," remarked Bridget. "Soon they'll be popping the buttons off her—"

"Shut up, Brie." I glowered at her. "Mind your own p's and q's. They're my bosoms and if they go to England it won't be because of Kenneth's sons."

"You wouldn't sacrifice them on behalf of darling Mother?" asked Bridget mischievously. "Don't worry, Mother," she reported back into the telephone receiver. "Emily says they're just baby fat. Tee-hee."

While Mother was gone, Bridget and I made an amazing discovery. One afternoon, puttering around the library for something to read, we cracked open a block of ten large matching blue leather-bound books arranged in chronological order (Volume I, and so on). Compared to the sets of gold-embossed first editions surrounding them, they were drab and academic, so we'd never bothered with them before. After a few seconds of idly leafing through them, we looked at each other, shocked.

"Brooke," whispered Bridget, although there was no one else in the room, "do you realize what these are?"

Indeed I did. Carefully pasted inside, punctuated by Mother's comments in her own handwriting, smiling up at us from page after page, almost bigger than life, was every photograph—

whether personal or publicity—that had ever been taken of her. And not only photographs, but magazine covers, press releases; every review, interview, or article that had ever been written about her; every note, letter, telegram from anyone who had ever mattered to her; every single memento that pertained to both her personal and her professional lives since the days when she was a child in Norfolk, Virginia.

Bridget and I were overwhelmed, not only by our good fortune, but by the sheer bulk and content of the material, and most of all by the idea that Mother, always so offhand about any aspect of her life, had painstakingly, over a long period of time, amassed all tangible records of it into half a shelf of scrapbooks. Why? we wondered. For whom? Herself to pore over when she was old and gray? What was this intriguing new paradox? We'd thought we'd known them all.

We found, however, that we knew very little. It was a long afternoon. By the time we finished with Volume X, dazed but exhilarated, we had acquired our first real sense of the high regard in which Mother, as an actress, was widely held, and not only that, but how long and tenaciously she had worked for it. Also, we finally knew what it meant to be a movie star. And we were thrilled to discover that there were facets to her personal life that we'd never dreamed of, such as her marriage, after Hank Fonda but before Father, to Willie Wyler.

"Look." Bridget nudged me excitedly and pointed to an old London clipping that read:

MARGARET ("ONLY YESTERDAY") SULLAVAN

passed through our little village the other week, accompanied by Husband Bill Wyler (he directs Margaret's pictures). Because it was a honeymoon trip, the couple made their London agents promise that they would not be asked to see interviewers. . . . Margaret and Bill were married during the making of *The Good Fairy* (now at the Empire). It was a rather unusual courtship. Star and director wrangled continuously during the earlier scenes of the picture. One evening at six o'clock Bill told Margaret that she would have to work that evening. "Oh, no, I don't," said Margaret. "I have a date for the fights." (Fights are fashionable in film society.) She stamped off the set. A little while later Bill followed her into her dressing room and said: "I'm sorry. I should have told you earlier. We won't work." Margaret flared. "Now you've made it worse. I've just called and broken the date!" A few evenings later Bill took Margaret home from work, but they didn't go home. Instead they drove to the aerodrome, flew to Arizona, and got married. . . .

"Imagine!" exulted Bridget. "She sneaked in another marriage on us. Wonder why she never told us. Shall we ask her?"

"No," I answered, considering. "Since she's never mentioned it before, she'll get suspicious."

"You're right," said Bridget. "Otherwise we'll never get to see the scrapbooks again." For, having stumbled upon such a treasure, we had no intention of relinquishing it.

Many years later, William Wyler told me:

"*The Good Fairy was one of the first important films I was making at Universal. Maggie was a star and I was a very young apprentice director just starting, so for me it was quite a step to direct her. One day I looked at the rushes and Maggie didn't look good. I said to the cameraman, 'What's the matter, you're not photographing her well.' He said, 'Well, you two had a fight the day we shot that.' So I said, 'What's that got to do with it?' He said, 'Well, when she's happy she looks pretty, when she's upset she doesn't!' I said, 'That's news; I guess I've got to try to make her happy.' So I made an effort. In order to get along, I said, 'What are you doing for dinner tonight?' And she said, 'Nothing.' And we had a dinner date, which was simply for the purpose of having her look good in the picture, and, well, we got along very nicely eating dinner. So, we had another date. Then I kissed her, and we began to like each other. Of course there were a few little obstacles: one night we were shooting a scene with her; she looked towards the camera and stopped acting. I said, 'Cut.' I didn't know what the heck she was staring at. Behind the camera was Jed Harris. He was a big successful producer on Broadway at the time, very influential. I had heard she and Jed were together in New York, but now we were already planning to get married. He'd heard about it; they were supposedly engaged, which I didn't know. Anyway, there he was. Out of the blue. Stood there. Like Svengali. And in those days flying out from New York was something. And he made her very nervous, but I think she was fascinated by him. He had a kind of hold on her. I think she desperately wanted to get away from him. For what reason*

I don't know. I think trying to get away from Jed Harris contributed to the fact that she married me. The morning we went to Yuma, Arizona—there he was again. She said, 'Let me talk to him alone.' I waited in the hotel lobby. I didn't know: is she going to come now or isn't she? A long time went by, half an hour; it seemed like forever. Down she came and said, 'Okay, let's go.' He was supposed to be a very persuasive fellow, but he didn't make it that day. So off we went. And it was a miserable wedding. Jeez. Awful. My lawyer had arranged it. I chartered this airplane, and flew to Arizona. We went to this justice of the peace; he stood there in a robe and slippers and said, 'All right, here, get together'—the radio was going all this time —and he married us. Then he said, 'Excuse me,' and went into the bedroom where his wife was still in bed and she signed the thing. Anyway we went straight back to the airport and the pilot said, 'Where do we go—Reno?' It was a good suggestion. After that wedding we should have gone straight up there. This was Sunday morning. Sunday night we were back and Monday we had to go on the set. And everybody was astonished. Here we had been fighting like cats and dogs and the next thing you know we're married. I was crazy about her."

As Bridget and I pored over the yellowing photographs and trophies of Mother's youth, we realized how surprisingly uninformed we were about that, too. Sometimes, looking amused, she had told us stories about herself, mostly disparaging. In all her schools and camps she'd always been undersized, the shortest and skinniest and the last to develop ("Why, I was eighteen and had given up hope for good that I would ever have a female figure— when overnight—let that be a lesson to you"), for which she compensated with her cherished tomboyishness and athletic prowess. She told us how she was, from the beginning, so stubborn (or, at least, so spoiled) that she refused to be weaned from her bottle until she was five. Then, on a sightseeing tour of Mount Vernon, as she leaned dreamily on the velvet ropes that partitioned George Washington's bedroom off from the public, she yawned for a second, and the ubiquitous bottle of milk dangling by its nipple from her mouth crashed to the floor, rolled across the priceless rug, and disappeared under Washington's bed.

Her memories of childhood were tinged with ambiguity:

deep pride about her Southern ancestry and customs, offset by a rebelliousness against that pride, as if any feeling so ingrained must also be pompous. Mother had hair-trigger reflexes about pomposity, particularly in herself, and never allowed it to go by without a few lighthearted jabs.

Although she scoffed at what she considered to be her family's overzealous obeisance to its lineage, she gave me her own middle name, inherited from her great-grandmother Priscilla Brooke Fleet Smith, wife of James Smith, State Senator, lawyer, and master of Smithfield plantation. ("You were doomed to have that name whether you were a girl or boy," she used to tell me, "if for no other reason than it's a good strong name that can't be abbreviated or tampered with.") A congratulatory letter written to Mother by her older half-sister, Lewise, at the time of my birth referred to her ambivalence and was, unwittingly, a perfect example of what caused it: "Dearest Peggy . . . I can hardly wait to see the baby. Leland said she was beautiful and Mother tells me you are going to name her Brooke. Mother also wrote me that you had asked about the family genealogy for possible names; so I immediately set to work to copy the old Smith and Fleet genealogies for you. . . . I have also in my possession a beautiful photostatic copy of a chart which traces our ancestry directly back through the Smith and Throckmorton lines to the early kings of France and England. . . ." ("Oh, my God, so what?" Mother would exclaim irreverently when confronted with this sort of information pertaining to her forebears. "Pugh. Who really gives a damn? Virginians. That's the best and the worst about them, their awful pride.")

We barely knew her parents. We saw them only once: they came to California for a few weeks while she was in England. Afterward we didn't feel we knew them any better. Mother's descriptions of them had never enabled us to form any clear image of what to expect—other than a thick syrupy drawl, which, as she warned us, would render almost incomprehensible everything they said. So in her absence we were unable to perceive them at all. Perhaps we needed her as an interpreter in more ways than one; this time she must have shied away from the role, and we must have known it unconsciously. There was nothing in the world at which Mother more excelled, in our eyes, than creating, with her own special blend of words and gestures and anecdotes, unforgettably vivid portraits of people. But she never attempted to portray her parents for us, and, picking up our cue from her, we never showed any particular curiosity about them. This lack of interest prevailed even when they were finally sitting right under our very own olive tree, strangers from Virginia, explaining to us why olives didn't taste like olives until they were pickled in brine like roe herring and spiced beef.

Cornelius Sullavan was spry and gay, and his wife, Garland, was plump and charming. Both were shorter than average; that seemed, at the time of their visit, to be the only respect in which Mother (who was five feet two) took after either of them.

Six months later, when Bridget and I came across photographs of Garland, aged twenty, taken in the mid-eighteen-nineties, we could see a passing facial resemblance to Mother, although we couldn't tell about much else, since Garland's loose hair—actually a full two thirds of her height—fell around her like a dark mantle, concealing most of her wedding dress, which swept, in turn, to the floor. She was so tiny that the actual dress, with its lovely satin panels interspersed with handmade lace and its long narrow sleeves (which she handed down to Mother, who kept it carefully guarded in a carton of tissue paper in the hope that one day Bridget or I would wear it), had an eighteen-inch waist. Consequently it made only one quasi-successful appearance on either of us; that was when Bridget was fourteen and at her skinniest. For the sake of a single fast Polaroid shot, Mother and I spent an hour cramming her into a waist cincher and forcibly buttoning hundreds of tiny satin buttons—mercifully leaving an inch here or there undone so that she could breathe—before she screamed that she would explode all over the house like goose liver if we didn't loosen her bonds instantly.

Garland's first marriage left her a widow after three months, since her young husband, Lewis Gregory Winston, contracted typhoid and never lived to see their daughter, Lewise. Seven years later, Garland married Cornelius Hancock Sullavan and moved to Norfolk, Virginia. In 1909, Mother, christened Margaret Brooke (and known to her family and friends as "Peggy," a nickname she loathed and changed to "Maggie" when she was twenty-one), was born.

Although Cornelius's produce business suffered from the slow postwar recovery in the South, Mother remembered a pleasant, gracious style of living: a cheerful house on Westover Street facing the park; wide porches, where, on hot summer afternoons, she entertained swarms of ardent beaus, to the vast irritation of her younger brother, Sonny (who would hover just inside the screen door and loudly stir the ice cubes in his iced-tea glass to drive them away); Sunday School at St. Andrews Church, where Cornelius was a vestryman; sewing and dancing classes; exquisite dresses stitched by the family seamstress; wonderful food; gay parties to celebrate her father's yearly hunting expeditions, from which he returned laden down with partridges and pheasant. Cornelius had a reputation for being one of the best shots in Virginia; from him Mother inherited a passion for hunting and her treasured Parker 28-gauge shotgun—its handle marvelously engraved with game birds and animals.

Mother told us that she had become an actress by accident. Her real ambition, when she was young, was to be a dancer. From those early photographs at camp and school, it was clear she would have made a good one, whether affecting the limpid, stylized poses and Greek tunics of Isadora Duncan, or perching merrily on a tree stump in the jerkin and feathered cock hat of Peter Pan. Of all the accomplishments in her life, I only heard her boast of two: her award, one summer, as best all-round athlete at Camp Aloha (a dog-eared, gray felt letter "A," carefully affixed to the scrapbook page with ancient Scotch tape), and her senior year at Chatham Episcopal Institute, in which she was elected president of the Student Council, voted the "most talented" girl in her class, and chosen to deliver the salutatory oration at its Commencement in 1927 ("O! so light a foot will ne'er wear out the everlasting flint"—M.B.S.).

After Chatham, she spent a year at Sullins College, Virginia, where she appeared to have excelled at every activity she undertook (not the least of which was flirting outrageously, to judge from the trail of dance cards and heartbroken letters in Volume I), and was named "most popular" girl in her class.

At the end of the year, she returned to Norfolk for her summer vacation. Suddenly life there seemed unutterably boring. Worse, the future, as projected by her traditional Southern upbringing and her parents' expectations, could only become more respectable and stultifying. She was young; she had determination, curiosity, ambition, and talent without knowing exactly how much, in what way, or how to measure any of those qualities against what standards. Her feet itched. Within a few months she left home and went north to stay in Boston with her half-sister, Weedie. From the Boston *Sunday Post*, May, 1929, was pasted a newspaper clipping of Mother in slacks and sneakers ebulliently executing a high kick: "High-steppers," read the heavily penciled caption under it, "of the coming Harvard Dramatic Club show, *Close Up*, to be given this week. . . . Peggy Sullavan of Norfolk, Virginia . . ." And there, in that show, her future began.

Josh Logan, later appointed one of our four godfathers, remembers:

"I must have been twenty and she must have been eighteen. I was a student at Princeton; I went up to Harvard one weekend to see a production of the Harvard Dramatic Society and the Hasty Pudding Club. They had written a musical; they were supposed to have Radcliffe girls to dance in the chorus; but they had found a girl from Sullins College, Virginia, who was up there for some reason." [As Mother explained it, "Pretending to go to secretarial school, but really taking dancing classes like mad and then trying to pay for them by selling books at the Harvard Coop."] *"She was one of the girls in the line."*

Another person in the cast who had nothing whatsoever to do with Harvard was Henry Fonda, who was about five years older than anybody else. He recalls:

"I was working in a repertory company in Washington, D.C., when I got a wire from a friend of mine, Bernie Hanighen, who was the president of the Harvard Dramatic Club. I used to do a little comedy character at parties, called him Little Elmer. Bernie had written Little Elmer into his musical, but he couldn't find an undergraduate at Harvard who could play him—this show was supposed to be strictly undergraduate—so he wired me. And he had cast, among others, a girl. . . . She was a character even the first time I met her. This was a typical burlesque type of comedy and one of the pieces of business was: she crosses the stage while I'm going in the other direction, I do a big take, make some gesture or comment, she turns and slaps me and just keeps walking. But when this girl

slapped me, every time in rehearsal and every performance, it was a solid-rock slap—you would have thought I could only say, 'Who is this bitch? Get her out of my sight.' But it didn't work that way, see. She intrigued me."

Josh continues:

"And I really think that's the first time I saw Margaret Sullavan. She was darling and she had this kind of husky, breathy, Southern voice. . . . I met her afterwards; Charlie [Leatherbee] took me aside; he'd invited her to be a member of the company that summer—that meant bringing her down to Falmouth, Massachusetts, to be in the University Players—as our ingénue. 'Isn't she wonderful?' he asked, and I said, 'She seems wonderful, but are you sure she can do all the big jobs like that?'

"The next time I saw Peggy, as we called her, and as I called her to the very end, was when we were building our new theatre at Old Silver Beach and rehearsing the opening production, a play called The Devil in the Cheese. She and Hank were the main characters. About four days before opening, Bretaigne Windust, who was directing the play—and always had a handkerchief tied around his forehead for some reason—said, 'No more rehearsals until the theatre's finished.' I said, 'We haven't learned our lines yet.' He said, 'We can't put on a play without a theatre. Go on, help work on it, we've got to get it finished.' So suddenly the whole company was nailing away, building scenery, installing seats: Fonda and I were way up on the grid for 72 hours putting in the counterweight system, Fonda face down most of that time, stretched out over the beams on his stomach, while I swung below him in a boatswain's gear with a mouthful of nails trying to thread the ropes through the sheaves; Windust was everywhere, still running around with a handkerchief around his head.

"It was a very complicated show, The Devil in the Cheese, one of the silliest and most difficult, and we had to have a lot of props. Just to give you an idea: the first act takes place in an old monastery on a Greek mountaintop and the only way to enter is to be hoisted up in a net from the earth below. Goldina Quigley, the part that Peggy played, is brought there by her mother and father on the pretext they are looking for Greek relics. The real reason is to get her away from Jimmy Chard, the boy she's fallen in love with (who eventually arrives by airplane and makes a spectacular crash landing), played by Henry Fonda. One of the monks gives Mr. Quigley an old amphora and a piece of cheese: 'Eat this cheese and know youth,' says the monk, so Mr. Quigley bites into the cheese, and suddenly there's a great green flash and out of the amphora leaps the Little God Min (some ancient Egyptian deity), who offers to take Mr. Quigley on a trip through his daughter's head. The second act takes place in Goldina's brain and consists of all her daydreams, enacted by Peggy and Hank: first they're on a sailboat, and while she washes dishes and drys them in a net strung out the cabin porthole, he catches a flying fish and pops it in the kettle for dinner; then they get wrecked on a desert island where they play the same scene, only this time he's found a turtle which she pops in the supposed dinner pot, and he brings her a monkey which they train—here there's a little time lapse and the monkey grows up into a gorilla—to take care of their baby. And so on.

"Well, you can imagine the props we had to round up. We never had any kind of dress rehearsal. Nobody had had any sleep for four days. The audience arrived for the opening; the curtain was six feet off the ground, so people could see us desperately trying to cover these white-pine steps that were supposed to be old rocks on the side of the Greek monastery. When we finally dropped the curtain, the audience applauded. I said, 'Windust, please go out and make a speech. Explain to them that we're not ready; maybe they ought to go home.' He said, 'No, no, I'll make a speech, but we're going to do this show come hell or high water. I've brought my full-dress suit and I will not make a speech without it.' He had to go downstairs; it took five or six minutes at least to put on a full-dress suit and white tie; when he walked out to make the speech, he still had that bloody handkerchief around his head. He made quite a speech, but the pounding of the nails was so loud the audience never heard what he said. There was such confusion, such hysteria; we were all in terror that this was going to be a failure, this, the beginning of all of our lives. Windust put on a monk's outfit over his full-dress suit (he had to be a monk along with me), we were ready to pull the curtain up, and he said, 'Wait a minute! We've got to get those lights out of the way. They'll cover everybody.' So the whole company came and pulled on the ropes but the ropes were twisted and the lights wouldn't budge. So Windy said, 'Put the lights on the floor.' Crash! When those lights hit, they made the biggest noise you ever heard. And the audience howled and applauded. The curtain went up.

"Unfortunately we'd never tested the apparatus for bringing up people from the cellar; Kent Smith, who played Mr. Quigley's butler, was supposed to be hauled up first, but the winches kept sticking and the basket that contained him started whirling at a dervish speed; it took ten minutes longer than we'd gauged to get poor Kent up high enough to be seen, so we all sang Greek chants until he finally appeared. And again the audience applauded. Now three people, the Quigley family, had to be brought up. A very old lady named Lily Jones was playing Goldina's mother; as the basket rose from the cellar below the stage, it whirled five times as fast as before, because it was so much heavier, and Lily Jones started screaming with the highest, most bloodcurdling scream that has ever been known, like a person being throttled to death. Finally the basket, still whirling, hove into view; two or three monks grabbed it, pulled it towards the stage for a landing, and out clumped the three Quigleys.

"This was Margaret Sullavan's début on the professional stage. And to my dying day, I will remember the first words out of her mouth. Just as though she were in the most successful play that had ever been written and she had the most wonderful lines to say, with the most aplomb I had ever seen, she said, 'Now don't get hysterical, Mother, we're here.' And I just thought, She must be the greatest actress who ever lived, because by rights she shouldn't be able to say anything at all. But she went right through the play, improvising with the same calm security, with everything around her going wrong, and that was just the beginning. It went wrong and went wrong ["Particularly the monkey," Mother used to tell us, "who, in the South Sea love scene between Hank and me, peed all over my very skimpy flowered bra." "She was absolutely magnificent," said Hank, "nothing fazed her"]. Finally the curtain went down. I should say, from then on we lived happily ever after, because although it was a disastrous night, the people who were there formed a kind of club, the audience that had seen the opening night of The Devil in the Cheese.

"After that, we began to put on really great shows. And Peggy became, within an instant, an accomplished actress. She went through thirty, forty, fifty shows with us over the years, playing every kind of part, every age, mostly leading ladies or ingénues, but the extraordinary thing was she'd never really had a great deal of training. If there was ever a natural, she was it. She had, from the beginning, that magic, that indescribable quality that is just extremely rare and immediately makes a star of a person. She was a true star. She was a true original. And we were very, very lucky to have her, because in a sense she, more than anyone else, put us all on the map. The audiences in Falmouth fell madly in love with her, as later they did again in Baltimore. . . ."

Mother, who always thought of that period of her life as its happiest, was beginning to fall madly in love with Hank Fonda.

Hank remembers:

"My first meeting with her in Cambridge and then playing with her in The Devil in the Cheese added up to a kind of nightmare. But slowly through the summer it became a romance. Look, everybody loved her. She was fun-loving, fun on the beach playing games. If she found a water pistol, she was the one who squirted water on everybody. And very early it became obvious she was a brilliant actress. I don't know what kind of experience she'd had; I don't think any. She had presence, which is something you're born with, you don't acquire. You don't learn it. People just noticed her whether she was walking in a market or on the beach or on the stage. And soon it was clear she was the talent; she played all the good parts, but the one I remember most was as Tessa in The Constant Nymph. She was unforgettable in that. . . ."

Josh continues:

"And several years later, when we did The Constant Nymph in Baltimore, she and Hank Fonda had to sing a little duet which was a very complicated bit of harmonizing. Peggy, who was always terrified of singing—although I don't believe that she was as unmusical as she always pretended to be—had to sing the melody while he sang the harmony, but she would always drift into the harmony the minute she heard him and then he would dominate it. Now, Fonda had a true musical ear, except he had the strangest voice *when he sang, the same voice he has when he laughs. It was kind of like a strangled sob, as though he were weeping at the top of his voice. It was a terrible sound. Anyway, the song was called 'Ah, Sigh Not So,' and even with the bad singing, the two of them were so enchanting, so romantic, that everyone was moved. Through that little melody the characters they were playing were supposed to fall in love. And shortly after that, Peggy and Hank announced that they were going to be married."*

When the season in Baltimore was over, the Fondas moved up to New York. Mother was under contract to the Shuberts. She claimed that they put her in seven consecutive flops. A contemporary account of her initial meeting with Lee Shubert went like this:

A Shubert scout saw her [as understudy for Elizabeth Love in *Strictly Dishonorable*] and she was eventually haled into the presence of the great Lee Shubert himself. At the moment she was suffering so greatly from a heavy cold that she really cared very little whether she saw the great Lee Shubert or not.

"Who are you, and what sorts of parts do you want, and all that sort of thing?" asked the great man.

She told him.

"You're hired," said the great Mr. Shubert, getting up and reaching for his derby.

"What do you mean—hired? You haven't even heard me read a part."

"You have a voice like Helen Morgan, a voice like Ethel Barrymore," said the great Mr. Shubert.

"What I have is a bad case of laryngitis," said Miss Sullavan.

"Laryngitis or no laryngitis," replied the great Mr. Shubert, "you have a voice like Ethel Barrymore and you're hired. Report on Wednesday to Elmer Harris."

Which is how Mother had come to star in her first show on Broadway, *A Modern Virgin*. (She used to tell us, half jokingly, that after that interview with Mr. Shubert she coddled her laryngitis into a permanent hoarseness by standing in every available draft.)

Dinner at Eight was Mother's first real success. Suddenly Universal wanted her for a movie, *Only Yesterday*. Even then she was hard to get. In 1931, she'd signed up with the American Play Company. She was quoted at the time as saying, "I didn't want a manager, but I signed up with a fellow just so I could tell the others I had somebody." The fellow who talked her into signing the agency contract was Father. By the time Universal was interested in her, she had already directed him to turn down offers from Paramount and Columbia for five-year contracts. It took all of Father's skills to negotiate, on behalf of his recalcitrant client, a deal satisfactory to both her and the studio.

She wrote her brother, Sonny, whose college education in Virginia she was proudly financing with her various short-lived theatre salaries:

> Dearest Son:
>
> Here's a secret—for God's sake treat it as such—I think I'm really going to Hollywood. It means discarding what might be termed youthful ideals about Art—but when ideals get tangled around your feet they're not much good. Would you like a Stutz Bear Cat Roadster, model 1925?? If so, we left one in Baltimore, two-toned blue, lots of chromium, and very ritzy—probably has to have a new battery, but swell tires. Write me immediately. . . .

And, leaving behind her youthful ideals, her car, and her marriage to Hank, she arrived in Hollywood on May 16, 1933—her twenty-fourth birthday.

The Universal make-up department and Mother went to war immediately. Make-up wanted to remove a wart and to extract a snaggletooth; also, in line with prevailing fashion, to thin her eyebrows and bleach her hair. Make-up won on the eyebrows and wart, Mother on the tooth and hair. The studio heads conceded that a girl with brown hair might be a novelty. They took test after test, all of them disappointing. They changed the lights and took some more. The strain wilted the subject and frustrated the experts. They ran off the film with its monotonous close-ups of Mother's face.

Suddenly John Stahl, the top director at Universal, in whose hands the movie rested, called out, "That's it! Stop the projector! That's the way we want her!"

It was a profile. For that split second she looked marvelous.

Eight different cameramen tried to recapture that second and failed. The ninth got it.

Mother wrote of the incident:

It seems that the trouble was my shallow chin. It wasn't long enough, and threw my face out of balance. The ninth cameraman set lights higher than my head and put others down low, directed at my chin, and there I was at last, a beautiful girl with a nice long chin, so the experts said.

"You'll be a star when this picture is over," predicted John Stahl one day, after shooting sixty-seven takes of a tiny scene.

"Stop kidding me," replied Mother.

But he was right. "THIS GIRL'S NAME will be as famous as any star's on the screen when she makes her debut in JOHN M. STAHL'S 'ONLY YESTERDAY,' " blurbed a full-page advertisement. "A NEW STAR WILL ARRIVE!" proclaimed another. "BOW—GAYNOR—DIETRICH —GARBO—HEPBURN—NOW IT'S MARGARET SULLAVAN."

Much more interesting to Bridget and me were some of the magazine articles.

Colliers, March 17, 1934:

What will eventually drive the press department of the Universal Film Corporation of Universal City, California, entirely insane is the news that Margaret Sullavan, on the eve of the opening of her new Super-Super-Super Special, has been discovered acting the lead in a stock company [with Henry Fonda, as it happened] playing the American Legion Hall at South Amboy, New Jersey. Upon the opening of her first picture, *Only Yesterday*, at the Radio City Music Hall in New York, an honor of some importance in the amusement world, she was home trying to finish a jig-saw puzzle. She won't make personal appearances, she won't show up on opening nights when the flashlights are booming, and when she is in New York, she spends most of her evenings barging up and down on a Third Avenue streetcar, dressed in something which looks as if it had been discarded by the Salvation Army. . . . Just now she is back in Hollywood acting in *Little Man, What Now?* . . .

Radie Harris:

ORIGINAL! One-word description of the new screen sensation, Margaret Sullavan. Here's the only interview she has granted since her smash hit in *Only Yesterday*. . . . I had already been warned that this littlest rebel hated Hollywood . . . "They call this picture *Only Yesterday*, but it's insane!" she exclaimed. "We've been on it for almost four months now and I've had exactly one day's vacation—and that I spent in jail for smoking a cigarette in a forest region." As she sat opposite me in a pair of blue slacks, looking for all the world like Huck Finn's younger sister, it was hard to realize that this pert infant was a brilliant actress, who in her very first screen effort was being "supported" by such luminaries as John Boles and Billie Burke. Orchidaceous. Glamorous. Sextacular. None of the usual Hollywood labels catalogue her. In a land of carbons, she is as original as the "a" in the spelling of her last name. . . .

Her second film was *Little Man, What Now?* The third, *The Good Fairy*, was the setting for that short-lived marriage with Willie Wyler. *Next Time We Love*, with Jimmy Stewart ("HOLLYWOOD'S NEW LEADING MAN"), was next. It was the first of their four films together.

According to a movie magazine of the time:

When there was trouble finding a leading man to cast opposite her in *Next Time We Love*, Peggy went to the casting director and said, "Why not test Jimmy Stewart?"

"Jimmy Stewart?" He scratched his head. "Who's he?"

Peggy (that's what Jimmy calls her) became quite indignant. "Haven't you seen Jimmy Stewart in pictures yet?" she exclaimed incredulously. "Well, he's a great actor from the New York stage. He's had years of experience and he recently came out to Hollywood, where they've been trying him out in small parts first. Did you see *Rose Marie?*" Somehow Peggy made that bit in *Rose Marie* sound quite wonderful. . . .

After making the picture, Mother returned to Broadway to appear in Edna Ferber's *Stage Door*. I particularly liked the idea that, on my account, the run of the play was imperiled.

Louella Parsons:

STAGE STAR REPORTED "EXPECTING"—MARGARET SULLAVAN'S HUSBAND DROPS HINT ON COAST

Margaret Sullavan is going to have a baby! At least we hear a strong rumor that says so. Her husband, Leland Hayward, has just been in town and the proud father-to-be just couldn't keep from dropping a hint. Margaret will leave the *Stage Door* company in a short time to prepare for the blessed event. The baby will cause a lot of upsets in plans, for Universal would like Margaret to have made another Universal picture, and soon.

Following my birth, Mother made three films, the first of which, *So Red the Rose*, was a Civil War drama that presaged *Gone With the Wind*. King Vidor directed. Recently he told me:

"I was just thrilled with her. I think I would have done any picture if she was going to be in it; I wouldn't have even read the script. . . .

"She'd taken up motorcycle riding while she was married to Willie Wyler, and she rode her motorcycle to work every day. Blue jeans were not the 'in' thing then, but that's what she usually wore. She was playing a Southern belle, and of course all the dresses of the period had full skirts and petticoats; so when she had close-ups, she'd come onto the set with her hair all done and her blue jeans on. It was hilarious."

About Hollywood rumors that she was difficult and willful, E. B. Griffiths, who had been her director on *Next Time We Love*, had another perspective:

"Margaret Sullavan is far too intelligent not to understand the value of cooperation. She is rather carefree and independent by nature, but she does not lack self-discipline in her work. All during the weeks of production, she arrived on the sets nearly an hour ahead of time, and even on the days when certain scenes not requiring her presence were shot, she preferred to come to the studio and sit for hours quietly watching the work of the other players, in order to correlate it to her own.

"Between sequences I frequently observed her, high up in the rafters with the electricians, discussing the lighting of the next scenes. She was interested in everything concerning the picture, and though she is firm in her conviction of how she interprets a part, she never refuses to listen to another's point of view if she feels something constructive is being offered. Much of this bosh about her being 'high hat' is merely the result of her not conforming to Hollywood's prescribed formulas for the conduct of its celebrities. She doesn't happen to care about dashing from party to party, or putting on an act after the cameras have ceased grinding. . . ."

After *So Red the Rose* came a comedy, *The Moon's Our Home*, the most important fact about which, to Bridget and me, was that Mother starred in it with Henry Fonda. This reunion was celebrated by more than the usual number of stills of them together, both looking achingly beautiful.

Margaret Sullavan's leading man in her new Paramount picture, *The Moon's Our Home*, is none other than her ex-husband Henry Fonda. And in the story she falls desperately in love with him, marries him, becomes estranged from him, and is re-united with him at the end.

Hollywood gossips wondered whether acting together in these circumstances would embarrass Margaret and Mr. Fonda, but they took it as being all in a day's work. . . .

However, many years later, Hank told me:

"While we were on location, the romance sort of bloomed again. When we got back, we talked about marrying again, even looked at property to build a home on. And then, suddenly, it was off. I wouldn't be able to explain what it was about the combination of the two of us that didn't work. I guess it was our temperaments. We must have been ill-fated lovers. . . ."

Then came *Three Comrades*, for which Mother received a 1939 Academy Award nomination for Best Actress, the New York Film Critics' Award, and a telegram from Father:

CONTRARY TO GENERAL LEGEND LOCAL PAPER FILLED WITH STALE NEWS. FOR INSTANCE THIS MORNING EVERYBODY SCREAMING YOU ARE SUPERBLY GREAT ACTRESS. WHAT KIND OF NEWS DO THEY THINK THAT IS? HOPE YOU'RE MISSING ME—GUESS WHO.

Also, in 1939, Bridget made her entrance:

DAUGHTER BORN TO MARGARET SULLAVAN—Stork Brings Second Child to Screen Star in Hospital Here. . . .

By 1941, she'd made *So Ends Our Night,* with Fredric March; *Back Street,* with Charles Boyer; *The Shopworn Angel,* with Jimmy Stewart (directed by Hank Potter and produced by Joseph Mankiewicz); *The Mortal Storm,* with Jimmy Stewart; and Ernst Lubitsch's *The Shop Around the Corner,* again with Jimmy Stewart.

From their four-time collaboration, Jimmy Stewart remembers:

"Humor. She had great humor. It wasn't mechanical with her. It was a part of her. This was one of the things that made her great. When you'd play a scene with her, you were never quite sure, although she was always letter perfect in her lines, what was going to happen. She had you just a little bit off guard and also the director. I've always called what your mother would do planned improvisation—she could do just moments that would hit you, maybe a look or a line or two, but they would hit like flashes or earthquakes; everybody'd sort of feel it at the same time. It's a very rare thing. Your mother hated talk. Lots of times your mother said, 'We're all talking too much, we don't need all this talk.' She would never sit down and discuss a scene. Lubitsch would say, 'Now we'll do it,' and your mother would say, 'Yes, all right, let's do it.'

"The longest number of takes I ever did in the movies was forty-eight takes with your mother in The Shop Around the Corner. We were in a little restaurant and I had a line: 'I will come out on the street and I will roll my trousers up to my knees.' For some reason I couldn't say the line. Your mother was furious. She said, 'This is absolutely ridiculous.' There I was, standing with my trousers rolled up to the knee, very conscious of my skinny legs, and I said, 'I don't want to act today; get a fellow with decent legs and just show them.' Your mother said, 'Then I absolutely refuse to be in the picture.' So we did more takes."

. . .

Finally, as Colonel Hayward commemorated the event in the last square of his needlepoint alphabet, arrived The Boy Named Bill.

Mother made only two movies after 1941: *Appointment with Love,* with Charles Boyer, and *Cry Havoc.* Then she retired "permanently" from the screen, because, according to one publication of the time, she said:

"I have three children. I wish to dedicate myself to them. The best service that mothers can render their country in these wartimes is to take care of their children. I am doing that."

I sighed. We had come, practically, to the end. There was a whole book designated for *The Voice of the Turtle,* but we knew all about that.

The question of possession, of ownership, was, I mused, troublesome. To whom did Mother belong: herself, us, or her public? In any case, did it make a difference? *She* must have thought so or else she wouldn't have gone to such lengths to keep her public and her private lives separate. But how much mileage was that deception good for? Once she'd deliberately become a public figure, how could she go on being one without being one?

"She made a mistake," I said aloud. Bridget was putting the books back so that their bindings lined up with the edge of the dust marks on the shelves.

"More than one," replied Bridget, smiling impishly.

"No," I said. "Seriously. She made a bad choice back when she was eighteen. She should have become an English teacher instead. Or a camp counselor."

"Why do you say that?" asked Bridget. "If that was true, you wouldn't be here." Bridget's logic could be breathtakingly righteous.

"I know," I said. "But she should have gone back to Virginia all the same. She'll never be happy. Just wait and see."

Millicent Osborn:

"There was one very sad thing: at the time of the last play she did—the one she died in—while she was in rehearsal, she came here to dinner. We were alone and she was gay and charming; we were having a perfectly lovely time talking about all kinds of things, and suddenly she took me into my bedroom and she said, 'Millicent, I can't go on and I can't get out.' And I had such a sense of horror— there was something in the way she said it that implied more than the play. Because then I took her by the shoulders, and I held her, and I said, 'You must go on.' And I didn't mean the play. But there was that crazy confusion, that ambiguity. . . ."

5

Growing Up

ogether

Johnny Swope:

"I'll never forget a remark your father made. We all went to a World Series game together, September, 1949. We were sitting at the table having lunch, the five of us: you and Bridget, Leland and Slim and I. And Leland looked at me and said—now at this time you were twelve and Bridget was ten—he said: 'You know, Johnny, these girls have reached the age when I can really enjoy them. I can take them to the theatre without having to take them to the bathroom or having to feed them; I don't have to hold their skirts up when they go to the potty and I don't have to tell them how or what to eat.' It was such a funny remark to make in front of you—as if he were rejecting the first twelve years of your life."

One sleepless night when I was thirteen or fourteen, following the exchange of some punishment or other on Mother's part for some provocation or other on mine, I finally accepted the idea that being a parent might be worse than being a child. Maybe Mother had bitten off more than she could chew. If I reversed our positions, as she was always adjuring me to do, I had to agree that I was impossible. "What would you do if you were me?" she'd query, at the end of her patience. I had no idea. It was one thing when we were adorable three-year-olds in starched organdy pinafores; quite another when we were erupting into puberty and chaos. "I loathe having to be a policewoman all the time," complained Mother. "Nag, nag, nag." (Then shut up and leave me alone, I'd think. From my point of view, it was *she* who was impossible, not I. The predicament was that I had a different point of view for every occasion.) "If you think it's fun to play God—" I didn't think it was fun. I overflowed with sympathy for her. What folly to perpetuate the human race; I, for one, would not make the same mistake. No children for me; no blood on my hands. I didn't want to live through this torture again.

The next morning, combing out my pin curls, I cheered up at the sight of myself in the mirror; was charming to everyone at breakfast, ate three helpings of sausages, got an A-minus on my English test, made left halfback on the field hockey team, spent

the afternoon recess learning dirty jokes in the eighth-grade coat-
room, scavenged twelve cents from my friends after school for a
vanilla burnt-almond Good Humor, and managed to have at least
six hours of happiness. My adolescence was a total delirium.

During the nineteen-fifties, Greenwich, Connecticut, was,
on the surface, an ideal place to be a teen-ager. It lay on the Long
Island Sound, not quite a suburb of New York City, but an easy
thirty-five-minute commute from it by either car or train. Greenwich was a wealthy community that prided itself on maintaining
the appearance of a small town. An expensive version of a small
town, to be sure, with spacious maple-lined streets radiating out
from the core of its township—a single shopping street, Greenwich
Avenue, where, in classical tradition, were located the post office,
the drugstore, the five-and-ten-cent store, and any other unobtru-
sive businesses that did not challenge the community's complacent
air of self-preservation. As for the maple-lined streets, they eased
quickly away from the typical New England houses near the center
of town toward the real heart of Greenwich: its vast country
estates, which grew vaster with each passing mile. All the intersec-
tions along the way were delineated by signposts set in large triangles of evenly clipped hedges. (Sometimes when Mother went
out to dinner, Bill and I would encamp in the middle of the
triangle where *our* road, Clapboard Ridge, joined the main artery
of North Street, and would spend the evening shooting our BB
guns through its protective hedges at the rear tires of passing cars,
hardly able to contain our pleasure when we hit our target and the
car swerved toward the ditch opposite.) That was Greenwich, with
businesses small, properties large and valuable, zoning laws tough,
and with enough clout from its citizens—many of them heads of
giant corporate interests in New York City—to keep it that way.

No wrong side of the tracks, no slums, robberies, rapes, or
murders—although I can vaguely recall one fatal car accident after
a big private débutante party that sobered everyone up enough to
question, for a while, the advisability of serving alcoholic beverages
at those ritual summer galas. For where its social life was concerned, Greenwich was no small town at all; it was tremendous.

We moved there in the fall of 1948. Mother had decided to
civilize us. The time had come to give priority to the serious
matters of education, culture, and social structure, none of which
was provided by Brookfield or California. But Greenwich had a
slew of excellent private schools (Greenwich Academy, Brunswick,

Greenwich Country Day, Rosemary Hall, et cetera), a slew of churches (Christ Church, Round Hill Community Church, et cetera), and access to all the cultural advantages of New York City. It also had a multitude of exclusive clubs (the Greenwich Country Club, the Round Hill Club, the Field Club, the Indian Harbor Yacht Club, the Belle Haven Beach Club), which was one aspect of life there that Mother found reprehensible. Despite our eventual importunings for her to join one (like the parents of all our friends), she drew the line and steadfastly refused. "I'm not a joiner," she'd say, "and anyway, I don't believe in that kind of *nouveau-riche* snobbism."

She also had grave misgivings about the bigotry in Greenwich; there were no Jews. I'd never heard the word "Jew" until we moved to Greenwich. One afternoon we were all drinking iced tea on the flagstone terrace when a friend of mine idly quoted *her* mother as being greatly relieved that the owners of such-and-such a house had held out against the irresistible bid of a rich New York Jewish couple who'd driven out *three* times to look at it—supposedly *very* prominent, too, but you know how that is: let one in, then another, and suddenly property values— Whereupon Mother exploded. It was one of the only two times I ever saw her really lose her temper (the other was when I punched Bridget in the nose for breaking one of my china horses), and I was extremely impressed. She sprang to her feet, her face purple with emotion. "There is one thing I will *not tolerate*—not in my house, not from anyone, not ever!—and that is discrimination of any kind, particularly anti-Semitism." She pounded one fist in the other hand for emphasis. "The finest, most brilliant people I know are Jews, my closest friends are Jews!" She paced agitatedly back and forth, superstitiously avoiding the cracks in the flagstone, delivering herself of a long impassioned lecture that not only detailed the entire history of the Jewish race, its accomplishments and persecutions, but also lamented the incalculable loss—cultural, intellectual, and scientific—that the rest of civilization would have suffered without it. Inflamed by her oratory, we felt a terrible collective shame at not being Jewish ourselves. "I find the only prejudice worth having," she concluded vehemently, "is against people who are prejudiced." Further to dramatize her point and to remedy what she saw as her personal neglect of our religious training, she thereafter, instead of sending us each Sunday morning to Sunday School, read the Old

Testament to us, starting with Genesis (and ending halfway
through Ezra, when her interest in the sessions lagged as much as
ours).

We were pleased that she'd backtracked about Sunday
School. Unbeknownst to her, we'd been playing hooky from it for
ages. All our friends went to Christ Church, with its sanctimonius
stone walls and rose window. But Mother had held out for the
Round Hill Community Church, because it was a Spartan Cal-
vinist structure, not a stained-glass window in the place, and the
rector, Dr. Prince, wore sensible steel-rimmed glasses. We were not
inspired by it. There was no pious ceremony, no incense or cushioned prayer stools, no Eucharistic chants, no dark shivering mystery. Mother thought all of that was baloney. Every Sunday she'd
drive us away from the center of town and Christ Church, where
our friends prepared for their first communion in virginal white
dresses, toward the country and Round Hill Community Church
with its simple wooden spire. She'd drop us off with twenty-five
cents apiece for the collection plate, and come back for us an hour
later, little realizing that we'd spent the hour playing hopscotch on
the deserted country roads with our quarters as "loggers."

Not only were there no Jews in Greenwich, before our family
there were, with one exception, no movie stars either. That exception was a miracle. The Fondas had preceded us there by a few
months; Hank was starring in the huge success *Mr. Roberts*, produced by Father, and with a long run ahead of him, he had brought
his family from California to live in Greenwich for much the same
reasons as Mother. Our first day of school—into which we awkwardly arrived at midterm, feeling more than the usual trepidation
because we hadn't been to school for years—was saved by the sight
of Jane and Peter Fonda. The ironic coincidence that brought us
all together once again in an unlikely town on a coast three thousand miles from home, the thrilling nuances of our parents' on-
going personal and professional relationships, the old feeling that
we belonged together tribally by some predestined ordinance endowed the five of us with a permanent sense of complicity. And
more: through each other's eyes we saw and knew everything there
was to see or know; we were superhuman.

On our property, at the bottom of a grassy hill, was a lake
overhung by two giant willows, beautiful trees that tolerated the
five of us perfectly. We would all somersault madly down the hill

head over heels until we were nauseated, giggling and shrieking
"Wahoo!" and grabbing handfuls of willow branches to swing
ourselves way out over the lake. Frog-hunting in the rowboat was
one of our major pastimes. Another was putting on plays for our
own private amusement. We would spend hours rehearsing them.
Nobody else ever saw a performance. Peter, who liked to cackle
evilly and drape himself in blankets, always played the villain; his
most treasured role was that of an old miser counting his money.
Bill had a running part as Peter's sidekick, Jane as the hero, and
Bridget as the ingénue; I was the director, also in charge of production.

In the sixth grade, Jane and I were kicked out of the
Brownies. It was a scandal; nothing like it had ever before occurred
in that chapter of the Girl Scouts. We went on strike and refused
to attend meetings with the rest of our classmates, preferring *any*
other form of recreation, even sitting alone in our classroom.
There, surrounded by empty desks and half-erased blackboards, we
devised a continuing fantasy about our illustrious careers, when we
attained the magical age of eighteen, as co-madames of a high-class
brothel fronted by a Chinese laundry, which fastidiously laundered
the shirts of our customers while they dallied in the spectacular
setting we'd provided behind the squalid façade. In every princely
suite would be a fountain splashing with wine, and for every patron
four or five of the most singularly exquisite girls ever seen by the
human eye: highly educated (often highly born) and expert in all
arts including sexual; multilingual, multiracial, hand-picked by us
on yearly trips to all corners of the world. They would drape
themselves across the opulently cushioned beds (the only furniture) or patter across the Moorish tiles with noble step, bearing
exotic drugs, ointments for massage, salvers of sublime culinary
delights, ivory lutes or lyres: whatever the occasion—and it went
without saying, a clientele worthy of our establishment—demanded.

We went to the Greenwich Academy, a private school for
girls in an august brick building on Maple Avenue. We wore
uniforms: in spring, formless green shifts; in winter, ghastly orange
lisle stockings, crepe-soled oxblood shoes with flaps over the laces,
green wool suits, and tan shirts sturdily tacked down with men's
green ties.

Bill and Peter went to Brunswick, a boys' school right around the corner. The main exchange between the two schools took place in the driveway of the Greenwich Academy each afternoon at 4:10, when our last gym class or study hall was over; school buses and cars, along with a goodly portion of Brunswick's student body, collected by the front portico where the older Academites primped and preened and fluttered in their gruesome uniforms. Also there were Saturday-night dance classes, socially mandatory, between the two schools, held in our gymnasium under the tutelage of Miss Something-or-Other, where, in respective taffeta dresses and dark suits, we learned the fox-trot, the waltz, the rhumba, and the Mexican hat dance. After several disastrous trial runs, those Saturday-night gatherings were boycotted by the Hayward-Fonda clans—until the eighth grade when Jane and I shifted our focus slightly from horses to the opposite sex, and were graciously able to overlook the fact that we were a full head taller than all the boys our own age.

In the seventh grade, Jane and I threw spitballs. We became expert. Pages of wadded-up semi-masticated notebook paper went into our daily stockpile of spitballs, which, at a prearranged signal, were fired off with devastating accuracy at any target. (Only our Latin and French teachers, burly and dangerous, were exempt.) We spent a lot of time in the principal's office. The principal, Miss Campbell, informed us that we were unruly, reckless, wanton, anarchistic, and natural ringleaders. We were responsible for the ruined health (heart attack) of our kindly homeroom teacher who'd taught upper-school English there for thirty years; for the dismissal (nervous breakdown), a few months later, of her unfortunate replacement; and for the last-ditch hiring of our first male teacher (to straighten out the rapidly disintegrating morale of our class). We came, said Miss Campbell, from fine families who had given us fine upbringings, and she knew she could depend on us, as we stood on the brink of disgracing both our parents and the Greenwich Academy, to rally.

The main reason we rallied was the male teacher. Centering our scattered competitive drives on him, Jane and I geared up to a creative frenzy. In the last semester of the seventh grade, we co-authored a short story laced with what we glibly assumed was authentic patois (inspired by my copious reading of Donn Byrne):

an old Irishman's account to his grandson of the time his decrepit mare won the Grand National. We diligently spent three nights writing it, and entered it in the school feature-story contest. To everyone's amazement, it won. We repeated our victory a year later with "Khangua" ("I remember that sweet Irish spring. Oh, the fresh green fields of daisies . . ."), a variation of the previous tried-and-true theme, this time with a gypsy as the protagonist. After that, until I went away to boarding school two years later, I never let the story contest go by without winning it. There was nothing in the world as pleasant as the long walk to the front of Assembly while I arranged my countenance into a haggard artistic expression.

I had made up my mind to be a writer. Unable to engage Jane's attention for such a prolonged venture, I persuaded another friend, Susan Terbell, to collaborate with me on a book. It was an ambitious undertaking, but I smelled money. My scheme was to write a book for and about twelve-year-olds *by* twelve-year-olds. During weekends for the rest of the seventh grade and over the next six months, Susan and I battered away on legal pads until the project was complete. It was entitled *The Riders of Red Devil*; the main action took place on a plantation and its climactic sequence was the upset winning of the Kentucky Derby by a pair of black twins (their combined weight that of a single jockey) improbably aboard the plantation owner's prize three-year-old (trained from colthood by the boys' father). I also executed a series of illustrations in watercolor. After reading it, nobody in either of our families took this enterprise seriously, but, out of kindness, Kenneth Wagg sent the finished manuscript to a friend at Simon & Schuster, where it created quite a stir. ("As to Brooke Hayward's manuscript, everyone agrees that it's wild, wooly, and quite wonderful. . . .") Mother, however, alarmed by the idea of the ensuing publicity, which, she felt, would capitalize on her name and have a negative influence on my budding career, vetoed the book's publication. I was furious, mentally having banked my first million.

But along the line I had become a good student. Bridget already was one. While I was out testing my new environment and rebelling against its restrictions, she had settled in. Methodical and industrious by nature, she always got excellent grades in every subject except gym. The only physical activity she enjoyed was modern dance, and she was good at it, with her agile, bony, double-jointed limbs, and saber-shaped legs, as Mother called them.

Wrapping them behind her head like a contortionist, she would, on request, manipulate herself hideously across the floor upside down on her hands and knees. She was well liked by her classmates and adored by her teachers, but kept very much to herself. She liked to be alone, preferred solitary amusements: painting, sketching, writing, sculpting, needlepoint—and was talented but very shy about it. "I have an inferiority complex," she used to say. Yet she could be gay, witty, charming. And at thirteen, with her fastidiously typed daily news bulletin, still the family chronicler:

SUMMER SUMMARY
June 16th, 1952
Editor
Bridget Hayward

SOCIETY

Mr. and Mrs. K. A. Wagg, of Clapboard Ridge Road, were present last night at a dinner party given by Miss Ann Seymour and her mother, Mrs. Ekert. It was a most enjoyable evening, but Miss Seymour left when the party was in full swing to attend a dance next door, given by Miss Vicki de Castro. Mrs. Wagg's daughter was not invited because of a feud between the two families.

. . . .

130 people were at a charming dance given by Miss Brooke Hayward last Wednesday night. Among the guests was Mr. Danny Selznick, who was the Waggs' house guest for the night. Many people said that the dance was a great success.

. . . .

TRY A CAN OF
HORLICK'S
PUFFBALLS
DELICIOUS—NUTRICIOUS
ONLY 50¢ PER CAN

. . . .

AGRICULTURE

Miss Seymour and Mrs. Ekert are using on their roses a new fertilizer. Among its revolting ingredients are fish meal and dried blood. Although these ladies have great faith in their fertilizer, the feeling is not mutual in the Wagg home.

. . . .

SWIMMING

Many of Bill Hayward's young friends are expected to invade the swimming pool this afternoon. We hope the damage will not be great.

. . . .

NOTICE

For the benefit of anyone who likes apple pie, there is some, freshly baked. We might have it for dinner.

. . . .

The Hayward children had their trunks sent off to their camps today.

. . . .

GONE WITH THE WIND
EXPEDITION TURNS BACK
FOR DIRECTIONS . . .
Yesterday Mr. and Mrs. Wagg, Brooke and Bridget Hayward traveled into N.Y. to see Gone With the Wind. When halfway into New York, it was discovered that the directions were missing. So the four

turned back and recovered them. Then Susan Terbell, a SLICK CHICK, was picked up at her house. Spelling games were played en route, and they had lunch at McGinnis' restaurant. Then the party went to the preview theater where they were to meet Danny Selznick. But he was not there! Finally he appeared, but he had forgotten Mr. Wagg's pants which he had taken by mistake when spending the night with the Waggs. Well, he promised to return them at the St. Regis Hotel where Kenneth could pick them up. Then the movie started and everyone was thrilled but tired when it was over (it took four hours). Everyone was very grateful to Mr. Selznick for arranging the screening.

Bridget and I were alternately best friends and archenemies. She was both repelled by and envious of my recklessness. I thought she was pallid and craven. The more flamboyantly I sprawled in every direction, the more righteously she pursed her lips and withdrew into herself. She became secretive. Her room was sacrosanct. Nobody was allowed to enter without her permission. This filled me with disgust, a disgust tinged with satisfaction; her behavior conceded my superiority. As we grew further apart, I was able to look back and recognize her ambivalence about me. For if, in the grand scheme of things, my chief combat was with Mother, Bridget had two dragons to slay: Mother and me. I didn't envy her that. Every so often I took Bridget's part against *us* (confusing, as I was apt to do in those days, myself with Mother or Mother with me). On Bridget's fourteenth birthday, Mother gave her another doll. Bridget may have loved it, but I was incensed. I thought she was too old for dolls even if she didn't look it. To add insult to injury, her first evening dress, which accompanied the doll, had polka dots and little sleeves. The temptation to treat Bridget as a baby was hard enough for me to resist without Mother making matters worse.

There was no longer any way to describe our feelings about Mother, not even among ourselves. Sometimes in Bridget's room after dinner—or at dinner, if Mother and Kenneth went out—we tried, but it was useless. We didn't have the vocabulary. Our feelings had lost all logic; conflict had rendered them blotchy, convoluted, and impressionistic, and without any training in any method of expressing anger or frustration—except not to—we were stumped. We certainly couldn't express them to Mother. "I'm your best friend," she would say, "and if you have *any* problem, you should come to me first." But that was a trap, because whenever we presented her with a disagreeable fact, or argued with her, or crossed her, or chafed at a policy we thought unfair, she would do one of two things. Either she would override our dissent with a twenty-minute sermon or lapse into wounded silence, a silence that was anything but passive. We knew, subconsciously, that it was a form of repressed anger, but it didn't make our own anger any easier to blurt out. There was no way to win. Once I said that to her, and she was quite taken aback. When it came down to it, I was more argumentative than Bridget and Bill; they were cleverer, although no less resentful. I fought a lot of battles, theirs as well as mine, and spent a lot of time in my room, working off the punishment for my insubordination.

Sometimes, however, in that suspended time before all was forgiven, Mother would visit my solitary confinement, and push things along. "Perhaps," she would muse, "you would be happier living with your father." Although she made that sound like a punishment, too, I sensed that she was just momentarily anxious about her inability to be a perfect parent. As usual, she was over-zealous. Her standards were too high. "No," I would answer, "I don't want to go and live with Father." Even though it was a very appealing idea. "Why not? Clearly he can offer you a lot that I can't. . . ." That was true, too. But I wouldn't have betrayed her for anything. "I want to stay here. I have all my friends, I'm doing well in school, this is my family, I'd miss Bridget and Bill." Molli-fied, she would leave my room and wait. For my apology.

Bridget, Bill, and I often puzzled over whether we were what had changed or Mother. We thought maybe she'd been different before the divorce; now it was hard to believe she and Father could ever have been in love, let alone involved in the kind of intimacy that might result in three children. Mother had established, in the last few years, a *modus operandi* that eliminated her speaking to Father at all. She would make arrangements to leave the house before his arrival, on the rare occasions he visited us there, and to return after he'd gone. The obligatory details of our visits to him were handled by Kenneth Wagg over the telephone. Mother was adamant. She said it was too difficult. We couldn't figure out how we'd been born. We were confused and ashamed, when we did go to see Father (never often enough), about enjoying ourselves thor-oughly; it seemed an act of deliberate disloyalty to Mother. For her sake, we'd misrepresent the extent of our pleasure, respond too casually to her questions. "Tell me everything!" she'd exhort us breathlessly. "Well," we'd say, having trained ourselves to look straight at her when we lied, "it was okay." If we raved, she was bravely crestfallen. If we'd told her how splendid Father's house was, how beautiful and generous our stepmother Nan, how thrilling the entire weekend had been, the look on her face would have been unbearable. One of the keynotes of Mother's personality was her ebullient curiosity, but when it extended to Father its pitch was off center. In that area, she applied her acting skills to no avail; we refused to be duped by their charm. Our answers were nonchalant or evasive. Or lies. Once, when Father called during dinner to ask if we could visit him the following weekend, I burst into tears at the table and heard myself blurting that I didn't want to go. That couldn't have been more untrue. We leaned over backward to protect her, and ourselves, but from what we didn't know.

We had not quite forgiven her for letting Emily go. We were getting old enough to look after ourselves, she'd decided; besides, it was high time for her to shoulder all the duties of an average mother. Much healthier for all of us. Otherwise we ran the risk of being pampered and she ran the risk of having her impact on us undercut by a nurse. We'd become too attached to Emily; a change was in order. And so, just before we'd moved to Greenwich, Emily had gone back to California to work for David O. Selznick as nurse to his stepsons Bobby and Michael Walker. That was as bad as losing Father. We were insanely jealous and wept for days. Once Emily was gone, there was no buffer between the three of us and Mother. We tried to substitute our black cook of several years, Elizabeth Hill, in the role of chief confidante, but Elizabeth's capacity was limited. She rose at five o'clock every morning, did all the housework and laundry, and cooked three sensational meals a day. If we wanted to unburden ourselves of a grudge, we'd go to the kitchen and hang over the sink while Elizabeth made lemon chiffon pie or floating island. "Don't bother me," she'd grumble, "and keep your fingers out of my nice clean pastry." After a while, complimented by our rapt attention, she would soften up and listen to our tales of woe. It was very soothing in the kitchen, very safe, mainly because Elizabeth snarled at anybody who entered it, including Mother. Mother was sufficiently intimidated by Elizabeth that she found it expedient to overlook both the radio—one of her pet peeves—on the tile counter, blaring forth Bing Crosby or the "Jack Benny Show," and the New York *Daily News,* to which Elizabeth subscribed, with its tabloid sensationalism spread across the kitchen table. Bridget, Bill, and I could be found any night of the week down in the sanctity of the kitchen, watching Elizabeth make dinner. We learned to cook, not by lifting a finger—she was too proud and possessive for that—but by years of hungry vigilance while she (pretending not to notice us) prepared one spectacular Southern dish after another. We loved her radio and her *Daily News.* "Elizabeth," I'd say, daydreaming, "someday I'm going to marry Marlon Brando." (It was unbearably distressing to me when Marlon married Anna Kashfi instead. But I forgave him and temporized. After all, we'd never met.) "You're not taking this seriously, Elizabeth. Wait till I'm eighteen. He'll divorce her, you'll see." Elizabeth would glance at me across the egg whites she was beating for meringue; her nod was worth pure gold. "Hmm," she'd capitulate, swayed by the ferocity of my determination. "Maybe." When she was in a good mood, she was a wonderful audience.

Shortly after we moved to Greenwich, a heavy crate was delivered to our house with a lot of hoopla. In it was a gift from Father: one of the first television sets on the market. From the moment of its arrival, Mother treated it like an unwelcome intruder and strictly curtailed our watching to no more than three programs a week, one for each of us. We began to look forward to the evenings when she went out to dinner; the minute she left the house we'd disobediently race for the set and, feeling giddy and light-headed, stay up way past bedtime watching the black-and-white cowboy movies that were heavily featured in the pioneer days of TV. As time went by, programming became more sophisticated and Elizabeth joined our clandestine nocturnal huddle. Occasionally, thinking she heard car wheels on the gravel driveway, she'd spring up and look out the window. "Just another five minutes," she'd say brusquely, and settle down for another hour. Best of all were the two weeks every spring when Mother went down to the Bahamas or the Virgin Islands to get some sun. She never understood why we didn't mind her being away. "My darlings," she'd apologize, "I hate leaving you like this—like a rat deserting a sinking ship. Will you be able to manage without me?" We'd extend her our sweetest long-suffering smiles and assure her that we'd make do somehow; off she'd go, down to the balmy coral-flecked beaches where she loved to sunbathe nude, and we, left behind, would blithely plump up our pillows in front of the television set. One night, Elizabeth, Bridget, and I stayed up until two o'clock watching *The Dead Don't Die*, a vampire movie that so profoundly terrified all of us that we went to bed in my room with crucifixes around our necks, our arms crossed over our chests as we lay rigidly staring up at the ceiling.

For all its shortcomings, television did link us to the rest of the world. When it came to covering events of consequence (Current Events, as the biweekly mandatory course at the Academy was called), television became a kind of animated newspaper. Although Mother herself was not a devotee of baseball, she tolerated—from a distance—our annual involvement with the World Series, then dominated by the New York Yankees and the great Joe DiMaggio. And even she had to admit, when it came to the first televised presidential campaign—Dwight D. Eisenhower versus Adlai Stevenson—that television wasn't all bad. I never thought I'd see Mother firmly entrenched in front of Father's "folly," as it was referred to, but all during the McCarthy hearings, she ordered lunch and dinner served in the playroom, to which she'd banned the accursed television set. That was quite a time. We children were treated to the privilege of observing Mother's rage, at its most imaginatively expressed, directed not at us but at the flickering images of Senator Joseph McCarthy, Vice-President Richard Nixon, and counsel Roy Cohn.

Meanwhile, Father was busying himself with a truly Machiavellian scheme. He'd determined to acquire a large fortune one way or another. So it was that Maisie Plant Hayward, the Colonel's widow, re-entered our lives. Father, as her stepson, was her most logical heir. After all, she had no other living family. Once or twice a year, we children, innocent and fresh-faced (so Father convinced himself for this purpose), were called on to remind Maisie of his existence. And at her signal we would collect for afternoon tea at the Fifth Avenue mansion.

Maisie had reduced her living quarters to a section of the top floor: an incredible domed conservatory where the elevator arrived, a sitting room, bedroom, bathroom, which I remember chiefly for its black onyx bathtub standing on four solid-gold claw feet, and Agnes's room. (Agnes was Maisie's faithful personal maid.)

More interesting by far than the obligatory visit and tea (vanilla ice cream for Father and us) was the rest of the house. The servants' quarters in the basement particularly caught my fancy; the servants' dining-room table was always set for twelve, with twelve half-grapefruits topped by maraschino cherries.

"Twelve!" I would invariably gasp. "Twelve people to take care of one!"

"Goddamn barmaid," was Father's stock reply.

A ballroom took up one of the six floors. It stretched clear from Fifth Avenue on one side to Madison Avenue on the other. We found it incomprehensible that Maisie had holed herself up in three or four of the least amusing rooms of her domain—along with an odd assortment of card tables on which to display an even odder assortment of pillboxes and jigsaw puzzles.

"Father," I'd whisper after a while, placing one hand delicately over my favorite ruby-studded box when Maisie wasn't looking, "do you *really* think she'd notice if this disappeared?"

"Yes I do. She probably counts them every morning."

I never dared ask her if she'd leave it to me when she died. She wasn't like Grandsarah at all. Afterward in the checker cab on the way down Fifth Avenue, Father would stretch with relief.

"Got it all sewed up this time," he'd say. "You kids were a tremendous help. Can't stand to go there by myself."

But when, several years later, Maisie did die, Father's hope died with her. She didn't leave him a cent. Her vast fortune went to charity and Agnes.

In the fall of 1950, Mother and Kenneth were married. It had been a long courtship, quite long enough, we thought, having tried every trick in the book to get Kenneth to propose in front of us. In the end, our feelings about him as a stepfather were mixed. We had reservations about his ability to keep Mother in line. The problems we expected him to solve were insoluble. "She walks all over him," Bridget used to say, sniffing. "He's so dotty about her he never takes our part even when she's wrong. It's unjust." But he was a kind man, with a gentle sense of humor and awesome reserves of patience; sometimes I couldn't help wondering if matters wouldn't be much worse without him around. He gave to our lives a semblance of structure and continuity if not the excitement we longed for. And there was a bizarre side to the mild-mannered, slightly stuffy Englishman the world saw: he was a crack gambler who had once supported himself handsomely by winning at chemin de fer in casinos all over the South of France and private clubs all over London. Although he'd long since kicked the habit by stringently disciplining himself to stay away from places like Le Touquet and Biarritz, there was no card game at which Kenneth did not excel. "I've always held better cards than anyone I know" was his modest way of putting it. As a result, Mother, who was a natural cardsharp, took up bridge, and two or three times a week invited various of their Greenwich cronies over for dinner and a cutthroat match. On those evenings, Elizabeth would really outdo herself, and we'd start hanging around the kitchen the minute the school bus dropped us off; also, with much fanfare, we'd be offered sherry before dinner and wine instead of milk, a privilege to which Bridget and Bill held their noses but of which I took full advantage. ("I can see you're going to turn into an alcoholic someday." Mother's prediction was only half joking. "All the same, my theory is it's better for you to get drunk under parental supervision than out at some wild party. Promise me one thing: if you ever have the misfortune to find yourself in a car with an inebriated beau behind the steering wheel, hop out—even if you're in the middle of the Merritt Parkway. And don't hitchhike home." "What'll I do?" "Carry a dime and call a taxi." "In the middle of the Parkway?" "Don't quibble.") Also, in spite of his pudgy physique—Bridget's nickname for him was "Uncle Barrel"—Kenneth was a champion racquets player and belonged to the Racquets Club in New York City where he could pursue a game of backgammon between matches. Good-naturedly disregarding our merciless teasing about his potbelly, he retired gigantic silver trophy upon trophy from which we drank champagne loving cups at Christmas.

The four Wagg boys remained in England for their schooling at Sunningdale and Eton; Kenneth worked out a set of logistics that kept him in perpetual rotation between their holidays in England, his job running Horlick's Malted Milk in Racine, Wisconsin, and his second family in Greenwich, Connecticut. This routine was not entirely to Mother's satisfaction. She likened it to Alec Guinness's in *The Captain's Paradise*, playfully feigning jealousy about a consortium of imaginary mistresses. Eventually Kenneth gave up Horlick's and joined a travel agency in New York City to which he commuted daily. In the summer of 1951, he fulfilled one of his fondest dreams by arranging to bring his four sons to this country for part of their holiday. The plan called for them to join us at a family camp on Squam Lake, New Hampshire.

That also happened to be the summer Mother decided to build a swimming pool. Typically, she exhausted herself overseeing every inch of the construction. ("Why, when I am having a pool built, do I have to enter so fully into pool building, do I have to identify myself with every workman? Why do I have to give the whole of myself to whatever I undertake, whether it's to you children, the house, acting, packing, reading, loving—or hating? Why, whenever someone tells me a sad story, do I suffer so much more than the sufferer? There must be a flaw in my character.") After a few weeks of throwing herself into camp life at Squam Lake, organizing picnics, tennis matches, expeditions, games, and so on, she announced that she had to go away for a rest; she was tired of friends and children, of feeling neglected, of being cooped up without a breathing space. "All I need is a week," she said, "of being selfish eight hours a day." So she drove back to Greenwich alone to recuperate. A week later, fully refreshed, she was back as if nothing had happened.

Although she had never done anything like that before, we were not, at the time, remotely unsettled by her behavior. It seemed a natural extension of the ordinary. We'd become accustomed to, charmed—when not irritated—by the way her emotions rose and fell, cyclically, like the tides. And always she was so sure of herself, so *positive* even about the negative, so uncompromisingly opinionated, we accepted many of her eccentricities without question. She lived by them. "It's my nature," she warned gaily, "to go around in high spirits most of the time and then to collapse." A few years later, I remembered that piece of self-evaluation with a chill.

Periodically, Mother would go through her accounts and conclude she was going bankrupt. Nothing was further from the truth, but when she'd announce she was broke and would have to go back to work, we, in turn, would commiserate out loud and smile to ourselves, knowing that she'd read a script that excited her. The first time she came out of retirement was in 1949, to make a movie, *No Sad Songs for Me*. Her explanation to the three of us and to Kenneth was both earnest and self-mocking: "I feel I should earn the money while I can; forget my principles, sacrifice my integrity, and go back to Hollywood. This means being a career woman—and a neglectful mother—for two years in order to get some security. This plan will be known as my two-year plan and certainly excludes marriage—much too expensive and distracting. I'm meeting Cohn, head of Columbia, on Tuesday, and think I'm about to cry. It's sort of like goodbye forever."

Forever was three months in Hollywood. During the shooting of the film, Mother's letters and phone calls exemplified what we came to recognize as constitutional extremes of temperament, more pronounced when she worked than ever before. Everyone was so kind and complimentary it frightened her: secretaries came out of their offices to say how proud they were to have her on the lot; the producer and director were wildly enthusiastic; they all seemed to have such high expectations that she wanted to crawl back into her little Greenwich home. She felt she was posing as an actress. Her acting was phony, old-fashioned, theatrical; if she continued to be as bad, they would have to replace her. One day she was wonderful, the next she stank.

No Sad Songs for Me was the last movie Mother ever made. It was our undeniable right, we argued vociferously, to be allowed, this one time, to see her on the screen; we were old enough not to be warped by the experience and it would be our last chance. Kenneth, similarly disadvantaged, backed us up. Mother's capitulation was based on the premise that her performance was so awful we would all be disappointed enough to discourage her from working again. Adhering to a rigid policy that she never see herself in a movie, not even in daily rushes, she waited nervously for us outside the Radio City Music Hall where *No Sad Songs for Me* was breaking records as the Easter attraction. We emerged dazed and shaken, unable to differentiate between our mother and the woman we had just seen die of cancer. For the next few weeks we treated her with inordinate tenderness ("Never have I known any of you to be so dear and well behaved"), and insisted that she go to the doctor for a thorough checkup.

In 1952, again claiming she was broke—but, according to our private appraisal, just plain bitten by the bug—Mother returned to the Broadway stage after almost nine years of absence. The play was Terence Rattigan's *The Deep Blue Sea*, brought over from London by Alfred de Liagre, her old friend and producer of *The Voice of the Turtle*. Never able to justify any half-measure undertaking, she "adored" the play, "adored" Terry Rattigan, "adored" Delly.

We were far more excited than she. At last we were going to witness the revelation of her most profound secret: what she was really like as an actress. She was about to breathe life into those old press clippings that lay yellowing and collecting dust—concealed from whom did she think?—behind the blue leather covers of the ten or so scrapbooks. We were going to have the chance to sit in a theater filled with anonymous people all paying for the privilege of sharing her with us. We would hear the applause, the oohs and ahs, the sighs, the comments, the coughs all around us; at the sound of the familiar husky voice, we would smile, titillated by the bitter-sweet pleasure of knowing her in a way nobody else could. We took turns cuing her with her lines; she was word perfect when she went to the first cast reading. We were not taken aback at the discovery that she was even more self-demanding as an actress than as a mother. Nor were we baffled by her protestations of hatred for what she was doing, nor by her nightly fulminations about the rehearsal, the director, the two leading men, the part, herself in it, and anybody, everybody who could not immediately rectify matters with the most constructive criticism—which to her meant telling her, line by line, scene by scene, how lousy an actress she was. It all made beautiful sense. It all added up to the intangible whatever-it-was we already knew about Mother.

But what was amazing, stupefying, stunning was the impression we had of her on opening night. We were unprepared. We had no idea, no idea at all. She was absolutely wonderful. "I rely on you to be my harshest critics," she'd said wistfully when we'd kissed her backstage beforehand. And she was right; Brooks Atkinson was no better equipped than we. Exposed to every nuance, every trick in her performances at home, we were primed to pick her performance on stage to pieces. But on stage all the tricks fell into place. Gestures, movements, voice inflections that might seem a shade too broad, too histrionic for the business of everyday life were totally right when mounted on a proscenium, bathed in intense light, and viewed from a distance of thirty-odd feet. We were shocked that she had ever given up—for whatever reason, even if it happened to be us—a profession at which she excelled.

"Damn," I growled out of the corner of my mouth at intermission, "it works better here than in life." Bridget jabbed my ribs with her elbow. But it was true. I resented Mother for alleging that her talent was less important than the happiness of her three children. Given a choice, we would have been just as happy all these years if we could have cued her and watched her go out where she belonged.

Afterward, I told her that. Not in her dressing room with clumps of friends and well-wishers squeezing through to congratulate her, but out on the street, past the stage door jammed with autograph seekers—through which she strode looking neither left nor right, even when they squealed, "Miss Sullavan, Miss Sullavan!" and plucked at her coat and beseeched her with their outstretched autograph books—as we accompanied her to Sardi's or wherever the traditional celebration was held that night.

"Mother," I said, trying to keep pace with her, "how could you ever retire? Was it really to raise children? We don't want that excuse hanging around our necks—you're no housewife and we didn't ask you to be. We were well enough taken care of—what about all those nurses and cooks and gardeners? Now we feel gypped."

"*Gypped?*" She swung around, her voice cracking with amusement.

"Well"—I gulped, thoroughly excited by my daring—"cheated. You *are* Margaret Sullavan. What's wrong with that?"

The answer, which came later as we were driving home along the Merritt Parkway and which was revived in one form or another whenever the subject of acting came up again, was: "Most actors are basically neurotic people. Terribly, terribly unhappy. That's one of the reasons they become actors. Nobody well adjusted would ever want to expose him or herself to a large group of strangers. Think of it. Insanity! Generally, by their very nature—that is, if they're at all dedicated—actors do not make good parents. They're altogether too egotistical and selfish. The better the actor—and, I hate to say it, the bigger the star—why, the more that seems to hold true. Honestly, I don't think I've ever known one—not one! —star who was successfully able to combine a career and family life. The children usually grow up to be delinquents. That's why"—she was addressing us from the front seat of the Nash Rambler as Kenneth drove, and her face, as she twisted in her seat, was very earnest— "I didn't want to delude myself that I could do it either. Hold down the two jobs simultaneously. And I so much wanted to have the fun of being just a mother and nobody else. Believe me, I've never for one day regretted forgoing my career to spend time with the three of you. Never. It was much more important to me to be with you during your most formative years. Besides"—she yawned and smiled—"you know how I hate hard work."

"But," I persisted, "you must have liked it once."

"Yes," replied Mother, serious again. "When I began. It seemed very natural then. Now—I can't explain why—my zest is gone. I suppose there's a love-hate feeling. I do love rehearsals; at least they're less dreary than playing the same part night after night. I used to think that acting was a kind of therapy, but now I think it creates psychological havoc. Actors become accustomed to being the center of attention, come to believe they're *special*, set apart from other people. That's dangerous and lonely. Actors *suffer*; look at all the instances of alcoholism, slit wrists, God knows what. As a result of which everybody else around suffers, too. Madness! And the built-in competition to be *special*, to be *different*, is deplorable. There are many fine, talented actors you've never heard of, while some of the most successful have no talent at all; they're just better at getting attention. If *any* of you ever decides you want an acting career, I warn you I shall do everything in my power to prevent it."

One of the fringe benefits of *The Deep Blue Sea* was the routine that it imposed on Mother's life, one that was as much a grievance to her as a godsend to us. She arose long after we'd left for school, which freed the breakfast table for reading or arguing to our hearts' content. Then, in order to get to the theatre in time to apply her make-up, she caught the 6:25 train into New York. This facilitated illicit television viewing and two-hour phone conversations with friends. Before matinée days, she would spend Tuesday and Friday nights in the city, which was a real boon. Normal discipline broke down; Elizabeth was mostly bark and no bite.

Another benefit was the new stature we gained socially from having a famous mother at work. Whereas before, few of our peers had had the opportunity to see her in anything (the days when first-class movies would be rerun on television were yet to come), now they could judge for themselves. Or their parents could judge for them. Besides, there was publicity to be sopped up; although Mother shunned publicity, she couldn't completely curtail it. *Life* magazine came out and photographed her for an article:

CITY CELEBRITY IN COUNTRY SETTING

Margaret Sullavan manages with no trouble at all to lead a happy double life. Six nights a week she is a grand lady of the Broadway stage, taking curtain calls to tidal waves of applause after her great personal success in *The Deep Blue Sea*. Ten minutes later her other life begins. She runs out the stage door into a waiting taxi and catches the 11:25 commuters' train for her country house near Greenwich, Connecticut. There she becomes Mrs. Kenneth Wagg (husband is in the malted milk business) and busies herself with a hundred household chores having to do with her three children, her servants, kitchen, garden and dog. . . .

We were all photographed eating Virginia ham and skating on the frozen pond. And then, in the spring, when the pink dogwoods were at the height of their glory and the garden was solid tulips and daffodils, *Life* came back and photographed me in a strapless evening dress for an article on daughters of the stars.

That Mother would give her blessing to this latter idea was extremely odd, but, breaking her own rules with as much verve as she kept them, she even added a touch of mascara to my lashes and powdered my nose. ("I thought you forbid us to wear make-up on penalty of death." "Absolutely *verboten*; most unbecoming. Hold still and don't bat your eyelids. You're so lucky to have the sort of face that won't ever need much touching up; this is an exception; don't get any ideas. In photographs, details can get washed out.") Afterward, when the fashion editor offered me the strapless dress as a gift, Mother, to my further astonishment, let me keep it.

Then, one afternoon a few weeks later, she mysteriously called me into the living room after school. "I have a surprise for you," she said, and handed me the June 1st copy of *Life*. I was on the cover. "Margaret Sullavan's 15-year-old Brooke," read the caption. I felt as if the breath had been knocked out of me.

"But, Mother," I gasped, inanely scrutinizing the life-size photograph of my profile under the red-and-white *Life* banner, "did you know? Did you give them permission?"

She smiled, very pleased. "I felt I owed it to you" was her answer, and she would not elaborate.

As this occurred just before school let out and the annual summer country club dances began, I was able to derive a maximum of attention from my cover. Fellow tenth-graders were reverential; snotty juniors and seniors nodded to me in the corridors between classes. A new delegation of boys from Brunswick, older and more sophisticated, with drivers' licenses and their own cars and a practiced way of dancing close, of kissing good night, of introducing themselves to Mother and Kenneth while everyone

waited for my grand entrance down the front stairs, began mate-
rializing. "Sniffing around," Elizabeth grunted. Bill surreptitiously
took a roll of nude pictures of me skinny-dipping and sold them to
Brunswick students for black-market prices. He had quite a profit-
able business going until Mother confiscated the negatives. And
Bridget, although she never said a word, was envious; I could tell
by her silence.

Bridget, at fourteen, was becoming as impossible in her own
way as I had been in mine. (Mother and I liked to think I had, by
now, passed through the most acute fevers of adolescence.)
Bridget's way was quite different. Her rebellions took the form of
strange fasts and silences. She hid her uneaten food in the playroom cupboards. Once when I searched there for paints, I came
upon a lump of desiccated liver wrapped in paper napkins. By
mentally retracing our dinner menus as far back as I was able, I
reckoned the age of that petrified scrap at two months.

Bridget's silences drove Mother crazy. Mother did not like to
be ignored. And Bridget did not like to be criticized. She might
withdraw to her room and not be seen again for many hours. Nor
did she like what she considered to be Mother's insincere, larger-
than-life charm. What, in fact, Mother thought of as Southern
graciousness, Bridget saw as strained, fake, hypocritical.

For instance, Mother might hurl down the telephone and
exclaim, "Good gooby, what a bore Helen Dodge is. She's on her
way over here right this minute with a smoked turkey—I'm
trapped! There goes my beautiful selfish morning, my nude sun-
bathing, and my fingernails, my toenails, my clean hair, my
checks!"

And then, when Helen Dodge rang the doorbell ten minutes
later, Mother would embrace her as if they were long-lost sisters
and beg her to stay for lunch. At lunch, increasingly offended by
Mother's effusive high spirits, Bridget would say less and less,
barely answering poor Helen Dodge's well-meant questions about
school.

Mother would cringe with shame, which she contrived to
conceal with sparkling bravado: "Speak up, darling! You're mum-
bling and you know how deaf I am."

Slowly, as if a shade were being drawn over a window,
Bridget's face would withdraw from the conversation as well. Move
by move, she would match Mother's act with her own. It was

unsettling to witness. The more animated Mother became, the more expressionless Bridget. Her unmistakable aim was to become invisible and vanish.

"How could you do this to me?" Mother would fume afterward. "You know perfectly well that *any* and *every* guest in my house is to be treated with respect *whatever the circumstances*—in the middle of an earthquake, for God's sake! You've been brought up to have good manners, you've been set a good example by both your father and me—in this respect, at least, we concur— Where do you think you're going? Don't roll your eyes up to heaven and leave the room when I'm talking to you!"

Bridget remained but, without saying a word, made it clear she was no longer present.

It was decided that I should go to boarding school for my junior and senior years. A Swiss boarding school had long been one of Mother's dreams: "You're so lucky that I can afford it; oh, I would give anything to have the opportunity to ski beautifully, to speak perfect French!" But, because I was swept up in the Greenwich social whirl and couldn't bear to leave it, I scotched that dream in favor of something closer to home. Bridget, on the other hand, suddenly professed a desire to get as far away as possible. To everyone's surprise, she announced that she would actually prefer to go to Switzerland. Then Bill, having considered his life alone without his two sisters, decided he, too, wanted to go away to school. So, in the fall of 1953, the three of us left home.

I was sixteen, Bridget fourteen, Bill twelve. It never occurred to me it was the last time we would live together as a family.

For all my resistance to the idea of leaving my beloved friends, my feature-story contests, my pink-and-white room, my role as troublemaker and provocateur, my convoluted flirtations, I'd begun to look forward to the novelty of freedom. Mother— after a winter of hauling me up and down the Eastern seaboard to investigate all the blue-chip girls' schools, and of glossing over my bothersome candor when interviewed by their eager headmistresses ("No, Miss St. John, actually I *don't want* to go away to school; I'm happy where I am")—had, on her own, entered me at the Madeira School, located in Greenway, Virginia, just outside Washington, D.C. Madeira was reputed to be very strict and academically tough; it also satisfied certain social and geographical requisites. ("Lucky you to be in Virginia, my home state!")

Greenwich had come to fit me comfortably. I'd broken it in, maybe outgrown it. Crucial events had taken place under its sheltering sky. My first evening dress, properly virginal—white organdy, ruffled, off-the-shoulder—followed by many other evening dresses, graduating to a strapless tulle, nipped in above by a painful waist cincher that left its hook marks on my flesh and a bone-stiffened bra that jabbed into the tender spot between my breasts, with its skirt belled out below by a set of crinolines modishly collected like silver bracelets. It was a time when countless orchid corsages were left to shrivel in the icebox.

Then there were my first stockings, sheer and seamed, and black suède heels—now, that had been some fight! Mother forbade them both until everyone else in the eighth grade had been sporting them for a year. She violently disapproved of all those emblems of budding eroticism. "You won't have anything to look forward to when you grow up," she'd remonstrate. "You'll become hardened and blasé. *I* didn't wear high heels till I was seventeen. And as for bras, it's pointless for me to waste money on a bra if you have nothing to fill it with." Consequently, my first bra was also the last bra to make an appearance in my class. I also had my first menstrual period, for which the fashionable euphemism at school was "falling off the roof." In those days we had euphemisms for anything remotely sexual.

My first kiss prompted another skirmish with Mother, when, after a Saturday-night party at Jackie Hekma's that started innocently with Ping-Pong and ended in the dark with a lot of rubbery, fumbling, spin-the-bottle-group embraces, I charged into the living room where Mother and Kenneth were playing bridge with friends to give them the good news of it. "I guess the time has come to explain promiscuity to you," said Mother ominously, squelching my enthusiasm.

Another problem was leaving all my romances behind. I fell in love every other week with someone new. And, of course, I liked to keep the discards hanging around. Ken Towe was my first older man. He drove a blue Ford convertible, and after I caught his eye, he used to speed up and down Clapboard Ridge Road, buzzing our house. One afternoon, I repaid his attentions by lining up Bridget, Bill, Susan Terbell, and myself on the side of the road with glasses of water snatched from the swimming pool. As he turned the car around and came toward us for the third time at fifty miles an hour, I gave a signal and we all threw our water at him. Mine hit his windshield and the blue Ford crashed into the traffic island at the bottom of our hill. Ken was furious; he had a broken nose and the steering wheel looked like an accordion. He yanked it off and threw it in the back seat. Mother came storming down the hill and, to my great mortification, Johnny Gladstone strolled toward the wreckage with a pipe between his teeth. Just out of college, and recently returned from a six-month research project in the Brazilian jungles (on a more fortunate occasion, he'd shown me his brace of pistols), Johnny was *truly* an older man, and this incident seemed to place him unequivocally beyond my reach. He calmly wiped the blood off Ken's face while Mother raced back for our car; then we hustled Ken off to the hospital emergency room. For some reason, Ken's ardor was in no way diminished, and he appeared at our house a few hours later, nose heavily bandaged, to escort me to a party. He was as smitten with Mother as with me—as were all my beaus, not surprisingly, since Mother could charm anyone, male or female, when she chose to—and long after he and I went our separate ways, he would come by to pay her a visit (and to sample Elizabeth's cooking).

Bridget regarded my romantic adventures with disdain. She claimed that my flirtatiousness was a bad habit and that it lacked finesse. Mother's, she admitted, at least had finesse. Bridget stayed away from boys, yet it was Bridget who had the courage to buck Mother's ban on leg-shaving. I found her in the bathroom scraping off blond fuzz with soap and a razor. "It's *my* body," she said airily, dotting her blood-specked shins with pieces of toilet paper. "I'll bet she doesn't even notice." But she did. Mother was outraged.

"Bridget Hayward," she began, building to hurricane force, "come here. Let me see your legs. My God, you've done it, you've disobeyed me and ruined your legs! How many times have I told you—from now on until you die, you will have *coarse black hair* sprouting all over your shins! I can't bear it, I can't *bear* it!" But Bridget never blanched. It was a landmark victory.

The fear of pregnancy was enough to effectively back up the code of sexual behavior our mothers prescribed for us. Heavy petting at the local drive-in theatre, or "passion pit" (another of Mother's bans), was considered racy. A far greater peril to our health and welfare was alcohol. I was beginning to run around with an older crowd, and Mother was justifiably concerned. More than once she reprimanded one or another of my suitors for carrying a bottle in his car. Once, spotting from her upstairs bathroom window young Scot Pierson transferring a case of gin from his car to another, she notified him at the top of her voice that he was never again to set foot on her property. Her dictums were not only stricter but more purposefully enforced than those of other parents, which was always a source of embarrassment to me. "Now, look," she'd say consolingly, "I understand how awkward it is to make explanations about being a nonconformist, I really do. But you have a perfectly legitimate excuse: blame me. Tell your friends that I'm eccentric, old-fashioned, whatever you wish. . . ." Of course, that was a specious argument since my identity was totally wrapped up in hers, but I couldn't articulate that. Besides, I was awed by her code of ethics, her skill at defending it, and her contempt for external opinion. I admired her even at my own expense. Once she took a position, she never yielded it. We found that the best way to get around her was deviously. J. D. Salinger's *The Catcher in the Rye*, the biggest best-seller of its time, was forbidden to me because, Mother maintained, it was so convincing, so *contemporary* a piece of writing it would seduce me. Into what I couldn't determine without reading it, so I filched a copy from Father, who was desperately trying to buy the movie rights. It remained hidden in my underwear drawer for years.

A *Streetcar Named Desire*, with my beloved Brando, was another example. Too provocative, she said, too overstimulating for someone my age to handle emotionally. All my friends went to the Saturday matinée at the Pickwick Theatre without me. (Ironically, Irene Selznick had offered my mother the role of Blanche du Bois in the original Broadway play, but on Father's advice she'd turned it down, another reason for my interest; Mother, however, was not to be swayed by that rationale.)

Had *she* ever been young and crazy and susceptible to ill-considered escapades? Heedless? Flighty? Had *she* ever been awakened in the middle of the night by pebbles thrown at her window? Rocky Fawcett used to climb up the tree by the side of the house, I'd wriggle out the casement, and we'd recline side by side on the sloping shingles of the roof until dawn, Rocky with a six-pack of beer and I with my heart in my mouth at the idea of what my punishment would be if either our German shepherd or Elizabeth heard us whispering. Had *Mother* ever eaten a live centipede? On a ten-dollar bet, *I*'d chewed and swallowed one during the intermission of the school's annual modern-dance program at the Greek amphitheatre; crunch, crunch; the audience was riveted. "Oh, my God!" hissed Mother. "Why do you always do these things for effect?" Had *she*, on a dare, ever boldly courted the town prostitute, rung the doorbell of her small frame house, admired her bottle of Chanel No. 5, and talked her into buying tickets for the school production of *The Pirates of Penzance?* This resulted in my being called into the principal's office again. "Brooke, dear," said Miss Campbell, with a sigh, "I have here a check for four dollars made out to the Greenwich Academy and signed 'Patsy Pine.' Is this—em—a valid signature?" "Yes, Miss Campbell." "How did you happen to obtain this—woman's signature?" "Well, Miss Campbell, during lunch hour I thought I'd apply myself to winning the ticket contest, so—" "Brooke, dear, I'm going to ask you to return this check: we can't have people like Miss Pine at school functions. You know what I mean." "But, Miss Campbell, she lives all alone and has no friends." "I'm sorry, Brooke, I can't bend school policy because Miss Pine is lonely."

Had *Mother* ever been an intrepid shoplifter? Not likely. *I*, on the other hand, was celebrated among my friends for my cool savoir-faire when it came to scooping up scarves—as many as twelve at once—from the counter at Woolworth's and exiting the store without any telltale ends peeping through my fingers. Once, finding myself penniless on Mother's Day, I enjoyed the pleasant irony of shoplifting the biggest potted plant I could carry out Woolworth's front entrance (not only to take home to Mother, but to satisfy my theory that, by exuding an air of complete authority, anyone could get away with anything).

Had *Mother* ever lain awake half the night dreaming about how Marlon Brando would make his first appearance in a green M.G., tires grinding up the gravel (I could definitely hear them if I listened carefully); how he would charge up the front stairs, brushing aside our dog's vicious attack, and gather me up in his arms? "Goodbye, everyone!" I would cry with glorious abandon, and out we would sweep to the M.G., never to return. Had *Mother* ever really been in love?

Had she loved Father madly, impetuously? Bridget, Bill, and I wanted it to be so. We badly and unrealistically wanted to believe that if Father came to the house for a visit, there might be some reconciliation between them. On one occasion we thought we might actually see them together in the same room again.

"Your father is driving out here Friday night," announced Mother. "Kenneth talked to him this morning, and he said to tell you girls he'd be delighted to take you to the Father-Daughter Dance at the Academy."

"Ooh, goody," we said, thinking we'd set up a foolproof encounter.

"He's coming early so he can spend some time with Bill, too," went on Mother. "You know how to offer him a drink and so on; Kenneth and I have made plans to go out to dinner that night."

"At six o'clock in the evening?" asked Bridget.

"Oh, come on, Mother," I said, exasperated. "Stop running away. He won't *bite* you. You act as if he's Heathcliff."

"Good God!" Mother clutched her throat melodramatically. "It's physically *impossible* for me to have the simplest, most prosaic conversation with Leland, but to have to be charming, here in my own house? I'm *much* too cowardly. Within minutes all my good intentions and control would desert me. No, Kenneth and I will go out to dinner."

As much as she liked to congratulate herself on her ability to refrain from open hostility, once after I accused her of making Father inaccessible to us, she replied, "Your father's one of the most attractive men I've ever known, but that does not presuppose his talent as a father. He should *never* have been a father. But, to be honest, he has no pretensions about that. I do think he cares about you and loves you in some abstract way, without knowing how to show you. Besides, he's so addicted to his work he doesn't have the time. The brutal truth is his requests to see you are not as frequent as you'd like to think."

When asked about this, Father answered, "Goddamn right, all that red tape every time I want to see you kids. Why does Maggie make a goddamn Dreyfus case out of everything? Simple plans, dinner. I used to ask her where she'd like to have dinner and it would take two hours to resolve what restaurant. Must drive you kids nuts. Thank God that's not my problem any more. It's funny, too, you know, she could be the most sensational dame in the world when she put her mind to it. Well, if the going gets too rough, you can always knock on my front door." It seemed we were caught between two diametrically opposed points of view. Or three or four.

Therefore, when Mother let Bridget and me (Bill was at camp) visit Father in Bermuda for two weeks in the summer of 1953 before going off to boarding school, we were thrilled. We found him irresistible, although we hesitated at coming out and saying so. Somehow we believed a precarious balance might be disturbed if we opened our mouths. We foresaw two possible outcomes to any impulsive expression of love for Father: one, Mother would feel slighted, which would be bad enough; or two, she'd disapprove, and not let us see him any more. Either way we'd be jeopardizing the status quo, so we didn't even let *Father* know how much we loved him.

That two-week trip was the longest stretch of time we'd spent with him in seven years. He was then at the height of his career. A series of hits like *Mr. Roberts, South Pacific,* and *Call Me Madam* had followed one right after another. He'd also, since 1948, presented *Anne of the Thousand Days, The Rat Race, The Wisteria Trees, Daphne Laureola, Remains To Be Seen,* and *Point of No Return.* The pressure of working on one of his productions, probably *Wish You Were Here,* had worn him out. Whenever he opened a play, Father went without sleep for days on end, and then, having pushed himself into a state of exhaustion, got on a plane to someplace quiet where he could sleep and sleep until he'd revived. In Bermuda, he'd rise about noon, putter around the bungalow kitchen making a batch of brioches or croissants, and go back to bed until dinner. Bridget and I were in heaven. We weren't accustomed to the luxury of hotel living, of unrestricted room service, of unsupervised time, of coral beaches and green seas right outside our window. At dinner every night, we ordered daiquiris and filet mignon—no questions asked, no expense spared.

This regime, or lack of it, was completely at odds with Mother's stringent attempts to see that we led a relatively un-spoiled existence. "Who the hell's going to spoil you if I don't?" asked Father, pleased at the effect our vacation was having. "Good for you to be spoiled once in a while. God, Maggie's a tightwad—I wish to hell she'd buy you some decent clothes. Whenever you come to see me, you're all wearing the worst-looking rags. I'm sure she sends you off like that deliberately. She knows I'll have to outfit you from top to bottom before I can set foot on the street with you." (This was true; we always came back from our infrequent weekends together with a new wardrobe from Bonwit Teller's and Brooks Brothers, which Father would have devoted all Saturday to selecting.)

Perhaps the most important factor in any of our visits was the influence of our stepmother, Nancy. Father called her Nan, and that's what she was to us. She was wonderful to look at, very tall and angular, with legs like a giraffe, yet in spite of that, she had a surprisingly voluptuous quality. Maybe it was her lips, or laugh, or just the way her flesh was attached to her bones. Nan wore a lot of Mainbocher. Her collection of shoes rivaled Father's. She was a connoisseur of style, however it was packaged, and had learned, long ago, to define her own. When bad permanents and nightly sessions with curlers were in vogue, she wore her hair parted in the middle and austerely pulled back into a sleek chignon, and as if that weren't gumption enough, she sported huge horn-rimmed glasses. ("I might as well *see*—don't you think?—since my plan is to be around for a while.") So there was a startling ambiguity to her presence; the spare and the sensual. Even her jewelry, each piece of it, evoked a sense of its owner: heavy gold and diamond earrings so oversized she had to unclip them to talk on the telephone, and a pin fashioned to resemble a boutonnière, set with a stone an inch or two in diameter—as big as an actual flower—a sort of boldness that nobody else could carry off.

Bridget and I loved to browse through her closets, and Bill loved to bask in her attentions. "Have some more pepper, Billy," she'd say, with a chuckle, watching him grind black pepper over his smoked salmon until there was no pink visible. "You're a man after my own heart. No bland diets for you and me. Load everything up with spice—that's what life should be about."

We also had a stepsister, Kitty, Nan's daughter by Howard Hawks. Kitty was a pretty child, about nine years younger than I. She adored Father and, for a while, changed her name to Kitty Hayward. Although we were very fond of Kitty, we envied her the life we would have liked: a beautiful, chic, smart, funny, doting mother married to, of all people, our father. By comparison we felt unlucky, and we couldn't help making comparisons. Father's extravagance was legendary. He lived like a prince, and loved every minute of it.

"Leland's always had a compulsion to live beyond his

means," Mother once remarked caustically when we returned, flushed with pleasure and weighted down with gifts, from his house in Manhasset, Long Island. "If his income were a million dollars a year, he'd spend a million and a half." That may have been somewhat exaggerated, but we thought it was glorious.

"That's his affair," Bridget mumbled under her breath.

"Not entirely," retorted Mother, better able to hear some mumbles than others. "It's *my* affair when he sends you home with expensive cameras that would take you weeks around here to save up for, weeks of washing the car and mowing the lawn—when Leland casually hands you a twenty-dollar bill that represents a month of hard-earned allowance. It's really quite unfair, because—I realize he doesn't see you very often and it's perfectly natural for him to want to be very generous when he does, but—his generosity undermines the values that it's my responsibility to teach you. I would like to be able to be so cavalier—much more fun, I assure you. But I don't want you brought up with the impression that money is that simple to come by. Or that it can buy a good life. Or that it can buy—" She paused emphatically.

"What?" we answered, our hearts beginning to race with knowledge of what she was going to say next, and the fear of it.

"Love."

"Oh, Mother," I blurted. "He's not trying to *buy* our love—he knows we already love him."

"I'm not implying you don't," said Mother, a look of hurt outrage crossing her face (which reinforced my resolution never again to mention the word "love" as it applied to Father). "That's not what I'm talking about. I'm saying that by overindulging you on the *rare* occasions when you see him, Leland is—unintentionally, I'm sure—inviting you to correlate *money* and *love*. Very irresponsible of him. You're too young and impressionable to understand that love *can't* be rewarded by a two-hundred-dollar camera that you admired on his bureau this morning—and of which, incidentally, he happens to have twelve more. Don't look so guilty, darlings; it's not *your* fault. You can't help it if you come to that conclusion."

"Here we go again," said Bridget, her eyes fixed on the braided rug at her feet.

"*I* didn't come to that conclusion; *you* did." I shook my head and, ignoring Mother's protests, stalked grandly upstairs to my room. Maybe Father *was* just trying to make up for lost time, for affection he didn't know how to bestow on us any other way. If so, did it really make a difference? What counted was that he loved us, not whether he did so wisely or well.

So when Mother, at last believing we were old enough to handle the disparity in their life-styles, arranged for that prolonged visit with Father in Bermuda, ironically her fears were borne out. Bridget and I began to play one parent against the other. Father had the advantage. Not only were the novelty and glamour of the experience in his favor, but also the timing. We were just at the age where we dared to abandon our usual caution. We wanted to have an effect, even if it took the form of sabotage. Our pettiest gripes about Mother were aired. We found Father to be a sympathetic listener. We liked the feeling that he was in collusion with us, that although he could do little to remedy our problems, he understood them better than anyone. "God, I wish my hands weren't tied," he'd commiserate. Also Nan, with her coziness and flair, became more attractive to us than ever. The idea that we had another family to fall back on, should we alienate the old everyday one, gave us a sense of confidence. And even if I didn't see Father as having anything but a backup position in our lives, I think Bridget did. From that moment on, her dissatisfaction with life in Greenwich was total.

For the next two years, however, the potential explosion of Bridget's unhappiness was delayed because of the distance between Gstaad and Greenwich. Bill was safely tucked away at Lawrenceville, and I at Madeira. And that fall Mother went into rehearsals for *Sabrina Fair*.

Apart

In "*Sabrina*," audiences were asked to believe that Mother, then forty-four years old, was a twenty-three-year-old girl. Not surprisingly, they did. Even at close range, Mother radiated the illusion that she was blessed with eternal youth. According to Bennett Cerf in his *Saturday Review* column:

Playwright [Samuel] Taylor describes Sabrina as a "vibrant beautiful young lady in her early twenties" and persuading Maggie Sullavan, born (according to *Who's Who*) in 1909, to accept the role required a bit of doing. "I'm too old to play Sabrina," she wailed. Director Hank Potter was inclined to agree. Taylor did not. The day of decision was a scorcher last July. Taylor and Potter journeyed up to Maggie's Connecticut house for a final powwow. They found her at the pool in a very fetching and abbreviated bathing suit, with her two daughters aged sixteen and fourteen. Sceptic Potter looked hard at the trio and asked quite seriously, "Which of you three is Maggie?" She signed for the part of Sabrina there and then.

I, the greatest skeptic of all, came up on the train from Madeira to see for my own eyes. She was flawless in the play, and not a day over twenty. I sat in the second row defying her to betray her age by a mannerism, an inflection, and she did not. It was the most extraordinary illusion I have ever seen. Yet, strangely, her grace and charm and youth were *real*. Her performance was distinguished by one ingredient Mother claimed no respectable performance could ever be without: honesty. And she could be merciless in her expectations, whether of herself or of any other actor.

In spite of the anguish with which she regarded her profession, Mother, when actually working, was fiercely dedicated to it. Joseph Cotten, who played the male lead in "*Sabrina*," was amazed by the way, one night, she was able to assimilate thirty-odd changes into her performance. Hank Potter, the director, remembers quite vividly:

"*It was even more remarkable than that. What happened was that she had allowed that little wistful (trademark) note to color far too many lines in 'Sabrina.' I spoke to her about it when I went round at half-hour one night. I did not want to confuse things by being too specific just before a performance, but I told her to try and keep it in the back of her head when she played that night. She told me I was a lousy director, never gave her anything specific. No one had ever made that particular accusation to me before, and so I got out my notes and showed her about fifty detailed instances where this was happening. So she got mad at me and asked me how I dared upset the applecart just before the performance. She went out on the stage, gave a brilliant performance, and made the necessary changes in every single case, without touching in any way her customary reading of any line that had not been noted. I don't think anyone else, before or since, could have done it.*"

. . .

She could also be dedicated in her loyalty to fellow workers and friends. During tryouts in Philadelphia the play wasn't going too well.

Joe Cotten:

"It had begun to disintegrate, get out of control. Hank Potter was working so hard with Sam Taylor, the author, that he was neglecting the play on the stage a little bit. Everybody decided that Hank better go down to the Labrador retriever trials near Baltimore for a little rest. Bob Sherwood came down from the Playwrights' Company; he was very good for morale but not much better as a director for this particular play. It was going right down the drain. They were fiddling around, looking for another director. And Maggie told me that Hank Potter had been fired on his last play (Point of No Return) by Leland, that his recent history in theatre had been a series of flops; she was of the opinion that if he was dismissed from this one, his career in the theatre would probably be over. She didn't think he deserved that and she wasn't going to be responsible for it. She made it clear that if Hank was fired she wouldn't open with the play in New York. They brought up Equity and Maggie said, 'Do whatever you want, kick me out, but I'll be damned if I'll be responsible for Hank Potter's being buried as a director.' So they brought him back, and everything turned out all right. All he'd needed was a change of scenery."

Mother claimed that *"Sabrina"* was one of the happiest theatrical experiences of her career. Out of it came many lasting friendships: Joe and Lenore Cotten, Cathleen Nesbitt, Sam and Suzanne Taylor. But her conflict about wanting to work and not wanting to work was greater than ever. Millicent Osborn told me:

"Before she and Leland were divorced, she went to this analyst in California and after she'd been going there for a while, she came to me and said, 'You know all that nonsense I've been talking about —how I hate being recognized and how I hate the theatre and how I hate acting?' And I said, 'yes,' and she said, 'Well, I've discovered I love it.' And I said, 'How did you discover that?' And she said,

'Through my analysis.' Maggie maintained that she didn't mind the acting, as such, but she hated having to take a bow, she hated the audience rapport, she wanted to go on and presumably act in a vacuum—which of course was not true. She was deluding herself, because the very essence of acting is that you have an audience."

In Paul Osborn's opinion:

"I think that Maggie was so conflicted about being famous that she was unable to see herself as a public person. Consequently she used this idiot ruse of pretending she wasn't who she was. Yet at the same time she had a very distinctive outward appearance, which she made no attempt to disguise. She both liked the adulation and hated it. Subconsciously she wanted it and she hated herself for wanting it, so she pretended she didn't want it at all. I don't think that's an uncommon trait in actors, but in Maggie it was terrifically magnified."

Millicent Osborn:

"Maggie was not a cruel person and yet she was capable of cruelty. One time, Paul and Maggie and I were having lunch at the Lafayette. The poor old chef came out—a little Frenchman with a high white hat; he walked over to the table where we sat and handed me an autograph book, and I said, 'No, this is Miss Sullavan.' He didn't speak any English, and Maggie confused hell out of him by insisting that I was Miss Sullavan. And in order to stop that, I finally signed it."

When the summer of 1954 came around, Mother agreed to let Bill and me spend it with Father in Los Angeles while she visited Bridget in Europe. We were thrilled. One of the reasons for letting us go was that Jane and Peter Fonda would be there with Hank; Father was making *Mr. Roberts* into a movie. Locations were to be shot in Hawaii, so Jane and I began making plans for our invasion of the beaches of Waikiki. Jane was also in boarding school, Emma Willard, and much more sophisticated than I. Everything about the Fondas' lives seemed "more" than ours. Jane and Peter's mother, Frances, had committed suicide; this, while tragic, was provocative. Mother had entered into endless discussions with Mrs. Seymour, their grandmother, about whether or not to tell the children the truth. Newspapers and magazine subscriptions had been canceled lest Jane and Peter stumble on some reference disclosing the real cause of their mother's death. They had been informed that Frances had died of heart failure. The entire student body at the Greenwich Academy was warned at assembly by Miss Campbell that it was to respect that story for an indefinite period of time. How Mrs. Seymour managed to keep the facts from Jane and Peter as long as she did was surprising. Some months later, during art class, Jane and I were leafing through a movie magazine under the pottery table, and we came upon a biographical digest of the stars, alphabetically listed. I flipped the page but not quickly enough. Jane turned it back and silently read the truth. Afterward she did not say a word about it to me, nor did I dare to bring it up. Now, at sixteen, she had passed through the most awkward stages of adolescence unscathed. Her skin was perfect, her face and figure beautiful, her personality original. She was, of all my friends, Mother's favorite. "Jane has remarkable character for one so young," Mother used to say. "She's incapable of telling a lie." (Since I was all too capable, this observation was artfully designed to strike terror into my heart, which it did.)

Peter was as singular an individual as any other Fonda. A year or so after Frances's death, Hank married Susan Blanchard, Oscar Hammerstein's stepdaughter. While they were honeymooning in the Virgin Islands, Peter accepted the invitation of his friend Tony Avery to spend the weekend at the family hunting lodge. Stepping out onto the roof with a sawed-off shotgun he'd found in the attic, Peter, unable to figure out how to load it, jammed the barrel against his belt buckle for leverage and the gun went off, blasting a hole through his stomach. His life was saved by a cool-headed chauffeur who drove him, unconscious, fifty miles to the nearest hospital. Peter basked in glory. Nobody else in Greenwich had ever had such an accident. In fact, he preferred to play down the accidental part and to impute dark subconscious motives to his trigger finger. (That was during the Korean War; Bill and Peter had fallen in with the Fawcett brothers, a wild crowd. The Fawcetts had substantial property nearby, which lent itself to the large-scale building of trenches and foxholes. Evil weapons were developed. Bill, who had a way with firearms, came up with a grenade that consisted of a cherry bomb dipped first in Le Page's glue and then rolled in BBs to give it the perfect weight for throwing long distances. Amazingly, only one of the gang sustained a major injury: Roger Fawcett, younger brother of Rocky, was accidentally shot in the eye with a BB gun.)

Eventually, the Fondas had moved from Greenwich into New York City. This had forced Peter to consider other outlets for his prodigious energy; he had taken up the trumpet and flower-arranging. It was then—across the tables in the Museum of Modern Art's garden, where our families met for lunch—that Peter (he claimed later) had fallen secretly in love with Bridget.

That summer of 1954, however, Bridget was in Switzerland with Mother and Kenneth. Bill and I were not particularly sorry; she could be something of a tribulation. While the rest of us were able, somehow, to express ourselves, she had remained, as in childhood, aloof. Not that she *felt* superior; the reverse was true. But to me—something I would never have dreamed of telling her—she personified the best qualities in all of us. I admired her integrity, and was afraid of her. I had the feeling that she had been dropped many times and glued back together but that the cracks still showed. I wanted to set her in the sun and let her turn a golden brown like Mother. To me that golden patina meant strength. At the same time, I was relieved to be rid of the responsibility. In a way I hoped that the school in Switzerland would do the job I wasn't up to.

At seventeen I was cockier than ever. I was also outrageously flirtatious. No man was exempt from my coquetry. Danny Selznick, a year older than I, took me to a small French bistro for escargots, and chastized me for flirting with his father. "There's a creature," he warned, "whose name begins with the letter 'V,' to which you bear a remarkable likeness." I was charmed by the notion that he saw me as a vixen. At David O. Selznick's annual Fourth of July party in Malibu, I set out to conquer all of Hollywood; much to Father's concern, Richard Rodgers told him I was delectable and Cole Porter gave me a cigar.

My greatest treasure that summer was my driver's license. For my seventeenth birthday, Father had promised me a car but weaseled out by temporarily substituting a very skimpy dress from a new Beverly Hills store named Jax. That evening I wore it to dinner—without a bra (quite shocking in those days), since it was too low-cut to accommodate one. My date was Warner LeRoy, son of Mervyn LeRoy, who was to replace John Ford as director of *Mr.*

Roberts. Afterward, Warner took me to watch Jimmy Dean shoot the Ferris-wheel scene in his first movie, *East of Eden*. "He's going to be the biggest young star in Hollywood," predicted Warner, whose brand of worldliness was quite unlike that of the average Eastern preppie. But Jimmy Dean's fate was far less interesting to me than Marlon Brando's. I had high hopes toward Marlon Brando that summer. For one thing, he was in Los Angeles making a movie, *Guys and Dolls*, which, for another, was being directed by an old friend of the family, Joe Mankiewicz. And if that wasn't luck enough, it just happened that I'd grown up with Joe's niece Johanna.

With me at the wheel, Josie Mankiewicz, Jane Fonda, and Jill Schary spent the better part of July and August zooming around Los Angeles on the trail of Marlon Brando. Although my optimism never flagged, the closest we came to him was the night I took everyone downtown on the half-finished freeway to see *Viva Zapata!* in a flea-bitten movie house. I was in such a rush to get us there that I drove, whenever traffic was bad, along the sidewalks. The others wouldn't get back in the car with me for a week.

Whenever I saw the Fondas, I was reminded of Mother, although she was nowhere around. Hank, it pleased me to observe, was as strict with Jane as Mother was with me. The quality of that strictness was identical: fervent, almost puritanical. Jane and I were given to speculation about their past romance and marriage. We liked to suppose that beneath their rectitude smoldered a still unbridled passion for each other. The idea of a renewed love affair—unconsummated, of course, on our account—did not seem as far-fetched as all that. In Greenwich, sometimes, after Hank had come to pick up Jane and Peter, he and Mother would demonstrate headstands together for what seemed to be longer than necessary. We children would eye each other reflectively: they were still madly in love! (Whether or not they were, we preferred to believe it.)

However, I never did get to Hawaii with Jane.

Hank, about to start *Mr. Roberts* for Father, was staying with his family down in Santa Monica at the old Ocean House. We were in town with Father, Nan, Kitty, and nurse, at the Bel Air Hotel. One evening, Father offered to take me to *Matador*, a documentary about bullfighting. I was obsessed with bullfighting, having read all of Hemingway; my ardor was in no way diminished by a recent introduction to Luis Miguel Dominguín, whose entire body, I was fascinated to note—when he appeared in a brief bathing suit at the hotel pool—was covered with scars. That night, Nan was up in Monterey visiting her family. While Father finished off a business meeting in his room, Bill and I, elated at the opportunity to order Châteaubriand for two at $22.95, ate an early dinner alone in the hotel dining room. Afterward we waited for Father on the path by the lobby. It was still daylight, though about seven o'clock; people were arriving for cocktails. Father came toward us in a dark suit with a business associate on either side. Just as the three of them came abreast of us, he fell to his knees, and then slowly, like a mortally wounded elephant that didn't belong there at all, sank to the pavement. There was pandemonium. A bellboy appeared with a huge bowl of ice; the desk clerk, the manager, guests gathered around him.

"Brooke," he said desperately, regaining consciousness when I splashed ice water on his face, "I'm bleeding to death."

"No, you're not," I said, equally desperately. I sat down on the pavement and put his head on my lap.

"Yes," he insisted. "There's blood on my pants. Call the doctor, not the goddamned hotel doctor—I want Dana Atchley. My telephone book—look under New York City—"

"That's not blood, Leland," said somebody else. "It's just ice water."

"I'm hemorrhaging, goddamnit," said Father. We carried him back to his hotel suite. By the time we got there, it was evident he was right. There was more blood than I had ever seen, more blood than I thought the human body contained. The heavy sweet smell of it was everywhere; the white carpet was strewn with dark clots. Later, we burned his pants. The living room quickly filled with people; word got around fast. When I heard the ambulance siren, I went back into his room and shut the door behind me.

"Come here, Brooke," he said, without opening his eyes. I sat on the edge of his bed, wondering how he'd known it was me. His skin was a terrible color, the same pale green as Christ's on the cross in the middle panel of the Grünewald Altarpiece.

"Do you love me?" asked Father, still without opening his eyes.

"Yes, Father." When I was six or seven, I'd come across the Grünewald Altarpiece in an art book, and it had scared me to think about ever since.

"That's good," said Father. "I love you, too. Poor little Brooke. Are you afraid I'm going to die?"

I certainly was. I didn't see how anyone could lose that much blood that fast and live. There was no way to stop the bleeding, no way to plug him up.

"You're not going to die, Father, I promise you. The ambulance is here. Besides, I won't let you." I was still invincible in those days, strong enough for both of us. The big question was whether I was strong enough not to cry. I rolled my eyes around furiously to disperse the tears, clenching my teeth with effort.

"Attagirl," said Father. Only his lips moved, and his voice seemed to come from far away. "Well, I am. I'm afraid as hell. You must forgive me, darling."

"What for, Father?" I asked, panicked, thinking I was about to hear his last confession. He *couldn't* die. He wasn't mortal like the rest of us: he was my father.

"For getting sick tonight, not taking you to that movie. The bullfight movie. What a terrible evening. I'm so sorry, darling, I know I promised you. . . ."

Father did almost die. He received massive transfusions every day for weeks, gallons and gallons of blood, according to Nan, who moved into the hospital with him. Then, after he began to recover, the doctors recommended that he take it easy for a while and retire. It was the work, it seemed, the pressure that made him hemorrhage. But Father got so cranky with enforced leisure, and it became so apparent that retirement would be, for him, a form of death anyway, that he was slowly allowed to resume *Mr. Roberts*. When the danger was over, Bill and I were sent home. It was almost fall, and school was about to begin.

My senior year at Madeira was splendid. I worked very hard, and took the idea of myself as a scholar very seriously. (An appealing vision of myself as a consumptive author, amongst dusty stacks of books and easels in an unheated Parisian garret, fueled my studies.) I ranked high on my college entrance exams, and was accepted by Vassar, Bennington, and Sarah Lawrence. Vassar was my first choice—or, rather, that of Miss Madeira, whose eightieth birthday we celebrated that year. Vassar was her alma mater. Father, fully recovered, came down to Washington and had tea with Miss Madeira. This charmed her into recognizing me from then on whenever we passed each other on the Oval. I sang alto in the select glee club and was inspired, during my weekly Sunday trips into Washington, to canvass a strange heterogeneous mixture of churches, cathedrals, and temples. While passing through a brief religious fervor, I was, at last, confirmed. Embarrassingly, this meant I first had to be christened, a rite Mother had overlooked in my infancy. The confirmation took place in St. John's Church, which met all of my requirements (the biggest rose window, the most vaulted nave, the most impressive altar in Washington), and was attended by all my friends. The high point was a fabulous breakfast in the rectory afterward, of codfish cakes and homemade baked beans made by the wife of the minister, Dr. Glenn.

"Dear Mother," I wrote. "Being a senior is both fun and difficult—I enjoy the privileges and prestige, but on the other hand, I loathe setting an example to the rest of the school. . . ."

This was quite true. I cultivated an image of myself as an artistic eccentric, outside the bourgeois concerns that governed the rest of the student body. In the spring, I spent two feverish weeks between mirror and canvas painting my masterpiece, a life-size self-portrait in oil entitled "Nervous Breakdown." I was often reduced to tears by the rigorous beauty of this creative endeavor.

I wrote, in typically florid style:

Dear Kenneth:

I just wrote, in one of my more energetic moments these last few days, a poem:

Awake! Bestir your senses drugged with sleep,
And rub the night from sand-filled eyes. To creep
In sluggish blindness by the Path of Shade
But dulls perception's edge, as rusts the blade
From disuse. Nature's torrents surging past
In irrevocable exuberance, last
A short breath only. Make your own ascent
A search of Life, until Life's flow is spent.

And Life was always full of drama. To a friend of Mother's, who was my kind hostess during spring vacation in Delray, Florida, I dashed off a tortured bread-and-butter note:

Have just gotten unpacked—hate to unpack—something so final and depressing about it. I hate school. Never has coming back been more miserable. The four walls have already swallowed us up again. Now the sinking feeling that I'm going into battle for a wasteful, useless cause is taking hold. Don't pay the slightest bit of attention to any of this. Tomorrow will be better, when the wonderful memories will have dulled a little. . . .

Parodying the style of one of my overstuffed letters, Mother replied:

Dear Heart—

Bedtime is imminent—the exigencies of my vocation demand that I avail myself of every possible wink—my soporific, Horlick's, stands awaiting me on my bedtable— and so, my beloved progeny, bonne nuit, gute Nacht, buenas noches, etc., ad infinitum.

It would be sheer rodomontade for me to suggest that all goes well with rehearsals—indeed, without prevarication, I can state unequivocally that I stink. Paradoxically I feel rather beatific. Your siblings are well.

Sanguinely yours,
Ma

Moody and mercurial, I fell in and out of love five times. Graduation was almost upon me, as was my June début at the Greenwich Country Club Cotillion. My letters were filled now with responses to Mother's queries about invitations, escorts, guests, dress, shoes, music:

Dear Ma,

To answer your last batch of questions, my favorite song is "Begin the Beguine." As for Jane Fonda, she graduates the 11th and would love to come. May she stay with me that weekend or will it be too hectic? Will arrange date for her. This makes twelve for dinner. Kenneth and I will have to practice dancing together. OH! Don't bother about white shoes—I have quite a nice pair of sandals from Calif. that went with that blue décolleté dress that was too suggestive.

Father was in Washington two days ago on business. He came out to school for a couple of hours. He was worried about young William. I hope the monster hasn't gotten himself into deeper trouble? I really feel sorry for him—he seems to have a knack for doing the wrong thing, especially with his school work. Almost a jinx. Father also said he would, if you approve, give me an M.G. for graduation. We are giving The Glass Menagerie in a week. It is extremely good in parts. . . .

My passing concern for young William was well founded. He had run into academic trouble at Lawrenceville and had been shifted to Eaglebrook, a smaller, less posh institution. Except for his skiing, he wasn't doing particularly well there, either. However, our school production of *The Glass Menagerie* was my major preoccupation; hobbling around the stage as Laura convinced me I should become an actress. Mother could not have agreed less.

"I forbid it," she said sternly when I called her to rave about myself. "Until you've finished college. What happened to your writing?"

Her allegiance to my writing seemed hypocritical; I pointed out that it was she who'd prohibited the publication of my book.

"That was probably a mistake," she admitted, "but I would be making a far graver one if I let you go to acting school instead of college. If you're still interested four years from now—so be it. I'll give you my blessing."

Also she was not pleased with the deal Father and I had made for my graduation present.

"Now I want to talk to you about another problem." (I scrunched up my face in the phone booth). "Leland called yesterday. It seems a year and a half ago he promised you a car for your birthday if you got good grades. You, of course, did not tell him I'd promised you a car if you didn't smoke. I've recently noticed cigarettes appearing for the first time. This, darling, is what I call playing one parent against the other. In other words, if Leland and I were not divorced, this situation could not have occurred." (I made a minute examination of my fingernails; it would have been foolhardy to interrupt her once she started.)

"You didn't tell Leland that I'd said you could have a car *if* you didn't smoke. This is being dishonest by omission." (Mother's voice sounded as if I were strangling her.) "Now *he's* in a quandary; he certainly doesn't want to break his promise. *I'm* in a quandary; I certainly don't want to be the policewoman you call on me too often to play. But also I've overextended myself on your various pleasures this year—skiing at Christmas, Florida at Easter, graduation, début, and, finally, a trip to Europe this summer. This, if you remember, was to have been my year for travel and leisure—instead of which, your expenses are so great I haven't budged from home. It's given me vast pleasure to do these things for you, but now I have to draw the line. A car's upkeep is not negligible; aside from the very costly insurance and running expenses—gas, oil, et cetera—we figure that each car averages around twenty-five dollars a month in repairs and extras. I cannot afford to keep a car for you now. I have arranged to give you a clothes allowance next year, and I feel it's a hardship to add a car—not only that, but I have to clear out the garage for a third occupant, which will sit out there all winter unused—your father and I are agreed you shouldn't take it to college. And all this for a girl who can't resist smoking!" (Oh, God, I thought, I can't stand these lectures—why did I call her?) "So we go to more expense and build a house to protect the furniture which the garage now holds. If Leland is willing to pay for the upkeep of your car, then I have nothing more to say. It's like that horse he offered you several years ago—the initial cost is small compared to the upkeep."

She paused momentarily; I didn't know what to say. "And one other thing." (Oh, *no!* I banged my fist on the walls of the phone booth.) "Leland says what you want, above all else, is an M.G. This I *cannot* allow. At least when, God forbid, you have that accident, you must have a fifty-fifty chance of survival. I don't have time now to explain to you why. Please grow up soon and stop creating these situations."

As usual, it was pointless to argue with her. Besides, there were more pressing things to think about. Events were rushing by, and, if possible, gathering momentum. I was pretty, bright, talented, confident, happy. I felt as if I'd come through a long dark tunnel into a sunlit meadow. Beyond that stretched the summer, two whole months of traveling in France and Italy and Scotland. Then Vassar. My whole life lay before me.

Although I had seen little of them in the last few years, the two people I loved most in the world were my sister and brother. It was an odd kind of love, one that did not demand much of my time or of theirs. I was not dependent on them, nor they on me. We expected nothing of each other, nothing at all. Perhaps we had deduced from the way matters had ended with Mother and Father that even the most committed relationships were not to be counted on. We couldn't damage each other if we wanted nothing from each other, not even rudimentary loyalty. The quantum "nothing" had its own value. Unhindered by what brothers and sisters ordinarily expected of each other, we were free to love without ordinary rules. We were free to come and go as we pleased. We were free to feel without demonstrating what we felt. By the same token, we were exempted from the need to regret what we didn't feel. Outsiders were often surprised that we didn't keep better track of each other. What they dismissed as cold or flippant or imperious behavior was devised by us as an intricately expressive sign language. All this is a long way of saying that however deeply we cared about each other, our care had a rogue quality. And occasionally, when it mattered most, our signals could get crossed.

In August of that year, 1955, Kenneth, three of his sons, and I were grouse-shooting in Scotland. We stayed at Yester, a beautiful Adam house with vast grounds, which belonged to the Marquess of Tweeddale, who was Kenneth's brother-in-law. I was deliriously happy. When we weren't shooting, we were mackerel-fishing. Marjorie, Kenneth's sister, presided over a breakfast table that never numbered less than twenty. At noon, there were elaborate picnics on the moors with hampers of food transported to the blinds by station wagon. In the late afternoon, there were seven-course high teas, and at night black-tie dinners at which we consumed a previous day's bag. Afterward, the men drank port with their savory, and the ladies, in their long dresses, retired to the drawing room to await the setting up of the roulette table. I had the feeling I was walking through a reel of Jean Renoir's *Rules of the Game*.

Mother was in Greenwich with Bridget and Bill. I felt sorry for all three of them. They had to be getting on each other's nerves. Greenwich had never been much fun in the sultry heat of August when everybody had left town. And, at best, Mother could be difficult. The one reliable soothing agent, Kenneth, was off with the one sure-fire distraction, me. Mother's letters sounded slightly oppressed. I could just imagine the general claustrophobia.

Although I hadn't yet seen her, Bridget had just come back from her two years in Switzerland. All her letters had begged Mother's permission to remain in Switzerland for her senior year, with the idea that eventually she might go to the Sorbonne or the University of Geneva. Her arguments were so persuasive that I'd taken her side. I realized that one of the factors in her reasoning was me. Several times, long ago, she'd confessed to Kenneth in the heat of emotion that she felt inferior. In Switzerland, with rivalry at a manageable distance, she seemed to be thriving. Her French was fluent and she had many friends. Amazingly, for one who had always been physically cautious, she had taken up skiing with a passion; her picture, with blond hair streaming over her red Alpine team sweater, graced the cover of a Gstaad travel folder. That spring she had written:

> Dear Mother,
>
> About school: I understand your reasoning, but what I would really like to do—and it isn't just a whim of the moment, because I have thought it out thoroughly—is to finish high school here. I love the school. The girls are wonderful, and for me, at this point, I would rather have contacts with girls from England, France, Germany, Switzerland, Jamaica, Singapore, Istanbul, Zanzibar, Southern Rhodesia . . . than Greenwich, Connecticut. Also it would be a shame to leave when my French is finally almost mastered; after all, it has taken me sixteen years to speak English as well as I do. And next year I could learn German and Italian. I still don't see what's wrong with the six years of European education you say I'm committing myself to; I like Europe, or what I've seen of it, and I think it's more interesting than America. Here there is history—and what is there in America? Even though it must be hard for you to realize that I'm sixteen, I really have thought this out, and I honestly and truly do want it. . . .

Mother, however, had chosen to disregard Bridget's plea. Against the advice of both Kenneth and me, she had insisted that Bridget return for her senior year. Her reasons were abstruse.

Bridget, she claimed, ran the risk of becoming a rootless expatriate. One year had been enough, two extravagant. Since it had been Mother's wish to send us both in the first place, I found this logic specious, and said so. I also pointed out that she should seize the opportunity to encourage Bridget's new-found independence. Mother, I think, found that the most subversive argument of all. In any case, she had recalled Bridget. Secretly, I was relieved to be as far away as possible from that homecoming.

Bridget and Bill were, under protest, both attending summer school at Brunswick. This, in their opinion, was a last-ditch recreation gratuitously contrived by Mother when she couldn't find something more productive for them to do. Mother did not like idle hands. It was a good opportunity for Bridget to catch up on certain credits, and for Bill to improve his poor grades at Eaglebrook. Mother was furious with him. He had a recent history of lackadaisical study habits. His motivation had been sluggish ever since the time, when he was nine, he had gone briefly to boarding school in England. That was the fall Mother and Kenneth had got married. Mother had felt that Bill would benefit from the same educational experience his four stepbrothers were having. He'd had a marvelous time in England but, after several months of the penetrating winter damp, had come down with severe bronchitis. In addition, Father had returned from London with horror tales about the lack of food and central heating. (Father's idea of minimum sustenance was a New York steak for lunch every day.) Mother had had visions of another mastoid operation like the one that had almost killed Bill in infancy, and had him sent home at once. After the rigorous curriculum at Sunningdale (algebra and Latin in the fourth grade), Brunswick must have seemed pallid. Bill had loved Sunningdale; now he lost all interest in school, and never regained it.

Mother wrote Father frostily in the spring of 1955. For her to have written him at all indicated an emergency.

> Dear Leland,
>
> Here are Bill's reports from Eaglebrook. He's also behaving very badly about money. I suggest that you don't give him, for a while anyway, vast sums. The $20 last time lasted for five minutes.
>
> I've given up policing the homework. He won out—I couldn't take the unpleasantness each day—and I saw no

evidence that he was developing any self-reliance or respon-sibility. I'm licked.

Bill's freshman year at Eaglebrook had followed a familiar pattern: he was off to a good start and then slowly lost ground. The one thing all his masters agreed on was that he was an interesting conversationalist. The reports to which Mother referred were summed up by the headmaster:

Bill is quiet but genial. His mediocre effort and indifference to achievement, however, detract considerably from his having a full school life. The results of his spring testing program rank him in the upper quarter of the independent school population, and in English, arithmetic, and spelling his work is on the public school eleventh grade level. It is odd that with these very good figures his actual school grades remain low, and in his class ranking he is in the lower quarter of all his classes. However we see that the high quality is there. . . .

It was hard for me to ascertain what Bill was up to, since his letters home, though affectionate, were few and spare. He was then fourteen. I thought he was adorable. When we'd seen each other during vacations, we had been mutually protective: I defended him to Mother and he, in a misguided effort to defend my honor, ambushed my beaus. One night he sicced our German shepherd on an admirer I'd spent three years trying to seduce; the poor fellow's pants were shredded to bits. Just before my graduation, Bill had sent me a note. I kept it in my jewelry box as the single piece of correspondence that I ever received from him:

> *I can't wait to see you!*
> *Mother and I were having a talk about your car (to be), and Mother says that she isn't going to pay for gas, etc., because of your smoking. She said she had found butts in your blue jeans, in your desk, and folded into your scarf. Happy Graduation and all that sort of rot. I don't know what to do for a graduate, but I'll think of something, just because you're my long lost sister.*
>

Lots of love,
Bill

One afternoon in August, I was sitting alone at the grand piano in the ballroom at Yester. The ballroom, though long unused for the purpose for which it had been built, was still the most compelling room in the house. It was on the second story with floor-to-ceiling windows that looked out over the estate, the village of Tweeddale, and, finally, the moors. I came there every afternoon to contemplate what it must have been like just before a dance; the now deserted parquet floor waxed and reflecting the room's lovely proportions in the candlelight that shimmered from wall sconces and the great chandeliers; I could hear the ghostly sound of bag-pipes as a breeze ruffled the pages of my sheet music. The only sheet music around was Noel Coward. I had already memorized "Mad Dogs and Englishmen" and "Bittersweet," which I bellowed into the echoing space while accompanying myself *molto espressivo* on the piano.

Kenneth came into the room and sat down beside me on the piano bench.

"Be quiet for a minute, darling," he said. He was very agitated. The letter in his hands was as thick as a pad of paper, and at a glance I could tell by the broad-nibbed scrawl that it was from Mother. "Something terrible has happened in Greenwich," he said. His voice was thick with emotion. "Your brother and sister have broken your mother's heart."

"How?" I asked. What had they done now? Flunked summer school? Set fire to the house? I couldn't help smiling to myself as I recalled the time Bill had arranged a box of .22-caliber bullets in a circle in the grass, so that when the sun's rays—

"They couldn't have picked a better way," said Kenneth bitterly. "They have gone to live with your father."

I stared at him aghast. He turned the pages of the letter.

"Shall I read it to you?" he asked. "Your mother—I'm worried about her."

I nodded. Bridget and Bill, deserters. Didn't they realize they'd left me, too? Sitting here innocently on a piano bench in Scotland? Or care? By God, they'd really done it, the selfish little bastards. Couldn't they have waited two more weeks until I got home to smooth things over? Idiots. Cowards. I despised them. My mouth filled with acrid fluid, my eyes burned. Craven, cruel, dumb. Didn't they stop long enough to consider the consequences, the destruction to their lives? To Mother's? Clearly that was intended. To Father's, then, and Kenneth's and, most of all, mine?

The letter had been written in the form of a diary over a

week's time. Mother had added to it every night. Events were recounted in chronological order. Her tone was frank, anguished, but without self-pity. Both sides were represented. It was a bravura piece of reportage. Even in the confusion of my anger, I couldn't help admiring its style. The cumulative effect of the details was shocking. By the time it ended, I was drenched in perspiration.

Mother did not blame Bridget and Bill at all. She blamed herself. This, more than anything else, made me want to cry.

The break, it seemed, had been precipitated by a note left on the hall table. The note was open and conspicuously intended, claimed Mother, to be read by anyone who passed. She did so. Bridget had written it to a school friend but it was clearly meant for Mother. (In Bridget's later version, this so-called note was, in reality, a locked diary, which Mother had pried open.)

The note outlined Bridget's disaffection from Greenwich. She found it provincial after the grandeur of Europe. She disliked the tedium of classes at summer school, but most of all she disliked being alone in the house with Mother. Everyone was on vacation, even Elizabeth. Bill was sweet but no help. The truth was she didn't love Mother; she hated her. The contrast between Mother and Nan, underlined for her on trips to Sicily and Rome and Paris with Father and Nan at Christmas and Easter, was more dramatically apparent now that she was actually back in Greenwich. She felt she didn't belong. She wanted to return to Europe immediately.

On reading this, Mother was outraged. When she picked Bridget up at Brunswick at lunchtime, she said, "You have made yourself very clear, my darling. I'm not so stupid I could fail to understand. You hate me and want to leave. Perhaps you would be happier living with your father?"

This was a test I'd encountered many times and ignored. To Mother's horror, Bridget's answer was, coldly, "Yes."

Then, a few minutes later, Bill came bicycling in from Brunswick. He was informed of this turn of events and asked if he, too, would like to leave.

"What about Brooke? Is she going?" he inquired cagily, apprehensive at the idea of holding down the fort alone.

"I assume so; why not?" responded Mother, implying she expected us all to desert her. (I could hear her martyred tone of voice as if I'd been there. Mother tended to cover her injured feelings with a first coat of icy aplomb and then, just to remind us of the courageous struggle *that* took, a second one that hinted at her unmentionable suffering.)

Bill and Bridget called Father. He was preparing to make *The Spirit of St. Louis*. Father was flattered at the notion that the two of them would like to live with him, but this was a bit sudden. Also it couldn't have come at a worse time. *The Spirit of St. Louis* was about to start shooting; there were locations all over the world. He would be traveling for the next six months: Boston, Nova Scotia, Newfoundland, Ireland, Paris. After that, he would be working on the editing of the film in California for a year. Nan was in Biarritz with Kitty. What was he going to do? Very inconvenient.

Discussions recommenced between Mother and Father. By now, Mother's initial fury had abated. She regretted her hasty and ill-considered suggestion. The game had gone far enough. But Bridget and Bill were adamant. No, they couldn't wait till Kenneth and I got home. The die was cast: they certainly didn't want to linger in that explosive atmosphere for two weeks while the situation deteriorated day by day. It would be agony.

There were two disastrous confrontations, one between Mother and Bridget, the other between Mother and Bill. She implored them to change their minds and stay. They refused; it was too late. Whatever accusations were then made on all sides were so vitriolic and damaging that Mother could not bring herself to report them. Suffice it to say that the children made the final preparations for their departure in secrecy. That night, Bill cracked open the safe and stole their passports. The next morning they were on their way to Boston.

Mother's letter went on to say that, circumstances being what they were, she expected me to join Bridget and Bill. Maybe it would be for the best, since events had proved her inadequacy as a parent. She hoped, however, that I would still go on to Vassar; she could arrange, if I liked, to send my trunks there. I shook my head; had she learned nothing from all this?

As Kenneth read me this, my anger did not subside. It grew. By the time he came to the last few words, in which Mother blamed herself for the whole mess, I was angry not only at Bridget and Bill, but at Mother and Father as well. It seemed to me they were all to blame; Mother for not having the sense to overlook

Bridget's sophomoric note, Bridget for not having the generosity to overlook Mother's behavior, Bill for not having enough gumption to overlook them both, Father for playing devil's advocate.

I went to my room and thought. Kenneth had suggested that Mother join us in Scotland. He'd gone off to send her a wire. I felt as if I were at a crossroads in my life. Certainly I realized that the rush of pure joy with which I'd entered that summer was over. Nor did I allow myself to believe it would return in the same measure again. I had to make a choice in which, no matter what, someone was going to be badly hurt. If I chose to cast my lot with Bridget and Bill—and it was tempting—it could be ruinous for Mother. I knew she took being a mother so seriously that if I failed her, she would see it as *her* failure, and that would be the last straw. Perhaps she would have a nervous breakdown, although I wasn't too sure what constituted a nervous breakdown. Still, if I caused this, I could never live with myself again. But if I chose to stay with her, something equally terrible might happen to Bridget and Bill. They were young and susceptible, and, whatever they thought, unlikely to snap back as if nothing had happened. For all his money, Father would never be able to lavish on them the time and care that Mother had. And their guilt would only snowball with time. Which of them was most vulnerable? Bridget? Bill? Mother?

In the end, instinct told me Mother was. Bridget and Bill were younger; they were more resilient. Other children had left home before and survived. Besides, maybe I was overestimating their guilt and underestimating Father's fatherliness. But Mother: I was afraid something truly calamitous might happen to her. Perhaps I could help stave it off for a while. Perhaps if I were around, her pride would keep her from shattering. She was a fighter, as long as she had someone to fight for.

I wrote her that I had no intention of leaving home and that I was insulted by her suggestion. Then (trying to sound as adult to her—and for her—as I could) I went on to say:

> *Kenneth and I have just been discussing Bridget and Bill. Not being there, I can only surmise that a vast amount of this business was concocted more out of a desire to play with fire than as a result of mature thought. They are both children still—and children can be the cruelest of all. Bridget, apparently, is snarling at life in general; this is not so very*

abnormal. And Bill is easily influenced; Bridget learned long
ago to profit by his weakness. The sad part is that you are
the nearest target. The family situation, chiefly the divorce,
would create friction in any case. Father's position makes
yours precarious. These conflicts have been encountered before. And surmounted. Other unpleasant factors enter in.
Ken says I'm one of them, that Brie feels I'm superior, etc.
etc. But I think some of that attitude is affectation on her
part. I wish I were there. Somehow I think none of this would
have happened. You say it's been brewing for a long time
and had to come to a head. We've all been idiots at one time
or another, so try to forgive their stupidity. I hope it's as un-
intentional as I think it is. And let me begin to atone for
mine. I know you must feel alone and low. Don't suffer at
home; we need you. Forget the expense and, for once, I beg
you, don't plan, don't staple yourself to a thousand petty
details; throw some junk in a suitcase and catch the next
plane. For God's sake, don't think any more, just come
along. I love you. . . .

But Mother was inconsolable. She thanked me for trying to
distract her, but claimed she was in no shape to travel. So Kenneth
and I flew home.

She met us at the airport. I expected the worst, but I wasn't
prepared for how bad the worst would be. Her face was ravaged.
Her clothes drooped on her. Her voice shook. As we stood in the
warm sunlight outside the parking lot, the air pleasantly whirring
with the sounds of planes taking off and landing like giant overhead fans, she held on to us as if she were a child. The look in her
eyes was one I had never seen and I thought I'd seen them all. It
was a look of defeat. I knew then that the worst was yet to come.

Breakdown

Jane Fonda:

"Here were two women, your mother and your sister, who had
infinite spirit—a certain kind of brilliance, a crazy brilliance, erratic,
difficult, neurotic, but still unique. I don't think society offers solu-
tions to people like that, especially women. They were never pro-

vided with a constructive way of harnessing that kind of energy and brilliance. It turned inward and destroyed them."

Bridget:

"I sometimes think there is only one way for me to resolve my struggle with Mother and that is to go down to Greenwich, push her in the river and then jump in after her to drown."

I didn't see Bridget again for another year. She came out to the house about a month later, but I was away that weekend. She stayed for a few hours, long enough to pack all her clothes and, to my fury, some of mine. Mother and Kenneth reported that she was civil but remote. Father's limousine brought her and waited in the driveway while she collected her books and trinkets for shipment to California.

I saw Bill once. He, too, came to gather his possessions. The fall term at Eaglebrook was about to begin. Apparently, while he was packing, Mother came into his room. Without any warning, she asked him to reconsider his decision to live with Father. She said it was a decision made in haste and anger and that it was all her fault. She had not intended to "drive him out." She asked him to forgive her. He said he had. She asked him to go away with her somewhere quiet for a week, Cape Cod, just the two of them, to straighten things out. She promised him that she would give in to him on whatever routine points distressed him; he could do this and wouldn't have to do that—anything if he would stay. Gently, Bill said no. He said he loved her but that for a little while at least he was committed to another kind of life; that for him to come back now would be difficult and strange. Mother began to cry. I had never known her to cry except for the time, before Mother and Father were divorced, when the ambulance had come for Father.

This time she couldn't stop. Even from my room the sound was so painful I went into my bathroom and put my hands over my ears. That evening I was supposed to go into New York to the theatre; it had been prearranged that Father's car would give me a lift in with Bill. Kenneth, white-faced, told Bill and me that we should go right away; he would calm Mother down.

On the way into town, Bill put up the glass partition between us and the driver, and we talked.

I was still unnerved by the scene earlier with Mother. It had been heart-rending to overhear a self-possessed forty-six-year-old woman pleading with her fourteen-year-old son, apologizing, bargaining, desperately trying to regain his favor. The balance of power had shifted. The fact that the woman happened to be my mother, and the boy my brother, was incidental. I had begun to have the disquieting concept of myself as a spectator, not a participant, in my own life. I saw myself as the audience, leaning back to watch my future unfold like a Greek tragedy. I already had presentiments of the ending. That, after all, was the classic form; it was not the surprise dénouement that one came to see, but the quality of the drama and performances.

Bridget, Bill was saying, had turned out to be a real pain in the ass. She'd started this upheaval and then refused (as usual) to do all the talking or to work out the logistics. And now everything had come down on his head. It was all blamed on him. One fine day he'd walked into an altercation between Mother and Bridget and the next thing— It was evident to him from the beginning that Mother didn't seriously mean she thought they should go live with Father. Certainly not as a permanent arrangement. But he was taking advantage of her moment of anger for purely selfish reasons. There was an enormous appeal to Father's life-style—the travel, the gadgets, the glamour, the fun. Mother refused to act like a rich person, always driving those Ramblers around. She was difficult, inconsistent. Yes, he'd proceeded out of basically selfish motives. He was aware of how incredibly stubborn he was, and he knew he'd hurt Mother deeply. But now he thought of himself as living with Father; the estrangement was complete. It would be hard to turn everything around again.

I looked at him carefully. His voice was beginning to change and down was sprouting on his chin. He looked underfed. I resisted the impulse to enfold him in a bear hug.

Bridget was absolutely no help in all this, Bill repeated, rattling on with his feet up on the jump seat; she was actually a hindrance. Since I, the traditional groundbreaker in most family arguments, hadn't been around to give orders, Bridget had initiated the debacle, and should have been able to deal with its aftermath. But she'd lapsed into one of her silences. Bill had had to organize the resistance and to carry her along as well. Matters had got even worse once they were under way. Throughout their travels from

Boston to Halifax to St. John to Gander to Biarritz, he'd had to take care of her. Just as if, he noted sourly, they were married. In the cramped proximity of hotel rooms, their relationship had disintegrated rapidly. To add to his other woes, he said, Bridget had a tendency to be light-fingered. She stole things, irrational things like his favorite pocketknife. She wouldn't use these things, or trade them, or do with them whatever you did with stolen goods. She just hid them. Maybe they had a symbolic value to her. She took a ten-dollar gold piece Grandfather had given Bill when he was born. Earlier that summer, she'd stolen a couple of hundred dollars out of Mother's purse, for which, Bill said indignantly, Mother had launched a big investigation and blamed him. Bridget was a fink. She always let him take the blame for her crimes until the day— the very day, in fact, that the final knockdown fight between Mother and Bridget had occurred!—that Mother had gone through Bridget's drawers and found a stash of items that had long been missing: odds and ends of Father's and Mother's and Nan's and Bill's and mine. Then Mother had finally pieced things together. And then Bridget had written that letter to her friend and left it on the hall table.

But, Bill concluded pensively, when Bridget and he had made the move to leave, he'd thought I would be extremely proud and pleased. He was stunned when I'd elected to stay, because he'd remembered several times Mother had threatened to send *me* to live with Father, and somehow he'd thought this time I would go right along with them. . . .

Then I did hug him. It was useless to do anything more. If we could have all been closeted together in one room and, at knife point, forced to speak until we were empty, it would have taken us as many years to undo the misunderstandings as it had taken to create them.

We held each other and promised to write, knowing that we wouldn't.

I went to the theatre and Bill went to a record store. That was the last time we saw each other for two years.

Although it took the next twelve months to come to a head, Mother's breakdown had begun that afternoon. I dated it from the moment Bill declined her peace offering. For Mother to swallow her pride, to offer blanket concessions by way of reconciliation, and then to meet with rejection, must have been more than she could bear. When I arrived home that night, our doctor's car was in the driveway and she was in bed under heavy sedation. Around dinnertime she'd disappeared. Kenneth had searched for hours, then taken the car and searched some more. He'd found her curled up pitifully in a ditch by the side of the road. She told him that she'd gone for a walk and fallen asleep looking for her lipstick. When he got her back to the house, she'd locked herself in her bathroom and refused to come out. That was when he'd called the doctor. All pill bottles had been removed from the medicine cabinets.

The next day she slept. The house was kept quiet and the doctor made several visits. Her powers of recovery were, as always, remarkable. The following day, Sunday, she came down to breakfast looking slightly wan and unsteady but determined. Monday was to be my first day at Vassar; though we tried to dissuade her, she insisted on driving me up to Poughkeepsie.

She had signed to star in a new play, *Janus*, and was now in no condition to do it. Kenneth and Delly, who was to produce it, met several times with Dr. Lawrence Kubie, an eminent New York psychiatrist. They discussed whether or not the distraction of hard work might overcome the hazard of an emotional breakdown. Mother herself was more apprehensive about the possibility of a physical breakdown. She maintained she was in a state of exhaustion and not strong enough to do the play. On the other hand, to withdraw from it once the machinery was set in motion would be a very serious and costly step. Even though she complained that she'd been deserted by everyone around her, including Kenneth and me, and that nobody was helping her to make a decision, typically she refused to let us. In the end, she made up her mind to go ahead.

The New York notices were good; under the circumstances, I thought they were amazing. But, even so, the strain became too great, and after Christmas Mother told Delly she would have to leave the play. At Easter time she was replaced by Claudette Colbert.

Slowly she seemed to be recovering from the terrible anxiety that she had failed as a mother. Then, in September, she decided to undertake a television show. She didn't like television, she didn't need the money, and there was no way to account for why she agreed to do it.

The show was based on the true life story of a nun, Sister Aquinas, who had not only a special talent for teaching mechanics and aerodynamics but also a pilot's license. Her ability was so singular that she was sent to Washington during the war to instruct in the assembling of planes and how to fly them.

Mother, always scrupulous about details, asked C.B.S. for the services of a Catholic priest to coach her in the subtleties of Catholic liturgy: how to genuflect credibly, how to make the sign of the cross, whether to pronounce "Amen" with a broad "A" or not. C.B.S. stalled. Finally, after much bullying from Kenneth on Mother's behalf, the network obtained a Methodist parson. Disorganization prevailed on all fronts. According to union rules, no actual props could be used until dress rehearsal, and Mother had to handle seventy-two props. The dress rehearsal was a shambles.

Mother informed the producer, Felix Jackson, that it was out of the question for the show to go on the air twenty-four hours later in such scandalous condition. He agreed diplomatically, but assured her everything would be straightened out by the next day. Mother said this would be impossible. She said she definitely would not do the show. She changed quickly into her street clothes, said goodbye to her theatre maid, and told her not to come tomorrow. As she left, she shook hands with Felix Jackson and told him the same thing.

Nobody, least of all Kenneth, took her seriously. Over dinner, he chided her for being sadistic and ruining Felix Jackson's sleep. Mother replied that she was being deadly serious. Kenneth pointed out that C.B.S. or Westinghouse would sue her if she walked out: they could hardly allow her to set such a precedent. She was, after all, not the best arbiter of either her own performance or the show as a whole, and what about the rest of the cast? Mother's answer was that AFTRA (the union) would see to it the other members of the cast were paid; she herself didn't care if she was sued, since actresses shouldn't be treated so shabbily. As a matter of fact, C.B.S. wouldn't *dare* sue her; they knew they were in the wrong.

The next morning Kenneth went to work without waking her. He assumed a night's sleep would restore her good humor.

He was mistaken. The final run-through had been called for 3:00 p.m. She did not show up at the studio. By 3:30, he was back in their apartment. He found a note telling him she anticipated that he'd return to convince her to change her mind. She was taking the car and driving off somewhere, she wasn't sure where exactly, but not to worry, she'd call him the next day; by the way, she was borrowing his book.

It was impossible to track her down. There was chaos. By 7:30 that night, the story was out and the press started calling. Mother, meanwhile, spent the night in a country motel. She was having breakfast at a counter the next morning when she heard a radio announcement that the missing actress, Margaret Sullavan, had still not been located. Disguising her voice and brushing back her bangs, she fled the coffee shop. She drove deep into the country, along the most inconspicuous back roads, until she reached the Osborns' house near Brookfield. Finding the house locked, she broke a pane of glass in the French doors and let herself in. Then she called her apartment on Riverside Drive. Paul Osborn answered the phone.

"Paul?" she asked.

"Maggie, where the hell are you?" he said.

"In your study," she answered.

"What are you talking about? You can't be," he replied.

"I am," she said.

"Hold on!" he exclaimed, and took a cab over to his apartment on Ninetieth and Park Avenue, but she wasn't there so he raced back across town and picked up the receiver where he'd left it.

"In the study?" he asked.

"In the country," she answered.

"Oh," he said lamely, and put Millicent on. Millicent asked if they could drive out to see her. Mother said they could on one condition: that they promise not to discuss the matter with her. They promised.

When they got to the house, they found that she'd stuffed the icebox with groceries and was treating the whole thing as a lark. Her plan was to hole up there for a week or two. Millicent persuaded her to call Kenneth. Kenneth drove out. He showed her the newspaper reports and convinced her that she should talk to her lawyer, Bill Fitelson, because there was some real question of a lawsuit. Gradually, as she realized the extent of the furor, she began to brood. While Kenneth was talking to her alone in the downstairs guest room, Millicent heard the sound of whimpering. She walked in and found Mother under the bed, huddled up in a fetal position. Kenneth was trying to get her out. The more authoritative his tone of voice, the farther under she crawled. Millicent took him aside and urged him to speak gently, to let her stay there until she came out of her own accord.

By the weekend, she was in a serious depression. Kenneth again sought the advice of Dr. Kubie. At his suggestion, Mother agreed to spend some time at the Austen Riggs Foundation, in Stockbridge, Massachusetts. Austen Riggs is a private mental hospital, one of the few "open" hospitals of its kind in the country. Its patients are all in some form of therapy but, depending on the individual situation, free to leave the premises as they wish or to live away from them altogether as outpatients.

Mother remained there for two and a half months. She grew to love it. When she left, right after Christmas, she put the Clapboard Ridge Road house on the market and auctioned off all its contents—the furniture, the silver, the china, the paintings that had taken twenty-odd years to accumulate. The time had come, she said, to make a clean sweep.

I breathed a sigh of relief. The worst had come and gone.

In the spring, a month or so after Easter, Father telephoned me. Would I, he asked cryptically, come into New York City to check out my brother Bill? Like that very minute? He was in a small private hospital, Regent. . . .

Bill was lying in bed, all doped up. He smiled at me idiotically. Suddenly I realized how much I'd missed him.

"Listen, you jerk," I said. "Why did the nurse frisk me at the door before she let me come into your room? Are you an armed suspect? She felt me up and down—searched my purse, held my gum wrappers up to the light—"

Bill laughed. "Razor blades," he said. "Possibility of suicide."

"Are you kidding?"

"Yes," said Bill. "Yes. That's not on my agenda yet. But I'm extremely incommunicado. That makes them nervous. You know. Also my spirit of cooperation leaves something to be desired—they had to cart me over here in an ambulance when I wouldn't come willingly." He peered into the carafe on the bedstand. "Want some? I read somewhere that drinking hospital water is a sure way to get strep throat."

"Bill, why are you in this place?" He seemed perfectly normal to me. "All I know is Father said you're angry at him because he thwarted some elaborate arrangements you'd made to run away from school. But this seems a bit drastic, doesn't it?"

Bill chuckled and tossed a cube of ice into his mouth. "That's not why I'm pissed off," he said. "I'm mad because I'm *here*. They got me here under false pretenses. They promised me I'd only have to come here for one night. It's been two weeks."

"Two weeks!" I exclaimed.

"That's not all," said Bill.

"Wait a minute—who's *they?* Father and Nan?"

"This big-shot psychiatrist, Dr. Kubie. Very highly thought of amongst those who think of these things. Kind of a family retainer." Bill chuckled again. "When Father found out about my plot to skip out on Lawrenceville [Bill had left Eaglebrook that year to return to Lawrenceville], he made a surprise appearance there and said he'd like to drive me into New York and have me talk to this old family friend named Dr. Lawrence Kubie. Part of my escape plan was to go to New York anyway, so I figured it would save me the train fare, plus Father had the biggest chauffeur I'd ever seen and I had the feeling there wasn't much refusing. I packed my stuff and came with him to New York to Dr. Kubie's office. We had a strange series of meetings: both Father and I, then one of us, then the other one, then both, then one, and then the other. Finally Dr. Kubie said that in his judgment, to relieve Father and Nan of the worry that I might disappear that night—I'd made it pretty clear my plans were just momentarily suspended out of inconvenience—it would be best if I spent the night in a small private hospital. And I refused to, and ended up in an ambulance, and here I am and it's been two weeks."

"Unbelievable," I said. I felt the same kind of isolation as when I hadn't read a newspaper in a very long time.

"Father and Nan come here every day," went on Bill. "I don't speak to them. Nan brings me books, which I must say is a boon. But I won't talk to either of them. Won't say a word."

"That's a dumb way to get revenge," I said. "If I were you, I'd be talking a mile a minute with every last breath in my body."

"There's nothing to *say*," said Bill. "I've already *said* it. Listen, I'm not being paranoid—I'm *here*. This is actually happening to me. I mean, they've taken my clothes, my money, my wallet, all my goodies—very underhanded of them. The night I arrived, they gave me a whopping dose of Tuinol—"

"What's that?"

"Half Seconal, half Amytal. Deadly. I was naïve enough to think I could power my way through, but it dropped me like a tree. Now they've got me on a steady diet of sleeping pills because my time thing is all turned around. There's a nurse on guard twenty-four hours a day; I have no privacy."

"Why the nurse, seriously?"

"In case I might try to break out—how do I know why? The place isn't equipped for this stuff— Father came here once with his stomach thing."

"Why are you in bed? Why are you just lying there?"

"Where else am I supposed to be? They won't let me leave the room. Haven't been out of it in two weeks."

"But, Bill, why were you running away?"

Bill crunched on another piece of ice. It was a very hot day and I could feel rivulets of perspiration running down my sides.

"Well," he said, "during spring vacation, I met this girl from Tulsa. Father took Bridget and me to Sarasota, Florida—he's got buddies there who run the circus, Harry and Johnny North. Strange place to go for a vacation, Sarasota."

He looked off into space.

"And?" Sometimes Bill's digressions were so convoluted he told the beginning of a story at the end.

"Oh, well," he said, sighing. "I fell madly in love with this girl. When I got back to Lawrenceville after Easter, I figured school was a waste of my time, better to get a job in some oil field driving a truck, so I bought a New York-to-Oklahoma airplane ticket with the cash I've been saving up for about a year. My best friend finked on me. The housemaster, a very nice fellow, called me in and asked me if it was true that I was leaving school. I said yes, it was. And he said he felt obligated to call my father and notify him. This was on a Friday night and I was planning to split on Saturday morning. I knew Father was premiering *The Spirit of St. Louis* in San Francisco that night, and that it would be totally impossible for the housemaster to get through to him. He had no idea Father was, first of all, in San Francisco and, second, in the middle of a theatre. Like a fool, I agreed to spend that night at the dean's house—so as not to be a bad influence on the other kids—before making my exit in the morning. The next morning, I was having breakfast with the dean's wife when Father walked in the door, which startled me enormously. The rest is history."

My heart ached for him. Oklahoma oil fields would have been much better than this.

"I mean, I would have been happier," Bill was saying, "they never asked me—going to a public school, living at home. This is my fourth consecutive year in boarding school. There's something creepy about all these Eastern prep schools anyway. But I've always envied the kids who go to public school and drive their own cars and go on dates and live at home, and I never have seen why I couldn't do that."

"Didn't you ever ask?"

"No. I guess not. We're programmed to the idea that boarding school is the only way to get into a good college, and that's what you have to do to survive." He smiled at me ruefully.

"When are they going to let you out of here? What do you want me to say to Father? Tell me what to do." Terrible, I thought; this place was enough to drive anyone crazy. Even if the idea of running away had never occurred to Bill before, this experience would take care of that. Run! I wanted to yell.

"Tell him—" Bill looked away. "Tell him to set me free. Tell him to call off Kubie. Tell him I'd understand it if I'd tried to kill someone or— No, it's useless. Don't tell him anything."

When I left Regent Hospital, I called Father and told him that I was very angry. I said that whatever Bill's problem was, it didn't warrant the extremes that were being taken to correct it, that just because he was going through his own brand of nonconformity didn't mean he should be locked up like a lunatic.

"He's acting like one," replied Father. "He's got a behavior problem neither Nan nor I is equipped to deal with. He's broken every rule at Lawrenceville: drinking, smoking, television sets under the sheets at night, Christ knows what else. They can't keep him. What am I supposed to do with him? He won't speak to your mother, he refuses to speak to me. His attitude is just awful."

"Yes," I said, feeling ill equipped myself to deal with the situation. "He thinks you're displeased with him—at the very least, unfriendly. He's discovered the most effective way to return hostility is by ignoring you."

"What do you mean?" snapped Father. "That just makes me angrier."

"That's the point. It's a good attention-getter. Why don't you just ignore him, too? If you stop trying to bend him to your own vision of what he should be doing with his life—"

"Brooke," responded Father impatiently. "Don't be a butt-insky. I have to tell you something. I've lived a lot longer than you and I'm a lot smarter. And you don't know what you're talking about."

A week later, Dr. Kubie told Bill they had finally found the perfect place for him: a clinic in Topeka, Kansas, named Menninger's, founded in 1920 by the illustrious psychiatrist Karl Menninger. Kubie showed Bill some fancy architectural drawings of the place that made it look very posh and luxurious, and told him there were no bars on the windows, that he could leave if he wanted to, but he wouldn't want to because it was really nice. Nan borrowed Bill Paley's DC-3, an executive plane with comfortable seats and a bar, hired two male nurses, and flew Bill out to Topeka. That's how my brother came to be at Menninger's.

Truman Capote:

"*I had been with Slim and Leland at the feria in Spain and we came back to Paris. . . .*

"*Bridget had come down from school to visit them. They had to leave for New York one day before she was due back, and Leland said, well, why didn't Bridget just stay with me? And I was delighted. I thought she was so beautiful, like some extraordinary Eastern enamel. I had just met her, and immediately responded to her more than I ever have to any girl that age. I loved her looks, I loved the way her mind worked, I loved her humor. She was a very straight-forward person, a little shy, but not really. She had a wonderful directness once you made contact with her; then she trusted you. I did feel there was some kind of permanent sadness about her, which was curious because she was so radiant-looking. I often wondered if she knew how good-looking she was. . . .*

"*In Paris, she hadn't really been around too much, so that first night I said, 'I'm going to take you to Maxim's.' She had never been to Maxim's, and the whole idea flattered and flustered and pleased her all at the same time. She went through all kinds of little-girl antics like 'I haven't anything to wear,' and she wasn't really a little girl, she was sixteen, but no ordinary sixteen-year-old girl by any means—not that I mean she was sophisticated—way beyond anything like that; I just think she was intelligent. We went into Maxim's and we had a very, very grand dinner. She loved the whole thing. We talked a lot about diaries. Curiously enough, she had read*

*a lot of diaries. And she asked me if I had ever read any of the diaries
of Anaïs Nin, which was odd because at that time nobody had heard
of Anaïs Nin. She said she'd heard of these extraordinary diaries,
had I read them? And I remember being quite startled, especially
since they hadn't been published. I knew Anaïs Nin, had known
her for about ten years, and I said, 'No, they haven't any of them
been published yet; how do you know about them?' And she said,
'Well, I read a book of hers called A Spy in the House of Love.' I
was quite startled by that, too. . . .*

"And then, one day, I went over to Gstaad. I wrote her a note
and told her I was coming. It was February, wintry, a dreary day. We
had lunch at a nice little place in town near the Palace Hotel and
went for a long walk. There was a school there, Le Rosay, and all
these boys were out playing hockey. We stood and watched them
and discussed which ones were attractive and which ones weren't,
and why. And she was very expert. 'Oh, no, no,' she said, 'he looks
attractive—wait until he runs; you'll see it's all very odd, the way he
runs.' She had a good time that day. We laughed a lot.

"After that, I was living abroad for four or five years and when
she—when that happened, I hadn't seen her in such a long time.
And I must say I really was stunned. . . ."

A few months later, I was told that Bridget was now at Austen
Riggs. The reasons for her hospitalization were not entirely clear.
She had spent that year as a freshman at Swarthmore. She'd
been doing very well there and had a roommate she'd liked enormously. Father and Nan had gone to visit her several times, but on
their last visit they had found her in a room by herself. When they
asked her why, she said she didn't know, she just preferred to be
alone. She didn't want anyone around her. And finally, she didn't
want to go back at all. The only place she did want to go was to
Europe, although when pressed for details, she was vague. She
appealed to Father and said she needed help; there was something
the matter with her. She was vague about that, too.

Once again the old family retainer, Dr. Kubie, was called in
to advise. Once again he advised Riggs. Mother supported him.
Father did not. He contended that he couldn't possibly afford it;
Bill's expenses at Menninger's alone were driving him to wrack and
ruin. (And what's more, he wasn't at all sure he was getting his

money's worth. Bill certainly didn't seem to be appreciative; he'd just cut his way to freedom through a steel-mesh window screen with his cuticle scissors.) Mother said she felt so strongly about the positive benefits of Riggs that she would like to finance Bridget's stay there by selling her own securities. Father said okay; what did Bridget think? Bridget said she thought it might be a good idea.

I, too, was asked what I thought. I said I was sorry; it bore out the old domino theory, which, for obvious reasons, I didn't want to believe in.

At the point when Bridget made the decision to go to Riggs, nobody knew there was anything physically the matter with her. Later, when they reconstructed events, Father and Nan realized that she'd had seizures they'd never known about. There had been indications. When she'd come home at Christmas vacation, she'd sent word down on Christmas morning that she didn't feel well and couldn't get out of bed. They'd brought her presents up to her and had had a Christmas party in her room. Afterward, she'd slept for two or three days. Looking back, it even seemed possible that her fanatic secretiveness was in some way related. Perhaps she didn't want her illness discovered; perhaps, for a while, she thought it might go away on its own.

After several incidents at Riggs in which she passed out and remained unconscious for forty-five minutes to an hour, she was transferred to the psychiatric wing of Massachusetts General. Everyone was alarmed; Mass. General was a closed hospital, and we thought if she ended up there she would be scarred for life. The results of the electroencephalogram and other tests were not conclusive. Bridget returned to Riggs.

I drove there twice to see her. The first time, she was living at the center itself; the second, in Stockbridge as an outpatient. On both occasions she seemed cheerful. Our past differences were overshadowed by the present situation; we did not discuss them. She introduced me to her friends and to several doctors, showed me around, asked me to stay to lunch.

She told me that she was making progress. At first she'd refused to talk to the doctors; she would sit in silence until the scheduled hour was up. Now she had a wonderful doctor, a woman, Margaret Brenman, who was the foremost hypnotherapist in the country. Margaret Brenman, incidentally, was married to Bill Gibson, the playwright (*Two for the Seesaw*), who had written a

novel, *The Cobweb,* about a mental institution. Bridget said Dr.
Brenman was the only person in the world she completely trusted.
She had come to like Riggs and its routine; she was so busy she
rarely had any time. She had become involved with local theatre
production as a stage manager. One of her friends took me aside
and praised Bridget's efficiency; everyone was amazed that a girl
with such a delicate air about her could be so immensely practical.

Bridget confided in me that the main reason she had wanted
to come there was her fainting spells. They frightened her terribly,
particularly now that there seemed to be no conclusive medical
explanation for them. The first one had occurred while she had
been at school in Switzerland. The Swiss doctors' original diagnosis
had been that she had a possible dietary deficiency; after all, as I
knew (only too well), she had peculiar eating habits. She would go
on hunger strikes. At one point, much to the school's consternation, she had lived on nothing but cheese and chocolate for a
month; at another, Pablum. However, the recent tests indicated
that these spells might be caused by stress. But there was no way to
predict them, to prevent them, or, once under way, to control
them. In fact they had become more violent with time.

Because of this, she was glad to be at Riggs. She knew she
had emotional problems as well, but the doctors couldn't say which
caused what. Did emotions precipitate the seizures, or did the
seizures affect her mental stability? As long as she stayed at Riggs,
at least, she felt protected from herself. If she collapsed and went
into a comatose state, Riggs could handle it. And *privately.* She
was pathological about privacy. She didn't want people to know
about her sickness, to discuss it, to witness it. She didn't want to
talk to Mother or Father about it, and she didn't want me to,
either. For the time being, she didn't want to return to the outside
world. She felt more vulnerable there, and if she should have
another attack—she lived in terror of that.

Her relationship with Mother fluctuated. Mother and Kenneth had bought another, smaller house in Greenwich, overlooking
the Byram River. Occasionally Bridget would drive down for a
weekend. These weekends were sometimes comfortable, sometimes strained. By now, Mother had been told that Bridget's
fainting spells were more serious than she had supposed, that they
were really seizures. Still, our understanding was confused. As it
was explained to us, a convulsive seizure is the physical evidence of

an electrical storm within the brain. This abnormal electrical activity is a phenomenon caused by the physical and chemical make-up of the discharging nerve cells in the brain. The overactivity of these cells produces disturbances in consciousness and in muscular coordination. Therefore, the fundamental or primary cause is chemical (or really electrophysicochemical). But the chain of events leading up to the brain's chemical reaction can be infinitely varied. That variety was what made all the doctors evasive about giving pat answers when asked what Bridget really had. They told us that about 10 percent of the population had a predisposition to seizures but would never know it unless one or more of the contributing causes were also present. Some doctors believed that the causes were hereditary, some believed that they were symptomatic or acquired—by, for instance, some injury to the brain. Bridget remembered a concussion she'd had after a skiing accident; perhaps that had triggered the seizures. In any case, at the top of the list of contributing causes was emotional stress. Most seizures occur, we were told, immediately after some unpleasant or terrifying experience. There might be an increase of seizures during periods of worry or unhappiness. In Bridget's case, the possibilities were endless.

The shame and the fear she felt about her seizures were as old as history itself. The very word "epilepsy" comes from the Greek word meaning "to be seized." Martin Luther called it the "demon disease." The supernatural interpretation of seizures is centuries old. And over the centuries, the casting out of the responsible devils took many forms. In Christ's time, people spat on epileptics as a precaution against being possessed themselves; from this custom arose the name "morbus insputatus" or "the spitting disease." In the Middle Ages, openings were sawed in the skulls of those suffering from unbearable headaches or convulsive seizures to let the evil spirits escape. Not until the eighteenth century did leading European physicians abandon a belief in demon possession. In many parts of the earth, men still continue to treat seizures by exorcism. And even now, when the image of the demon as an evil force is no longer valid, the most civilized and educated man still fears being rendered unconscious by something that seems irrational and uncontrollable.

With Bridget, we knew that after a seizure the length of time it took for her to return to normal was commensurate with the length of time she'd been out—which could be a matter of minutes or days. If, say, she passed out for half an hour, it might be six hours before she was herself again. We also knew that before one, she was given a warning that manifested itself by feelings of mental confusion or stupor, nausea and dizziness. During the time she was unconscious, her pulse rate was drastically lowered and her respiration slowed; muscular rigidity set in; her body became cold; all the symptoms of catatonia were present. Catatonia, or catalepsy, is a syndrome most often seen in schizophrenia, so Dr. Brenman asked that Bridget not be subjected to situations which might cause severe emotional agitation. On several occasions, therefore, when plans had been made for Bridget to drive down to Greenwich, Dr. Brenman telephoned Mother and canceled the visit; she suggested that Bridget might be in no state, at that moment, to risk any further emotional disturbance.

These calls from Dr. Brenman left Mother depressed. She correctly interpreted them to mean that Bridget didn't want to see her. The implication that Bridget's seizures could be triggered by the vagaries of her relationship with her mother was a terrifying one. Dr. Brenman, positioned between Bridget and the outside world as a kind of intermediary, became, at these times, the object of Mother's frustrated rage. Dr. Brenman religiously adhered to the sacred principle of the doctor-patient relationship and refused to reveal any of Bridget's most intimate confidences. While Mother, on the one hand, expressed her endorsement of this principle, she was, on the other, subconsciously threatened by it. It placed her in competition for her daughter's soul. As much as she truly believed in the process of psychoanalytic therapy, there were moments when she now came to doubt its efficacy. Maybe it was all a futile stab in the dark. Always haunted by the specter of failure—failure as a mother, and therefore as a human being—she began to alternate between periods of high elation and quiet but grave despair.

Her letters to Bridget reflected these swings even more precisely than her spoken expression of them.

Dearest Bridget,

I want you to know that if I appeared cold to you today that it was because I was afraid of crying—and of having to leave the house. I love you as much as I ever have—which, my Brie, is as much as it is possible for me to love anyone—

and nothing can ever change this, not even if you go on hating me forever. No one in your whole life will ever love you as unselfishly as your mother. I want, at any cost to my personal happiness, your welfare and happiness. I hope that you will remember this no matter what happens. . . .

Dearest Bridget,

Perhaps you have noticed that my letters have pretty well stopped? It has finally occurred to me that if you don't want to see me, or talk on the phone, or even answer my letters, you certainly can't want to receive them. I am sorry, I hate for there to be no contact between us whatsoever.

I have heard from several sources that you feel you have no home. Perhaps you only say this to people for dramatic effect. I hope so. But in case you are fooling yourself, too, I want to remind you that you chose to leave your home, that where I am I will always consider you belong, whether you want it or not. You can choose not to behave like a daughter, darling, but you can't choose not to be one, just as I can't choose the kind of behavior I would most like from a child, or the kinds of looks, or the size, or the personality.

There is nothing you can do to stop my loving you, and worrying about you, and hoping always for your return. Perhaps you feel some guilt about going to live with your father three years ago, but please don't delude yourself as to the reason you went.

Have a lovely summer. I shall miss you as always. . . .

Dearest Bridget,

I'm glad you wrote that letter, and I know how hard it was for you. I've always known that you haven't hated me, but that it was an excuse to cover up other feelings you couldn't explain or couldn't face. But so long as you believed it was hatred, the result was the same.

The confusion and conflicts in your hearts that led you and Bill to leave your own home for your father's had been growing for several years, while I seemed to stand helplessly by and watch—hoping that you would see clearly some day before any real harm to yourselves resulted. If only I could have averted that final crisis three years ago—

not for my sake, but for yours—then I believe that Bill would not be at Menninger's, nor you at Riggs. But in those days you would not have believed the truth; it didn't fit in with your resentment—that I was influenced by jealousy.

And make no mistake about it, my darling, I was jealous—strongly, furiously—but only of your well-being—which I saw constantly threatened.

Anyway, it's not too late for you, that's certain, and I still hope not too late for Bill. . . .

Dearest Brie,

Your father reports that you have agreed to discuss your finances with him if he comes up on Wednesday, and that you deny you have been unwilling to give me an accounting in the past. . . .

When we made this arrangement, you were planning to become an outpatient [this was circled in red pencil by Bridget with the marginal note "Not immediately or even in the foreseeable future"], which would reduce your expenses quite a bit. You agreed to give me an accounting in February and monthly thereafter [again encircled by Bridget with the notation "Never discussed"].

Since any form of inspection, supervision, or advice—in fact, any relationship with me—appears to be difficult for you at this time—and since I must have same in order to provide for you, I am wondering if you wouldn't very much prefer to return to the status of '56 and '57—i.e., your father's supervision [Bridget's note: "What does that mean?"]. If you remember, I only took over because you wanted to run away to Europe; whereupon Kubie agreed with me that this could be disastrous for you, advised Riggs instead, which your father felt he couldn't afford. . . .

Dearest Brie,

Your father's visit to Riggs was highly successful, I gather—from everyone's point of view. For the first time he appears to be wholeheartedly for Riggs. Because he didn't know the place, or the doctors, he couldn't share my respect for its policies, and I so needed his moral support—without it the responsibility was too great for me alone. Often, in

these last months, I had begun to doubt my wisdom in
bucking him.

Now everything's going to be different! Peace, Praise
the Lord! And we'll advise you about your finances.

Kenneth returns on Monday from England after the
longest six weeks I ever spent. Nothing has been accomplished
on the new guest house/studio, just problems and crises all
summer. Our great elm fell across the river, creating a major
challenge to some 40 engineers, tree experts, city planners,
etc., and a nightmare for me.

Enclosing check and love,

Ma

Aftermath

"Brooke?" asked Father tersely. "Brooke Hayward? It's
damn decent of you to return my phone call. You're the hardest
person on earth to track down. Why don't you ever check in with
the office? Where the hell have you been for the last twenty-four
hours?"

"Oh, here and there." I grinned in the sweltering phone
booth, pleased by his familiar offensive. That was the summer I
started modeling. I spent a lot of time in phone booths, with a
fistful of sweaty dimes that kept slipping through my fingers and a
cavernous bag that held everything a job might require: make-up,
falsies, eyelashes, appointment book, shoes for all occasions—
everything except a pen with which to write down the next photographer's address. I was always ruining the sharp end of my eyebrow
pencil on whatever paper was handy, mostly the pages of the
Manhattan directory.

"Guess what? It's my lucky day. Avedon photographed me
for *Bazaar*."

"About time," rasped Father. "He's the best. Maybe I'll call
him—take a look at the proof sheets. What did they pay you?"

"*Bazaar* only pays fifteen dollars an hour for editorial work,"
I said.

"You should be paying Avedon," said Father, pretending to
be mollified. "He'll make you look better than you ever looked
before. By the way, have you any idea what's been going on in the
rest of the world today?"

"What?" I sighed, allowing myself to fall into the trap.

"It's July 5th, you nincompoop," said Father. "You're twenty-two years old. Christ, hard to believe. I just had Kathleen Malley make a reservation at the Pavillon for eight o'clock. Big celebration. Just the two of us."

"Neat," I said, surprised.

"Not too much of that crappy eye shadow," continued Father. "I'd like to see your real face for a change."

Where restaurants were concerned, Father liked the Pavillon for dinner and the Colony for lunch. Or, as an alternative, vice versa. The reason was very simple. Comfort. They made him feel at home. He had his own table in each. What had been, before he elected to have it, the worst table in the Colony—the one right by the kitchen door—became Mr. Hayward's table. A bottle of Wild Turkey was waiting on his table whenever he came in. He never drank too much of it but he liked to see it there. For a while he toyed with the idea of having the telephone company install a direct line from his office to the table, but was finally persuaded by his great good friend and lunch companion, George Axelrod (whose play *Goodbye Charlie* he would produce that fall), that that was *too* chic. Father and George put boeuf bourguignon on the menu at the Colony. They ate there so often they got tired of the usual fare. One day, George, who had been a mess cook in the Army, asked the maître d' to bring them whatever had been prepared for the staff's lunch. It turned out to be beef stew, much the best beef stew they'd ever eaten, and eventually it was elevated to a position on the menu.

At Le Pavillon, the night of my twenty-second birthday, Father was in an uncommonly jovial mood. He ordered two glasses and a bottle of champagne.

"Here's to you, kid." We smiled and clinked glasses.

"I'm flattered," I commented. "I've never seen you drink champagne before."

"Hell," he reminded himself after a sip or two, "the only way to drink this stuff is with good caviar." So he ordered some of that, too. It came with a double Wild Turkey, sent over by Henri Soulé, the formidable owner of the restaurant. By now, Soulé knew Father's preferences well.

Father leaned back expansively. "Well, darling, hold on to your hat," he said. "Are you old enough to keep a secret?"

"You know better than that." I laughed, twirling the stem of my champagne glass. Maybe he was about to give up producing to pursue his most extravagant ambition—running TWA.

"I've decided to get married again," he declared.

"But," I replied, stunned, "you already are."

"True," said Father. "First I'll have to get a divorce."

That was also the summer of the great Dominguín-Ordóñez *mano a mano* in Spain. My stepmother, Nan, was following it with a coterie of friends: Hemingway, Truman Capote, Harry Kurnitz. Father said he would fly there in a few days to give her the news.

"The reason I'm telling you tonight," he continued, "is because tomorrow Pamela is arriving here from Paris and I want you to meet her."

Pamela Churchill, it turned out ironically, had been introduced to him some months earlier by her good friend Nancy Hayward.

"You know I'm not a big fan of English women," said Father. "They all have bad teeth and talk through their noses; they're all also amoral, as opposed to immoral—big difference—all without exception. Don't know why that is. They all lead restricted lives until they get to be about sixteen and they start screwing *any*thing. So Nan had a helluva time, when she went off to Main Chance for two weeks, convincing me I should be polite and escort this dame—who happened to be visiting New York, didn't know her way around too well—to the theatre."

As a result of that reluctant theatre date, Pamela, who lived in Paris, was selling her fabulous apartment overlooking the Seine, giving up her staff of five, the bulk of her priceless Louis XV furniture, her life of incomparable culture and refinement and grace, to move to New York City on Father's account.

"That's romance," said Father.

There was no denying that. And his description of her was quite thrilling. She sounded like a mixture of Brenda Starr and Mata Hari. "Terrific auburn hair. Wonderful complexion. One of the most accomplished charmers of the century" was Father's summation.

He went on to explain. Born in 1920 to Edward Kenelm Digby and the former Honorable Pamela Bruce (later Baron and Lady Digby), Pamela had, at the age of nineteen, married Randolph Churchill, from whom she'd separated after the birth of their son, Winston. Thereafter she'd presided over a legendary salon, to which all the most illustrious diplomats, military figures, politicians, and foreign correspondents of wartime London had flocked. Over the next twenty years—right up to that time—although she had not married again, she'd lived a life of some considerable comfort, given her friendships with some of the world's wealthiest and most powerful men, including Averell Harriman (currently her husband), Gianni Agnelli, the Baron de Rothschild, and Ali Khan. ("It cost ten thousand dollars a year just to keep her apartment in fresh flowers," marveled Father.)

So vivid was his account of her, so boyishly gleeful and amorous, that it upstaged the moment, a day or so later, of our actual introduction, and remained fixed in my mind as the night we met.

Diana Vreeland, editor of *Harper's Bazaar* in the fifties—in which capacity, that summer of 1959, she'd given me my start as a model—editor-in-chief of *Vogue* in the sixties, and now Special Consultant to the Costume Institute of the Metropolitan Museum, had been a close friend of Father's and Pamela's separately, long before they knew each other.

When, in 1960, they were about to get married, she had it out with Pamela: "Pam, you've got to realize that he's a terrific *père de famille*. Before you came into his life, these three children were there. And there are difficulties. . . . Are you taking this into consideration?"

And Pamela replied, "I adore the children."

Diana went on, "It's a pretty tough life, that theatre life, and if you want to sit around the hotel in New Haven and smell the cigar smoke of fifty years coming out of those carpets while he's trying to get a show into New York, if you can stand that, Pam— What makes you think you can stand it? You've only spent the most beautiful time in the most beautiful places, always in fresh air."

But Pamela was oblivious. She answered, "I'm going to marry him because I've had everything in my life, but I've never really had a husband, and Leland is going to be my husband."

Just as Father liked all nursery food—puréed peas, creamed chicken, mashed potatoes, ice cream—he liked being taken care of. He loved Pamela because she took wonderful care of him. English women, far more than American women, are built-in nannies, housekeepers, gardeners—with the lightest touch in the world. Pamela had a great gift: she understood the men she loved. That was where she began and ended; it was the only life she had. No man could ever leave a woman like that. Where could he possibly go?

Diana Vreeland:

"Your father has always been a great romantic. I've known him forever and he hasn't changed by a hair. I'll never forget the time I first met him: 1922. Cedarhurst, Long Island, at a party. The heat of the collegiate days of 'Saturday night at the country club.' I'm very interested in this type, who is standing: he doesn't speak to any of the girls, he pays no attention to anything; the party goes on; he is obviously waiting for someone, but he doesn't kill off time with another chap or with anybody. I remember him because he was quite pale and his eyes were very avid and very searching. He was waiting. Then, in the dark—it was in the days when we wore big evening dresses—a girl comes in and she has on a navy-blue serge suit. And she has the most beautiful face I've seen in my life. Where she had been, why she had come at that hour, why she wasn't dressed, I have no idea. They said hello, they went straight onto the dance floor, and they danced the rest of the evening alone. Just the two of them. That was Lola Gibbs, who became his first wife. She was very beautiful. Very unusual. The face was small and very special. Also, the fact that she had on a blue serge suit and a shirtwaist made her look very racy, as she was in no way involved with evening clothes, nor did she give a damn. Nor did Mr. Hayward give a damn. They had their own ball, their own party, and that was all."

It was not so very hard to believe the popular legend that Father once, unable to resolve some lovers' quarrel with Lola on the way to Europe, jumped off the boat mid-Atlantic in despair and had to be rescued. He admitted to being not only a romantic but a man who truly preferred the company of women. Even when he most disapproved of the way I was leading my life, he still adored me, not because I was his daughter but because I was a female. I wanted him to be an archetypal father, and he couldn't be. He knew it, too.

He also was capable, at times, of a certain kind of cruelty. But although he could and did say savage things, his intention

never was to hurt. His cruelty was unthinking, childlike. He just
said what he thought was obvious; quickly and only once, because
the idea of saying it over again bored him. His mind would already
be on something else.

Like most children, he tended to speak very directly. But in a
Freud-oriented world, it was hard to take Father at face value, even
harder as I'd grown older and more sophisticated. He'd say,
"You're acting like a goddamned fool," and I'd think, He hates
me. But he'd meant nothing more than what he'd said. It didn't
really bear decoding. "I want a darkroom" did not mean he had
some buried passion for his mother. It meant he wanted a new toy
from F. A. O. Schwarz, a grownup's version of a huge electric train.
Exactly like Bill and his cars. It also meant that he wanted it
immediately and was prepared to go to any lengths or to any
expense to procure it. He had a childlike need for instant gratifica-
tion coupled with a childlike disregard for the impossible. Introduced to Loel Guinness's private helicopter on a visit to Palm
Beach, he coveted it on sight. So, undaunted by the fact he was in
his mid-sixties, he took up helicopter flying, managed to pass the
stringent physical requirements for getting his license, and converted part of the lawn at his house into a helicopter pad.

"What in God's name do you want to be an actress for?" he
used to ask me when I came up to his office for a friendly visit
between rounds. "For a smart girl like you—dumb, plain dumb."

His fingers would twirl a matchbook exasperatedly around
the edge of his desk. "Awful profession. Wait a sec—don't go
away, darling, sit down. Gotta finish this phone call—" He'd slam
down the receiver, punch another button. "Crummy connection—
bastards cut me off."

He had a way of leaning back in his chair that was more
ominous than if he had leaned forward. "What the hell was the
point of giving you an expensive education? Colossal waste of my
money, not to mention your time and brains." He'd fix me with a
stare so dark with oppression and injury that I'd swear to myself I'd
never come back. Then the intercom would buzz and he'd cheer up
again. And my resentment would subside while I played with the
new gadgets on his desk, and looked at the silver-framed photographs on the piano, and reminded myself that naturally it was
much easier for him to deal with a machine than a daughter, a
daughter being synonymous with emotion, and that the more he

loved me the more ferocious he was apt to become; in short, that I should be flattered.

"Your brother, Bill," he once announced to me on the telephone in the angriest voice I'd ever heard him use (Bill had just been returned to Menninger's after his most famous "elopement" had landed him in jail), "is going to be worth just about a plugged nickel. That is, if he's lucky. That bughouse is costing me a staggering sum of money—thirty thousand dollars a year after taxes; that's really, let's say, a hundred thousand bucks—and the little son of a bitch spends all his time there breaking out. I just finished telling him that in all fairness to his two sisters, I'm going to have to compensate by rearranging my will."

"Father," I said, thinking it was much easier to stand up to him long distance, "we both know you don't care about money and never have."

"That's almost true," he half shouted, "but not quite."

"What you mean is you care about Bill and he's hurt you."

"You're goddamned right," agreed Father. "Look at it from my point of view. I ought to kill him."

Perhaps there was even a redeeming quality to his cruelty, once one got used to the idea that it camouflaged his deepest feelings. The epitome of sophistication, he was also wonderfully naïve. I'd come to think of him as a castle. He'd built a wall around himself, a superb wall. He'd built it to keep people out. Although he seemed to have a marvelously outgoing personality, he'd built it to protect something very vulnerable, the most secret part of himself. It was quite a fortress. Walls work both ways; sometimes he couldn't get out himself. There were bottomless moats around the castle and forests of thorny brier. His drawbridge to the outer world was the telephone, and to that world he presented the image of a fast-talking, generous, charming, debonair entrepreneur.

"The Toscanini of the telephone," George Axelrod called him.

One of my favorite stories about him came from Josh Logan:

"There was a time when—before we did Mr. Roberts—I was in Cuba. I decided to take Jo Mielziner [the set designer] to a town on the south coast, Trinidad, an eighteenth-century coffee town that had died when sugar cane took over. It was very hard to get to. We drove up, and then couldn't even reach the town by car, because

*we had to park on the opposite side of the river. We took off our
shoes and waded across, put our shoes back on, and then started
into the town, this magic town; looked like a forgotten place. There
were palm trees and little, wonderful, colonial buildings painted light
blue and yellow and chalky red. We were enchanted and began
taking pictures. All of a sudden, a man came up to me and said in
español, said, 'You Logan?' I said, 'Sí, sí.' He said, 'Hayward want
talk—telephone.' It was absolutely impossible. How we had been
able to get there, how that phone could be there, how Leland could
ever have located both it and us, I still don't know."*

To me, that was more than a story, it was Father. Whatever else
happened in my life, I was confident that he could and would
find me. I knew that if I was lost in the darkest part of Africa, a
telephone would materialize, with Father at the other end, in-
structing me how to get home.

That summer, the summer of my twenty-second birthday, was
important to me for many reasons. (I tended to measure my life by
its summers, perhaps because I was born in one.) I felt, for the first
time in four years, a sense of resolution not only about my future
but about my family. Although Bridget and Bill were still hospital-
ized, I was hopeful about them, too. I couldn't help wanting to
believe that the fever which seemed to have gripped us all had
broken. It had been such a long time; we were at our weariest.

I was living in Greenwich not far from Mother and Kenneth.
I had two children, Jeff and Willie, who were two and one. Nothing in her life gave Mother more pleasure. She adored them and
they adored her. She, who had always been wonderful with small
children, who had even, in the last few years, given serious consideration to the idea of adopting a baby—who still dreamed of
someday raising a chimpanzee—now had two grandsons at her
permanent disposal. It was a fresh start.

Early in July, Kenneth left for England to see his children.
He was gone for six weeks. That was when the mighty elm tree at
the edge of the river inexplicably uprooted itself and toppled into
the water. The property was daily overrun by municipal engineers
who couldn't determine how to remove it. Mother went into
mourning. She said she was reminded of the death of a family

patriarch. In the middle of this confusion, she read a play—*Sweet Love Remember'd*—and decided to do it. In the last interview she ever gave, to John Keating of *Theatre Arts*, she gave as good a reason why as any:

"I loathe acting," she said, when the subject of her erratic commitment to her trade came up. "I loathe what it does to my life. It cancels it out; you cannot live while you are working. You are a person completely surrounded by unbreachable walls."

KEATING: "But isn't that just during the rehearsal period and the hellish weeks of tryouts when you are trying to live your way into a part? Doesn't life resume again after you have settled down for a run?"

"No." The answer was definite. "Being in a long run is the hardest work in the world. I loathe it. When you have been playing the same role for months, saying the same words and repeating the same actions on the same cues, night after night, you find yourself replying to a speech almost before its over, putting the glass on the table a step before you should. There is nothing more difficult than keeping a performance fresh. In *The Voice of the Turtle*, which was the most perfect little play about nothing, I found myself hating it after we had been running a while. I was appalled when I recognized what I was feeling. Here is this enchanting thing, I said to myself, and I loathe it. Terrible.

"One day a ladder fell on my head. I was bruised and bleeding from every pore; I made no sense for a whole day. That was the day I read the play. And I knew I would do it; I wanted to do it. After I got over my wounds, I was afraid to read it again. I don't know whether I was afraid because I felt I would like it just as much the second time and feel compelled to do it, or because I feared I might *not* like it as much. But I did read it and I knew I would have to say yes. This is a play about good people—I mean people you have respect for. And it is a very affirmative play. It proves that marriage can be a very good thing, building up each person, not that terrible possessive business. And with this play, every time I read it, it makes me want to do something nice, loving, for my husband. I think it will have that effect on others."

The morning Kenneth went to England, she called me.

"Brooke," she said urgently, "please come over right now. Can you? Your father's coming to lunch and I've just driven Kenneth to the airport; I'm all alone in the house."

"Father?" I asked, amazed.

"Yes," she said, out of breath. "He's stopping by on his way up to Stockbridge. Thank God he's finally agreed to have a look at Riggs and also to sit down and discuss Bridget's finances."

She hesitated. Then, "I need a chaperone."

I drove over. How could I resist? I'd been waiting twelve years to see them together again. Her house was perched almost on top of the Byram River. A long brick terrace ran the length; one could sit on its stone wall and watch the two swans drift by.

Father's car pulled into the driveway just as mine did. Mother was standing in her oldest pair of shorts—her uniform, she called it—way down at the far end of the terrace. Father and I walked toward her. Father shielded his eyes.

"My God, Maggie," he said. Mother didn't budge. She just stared. I began to blush.

"My God," he said again. "My God, Maggie, you look good."

She laughed, and the years fell away.

My cheeks burned. I couldn't look any more; I felt as if I were intruding on the most intimate conversation. I leaned on the wall overlooking the river. She still loves him, I thought; she's loved him all this time. Behind me I heard them moving toward each other, talking about this and that. The sun beat down on my hair. All this time, I thought. Chairs scraped; they were sitting down. Mother laughed again, a low throaty laugh. The river swirled by, bearing leaves, swans, water bugs.

I thought of the summer I was eight, the first summer in Brookfield. One day Bridget, Bill, and I, inspired by Mother's nightly installments of *Huckleberry Finn*, had tried to run away.

While Emily made us some hard-boiled eggs, Mother got six bottles of chocolate milk out of the icebox and divided them up into three of Father's handkerchiefs. "I know you'll have a wonderful time," she told us. "But if you get bored, please come home, 'cause I'll miss you terribly."

The road was too hot to walk on barefoot, so with no prearranged destination in mind, we crossed into the alfalfa and corn fields on the other side. Warm green cornstalks swished over our heads like a dense thicket of bamboo. At the far end of the meadow was the pine forest. After looking back to make sure the house was still visible, we plunged into its cool Gothic shadows and remained there for the rest of the afternoon. When there were no eggs left to peel or milk to swig, we fanned out on the dead pine needles and took a nap.

Although we had no intention of ever going home, toward

dusk we were seduced by the sound of Emily ringing the dinner gong. In order not to appear too anxious, however, we took the long way home, along the crest of the hill past Andrew Tomashek's unkempt farmhouse where the pigs were being fed, past a bramble of ripe raspberries, over the fence and down through the meadow, ignoring Bridget's squeals about nettles and poison ivy; then back across the road—cool now—and up onto the stone wall that bordered our property. Already we could tell it was going to be a perfect evening for a firefly hunt. The air was thick with the hum of tree toads and mosquitoes, the rustle of squirrels in the maples, the flutter of bats. In the home stretch now, we moved more and more deliberately, creeping from stone to stone over the vines of shriveled morning-glories, snatching at the overhanging branches for unripe apples, testing them, spitting them out at each other.

"Get the hell over here," bellowed Father. "What in God's name do you think I drove out here for, peace and quiet?"

Mother, Father, and Emily were waiting under the maple trees on the front lawn. All around us the earth was dissolving into sky, cobalt blue shot with opalescent fire, and just where the pinks and greens and yellows evaporated into night hung the new moon.

I climbed onto Father's gleaming shoes with my bare feet, and we swayed clumsily across the grass, circling faster and faster until my legs flew out from under me and I howled at him, between convulsions of laughter, to stop or I'd wet my pants.

The screen door banged; everyone else was going in to dinner. Father gradually lowered me to the grass.

"Now make a wish," he said, pointing my head toward the moon.

"What's yours?" I asked, rapidly discarding one idea after another.

"I've narrowed it down," said Father. "We stay here, right here in this very spot—here and now—for the rest of our lives. What do you think? When you were born I was thirty-four times as old as you, when you're thirty-four I'll be twice as old as you, and someday, at that rate, you may catch up. But for now, let's just stay here the rest of our lives."

Father and Mother, behind me, were still talking. I stretched out in the sun and gazed down at the water, letting myself lap against the stones. All this time, I thought over and over. All this time.

6

Bill

In the next decade, Father became a sick man. A stroke only temporarily slowed him down; more insidious was the excruciating attack of pancreatitis that put an end, once and for all, to cigarettes and liquor. Uncomplainingly he substituted Diet Rite Cola for Wild Turkey, and photographing the night skies for flying them. But he was not so uncomplaining about the lives of his remaining two children. After Bill's time as a paratrooper was up, he went from Germany, where he was stationed, to New York. Father and Pamela were not particularly enthusiastic. As a result of Father's cold shoulder, Bill came out to California to see me ("and bum around," said Father). He stayed on. I had removed myself to the comparative sanctuary of the West Coast upon my marriage to struggling actor-director Dennis Hopper; Father's disapproval of that union was exceeded only by Pamela's. (She was offended by the way Dennis dressed; he couldn't be relied on to turn up in the proper raincoat for the proper occasion.) The day of our wedding Father had called me up at 6 a.m. to remind me I still had time to call it off. When, in the 1961 Bel Air fire, Dennis's and my house burned to the ground, Father's response, by long-distance telephone, had been, "Christ, I hate Los Angeles; why the hell didn't God burn down the whole city while he was at it?" Although the next year Dennis and I produced a daughter, Marin, Father was not pacified. The day in 1967 that I decided to get a divorce, however, he called again. "Congratulations," he announced to me in Los Angeles from his office in New York City—I could tell by the sound of his voice that his feet were up on the desk—"on the first smart move you've made in six years." But he didn't let his dislike of Dennis (which survived the divorce) dampen his enthusiasm for the huge success of *Easy Rider*, which my brother, Bill, and Peter Fonda co-produced and Dennis directed.

On the night of February 3, 1971, Bill was skiing in Alta, Utah ("Terrific powder," he said wistfully), when Father was rushed to the hospital. Pamela finally caught up with Bill by telephone—no easy matter, as he put it—to report that the subsequent operation was an unqualified success. Father was already insisting that he be released at once. A good sign.

I had been easier to reach. I was walking out my front door in Los Angeles when the phone rang. Father, in rehearsal with Father Daniel Berrigan's play *The Trial of the Catonsville Nine*, had suffered a small stroke. A warning.

His decision to produce *"Catonsville Nine"* had provoked a certain amount of controversy. It was unusual for Father to commit himself to such an unequivocal, fervent, anti-war statement. Admittedly a WASP of the old school, he backed away hurriedly from anything radical. And during the year since he'd first read Dan Berrigan's adaptation of his book about the trial, Berrigan had gone on to federal prison, to serve out his term. In addition he faced co-conspiracy charges in an unlikely alleged plot to kidnap Henry Kissinger.

Father was also meeting with some resistance from Pamela. Pamela didn't condone Dan Berrigan's plan to go into hiding for those months before he finally faced his prison sentence. Not only was he a fellow Catholic but more, a Jesuit priest, and Pamela, who wasn't sure she approved of his burning Selective Service files in the first place, was positive she approved not at all of his going underground once he'd been convicted for it. She felt it was unethical. But Father loved the material. "Very gutsy man" was his opinion. "A lot braver than I could ever be. Besides, I don't think he's guilty. And if I only produced plays that followed my own political beliefs—God, how limited." *"Catonsville Nine"* was due to open on February 7th. Father's main beef, when he entered the hospital, was that he might not be able to attend the opening night of his play. Maybe he knew it would be his last. He did know that sooner or later he was going to end up in the hospital for some extensive tests; he'd been having trouble with the circulation in his legs and was buying time until after the opening.

On the night of the third, just before leaving his apartment at the Beekman to go to one of the last previews, he suddenly stopped talking in the middle of a telephone conversation with his secretary, Kathleen Malley. Kathleen had got through to Pamela on the other line, and Pamela had run into Father's bedroom to find him unconscious.

I called him from California right after he came out of surgery.

"How do you feel, Pop?"

His speech was still slurred from the anesthesia. "Groggy as hell," he answered faintly. "Hurts to talk. Big bandage stuck on my neck."

"Don't talk, Pop. You're not supposed to. Good luck with the play. I hear it's terrific."

Then he woke right up.

"Where'd you hear that?" (I could almost hear his head snapping around.) "Goddamned right, terrific. Did you ever get to meet Dan? Marvelous fellow. Play opens in two days. Don't forget to call Kathleen; she'll read you the reviews. I can't stand it; they won't let me out of here for my own opening. First one I've ever missed. Do you realize? Two days. What luck. Just kills me."

The morning after the play opened, I called him back. He was in wonderful spirits.

"What about those notices!" he shouted into the phone. "Great, huh?"

Then suddenly his mood changed and he launched into a long philippic, laced with colorful language, against doctors and hospitals and operations and anybody or anything that would conspire to remove him from the main action at a time like this.

"But, Pop," I protested. "The operation's a success and the play's a success. What more do you want?"

"To get the hell out of here and go straight to the theatre," he replied at the old staccato pace. "This bedpan routine stinks. I'm going home tomorrow."

"Well." I hesitated, knowing that was out of the question. "Isn't tomorrow a little soon? Shouldn't you be taking it easy? How are you, anyway?"

"Just sensational," he barked. "And that's the way I want to keep it. Another day in this clip joint will be the death of me. Lousy ice cream, too. Inedible crap. If you had any style, you'd air-mail me some Will Wright's chocolate mocha. I'll be out of here faster than you can say Jack Robinson; it's either that or starve, take your pick. They'd better not try to stop me or I'll walk out in my birthday suit."

"It's hopeless to argue with him," said Pamela a few days later. "Last night the poor nurse on duty couldn't keep him in bed. He was too strong for her. He wrestled with her, ordered her to pack his bag and help him check out. What can we do?"

And so it was that Father left the hospital four days after the operation. His doctor advised him to stay a couple of days longer. Father refused. He was recovering nicely. He vowed that if he was allowed to return to his beloved country home in Mount Kisco he would behave himself and stay in bed. Mount Kisco is about forty miles from New York City; it was suggested that he make the trip in an ambulance. He refused that, too. At his insistence, his limousine and driver picked him up and drove him home—to Haywire House.

He'd named the house after his cable address, an ingenious logo he'd devised thirty years earlier and had incorporated ever since into the letterhead of his blue-on-blue stationery. It was also imprinted indelibly on my mind. "Get it?" he'd pointed it out with pride when I was a little girl. "Haywire. Hay-wire. Damn clever. Means kind of nuts. Never forget it. That way you'll always be able to reach me day or night, wherever you may happen to be in the crazy old world."

On his way home, he complained of terrible stomach pains. Fortunately, Pamela had arranged for a doctor to be there on his arrival. As it turned out, Father was home only a few minutes and, although he had refused to leave the hospital in an ambulance, less than two hours later he was on his way back in one.

This time the stroke was not a minor one.

He was back on the operating table, six days after the first operation, as soon as the results of his second arteriogram were known. An arteriogram, it was explained to me on the telephone, is the painful procedure that outlines obstructions in the body's arterial system.

It took four or five hours, crucial hours in which, owing to the size of the new clot, the blood supply to Father's brain was minimal, practically nonexistent. The damage was done. The wonder was that afterward he could speak at all.

"Shit," said Bill through his teeth.

"What's the matter?" I looked up sharply from the *Sunday Times*. We were alone with Father in the hospital room; the nurse had gone out for a few minutes. Father was asleep. His breath rattled in his throat and whistled through his lips.

"What bothers me most is his stomach. Really hurts him. He's been complaining all day. Look how bloated it is." Bill sagged against the window. It was starting to snow.

"What did the doctor say this morning?"

"Oh, God, which doctor? I get so confused about their different functions, who's in charge of what, I can hardly remember their names. I think the internist—what's-his-name—said it was gas."

"Dr. Cox, you fool."

"Yeah. Enough gas there to fly a balloon around the world. Fly him to the moon."

"Forget the gas, Bill, and concentrate on his *mind*. Tell me what the hell we're going to do about that?" It was a week after the second operation and our initial optimism had worn off.

Bill shook his head and rocked back and forth against the window. His body seemed to move in sections; he had the characteristic Hayward build, tall and thin. But while Father had always carried himself with military erectness, Bill, who had actually been in the military, slouched.

"It's all so ill-defined," he said, peering at me intently over his steel-rimmed glasses. Bill was the only person I knew capable of throwing me looks that were in no way dissipated by the space of a room between us.

"There's no sense of reality," he went on, "because most of the intelligence we're getting here is filtered through Pamela, and that's whatever *they're* laying on *her*. Pure doctors' rhetoric. Propaganda. As I said before, who knows who's in charge of what around here? I mean, at some point you're still under a surgeon's care, and at some point the other doctor takes over, and then the head of the hospital wanders in for a look and issues a bulletin. We're staggering around in this no man's land in the middle of a pitched battle and our side is losing. I feel shell-shocked. No leadership, I tell you."

Once Bill got going, he could talk for hours. Monologues.

"We could set up a counter-offensive, but—" He sighed. "I think it's too late."

"What do you mean by that?" But I knew what he meant. He sighed again. "Well, you know."

"Sort of."

He was wearing a dark suit and tie—his hospital outfit—with cowboy boots. He usually wore cowboy boots. More comfortable, he said, with superior soles for striking matches on. As a concession to Pamela, he'd had the worn tooled leather polished.

"I guess it's not all fair to blame doctors, really." His eyes, behind the glasses, flashed blue fire. "It's what they're getting paid—a bundle—for. Lucrative way to make a living. Christ, no wonder they don't want to boogie in here and say, 'This is a total fucking failure—go home, folks, we screwed up this time.' "

"Horrible, isn't it? What do people with no money do?"

Bill began to pace up and down past the row of jars hanging upside down by Father's bed. "Well, these cats honestly don't think they're lying. They have different priorities from us, that's all."

There was a long silence. Father was snoring. His chest rose and fell with an irregular rhythm.

Bill moved back to his window, one boot in front of the other: heel, toe, heel, toe. "It's really quite simple," he said at last, turning to look at me. "A young hot-shot surgeon did this relatively experimental operation. The dude wants very badly not to go wrong—in the sense that if he does, Father could die. And Father's not exactly a nobody, either. Bad publicity."

He rubbed his back vigorously along the sharp juncture where the window and wall met.

"Do you want me to scratch your back?"

He smiled. "Doesn't sound all bad."

"Well, come over here. I'm too lazy to get up."

Bill came over and presented his back to me, blocking my view of Father. My chair was at the foot of the bed. Bill grasped the iron footboard and leaned back into my fingernails.

"Ah. God, that feels good," he groaned. "Over to the left and up. Feels like I've been bitten by a bedbug. Guess that's not too likely at the River Club, though, huh?" Bill didn't care for the Beekman and had moved over to the River Club because of the dining room there. He liked the view, at breakfast, of the boats on the East River.

"Just nerves," I said, trying to scratch through his jacket.

His back twitched disjointedly like a cat's.

"I really hate his stomach scene," he murmured, looking down at Father. "This could turn out to be the doc's first failure. That's the thing, you see. His whole objective is to keep Father alive. Ours . . ." He lapsed into silence again.

"To let him die?"

"Um. There's clearly so much brain damage." He straightened up and walked around to the side of the bed.

"Pop," he whispered, gently taking Father's hand. Father's hands were rather small-boned and slender. Mother had told us we were lucky to have inherited them from him, an opinion that had always pleased him enough to quote. Now his hand seemed like a child's in Bill's. He slept on.

I was reminded of the worst dream I could remember ever having had. I was six years old, and in the twenty-seven years since then nothing had equaled it in terms of sheer terror. Every night for weeks afterward, Emily had had to sit by my bed until I dropped off to sleep; it was in the days when my dreams were apt to recur.

I dreamed that one day an indescribably horrible monster rampaged through Brentwood, killing everyone in sight. Bridget, Bill, and I, forewarned by its dreadful roar, were able to save ourselves by hiding behind the blue sofas in The Barn. However, when we crept out in the silent aftermath, we found Emily, Elsa and Otto, and George Stearns gathered on the gravel driveway, weeping. The monster had killed Mother and Father. Then, abruptly, I was with my friends in the school cafeteria. With destruction all around us, the Red Cross had arrived and were passing out supplies and hot lunches. The food was extraordinarily delicious. It was a sort of fried chicken, succulent and delicate, quite unlike anything I had ever seen or tasted. While I was chewing on the bones, my teacher stopped by the table where we were all eating.

"Brooke," she said. "We've given you the wrong lunch. Let me take it back and get you another."

"Oh," I answered, "I'm so hungry and it tastes so good."

"But Brooke, dear, what you are eating," she pointed out, "are your father's hands."

I had awakened screaming and screaming. Emily said she'd never heard such a sound. It was strange, too, because I'd never heard of cannibalism. It wasn't until I'd grown up that the dream was interpreted as being a result of the spanking that Father, against his will and at Mother's insistence, had given me that summer in St. Malo.

Father's hand was so emaciated that when Bill held it up, light from the bed-table lamp passed through it, giving it the unearthly glow of a Georges de La Tour painting.

"Look," he said. "You can see the silhouette of the bones. Look how transparent his flesh is. Amazing."

He laid Father's hand back on the sheet and bent over to kiss his forehead.

Bill is wonderful, I mused. My kid brother. Who would have thought? Miraculous. Thank God he's here or I couldn't possibly get through another day of this torture. Crazy Bill. He really is still crazy but nobody knows that any more except me—and maybe a few other well-chosen people—because most of the time he acts saner than anyone else for miles around. Just sometimes . . . Of course, it had occurred to me that the reason I knew that Bill was crazy was because I was secretly crazy myself.

"Sometimes," I said out loud, "I don't know, I don't know. Do we *want* him to die? What we *don't want* is for him to go on living like this, but—"

"It's a bummer, no doubt about it." As Bill moved down the line-up of suspended glass jars, he tapped each one experimentally with his fingernails. The room tinkled with varying tones. "But, Brooke, he *is* dying. Face it. He can't possibly go on like this. When you come in here every morning and rap with him and there's no change, or he's worse—yes, worse. I remember when I first got here. At least he was coherent for a while, and then he kind of slipped into the—weirdness. Did I tell you what he said when he first saw me?" Bill came and sat beside me in the other armchair at the foot of the bed.

"Go on." I was learning more about Bill in these afternoons at the hospital than in our entire adult life. There was a strange urgency to our conversations, as if somehow we had been given a second chance to catch up with each other—but if we messed it up this time . . .

"Well, when I got into New York I went over to the apartment at the Beekman. And I was dealing with a beard, remember? A full-on beard, which Pamela had never seen before. It completely freaked her out." He threw back his head and laughed.

"I wondered what had happened to the beard."

"Well, she made me go to the barber, Father's barber at the St. Regis. What a hassle. She said if Father saw me in that condition, he might have a serious setback. Wouldn't do him any good to get him mad, irritate him. She felt my hair was a little long, too, so I put it in a ponytail and told her I would dialogue with Father full-face only, so he'd never see it." (He laughed some more, his zany laugh, which always made me giggle.) "And we came over here. To the hospital."

"Well, at least you still have your mustache."

Bill stroked it fondly.

"He was conscious at first," he went on, "and coherent. We talked for a minute and he said that his play was terrific. He asked me what I was doing, and I told him *Idaho Transfer* [after *Easy Rider*, Bill and Peter Fonda figured they were a winning combination and had produced and directed two more movies together], and he said that was a terrible title. Hated it. Then he asked me how come I wasn't in uniform—was I on leave? I didn't want to remind him I'd been out of the paratroopers for ten years. I could have walked in with a full beard and dark glasses and smoking a joint, and he wouldn't have known. His vision thing wasn't happening. He was laying back, looking awful with the bandages and shit. He asked me if I had a gun. I said, 'Yes, I do.' He said, 'What kind of a gun is it?' They seemed rather strange questions. And I said, 'Well, it's a Smith & Wesson thirty-eight special,' and he said, 'Oh, good.' Bizarre fragmented dialogue like that."

We were definitely flip sides of the same coin. I knew that much. I felt better whenever Bill's life touched mine. I felt, when I saw him, as if I were coming home after a long journey. As unreliable as he might be (and was) where anyone else was concerned—as eccentric, as fundamentally off center as I knew him to be—at that moment, he was the only person left in the world with whom I would unequivocably trust my life. We sat side by side in the armchairs at Father's feet, and I thought irreverently it was unfortunate Bill was my brother; if it weren't for the taboos about incest, I would have married him. It wasn't so much sexual attraction (although I'd never pursued this line of psychological investigation: the taboos were thicker than blood); it was much less complicated than that. We had a tacit understanding.

"I feel alone," I said to him. "Do you ever feel alone? I mean *alone*? Way up high where the air is so thin and cold nothing much can live? And besides, my mind is going. I'm turning into a manic-depressive right here. Whenever I come into this room, it happens. Up and down. Up and down. Both at the same time. It makes me queasy."

"Don't worry," he said. "That's normal."

Normal, I thought. It was cold in the room. A bracing climate. Freezing, actually. My skin hurt as if I were walking naked through a driving blizzard. Father's body lay before us like the mound of a newly dug grave beneath fresh snow. All that white.

All we could see of him, from where we sat, was his swollen belly looming toward us. A great white whale. Moby Dick beached.

Normal? There was definitely something in the air.

"Stop worrying about it," said Bill. "Your senses are more acute than usual, that's all. They're probably more acute than the average citizen's, anyway." He paused. "You're right. You are a manic-depressive." He grinned at me. "Join the gang." He went back to staring at Father's feet beneath the ghostly bedclothes.

"By our standards," he said without interrupting his contemplation, "most people don't know the meaning of the word 'depression,' although it's become fashionable to bandy around. But we had a superb education; our family wrote the textbook. We could probably give courses in it. Carry on the tradition. Those lows. Jesus, I think I know what Hell looks like. I've charted it, every square inch of it. I've been in states so bad I've been paralyzed with fear. Literally couldn't get out of my bed for *weeks*. Totally wasted time. Pillow over my head. Really rank. No showers, no food, couldn't talk, couldn't read—couldn't even concentrate on the TV. No relating to my life at all. Total stupor. Bad. I *never* want to go through that trip again. But you have to remember one thing: most people don't spiral down as low as we have, but they sure don't get up as high, either. No way. They mosey along on relatively level ground, a little happy, a little sad."

"Sounds good to me," I said. "I'd like that for a change. Sounds peaceful."

"Boring," said Bill. "Boring. You'd get sick of it. We've been exposed to too much. Overexposed. Once you've been there—those highs!—my God, they're like Mount Everest. Hard to scale but worth it when you get to the top. Dizzy stuff." Bill liked challenges. He was a mountain climber. He liked mountains, climbing up them and skiing down them. He'd been up and down the Amazon in a friend's boat and over the Snake River rapids in a raft. He'd run guns down through Mexico and smuggled cocaine up from Bogotá. Lived off stolen credit cards. Lots of nefarious adventures. He'd wrangled horses, raced motorcycles, had sailed the seven seas.

"On the whole," continued Bill, so softly that I thought for a moment he was talking to himself, "if I dropped dead tomorrow, and had that moment to look back and decide what more I wished

I'd done in my life, it would be hard. I've done an awful lot of the things I've fantasized doing. I've led a pretty exciting life."

He stood up and stretched. "Got to keep moving."

"Not bad for an old man of twenty-nine. Like what fantasies?"

Ping! went the glass jars as he passed. There was a slight gurgling aftermath as the pale fluids in them trembled.

"Oh, I think the fantasy of being reasonably successful in a fairly competitive business, making a lot of bread without having had a formal education. All kinds of possession fantasies, like being able to travel here and there, being able to do all the inane things you want—not feeling trapped because you can't afford this or that. The ones you have when you're a teen-ager, of where you want your life to go in terms of success or material trips. I've skated through most of those. I mean I've done it. Flashy cars. Being a rich bachelor, marriage, kids. Then the fantasies you have when you're married, of being a bachelor again. Being in love. It hasn't been all bad. Can't really complain. I had the opportunity to make my own mistakes. Made every one." I loved him dearly.

"But Bill," I sighed. It was really snowing hard now; we would have trouble getting a taxi to the theatre that night.

As he'd said, he'd had more opportunities to do more things than most people. What he'd chosen to do with those opportunities—that was another matter altogether, a matter of some concern to everyone in his family except me. What was to Father, for instance, patently erratic, if not downright demented, behavior was to me Bill's saving grace. Literally. He was always moving on. An aberrant knight. He was always disappearing without trace or warning. He was even hard to find when he was around. Once he'd been sighted, he was hard to keep in focus; he kept slipping over the horizon. And he never looked back. Then unexpectedly he'd reappear. "Heard from your no-good crackbrained brother," Father would say with gruff affection. "Turned up again the other day like a bad penny." As an escape artist, Bill ranked with Houdini. Father and I argued about it: Father insisted that Bill's demonic elusiveness was a fatal flaw and I claimed it kept him alive.

"But, Bill, tell me which ones—the fantasies—you *haven't* lived out."

"I'm not going to tell you all of them. But they are almost all related to being outdoors. Never got to be a commercial airplane pilot—that was always one. Let's see, what others do I have? Actually, what I've always wanted to own and be able to operate properly is a commercial tuna-fishing boat. I've always had a thing about boats and working on them; fishermen—I don't know—the ocean, independence, the whole thing, whatever it is. I've had that one for fifteen years. I still flash on it from time to time. The only thing that stops me is that I really wouldn't know how to find a school of tuna." And he laughed, carrying me with him. "But I still hang on."

Father moved in his sleep. It was getting very dark. Bill turned on another light.

"Pop," he said. "Are you okay?"

If I'd had to distill my feelings about Bill into a single image, it would have been rooted in the mythology I'd loved as a child. Jason and the Argonauts, Odysseus sailing on. And Hermes, with winged sandals, who was, from the day he was born, the shrewdest and most cunning of all.

Father opened his eyes and looked at us for a minute, then closed them again.

"Do you realize we're going to be orphans?" Bill asked me, his hands clenching the iron footboard of Father's bed. "That'll be a new one."

He'd read my mind.

"Aren't we too old to be orphans?" Past the statute of limitations. But we still thought of ourselves as children. Bill's question was interesting. Would we ever grow up? It didn't seem likely, at the rate we were going. Hansel and Gretel without a father any more, just a stepmother. Ridiculous. Why was it that we—and all my friends, the ones I liked the most—had remained, at the core, children? Why did we all seem so much less mature than our parents—as we remembered them—had been at the same ages? Why, when our prime ambition as children had always been to grow up, were we now so protective and appreciative—in ourselves and each other—of our most childlike characteristics?

Maybe it was how we'd managed to survive. Protective coloration, like a permanent case of Bambi's spots.

"How did we survive, anyway? How did we get this far? Don't you ever wonder about that?"

Bill smiled ruefully. "Just lucky, I guess. The old whatcha-macallit. Pioneer spirit. Staying power. We must have inherited something from the Colonel and Grandsarah, after all. In a rene-gade form, a mutation; may be troublesome to our public and even to our near and dear, God bless them, but—here we are. Fit as a fiddle."

"What do you mean? Crazy as a coot is more like it. Look at the whites of your eyes. Here, I'll get out my compact if you like."

"Crazy is *bueno, muy bueno*," chuckled Bill, rolling his eyes in their sockets.

"Come on, Bill, cut it out. They'll get stuck like that, as Mother used to say." *As Mother used to say.* Not a single day of the last eleven years had gone by that I didn't wonder what Mother would have been doing right that very minute.

"Crazy keeps us young." He thumbed through the pile of notes and telegrams on the table.

"In that case, we'll live forever."

"God, I hope so. Ah. Look. Here's one from Kate Hepburn."

The nurse had just come back in and was looking at us both strangely. "He's still asleep, I see," she announced briskly.

"Superior deductive reasoning," muttered Bill under his breath, his face buried in the latest flower arrangement. "Keenly observed. Look where sanity can get you—"

I stuck my elbow in his ribs. "Bill." I could feel hysterical laughter coming on. "Be serious. I want to ask you a serious question."

"What?"

I'd never dared ask him, perhaps because I was afraid of the answer. There was no telling why I was curious enough now.

"Well, have you ever been so depressed you wanted to kill yourself? I mean, have you ever thought about what would make you . . ."

"Hmm," replied Bill, becoming serious very quickly. "Let me take you away from all this, my dear." He extended his arm to me.

"Hold down the fort for us," he said to the nurse; "we'll be back." He winked at her.

We walked down the corridor and around the corner to the elevator.

"I must be going stir-crazy," I said. "It's awfully nice to be out here, hideous as it is."

"Let's chow down," said Bill. "I'm starving. I see a double Bloody Mary in my immediate future."

"What about Father?"

"We'll check on him after the play. Tell him what we think."

"They won't let us back in."

"Private room. Different rules." He snapped his fingers. The elevator doors opened.

I felt very gay (as if we were playing hooky) and, at the same time, guilty. Unfairly privileged. Charmed. And running the risk of missing something.

"Well, have you?"

"What?"

"Ever thought about committing suicide?"

"Often." He ignored the riveted gaze of the other occupants of the elevator. "I've always held on to it as an alternative. If things got really screwed up—the idea of having another choice. I've never tried it, although I've spent a lot of time thinking about it. But thinking about it is a way of recognizing there is a choice. I'd like to think that my affairs would be in order. But, of course, if my affairs *were* in order, I wouldn't be thinking about suicide."

He chuckled to himself. Bill tended to communicate information in a way that was meant less for other people's enlightenment than for his own private entertainment.

The elevator let us out into the lobby. Now he was lost in thought.

"Where do you want to eat?" I tugged at his arm. We moved toward the night.

"Shit, I don't have any of the right clothes. I left Los Angeles too—uh—precipitously, you might say. It was seventy degrees there. I didn't have a chance to unpack my ski gear. I need warm gloves desperately."

"Russian Tea Room, please," I told the cabdriver. "I wonder where Pamela was this afternoon."

"Legal crap," said Bill, rubbing his hands together. "Once I got frostbite skiing, and that screws your hands up whenever they hit the chill winds afterwards. Wanted to be a surgeon, too, oddly enough."

"How would you do it?" I asked, staring out the window.

"What?" Bill glanced at me. "Kill myself? You do persist in these morbid notions."

But I knew he was secretly pleased to be asked.

"I've always thought if I did it I would shoot myself with a pistol," he replied matter-of-factly.

I wasn't so sure about that. "What, shoot yourself in the head? Terribly gory."

"No, I figure I can find my heart." He laughed. "*Quick*. That's the trick. Bang. Whatever pain there was would be so instantaneous it wouldn't count. I decided a long time ago—back in the Menninger years—that if I did it, it would have to be one hundred percent for real. No false attempts. Pills would probably be the most pleasant way, except so many people fuck up and leave clues and get saved. Another thing about pills is if you do get discovered, the recovery period in the hospital is extremely unpleasant—I mean from the stomach pump to all kinds of crummy aftereffects. If a strong enough barbiturate like Amytal is in your system for any length of time, you're futzing around with brain damage, kidney damage. Ideally, what you get is the spy pill. You just bite down on it—"

"Cyanide?" I could feel him opening up, relaxing.

"Yeah. Potassium cyanide. You're dead instantly. No pain, all that shit. It's funny, I have a thing about disfiguring my body. I suppose that's why I'd rather shoot myself in the heart than in the head. I guess anybody's who's really serious just goes and jumps off a bridge. Which I don't think I've ever had the urge to do."

The experience of Menninger's, I was convinced, had burned a small hole right through the center of his mind just the way a laser would, neat and clean. He'd spent the most formative years of his adolescence there. Wasted years, untold damage. A small hole in his brain that went right through his forehead and out the back. It wasn't that he was crazy now—he certainly hadn't been when he went in—but that empty spot explained a lot. It had been fashionable to send your children to places like Menninger's in those days, if you didn't have the time but did have the money. It took a lot of money. Bill had been sent up when he was sixteen. Two and a half, three years. I went to visit him once, flew to Topeka. Walked around the grounds. It looked like a country club, lawns as far as the eye could see. From the moment he'd arrived, he'd tried to escape. He'd broken out several times, stolen getaway cars, crossed state lines in them, landed in jail. Father had said, "This time I've had it with the kid. He's really loco. Let him rot there." And wouldn't bail him out. Nine days in jail. Bill knew better than I about emotional detachment, although we'd all been given an equal head start.

He sighed and fished through his overcoat pockets for a cigarette and matches. "I always thought I'd check into a hotel with some creepy desk clerk to find me. You know, to be the wife or husband— I never wanted anyone to find me, it's a bummer to be around. Notes can be very irritating, but I have always thought there should be a few instructions. I wrote the note once—I hadn't figured out how to do myself in, but I did write the note."

"What did it say?"

"Well, most people who commit suicide are trying to inflict some kind of pain on other people, which I've always felt was immoral. I think anybody's got the right to do it, to me it's not a mortal sin, but you ought to be kind of clean about it and not hassle too many other people. I've always felt you ought to check out with a little—"

"Style?"

"Yeah. But to try and blame it on somebody else is wrong, especially if you are successful. [We both grinned at that absurd bit of sophistry.] So I tried to make it clear, in my note, that there was absolutely nobody to blame, that I didn't feel there was any way to continue on my present road and couldn't see any way to get off it, either."

He began to laugh again.

"Cracking yourself up, aren't you?"

"I carried the note around for a while, figuring the precise moment hadn't quite come, but it was right around the corner—and then finally I got embarrassed and threw it away."

Somehow, this was all very reassuring.

"Bill, listen. I want to ask you another question." I knew he was thinking about it anyway, even if he didn't verbalize his thoughts without being prompted, or exhibit my kind of curiosity.

"When Mother and Bridget died, what did you think? How

did you feel? I hadn't seen you in so long. You were totally withdrawn at the time, do you remember? You never said much."

When I asked him the right question he'd talk all night. Sometimes he would hold forth about the most astounding trivia. He was a pack rat of information on every subject known to man, the more arcane the better.

"When Mother died"—Bill cleared his throat—"I think I was shocked that I was not as moved as I felt I should be, not at that time. I don't think I was aware of the reality for some time afterward. I've always buried that kind of trip. Because I remember being constantly stunned that I wasn't more moved. I think the only time I cried was at the service. And I don't know if that would have happened if everybody else wasn't unhappy."

He began to laugh.

"There you go again, you crazy galoot. I remember you flew in from Topeka in a rage because of the black-suit episode."

"Yeah. I'd just terminated Menninger's as an outpatient. I was engaged to Marilla and going to school, I think, and working, and about to— I recollect Mother died on the first day of 1960 and I went into the paratroopers on the fourteenth. I was visiting Marilla's apartment when the phone rang and I had one of those flashes about some impending disaster. It was Father."

"What did he say?" All those years ago. I had never forgotten how angry I'd been at Father for not telling me himself.

"He said she'd died of natural causes but that the papers were very likely to pick it up in some other manner. And obviously for me to fly back immediately. He told me to bring a black suit and all that—he didn't have to *tell* me—but I remember the dialogue. So the following day I went to a store where a charge had been set up for me to buy clothes while I was in Menninger's. I bought a black suit, shirts, ties, all the gear for a funeral. Hadn't been in there in several years, so when I went to charge it they said they'd have to get an okay from Father. They got off the phone and said, 'This charge has not been authorized.' I said, 'Well, who said no?' I couldn't believe that Father would have refused it. They said, 'Well, some lady answered the phone and she said no.' And I remember assuming the lady must have been you. I guess I was eighteen, yeah, and extremely irritated about the whole thing. Then before I took off for New York, I spoke to you on the phone and you clued me in about Pamela. Which was the first I heard about that business. I knew that Father and Nan had had some kind of problem; he'd told me that. But I had no idea there was another woman involved. And she nixed the charge. I flew back that afternoon, but I wasn't nearly as distraught as I should have been. And I was extremely pissed off about the clothes."

That memorial service in Greenwich, Connecticut. The family, according to the protocol of these things, had traipsed in, in single file, to be seated in the front row after everyone else. The church was jammed. We—Bridget, Bill, and I—felt more exposed at that moment than ever before in our lives. Afterward I'd sworn to myself I'd never go to another funeral. If it hadn't been for Bridget—

"Aha! That explains your filthy mood. You were really uncommunicative."

If it hadn't been for Bridget, two thousand horses couldn't have dragged me to another one.

"And when Bridget died, it was the same thing. I was married, stationed at Fort Bragg, rented house, the phone rang, and it was Father again. 'Natural causes,' he said."

Bill put his face up to the partition where change was made. "Driver, got a match?"

"We're almost to the Russian Tea Room."

"Thank God. I want caviar. Golden caviar."

"Who do you think you are, the Shah of Iran?"

"We deserve it."

"Is that all he said?"

Bill struck the match and let it burn almost to his fingernails before blowing it out.

"I can only remember both calls minimizing any question of suicide. The—Mother's thing—the only indication was that the press would probably pick it up because there had been a bottle of sleeping pills on the scene. Very underplayed to me. With Bridget —I think the line was the same; she'd probably taken two of the wrong drugs or whatever."

He was even vaguer about the details than I. Right afterward, I had been too numb to engage in the proper detective work, and later I didn't have the heart for it. Besides, as time went by, the explanations that we got from Father and Pamela had become increasingly elliptical.

"I didn't even know she had epilepsy," Bill was saying. "I'd no contact with the outside world for a couple of years. But I do remember the funeral. And the church. It was dark during the service, late afternoon and raining. Typical funeral."

The only funeral I'd relented about going to after that was David O. Selznick's, because he was almost like my own father. *My own father—*

"Oddly enough, I still flash on Mother from time to time—"

Bill struck another match and aimlessly let it burn.

"I mean the reality that you'll never see somebody again never struck me fully. You just get a taste of it from time to time."

"Bill, listen." The cab was making a U-turn on Fifty-seventh Street to land us at the door of the restaurant. "Listen."

This was the crux of the situation.

"Do you think the possibility that Mother and Bridget . . . killed themselves has ever affected your feelings about suicide? Your own, I mean?"

"I'll tell you," said Bill, scrunching the lower half of his body forward so that his hands could root for change. "It's possibly been, on some small level, a preventive, only because I feel that it would be more of challenge *not* to do it. Since it seems to run in the family. It's like trying to beat the system. There must be something inherently weird—the family drops like flies."

The sound of his laughter, as we emerged from the cab, rang in my ears for the rest of the evening. There had been times, in the last eleven years, when I had been furious with Mother and Bridget. When I stopped to analyze my feelings, I knew it wasn't really important to me how they died, and never had been. What made me angry, though, aside from the primary fact of their deaths, was the dark realization that *whether or not* they killed themselves, they had tinkered with my mind. They'd given me a double whammy. They'd planted it like a minefield with the idea, the *concept* of suicide—but also, by that perverse act, had disarmed the tricky little mechanisms set up to explode. Leaving it strewn with litter. Leaving me with the feeling that although the two things canceled each other out, I had been victimized, raped. Betrayed. The feeling of impotence. Yes? No? Would I ever dare? As Bill said, although it was a free country and we had a choice, we didn't really. Suicide was a luxury we couldn't afford. Not with that background. Not with those odds. For me, it wasn't out of the question because of grave moral considerations but because I always resisted the predictable.

7

---◦◦◦---

Father

$\mathcal{J}$immy Stewart:

"Your father did a funny thing. He was always trying to get me married. When I got back from the service, he came to me and said, 'Now, look, you've been away for five years and the movie business is all changed and God knows what, you don't know what you're gonna do—what you ought to do is marry a rich girl and take it easy. And I know exactly the one. Take her to dinner and the theatre and marry her and take it easy, because now you've had five years—and as I say, I don't know what's going to happen in the movie business.' I said, 'Well—' He said, 'Now do as I say, here is her number and call her. So I did. I went and picked her up, asked the doorman to get a taxi—this was in New York—and she said, 'Don't we have a car?' That was my first mistake. Then we had dinner and we just—didn't seem to have much to talk about, and she ordered something that she didn't like. Then we went to the theatre and it wasn't a very good play. After the theatre we had a terrible time getting a cab, and she said, 'I'd like to go home,' so we went home. She said goodbye and left me in the lobby and that was it. Your dad, the morning after, called me up and said, 'How'd it go? How'd it go?' 'Well,' I said, and I told him my story. He said, 'How many flowers did you send her?' I said I hadn't sent her any flowers. He said, 'I'll send her the flowers.' He sent her the flowers and I got the bill. She called me up about the flowers he sent—there must have been a thousand flowers. She said, 'I've never had so many flowers, the flowers absolutely cover the whole room. I don't know where to put any more flowers. There are more flowers than I've ever seen in my life. Thank you very much.' And hung up. Your father said, 'You can't fool around with a thing like this. You get a thing going, send the flowers.' And I never saw her again. . . ."

At least my father died with his boots off. He was sixty-eight years old. There were many things, he said, that he wished he'd done or hadn't done but, on balance, it was hard to see how he could have packed any more into sixty-eight years than he did. He looked his age. And he looked tired. The last ten years had been rough: he'd pushed the machinery at stress capacity for so long it had begun to break down. "I thought it was guaranteed to last a lifetime," he commented. "I smell a bum deal here. Son of a bitch, didn't have time to read the fine print. Some lousy contract. Christ, I feel cheated."

As he lay in the pleasant, sunny corner room of a New York hospital, I had plenty of time to wonder what my life would be like without him. After that first vascular operation, when the young surgeon who had performed it a hundred times before without mishap sliced neatly into Father's neck, replacing an inch or so of blocked artery—right carotid, to use the correct terminology— with a more efficient (impervious to shrinkage and hardening, unlike the real flesh and blood which constituted the rest of his body) segment of plastic—after that, there was the strain of the repeat operation, six days later, to remove the clot that had developed in his contralateral left artery. For a more sweeping diagnosis: what we had here was occlusion of the carotid vessels— two great arteries, I remembered from biology, one on either side of the neck, which carry blood to the brain. Or, in a grandiloquent summation: "Extensive arteriosclerosis"—i.e., thickening of the blood vessels—"of the entire vascular system, most marked in the region of the brain and the blood supply to the heart and aorta"— that last being another of the big guys, the main trunk of the arterial system. And certainly after *that*, it didn't look as if this particular time this particular surgical intervention was going to be an unqualified success. It didn't look that way to us, although the surgeon was insuperably cheerful every morning as he made his rounds.

"Seems to be a slight improvement since yesterday."

And, "We simply don't know enough about the brain's ability to regenerate itself. Remarkable organ, the brain."

We—Pamela, Bill, and I, and, later, Pamela's son, Winston —would stand, arms crossed, unified for the first and last time behind the impenetrable revetments of family crisis.

Yes, our eyes would answer the brilliant young surgeon, do go on. Tell us more. Tell us why, if he's better this morning, there are two new catheters running out of his nose and mouth or arms and legs or urethra and colon that simply weren't there last night; seemingly more yards of flexible plastic tubes flowing out of him than of arteries circulating within him. And to think it was all because of that one little inch of plastic tubing we allowed to be implanted in his neck and grafted to his right carotid—a miracle inch, we were advised, that would save his life.

Daily we waited for the doctor to wind up his cheery fore-cast. Then—politely—it would be our turn. Father, we pointed out with all due respect for the doctor's chipper medical prognosis, was getting worse instead of better.

One morning, Bill, Winston, and I were gathered in the hall by the elevators when the doctor breezed out looking as if he'd come from a bracing game of tennis. He was a good-looking man in an Ivy League way; he always looked appropriately scrubbed down and disinfected. His eyes looked directly at us without wavering or blinking, an attitude that may have reassured some of his other patients' kin but had the reverse effect on our group. "I don't trust folks who don't blink," remarked Bill. To which I'd said, "Well, he's wearing blinders; how else can he wade through the drek he has to face every day?"

"Good morning, Haywards. And Mr. Churchill. How is our patient this morning?"

"Worse," I said.

"Well, now—"

"Now, look, Doctor," interjected Winston, whose sober pin-striped suit and Turnbull & Asser shirt lent Bill's and my appear-ance a measure of respectability, "I haven't been here all along, I admit, but it is evident to me that Leland doesn't seem to be making any sense. It's not that he's delirious and he's not potty or senile. It's something else. And he's not improving."

The doctor looked serene. "We can't tell at this point whether or not—"

"Oh, yes, we can," I interrupted. "That is to say, we can. We ought to be able to, we've known him for thirty-odd years. And since one or another of us is in the room with him all day every day—"

"Our empirical observations should have some value," drawled Bill.

"He was definitely improved last night," said the doctor imperturbably. "We talked at length about photography."

The vein in Bill's temple began to pulsate. "Look, Doc, you're not in there all day. Stick around. You'll see what we're talking about."

"Oh, I'm sure there are moments—"

"Moments, hell," said Bill. The passion in him that I some-times thought had solidified into ice was flowing. "Look, we know all about the trauma to his brain. It's a wrap on that dialogue. We also know that the consensus is we should cool it because there is this possibility he may regain some of his faculties. But let me tell you that the gray matter in the middle is *dead*—and there ain't no way—"

"D-Doctor." Winston was stuttering slightly. His face was flushing as red as Bill's was getting white. "Every day the family comes here and looks to see—it's been weeks now—if there's any improvement—"

"To his head, Doctor." I re-entered the fray. "To his head. You can understand that's what really scares us. It's bad enough dealing with the physical stuff, the surgery and bandages and so on, the by-products, but that's secondary when we're faced now with something that's happened to his mind. As a result of all this."

The doctor shook his head and a bemused smile flickered at the corners of his mouth. He looked like a beleaguered math teacher.

"You know, I don't understand your family at all," he said. "I've never encountered anything like it. Most people would be grateful to have him *alive*."

"But, Doctor," I said, feeling my intestines tighten, "what possible good is it for him to be *alive* if he can't use his mind? How do you think—if he were given a choice—*he* would feel about living like that? This is no dimwit, this is a very intelligent, active man."

"Certainly he's still aware enough to know what's going on," said Bill, "and to hate it. Poor son of a bitch just doesn't happen to have a gun lying under his saddlebag or the wherewithal to use it anyway."

"Most people—" responded the doctor earnestly.

"Well, we're not most people, thank God," Winston interrupted.

"What happens when we take him home?" I asked, wanting to clutch my stomach and rip it out. "He just sits in a wheelchair with a lap robe, unable to see, to speak or walk, to *think*—for the rest of his life, however long it is that he lives?"

"A vegetable," said Bill, studying his watchband with fixed interest. "He won't even be able to see the stars at night. He loves the stars."

"Most people," the doctor tried again, "would be grateful to be able to take their fathers home at all. Even if his mind isn't as acute as it was, things won't be as bad as you anticipate. It's like having a pet—a cat or a dog—around the house. I've known cases where the woman of the house told me she was happy to have someone to take care of—"

"A pet!" we exploded. "Doctor, you have to be kidding! A cat or a dog! Woman of the house to take care of!"

And that was the end of it. He moved on to make his rounds.

"I do not believe what I just heard," I seethed. "I did not hear it."

"Wait till Mummy hears about this," said Winston, shaking.

Bill's laughter began again. "Spooky dialogue," he said. "Guess saving someone's life is all he thinks of. Guess he thought he did enormously well from the surgical end of the thing. Absolutely bananas conversation. They're even more bananas than we are."

But that didn't seem to matter. It was more and more horribly true that Father could be less and less relied on to recognize all of us all of the time or, at the scattered moments when he did, to make any sense. However, on those increasingly rare occasions when he did make sense, there was a single sentiment that he expressed lucidly, vehemently, and with unremitting clarity of articulation. He wanted to go home.

Father lay immobilized, wrists bound down with strips of sheeting in case he might gesticulate and displace a tube or two, in his adjustable iron hospital bed for about four weeks.

Then Pamela, outraged and horror-struck by the barbaric customs in this country when it comes to death, spoke up. It was another of those dramatic morning conferences.

"Children," she said after the doctor had left, "please help me. In England when someone is fatally ill— My father died at home. He was very old, and when he became ill, that's where he wanted to die. And of course we respected his last wishes. The situation had some dignity. He was surrounded by the people who most loved him, in his own bed in his own house. But this—I don't understand."

I was grateful. After all the empty proselytizing for life at any cost and the emphasis on stuffing everything handy into that life even at its end, with total disregard for the quality of the end itself, it was nice to hear a sane voice.

I broke the silence, swallowing hard: "The problem is that euthanasia is illegal."

"Unless we take him out of the hospital," said Winston. "That in itself would be a form of euthanasia. They couldn't stop us from doing that."

"What do you think, Bill?" asked Pamela. There were tears in her eyes.

Bill unraveled himself from the tangle of some sort of labyrinthine inner contemplation.

"Well," he said slowly, "my guess is the surgeon is not going to go for that one at all. Don't forget, his reputation's at stake. But a certain amount of time *has* passed since the operation—so Father is out of his responsibility or jurisdiction."

And so we got over that stumbling block, and Pamela, with our thankful consent, took Father home.

But first she had to make the agonizing decision to sever Father's lifeline. Some lifeline, Bill and I remarked to each other. To us it looked like a cocoon of man-made webbing spun over and under and around Father's body to pin it down to the hospital bed, a closed circuit that conducted God knows where or why a pitiful trickle of God knows what. We didn't trust it any more. We had begun to suspect that Father's lifeline really led neither here nor there, maybe nowhere.

It had taken us the month since that second operation to admit it. Plenty of time for me not only to think about what was happening right in front of my eyes, but also to look back at everything that had ever happened and to imagine everything that was to come.

It was a new experience, although one I hated. Well, I thought, you should be grateful for the chance to know (much more than you ever wanted to) about the mysteries of death as they relate to yet another member of your family. The titular head of it, in fact. Just thinking that way made me shiver. Well, I comforted myself, this time you'll be able to follow right along, assimilate all the medical expertise, see for yourself that the mysteries of death are really exaggerated. See it all as a long, exploratory, circular journey where the end runs into the beginning like the great serpent that coils back on itself and swallows its own tail.

You know very well that the process of dying is part of the process of living. This time, at least, you can observe firsthand the natural conclusion to a first-rate life (only why does it have to be my father's? And why, if it's so natural, does it seem so artificial?), a life that's just going by the book, doing what it's supposed to do in the end: shed its last trappings one by one, the way a tree sheds its autumnal leaves.

This is a good opportunity to observe firsthand all the miracles of nature. Remember when Mother used to say that, years ago, on the farm in Connecticut? Remember Agnes the cow calving? Stewart the dog being run over? Chickens flopping with their heads left behind them in the dust? Do you remember *Mother?* What a twist. And Bridget? Well, no surprises this time, even though this time was definitely not one that I, Brooke, would have picked as ideal—meaning that Father's death could have been considerate enough to have scheduled itself after mine, so that I wouldn't have to deal with it. Father would understand best of all what I felt; except that Father, for obvious reasons, wasn't going to be there to help me this time.

Until my early twenties, I had believed—not believed, really, blithely *assumed*—that I was immortal, under the brooding protection of my own private guardian angel assigned by God to watch over me day and night. I could even feel my angel's wings brushing my face just before I fell asleep; in times of danger I imagined his shadow hovering just above my head. When I no longer knew whether or not I believed in God, my angel left his post. Then I no longer believed that I was specially blessed and immortal. Bereft of that romantic conceit, I had more respect for—and fear of—life.

Until my early twenties (when Bridget and Mother died deaths that were still as mysterious to me now as then, that people still mentioned—if the subject came up at all—with hushed questions in their voices), I had my guardian angel, and never wondered what life would be like without anyone. Life was forever. Here we go again: that terrible elevator ride in the pit of my stomach. ("Take it easy," said my pounding head to my pounding heart; "no surprises this time. You know so much more going in.")

The truth was these conversations with myself didn't help at all.

The truth was this time was much worse than either of the other two, even if it was more logical.

The truth was logic was useless. The feeling of abandonment

prevailed against all emollients, tranquilizers, anodynes, and razzle-dazzle philosophizing. Feeling abandoned was an insidious, incurable, cancerous feeling, and a cumulative one.

The truth was death may not be so bad, but watching Father die was awful.

He lay in that pleasant, corner hospital room, with belly distended, flesh sunken, the shipwrecked hulk of what had been a magnificent man. And still, probably thanks to my childhood reading of all those beautifully illustrated books he'd commandeered, I clearly saw him as a distinguished old general from the *ancien régime*, who had weathered the maelstrom of the Revolutionary Wars and was preparing himself for a brief nap on the eve of the Battle of Austerlitz. He was having trouble getting his boots off. He'd already sat down ponderously on the edge of his iron Napoleonic campaign bed and, grunting, had found that he couldn't bend over to unbuckle the polished leather straps. With a long sigh, he had leaned back into the pillows and called for his beloved aide-de-camp, Lucio (the butler). Lucio, by now, had loosened all the brass buttons on Father's jacket—heavy as armor with the weight of its decorations—and had covered him with a warm army blanket.

"I think I'll sleep for a little while," murmured Father apologetically to Bill and me as we stood at the foot of his bed. (Lucio had removed the boots as gently as possible and they lay crumpled on the floor.)

"That's good, Pop," said Bill, walking around to the side of the bed where—to judge from the way his head followed movement—Father could still distinguish shapes with one eye, although that, too, had lost its acuity.

"Water," croaked Father, clicking his tongue against his dry palate. Sometimes the corners of his mouth crusted up now that the tubes had been stuffed into it.

"Water." The word was barely intelligible.

"He wants water." I moved toward the metal pitcher by his bed.

"Not too much," remonstrated one of the omnipresent nurses.

"Why not? He's thirsty."

"Bad for his stomach, Brooke," said Bill. But Father only wet his lips on the glass anyway.

"Thank you, darling," he said with effort, making my heart

turn over. For a fellow who had grown rather crotchety (the first stroke, a few years earlier, had partially paralyzed one side, and although with intensive physical therapy Father had managed to thwart most of its physical effects, it left him irritable, something of a curmudgeon), he had now become amazingly polite. Very courtly. With people to whom he might have been very rude before—nurses, doctors—he now went out of his way to say please and thank you, like a small child. The more indignities he suffered, the more pain he endured, the closer he came—with fear—to death, the more gentlemanly he behaved. His disposition regained its former sweetness. Once Bill and I got over the initial shock of finding out that, in his head, he was living in a different time zone—the thirties, mostly—and conscious only in a more primary way, we started to enjoy talking to him. It could be kind of fun. We didn't have to make a lot of sense or try to impress; we could trip around in pleasant conversations that didn't relate so much to us as to another time.

"What are you thinking about, Pop?" I'd ask him idly, noticing that on these bright days he would turn his head toward the window and stare at the sky with his half-good eye.

"Pretty day," he'd mumble. "God, it's a good day for flying. I wish I didn't have to stick around the goddamn office on a day like this."

Many people came to see him before Pamela took him home. He always recognized the friends who went way back, if only by their voices. Jimmy Stewart stopped in New York on his way from Los Angeles to Boston and took a car in from the airport to pay him a visit about a week before he died.

"I'm glad I got to see him," Jimmy said later. "It had been a long time."

"Did he recognize you?" I asked.

"Yeah, he recognized me. First thing he said was 'What the hell is going on?' I said, 'Nothing much, just passing through, thought I'd stop and say hello.' We talked. We had a half-hour visit, maybe three quarters of an hour."

"And he seemed rational to you?"

"Yeah."

"What did you talk about?"

Jimmy paused for a long time and looked away, far away.

"Flying," he whispered at last.

Of course, I thought.

"When I came back from the war," said Jimmy, "I'll never forget—he was standing at the foot of the gangplank with a bunch of red roses. How he got onto the pier, I don't know—absolute top-secret, no one was allowed—but your father could always get in anywhere. There he was, first thing I saw. I'll never forget that."

While Father didn't seem to be living in the present and to have much interest in, or sure recollection of, the more recent events in his life—one evening, to Bill's and my intense pleasure, he called Pamela "Maggie"—the farther backward in time our conversations took him, the more incredible his memory. One of those days, when Bill and I were asking him about different things he'd done in his life and were trying to piece them together chronologically, he suddenly announced that his first job had been working as a brakeman on a railroad. Bill and I looked at each other incredulously.

"Come on, Pop," we said, amused at the preposterous image that sprang to mind, "a *brakeman*. Why did you never tell us that before?"

"Don't know," muttered Father, moving his head restlessly from side to side. "Forgotten."

We didn't believe him at all. We assumed it was wishful thinking, one of the tricks his mind could play. Much later, Bill would check it out with Grandsarah (who, at eighty-nine, was to outlive her only son), and she would recall vaguely that one summer when Father was sixteen or seventeen he *had* worked for a railroad.

We could tell that there were days when he couldn't *see* us. But he always recognized our voices. In that last month, Bill and I would meet at the hospital in the morning and spend most of the day there. Pamela, who was usually the first to arrive and the last, in the evening, to leave, arranged for Father to have shifts of nurses round-the-clock; even so, she felt better knowing that some family representative was there as well. That way, if the nurse on duty wanted to go out for coffee, or if she herself had something else to attend to, Father would not be left alone. Father's room and the hall outside, where there was a pay phone and a couch and where all the morning conferences were held out of his earshot, became as familiar as a recurring nightmare. We were now faced with the irony that as fearsome as it was to continue with the nightmare, the fear of ending it was even greater.

"Hiya, Pop. How's it going today?"

Some days he would look straight at me and say, "Hi, darling, much better thank you." ("He had a good night," the nurse would whisper.) Some days he would scan the room for the source of my voice; then I would move deliberately across his line of vision.

"Oh, Pop, you didn't sleep well last night, did you?"

"Darling little Brooke. I want to go home. Take me home." He would struggle vainly to wrench his body from the sheets.

"Oh, Pop."

"Home."

"Pop. Don't try to sit up, Pop."

"My gut hurts." Sometimes he swallowed again and again as if a bone had stuck in his gullet. I had to fight the instinct to pound him on the back.

To the nurse: "His stomach is bothering him again. Shouldn't he have a pain-killer?"

The nurse would shake her head. "He's getting Demerol intravenously." Ah, that must be the new tube taped to his arm.

But there were afternoons where Bill and I found that we could ease into discussions with him about the past, where we could really get him going on and on, comfortably ask him intimate questions about his various love affairs and marriages that, ordinarily, we wouldn't dare bring up.

At the suggestion of our ex-stepmother, Nan, who was following all this very closely, Bill wandered into the hospital room one day and asked Father for his list of the ten most beautiful women that he'd ever known. It was just the sort of question Father liked best. He was terrific. A trace of color appeared in his cheeks.

" 'Beautiful' is the most misused word in the English language," he stated, with near-perfect articulation, "next to 'glamorous.' Very hard to define. Goddamned elusive. In my book, to be beautiful a woman has to be more than beautiful—you know what I mean? She has to have this quality of glamour, which is also impossible to describe. A certain look in her eyes, a style—an awareness of her effect on people—the way she holds herself, moves, a sense of her own mystery. A blend of all those things. And then some. Damn few women are genuinely beautiful. A handful. I must have come close to knowing them all, as close as any man alive. Fell in love with half of them, married three—"

"Whoa, Pop, you're going too fast. Three of your *wives* on your all-time list?"

"Ya. You're goddamned right. Lola; I guess she was the most beautiful woman I ever knew. She taught me how to fly. Did you know that? Got me interested in planes. Married her twice, I thought she was so beautiful. Maggie—not beautiful in the classic sense, but I don't subscribe to the classic sense. Nan, definitely. Kate [Hepburn], definitely. The best. God, yes." He turned toward the window and seemed to drift out.

"Go on, Pop, who else?"

"Oh, well. Garbo, of course. Most beautiful eyes I ever saw. Great face, strange body. Huge feet. Size ten, something insane like that."

"Could you ever have fallen in love with her?"

"Not possibly. She was kind of sexless. Moved clumsily. Not smart enough for my taste. But my God, that face. When I was her agent, I had to go up to her house to talk her into some deal—I was simply mesmerized by her face, I wanted to fall into it. Your mother was insanely jealous, or pretended to be." He chuckled to himself.

"Let's see, that's only five, Pop."

"Hold your horses, hold your horses. Fay Wray."

"Fay Wray?" Hmm, that was unexpected. When David O. Selznick died, his son, Danny, had given me some old photographs he'd found of Father as a young agent; there was one with Fay Wray standing in the background, laughing.

"Ya, ya, gorgeous. Marlene [Dietrich], gorgeous. Isak Dinesen. You know, *Out of Africa*. Fabulous. An old woman when I met her. How many is that?"

"Eight," replied Bill and I together.

"Not so sure there are ten," he mused. "I guess Justine Johnson and—Esmé O'Brian."

He was pensive now; his hands plucked at the sheet involuntarily. (Who were Justine Johnson and Esmé O'Brian? We didn't know, and Bill had to take the list to Nan to find out.) "God, I love women. Much more intelligent, much stronger, much braver. Nicer than men, not as mean. And so much more beautiful. There's not a single inch of the female body that is not beautiful. Think of that. They're luckier, too. I have a theory about women. . . ."

We leaned closer; his energy was fading and so was the color from his face.

"What, Pop?" asked Bill. "Do you want something to drink?"

"No, thanks, son." Father's voice caught, as sometimes it did, on one syllable or word. What made that terrible was his subsequent struggle to rip the word from his larynx, to hawk up something more than a throttled exhalation. His entire body would heave spasmodically with the effort. There was no way to help. We would wait, panicked, for him to exhaust himself. Slowly the glottal sounds would subside into a wheeze. He would lie still, looking over in our direction with a confused expression on his face, as if he hoped he was imagining such a lapse of control.

"Women," he choked finally. "You know what it is about them that men envy most?"

"The fact that they shall inherit the earth?" said Bill.

"You bet," Father closed his eyes. "They'll outlive us all. Aristophanes was no fool."

Diana Vreeland:

"*I always, during those last ten years, kept thinking: This man is so terribly brave. But, you see, he was built as a gentleman. Consequently, even illness—and pancreatitis is supposed to be the worst, isn't it, because it affects the emotions so much; everything to do with that department, gall bladder, bile tract, affects the emotions. I would go up to Mount Kisco quite a lot and sit with Leland and talk to him, and God, he was so— Every time I'd leave and go home I'd think, That's the brightest man I've ever known. I mean what's he carrying on on? No man could have been a more charming gentleman in anyone's life than he was in mine. He really was a courtly gentleman. It's an effective phrase because it makes you think of the Civil War or something. But that's what he was. Even the deep illness of his late life couldn't take that away from him. Even when he was telling you the craziest story that ever was about his stepmother, Maisie Hayward, and his father, the Colonel—even if he was making a bit of a nut out of somebody, it was never done with malice, never. It was always done with great courtliness and richness of spirit.*"

It had taken me such a long time, my entire life, to learn how to interpret him. The knack was to unlearn everything except my most primal love. He was so ingenuous he was hard to figure out. One attributed to him layers of deviousness, subterfuges that would never have occurred to him. And because, to me, he'd always been not only a grownup but my *father*, I'd spent my adolescence and early adulthood trying to communicate with him on that level. A mistake. His parenthood was a conditioned idea that had been wasted on both of us. Worse—with time, it had separated us. As I'd grown older and bigger, he'd grown proportionally farther away.

"Brooke, darling, is that you?"

"Yes, Pop."

"That's good. Where's Bill?" His eyelids twitched open.

"He'll be right back. He's just gone down the hall."

"Don't go away."

"I won't, Pop."

And if all children see their fathers as personifying power—a notion that is usually dispelled by a little time under the belt—I had perceived my father as being even more powerful than anyone else's. In fact, he was.

How do you live up to that? With your heart in your mouth, that's how. How close can you come to the sun before it melts your wings? And why, as I stripped back the years and memories, did I have the feeling that the younger I'd been the closer I'd come? Later, I would say to myself, "Nobody this powerful can also be this simple." But Father was that simple. Deep down he was a child, too, and that's where he won.

"Do you love me?" He looked toward me blindly.

"More than anything in the world." I felt the tears beginning. Oh, no, I thought.

"That's good," he said. "I hate this, though."

"Yeah, it stinks," I agreed, sputtering slightly with nervous laughter.

"Don't cry, for God's sake; are you crying?" His eyes were closed and he couldn't possibly see me anyway.

"No," I choked, tears streaming down my face.

"I'm sorry, darling. I'm so sorry."

"Don't, Pop. Why?"

"I broke my promise." He stirred restlessly under the sheet. "To take you to the bullfight movie. I promised . . ."

What on earth had made him think of that? "Pop, do you realize how many years ago that was?"

Even after I'd grown up, the implicit threat of his authority was able to scare me. It was only now, as I sat musing at his deathbed, that he became again what he'd once been; when there were no demands on either of us and I was very young; when I was just a child and he was just my father, and sometimes those two states of being seemed almost the same.

"A helluva long time ago." He roused himself to glare at me. "What?"

"All my promises." His voice softened. "I did keep one, though. The time your mother made me spank you. Promised I'd never do it again."

"Yes," I whispered. For a moment I'd almost asked him for his handkerchief.

"I never did, either."

There was a telephone in the hospital room, but Father wasn't allowed to use it. He wasn't even supposed to know it was there. Accordingly, it never rang. Out of respect for him, we made all our calls in the phone booth down the hall. To use a telephone in his presence, when he himself didn't have that privilege, seemed heartless. He was the master; it was one of his glories. Our most crucial communications had taken place on the telephone, and our most comfortable. For me, his disembodied voice—whether spanning thousands of miles or just a few blocks—had more immediacy and meaning than his voice in person.

One day I stared at the telephone in Father's room, contemplating ways to kill it, indulging myself in fantasies of hurling it against the wall, extinguishing it with a pillow.

I even picked up the receiver to see if it could save me the trouble by going dead on its own.

"Let's yank it out, Bill. I'm serious. What the hell's it *for?*"

Bill shrugged. "Emergency."

After that, I couldn't glance at it without wincing. It had become more than an ugly black little reminder of everything that lay outside the hospital, of Father's past.

It had become a symbol of his impotence and ours.

And finally I knew that he would never call me on the telephone again, that that part of our lives was already over.

·   ·   ·

"I miss Emily," I said out loud, without opening my eyes.

"Emily Buck? Our old nurse?"

"Yes." I'd dozed off in my chair. It was a bad way to wake up. "Remember how she used to sit on our beds when we were sick? I miss the way she smelled—Clorox, tobacco, coffee, toast. If she were here now, I'd sit on her lap and she'd rock me . . ."

I peered at Bill through my lashes, not wanting to let in too much light. But the room was already dark. "What time is it? How's Father?"

"Still asleep. I wish I could sleep that soundly."

"Me, too. I'm afraid."

"Of what?" Bill's chair scraped close to mine.

"Right this minute? Everything. You name it." I closed my eyes again, longing for Emily. But Emily had died painfully of stomach cancer a few years earlier. "Of letting go. Of dying. Of living. Of going nuts. That's the most prevalent one. And you?"

"I suppress most of that stuff." Bill whistled a tune silently through his teeth. "Programmed myself a long time ago not to think about the shit that the future might be handing down to me."

"Don't you ever feel rage now?"

"You mean specifically at Mother or Father?" Bill swiveled his gaze to the hospital bed where Father lay. "I couldn't live long enough to discharge it. We were trained *not* to express anger. I got so good at that it landed me in Menninger's."

The room was steeped in twilight. I felt as if we were detached from the rest of the hospital, adrift.

"Extraordinary," murmured Bill, wandering back and forth in semicircles around Father's bed. "Insane what you go through— sixteen years old, being locked up—not because you've committed a crime, but because your parents think you should be. Absolutely one of the most impotent, frustrating, disastrous kinds of feelings, because there's no voluntary trip about it at all. Even though you know it might be doing you some good, and in the long run you might benefit from it. Never got over it."

Listen, I wanted to answer, what makes you think I got off scot-free? The marvelous act I put on to give that impression? The truth was I felt like a veteran of the wars. It was still inexplicable to me that Bridget and Bill had wound up in Menninger's and Austen Riggs and I hadn't. My guilt for *not* having gone through their ordeal was as great as my relief at having been spared it. Whatever had happened to my brother and sister had happened, in some way, to all of us.

Bill came to a halt in front of me.

"But, on the whole, I'm glad I went."

"Why?" He really was crazy.

"Well, it's weird. It's like—if you think you're neurotic or possibly insane, the idea is always lurking in the back of your head that the punishment for going crazy is being locked up in the loony bin. And it must be very frightening. But if you've already gone through it, it's not so bad. Besides"—he held out his hands to pull me up—"you can always bullshit your way out. . . . Here comes the sun." He flicked on the light.

"Ugh."

"Reveille," he went on cheerfully. "What do you want for breakfast tonight? My flight plan features Szechwan Tang Tang noodles smothered with those heavy-duty little black peppers that blow your head off."

When we leaned over Father to kiss him good night, he awakened instantly as if he were afraid to miss anything.

"What's up?" he croaked.

"Thought we'd nail down a little dinner, Pop," said Bill.

"Good idea." Father nodded weakly. "Let's go to the Colony."

"Of course—where else?"

I looked away from the tube of glucose fastened to his arm.

"No." Father struggled to lift his head. "Let's go home instead. Where's Bridget?"

"She—" I hadn't heard him mention her name in many years. "She'll be here in a minute."

"Please tell her to hurry up." He sighed and turned away from our voices. "I'm tired of waiting." Then he spoke very softly and as if he were miles away. "There's a clock in my head. It never stops ticking, but the hands don't move. Why does it take so long to die?"

A few days later, he went home.

The night of March 18th, I drove out to Haywire House. After Pamela's phone call, it took me about an hour to rent a car and get there; by the time I stood at the front door, I felt as if I'd been driving all night. Lucio, father's young Italian butler, opened the door immediately and grasped my hand.

"I'm so sorry," he stammered.

"Lucio. How is he?" Although I already knew the answer from the expression on his face.

Lucio gripped my hand tighter.

"Is he still alive, Lucio?" I wanted words, not touch.

"Ten minutes ago . . ." he began.

The familiar hallway melted around me, pulling me in. I fought numbly against its perfume, its plush burgundy carpet, its diffused light—as carefully regulated as a greenhouse thermostat—illuminating the colors of a painting here or a bowl of flowers there, and playfully flickering across the scintillant feathers of the two silver fighting cocks as they sparred in mortal combat on their tablecloth of rich rose velvet; a hum of conversation in the living room beyond, the phone ringing; was I really too late?

Pamela, in a coral silk caftan shot with gold, came toward me with a fresh whiskey sour in her hand.

"Would you like to see your father?" she asked cordially, as if nothing had happened. I nodded uncertainly and followed her down the hall.

Father's bedroom was located at the far end of the house, so I had plenty of time to hypnotize myself, by riveting my eyes on Pamela's robe floating from side to side a few feet in front of me. Nevertheless, when we entered the room, I managed, without looking, to see everything in it at once. The room was octagonal in shape; it had been designed by Father and was his pride and joy. Now its contents were suffused with the light I associated with small chapels. Otherwise everything seemed normal, except that on my right, along the side of the octagon where Father's bamboo bed had always been situated, was the intrusion of a hospital bed. Its covers formed an unbroken line over the body in it. I stared straight ahead. Okay, I told myself, this is it; on your mark, get set. Pamela was delivering me into the outstretched hands of Brother Paul. Brother Paul, she said, was a member of the Franciscan order and also a male nurse, who, luckily for us, had been taking care of Father since she'd brought him back. Brother Paul told me what a wonderful man Father was.

"May she see him now?" Pamela asked him.

He hesitated. "It might upset her," he said.

",Why?" I asked, suddenly wanting to reclaim control over what was happening to me.

"Because I've had to bind him up."

"What?" Strange horrible images flitted through my mind.

"A handkerchief—" He made a wrapping motion around his head.

"Did he hemorrhage? Is there a lot of blood?" I asked, terrified.

"No, no," Brother Paul gesticulated awkwardly. "We have to do that—it sets so quickly."

Then I understood. And at that moment, for the first time, I truly realized that Father was dead. I took a deep breath.

"Please," I said, letting it out. "He's my father and I want to see him." Not that I'm brave, I thought, because I'm not, but squeamishness aside, there's something else: I have to see for myself. Now. No obituary tomorrow or funeral in three days can have the same meaning. And how dishonorable it would be if I walked away without saying goodbye. Properly, face to face.

He nodded, and Pamela left the room.

We went over to the bed.

Brother Paul folded back the sheet. The only dead body I had ever seen before was an anonymous corpse being dissected in the morgue of the Roosevelt Hospital. I hadn't been allowed to see my mother or sister. Now I steeled myself to look down, thinking, I must be *sure*; this time I must *know*. I knelt beside the bed.

The most shocking sight, as Brother Paul had warned, was the blue handkerchief tied all the way around Father's head to hold his jaw in place. After I got over that, I forced myself to look at his face. Amazing, I thought, trying to stall my emotions with clinical detachment, the accuracy of every description, however trite, I'd ever read. I put my arms around his head and lifted it up. Amazing the aptness of hackeyed phrases like "deathly pallor" and "dead weight." Amazing how quickly life goes when it goes; how quickly everything empties, body temperature drops, flesh implodes into matter, skin becomes as hard and cold as a sea shell.

I looked down the length of his body: it, too, had altered. It was smaller, shrunken; his stomach, distended for so many weeks as if pregnant, was flat. He had borne his death and was free.

I imagined him traveling through space faster than the speed of light. Grounded far behind, I envied him. I wanted to let go of his head and follow, like a speck of dust, up past the moon and the sun. Where were Bridget and Mother at that very moment, I wondered, reaching out to him over the edge of some distant star? What address should I write in my telephone book after the name "Hayward, Leland"?

His head was very heavy. I cradled it against my chest and ran my hands over the stubble of his hair. Even it felt dead. I began to weep. My tears drenched his face, glazing it like ice. They soaked through the blue handkerchief and trickled in chilly rivulets back onto my hands. I sobbed and sobbed, soundlessly so that Brother Paul couldn't hear, holding on to Father's head with all my strength as if it were the last thing left in the world. I wept for my family, all of us, my beautiful, idyllic, lost family. I wept for our excesses, our delusions and inconsistencies; not that we had cared too much or too little, although both were true, but that we had let such extraordinary care be subverted into such extraordinary carelessness. We'd been careless with the best of our many resources: each other. It was as if we'd taken for granted the fact that, like our talents and interests and riches, there would be more where *we* had come from, too; another chance, another summer, another Brooke or Bridget or Bill.

I laid his head gently back down on the pillow and kissed his forehead. It was time to go.

I got as far as the middle of the room before I stopped, feeling him over my left shoulder. If I look back now, I thought, I'll never let go; maybe that's why Brother Paul keeps his vigil tonight—to guard the living as well as the dead.

So I started for the doorway and the dark corridor beyond, knowing, as I passed through it, that my only choice was to keep moving forward.

A Note on the Type

The text of this book is set in Electra, a typeface designed by W. A. Dwiggins for the Mergenthaler Linotype Company and first made available in 1935. Electra cannot be classified as either "modern" or "old style." It is not based on any historical model, and hence does not echo any particular period or style of type design. It avoids the extreme contrast between "thick" and "thin" elements that marks most modern faces, and is without eccentricities which catch the eye and interfere with reading. In general, Electra is a simple, readable typeface that attempts to give a feeling of fluidity, power, and speed.

Typography and binding design by
Virginia Tan